ACE® GROUP FITNESS INSTRUCTOR HANDBOOK

The Professional's Guide to Creating Memorable Movement Experiences

AMERICAN COUNCIL ON EXERCISE®

EDITORS

JESSICA MATTHEWS, M.S.

SABRENA JO, M.S.

TODD GALATI, M.A.

DANIEL J. GREEN

CEDRIC X. BRYANT, PH.D., FACSM

AMERICAN COUNCIL ON EXERCISE

Library of Congress Catalog Card Number: 2015960043

ISBN 978-1-890720-59-9
Copyright © 2016 American Council on Exercise (ACE)
Printed in the United States of America

B C D E

Distributed by:
American Council on Exercise
4851 Paramount Drive
San Diego, CA 92123
(858) 576-6500
(858) 576-6564 FAX
ACEfitness.org

Project Editor: Daniel J. Green

Technical Editors: Jessica Matthews, M.S., Sabrena Jo, M.S., Todd Galati, M.A., & Cedric X. Bryant, Ph.D., FACSM

Art Direction & Cover Design: Karen McGuire

Production: Nancy Garcia

Photography: Dennis Covey, Rob Andrew, Matt Gossman

Anatomical Illustrations: James Staunton

Stock images: iStock.com

Index: Kathi Unger

Exercise models: David Burnell, Angel Chelik, Jacque Crockford, Steve D'Addario, Priscilla Flores, Ashley Franz, Kyle Gosselin, Monika Lucs, Stephanie Perillo, Jay Petterson, Amanda Wigley

Acknowledgments:
Thanks to the entire American Council on Exercise staff for their support and guidance through the process of creating this manual. A special thanks to Rehab United for allowing us to photograph on location at their Sorrento Valley facility.

NOTICE
The fitness industry is ever-changing. As new research and clinical experience broaden our knowledge, changes in programming and standards are required. The authors and the publisher of this work have checked with sources believed to be reliable in their efforts to provide information that is complete and generally in accord with the standards accepted at the time of publication. However, in view of the possibility of human error or changes in industry standards, neither the authors nor the publisher nor any other party who has been involved in the preparation or publication of this work warrants that the information contained herein is in every respect accurate or complete, and they are not responsible for any errors or omissions or the results obtained from the use of such information. Readers are encouraged to confirm the information contained herein with other sources.

ACE's Mission Is to Get People Moving.

P17-003

TABLE OF CONTENTS

FOREWORD

IN THE MORE THAN 30 YEARS THAT THE AMERICAN COUNCIL ON EXERCISE HAS BEEN CHAMPIONING education and professionalism in the fitness industry, much has changed about the industry and, more specifically, group exercise instruction. What began as a means of improving health and fitness through the use of traditional dance and aerobic movements has evolved to include such traditional fare as step training and kickboxing classes alongside constantly emerging modalities such as equipment-specific classes, small-group training, and mind-body disciplines.

The *ACE Group Fitness Instructor Handbook* was designed to equip group exercise professionals with the skills and know-how needed to teach any modality of group exercise. Our goal was to provide not only the critical knowledge that all instructors need to teach safe and effective classes—the essentials of human anatomy and movement, for example—but also application-based content that teaches the reader how this information applies to the needs of every participant. For example, after presenting information about stability and mobility throughout the kinetic chain and movement in the various planes of motion, the "Understanding Human Movement" chapter goes on to explain how to balance these elements in a class setting and how they impact a participant's ability to perform activities of daily living.

Another hallmark of this new text is an emphasis on developing rapport, maximizing enjoyment, and facilitating true behavior change, all within the context of a safe and effective group exercise experience for all participants, regardless of their health condition or fitness level. Group fitness instructors hold a unique and valuable place in the allied healthcare continuum, as well as in the lives of their participants. Our goal in creating the *ACE Group Fitness Instructor Handbook* was to enable our certified professionals to positively influence people to have an enriching relationship with physical activity and develop a lifelong fitness habit— one day and one class at a time.

Scott Goudeseune
President and CEO
American Council on Exercise

INTRODUCTION

The American Council on Exercise is proud to introduce the *ACE Group Fitness Instructor Handbook*. As with all ACE texts, this new handbook offers the most current, complete picture of the instructional techniques, leadership skills, and professional responsibilities that instructors need to teach safe, effective, and enjoyable group fitness classes. In addition to serving as a study aid for the ACE Group Fitness Instructor Certification Exam, the *ACE Group Fitness Instructor Handbook* is a comprehensive resource for both new and veteran instructors that not only provides the critical knowledge you will need to effectively lead a class, but also application-based tools to help you master that content and then utilize it to create memorable movement experiences.

The handbook begins with **Part 1: Group Fitness Fundamentals**. In these three introductory chapters, readers will learn about the unique role group fitness instructors play in the allied healthcare continuum. The role and scope of practice of ACE Certified Group Fitness Instructors is examined, along with current industry guidelines. Part 1 closes with a practical guide to anatomy and human movement.

Part 2: Considerations, Design, and Preparation for Group Fitness Classes is made up of four chapters that teach readers how to design safe, effective, and enjoyable exercise experiences for their participants. After learning how to design a class blueprint and to anticipate and properly respond to unforeseen situations that may arise during class, instructors will walk step-by-step through day-of preparation for classes, including adherence to onsite procedures and responsibilities.

The heart of group fitness instruction lies in the ability to effectively lead participants of all experience and fitness levels through an exercise session. **Part 3: Elements of Leading Group Fitness Classes** introduces instructors to various learning and teaching styles, as well as techniques to create inclusive experiences for participants with specific limitations, whether they stem from musculoskeletal issues or various disease states. This part of the handbook concludes by teaching readers how to solicit feedback from participants, supervisors, and colleagues in order to continue improving as a leader and instructor of group fitness classes.

The final section of the book is **Part 4: Professional and Legal Considerations**. Participant safety should be the primary focus of any instructor. This includes effectively delivering well-designed multilevel classes and appropriately responding to emergency situations as they arise. Instructors must understand the professional responsibilities and legal guidelines associated with their professional role.

Finally, the appendices present the ACE Code of Ethics, the Group Fitness Instructor Certification Exam Content Outline, Principles of Nutrition for the Group Fitness Instructor, and the ACE Position Statement on Nutrition Scope of Practice for Fitness Professionals.

We wish you luck as you prepare for a rewarding career as an ACE Certified Group Fitness Instructor. We sincerely hope that this handbook serves you well as you prepare for the certification exam and remains a trusted resource throughout your career.

Cedric X. Bryant, Ph.D., FACSM
Chief Science Officer

Daniel J. Green
Project Editor

STUDYING FOR THE ACE GROUP FITNESS INSTRUCTOR EXAM

TO HELP YOU ON YOUR JOURNEY TO BECOMING AN ACE CERTIFIED GROUP FITNESS INSTRUCTOR, WE HAVE PUT TOGETHER A COMPREHENSIVE SET OF RESOURCES YOU CAN USE WHILE YOU STUDY.

The ACE Learning Center contains online study materials that include videos, webinars, learning activities, and quizzes for each corresponding chapter of the *ACE Group Fitness Instructor Handbook,* as well as a summary review of each chapter to help you focus your studies. The ACE Learning Center also includes an end-of-course exam review and practice tests with annotated responses to enhance learning.

FOR HANDBOOK AND ACE LEARNING CENTER

If you purchased an ACE Group Fitness Instructor (GFI) study program that includes the ACE Learning Center, you will use our online program to guide you through your studies.

The ACE Learning Center provides an online study guide designed to help ACE Group Fitness Instructor Certification candidates get the ultimate learning experience. With interactive lessons that bring the *ACE Group Fitness Instructor Handbook* to life through videos, demonstrations, webinars, reading assignments, learning activities, chapter summary reviews and quizzes, an exam review module, and practice tests, it will help you learn like you would in a classroom. You will also be able to track your progress and contact our study experts in the ACE Resource Center if you need help.

If you are utilizing the ACE Learning Center, log in to your My ACE Account at www.ACEfitness.org/MyACE to begin, and then take the following steps to best prepare for the exam:

- **STEP 1:** Read Chapters 1–3 of this book, *ACE Group Fitness Instructor Handbook*. These chapters cover the fundamentals of becoming an ACE Certified Group Fitness Instructor—from the role of the GFI in the health and fitness industry to an introduction to group fitness and human movement.

    After reading each chapter, complete the corresponding education, learning activities, and quiz questions in the ACE Learning Center.

    Also, review Appendices A, B, and D in this handbook, which cover the ACE Code of Ethics, the Exam Content Outline, and the ACE Position Statement on Nutrition Scope of Practice for Fitness Professionals.

- **STEP 2:** Read Chapters 4–7 of this book. This material covers the key design considerations and preparation for creating and leading memorable group fitness classes, including class blueprints and day-of preparation for group exercise classes.

    After reading each chapter, complete the corresponding education, learning activities, and quiz questions in the ACE Learning Center.

STEP 3: Read Chapters 8–10 of this book, which cover the essential elements of leading group fitness classes, fostering inclusive experiences for all participants, and strategies for enhancing instruction.

After reading each chapter, complete the corresponding education, learning activities, and quiz questions in the ACE Learning Center.

STEP 4: Read Chapters 11–12 of this book, which cover professional and legal considerations for group fitness instructors, including participant safety and legal guidelines and professional responsibilities. Also, review Appendix C, which presents the principles of nutrition for the GFI.

After reading each chapter, complete the corresponding education, learning activities, and quiz questions in the ACE Learning Center.

At this point, we also recommend that you register for the ACE Certification Exam by visiting www. ACEfitness.org. Setting a date will give you a clear goal to work toward while you complete your studies.

STEP 5: Complete the GFI exam review module and the practice tests in the ACE Learning Center. The results of your practice test will help you to assess your level of preparation and plan your remaining study time as your exam date approaches. Be sure to review the annotated responses to each practice test question to help you gain a better understanding of competency-based assessments and the professional role of the ACE Group Fitness Instructor.

IMPORTANT TIPS

- To register for your exam, do not forget that you must be at least 18 years old, have completed high school (or the equivalent), and hold a current certificate in cardiopulmonary resuscitation (CPR), and, if living in North America, proper use of an automated external defibrillator (AED). The course must include a live skills assessment performed in person; an online certificate course is not accepted. As you begin your studies, start looking into local providers and register for a course.

- As you make your way through your study materials, be sure to keep an eye out for the boldface terms in the chapters, which are defined in the glossary.

- As a general rule, ACE recommends that candidates allow approximately three months of study time on average to adequately prepare for the ACE Group Fitness Instructor Certification Exam.

- For additional tips and resources, check out the Study Center Facebook page at Facebook.com/ACEfitnessStudyCenter and the Exam Preparation Blog at www.ACEfitness.org/examprep. If you have additional questions, contact ACE at support@ACEfitness.org or (888) 825-3636.

PART 1

Introduction to Part 1:
GROUP FITNESS FUNDAMENTALS

ACE Certified Group Fitness Instructors (GFIs) hold a unique place in the allied healthcare continuum, leading engaging exercise experiences that serve a wide variety of participants. In this section, the role and scope of the GFI is examined, along with the core components of a group fitness class and current industry guidelines. In addition, a practical guide to anatomy and human movement is provided to ensure a science-based approach to designing safe and effective classes.

OVER THE COURSE OF THIS PART OF THE HANDBOOK, INSTRUCTORS WILL GAIN COMPETENCY IN THE FOLLOWING THREE AREAS:

The role of the group fitness instructor

The elements of a group fitness class

Anatomy and human movement

CHAPTER 1

CHAPTER 1

THE ROLE OF THE GROUP FITNESS INSTRUCTOR

SABRENA JO

LEARNING OBJECTIVES

- Explain how group fitness continues to evolve.
- Describe the group fitness instructor's role in the allied healthcare continuum.
- Differentiate between professional certification, certificates, and continuing education.
- Describe the role and scope of practice of the ACE Certified Group Fitness Instructor.

Group fitness has its origins in cardiorespiratory exercise via classes inspired by dance. In his 1968 best-selling book *Aerobics*, Dr. Kenneth Cooper promoted various modalities of aerobic exercise as a means to help prevent **coronary artery disease.** Shortly thereafter, participating in activities such as walking, running, cycling, and swimming became popular as a way to improve health. Included in this trend was a new form of exercise that combined traditional calisthenics with popular dance styles, aptly called dance aerobics. These types of classes were popular throughout the 1970s and early 1980s, and consisted mostly of high-impact movements. By the late 1980s, low-impact aerobics and step aerobics gained popularity because of the less-jarring movements used in the classes.

If your study program includes the ACE Learning Center, visit www.ACEfitness.org/MyACE and log in to your My ACE Account to learn more about the important differences among certifications, continuing education, certificates, licensure, and registration.

IN THE 1990S, CLASSES BEGAN TO EMERGE that incorporated more than just aerobic exercise, often with specific types of equipment, such as dumbbells, resistance tubing, and stability balls. Hence, the term aerobics was replaced by the term group fitness. Currently, a large number of varied formats exist, including equipment-based modalities, such as indoor cycling and rowing, suspension training, and kettlebell classes, as well as mind-body formats, such as yoga and Pilates. Additionally, classes that serve a specific niche for participants who desire vigorous workouts and a competitive atmosphere, such as boot camp and high-intensity interval training workouts, have become popular.

As the general public continues to access more and more fitness information via the Internet and social media, it is imperative that ACE Certified Group Fitness Instructors (GFIs) provide sound, science-based instruction to keep

> ## GFIs must continue to evolve

participants safe. With innovation in exercise equipment and programming, GFIs have a responsibility to stay up-to-date with current standards and established teaching techniques to provide their participants with safe and effective classes. Innovation is how the group fitness industry is evolving, and GFIs must continue to evolve with it to provide the class experiences that participants want in a timely and appropriate manner.

It is important to keep in mind that as an industry, the business of fitness is in its infancy. Specifically, health and fitness professionals have been operating as such for about 30 years. As awareness has heightened about the opportunities inherent in helping people improve their lives through healthy behavior change, sound exercise programs, and strategies for nutritious eating, consumers and health and fitness professionals alike have been drawn to the rewards of working in fitness. Accordingly, the profession has continued to develop its **standard of care** and refine its **scope of practice** with the help of education and credentialing organizations, such as the American Council on Exercise (ACE).

 [EXPAND YOUR KNOWLEDGE]

Standards of Practice and Organizations Advocating for Industry Best Practices

Common standards of practice for health and fitness professionals include:

▬ Assurance that the professional has been accurately assessed and maintains documented qualifications to practice in the specific professional role [i.e., earning a certification that is accredited by the **National Commission for Certifying Agencies (NCCA)**]

▬ Proper representation of academic achievement, skills, and abilities

▬ Practicing in accordance with standards and guidelines within the defined scope of practice of the profession

▬ Commitment to continued professional development

▬ Protecting client/participant privacy by not disclosing information to third parties unless required by law

▬ Maintenance of appropriate filing systems and documentation of all professional activity

▬ Implementing proper screening and evaluation, and acquiring medical clearance when required for the safety of the client or participant

▬ Referral of clients or participants to appropriate healthcare practitioners when needed

▬ Implementing risk-management strategies and services in accordance with business, industry, and legal standards and guidelines

▬ Avoiding conflicts of interest, improper distribution of information, or any other false representation

▬ Calling attention to unethical, illegal, and unsafe behaviors by other professionals

The International Confederation of Registers for Exercise Professionals (ICREPs), European Health and Fitness Association (EHFA) Standards Council, and, in the United States, the Coalition for the Registration of Exercise Professionals (CREP)—which is currently made up of the American Council on Exercise (ACE), American College of Sports Medicine (ACSM), National Council on Strength and Fitness (NCSF), National Strength and Conditioning Association (NSCA), National Exercise Trainers Association (NETA), Pilates Method Alliance (PMA), and the Cooper Institute (CI)— are serving health and fitness professionals through standards setting, professional advocacy, and industry best practices.

THE ALLIED HEALTHCARE CONTINUUM

The allied healthcare continuum is composed of health professionals who are credentialed through certifications, registrations, and/or licensure and provide services to identify, prevent, and treat diseases and disorders (Figure 1-1). Physicians are the "gatekeepers" of allied healthcare, evaluating patients to diagnose ailments and implement treatment plans that can include medication, surgery, rehabilitation, or other actions. Physicians are assisted in their efforts by nurses, physician assistants, and a number of other credentialed technicians. When ailments or treatment plans fall outside their areas of expertise, physicians refer patients to specialists for specific medical evaluations, physical or occupational therapy, psychological counseling, dietary planning, and/or exercise programming.

Figure 1-1
Who is the ACE Certified Group Fitness Instructor?

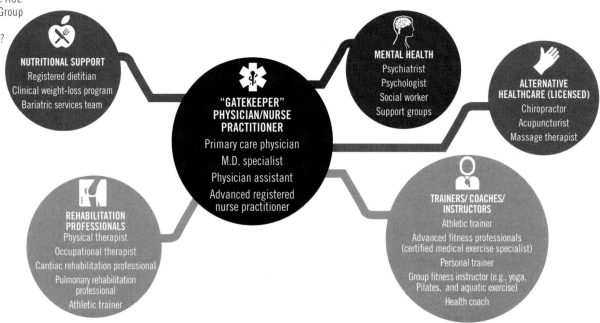

Physicians and nurses teach patients the importance of implementing their treatment plans. **Physical therapists** and **occupational therapists** lead patients through therapeutic exercise and teach them to perform additional exercises at home to facilitate rehabilitation. **Athletic trainers** teach athletes exercises to prevent injury and take them through therapeutic exercises following injury. **Registered dietitians** teach clients proper nutrition through recipes, meal plans, food-preparation methods, and implementation

of specialized diets. While these professionals might also give patients or clients guidelines for general exercise (e.g., "try to walk up to 30 minutes per day, most days of the week"), few of them actually teach clients how to exercise effectively. This is where health and fitness professionals, including GFIs, hold a unique position in the allied healthcare continuum.

The majority of GFIs will work with apparently healthy participants, helping them improve fitness and health. Not only do well-qualified GFIs lead safe and effective exercise classes, they also foster an environment wherein participants develop group camaraderie and engage in social experiences that potentially strengthen the motivation and adherence to exercise. The community aspect of participating in group fitness classes is a strong draw for exercisers who enjoy socializing while being physically active.

[EXPAND YOUR KNOWLEDGE]

Initial Insights Into Raising Fitness Professional Competency

An international movement focused on raising the level of professional competency and skill attainment among exercise professionals is currently underway. This movement began in 2003 when the board of directors of the International Health, Racquet and Sportsclub Association (IHRSA) recognized the need for legitimate professional credentialing. Following an assessment of credible accrediting organizations, the board made a recommendation that personal fitness trainers seek fitness certifications from only those organizations that have been accredited by the NCCA, the accrediting body for what was then called the National Organization for Competency Assurance (NOCA), now the Institute for Credentialing Excellence (ICE). IHRSA later updated the recommendation to include accrediting organizations recognized by the U.S. Department of Education, creating significant confusion, as education program accreditation is very different from, and not comparable to, certification accreditation.

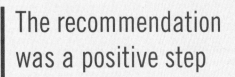

> The recommendation was a positive step

IHRSA's recommendation has had a tremendous impact on the way the industry views certification, particularly the organizations providing the certifications. Although the recommendation was a positive step toward legitimizing the credentialing aspect of the industry, the addition of organizations (e.g., the Distance Education Training Council) designed to evaluate education programs provided a means to circumvent the rigors of the NCCA accreditation, yet still earn the title of "accredited" for a process geared toward professional development, rather than professional competence, which is the goal of certification and licensure. The crucial point to understand is that an accredited education program (which offers narrowly focused content about a specific topic) is distinctly different than an accredited certification program (which provides a competency-based assessment of an individual's knowledge, skills, and abilities related to performing a job).

Important Terminology Related to Credentialing

There are several important terms related to credentialing that the GFI should understand:

■ *Professional certification:* A voluntary process by which a non-governmental body, such as ACE, grants a time-limited recognition and use of a credential to individuals who have demonstrated that they have met the criteria for required knowledge, skills, or competencies for safe and effective practice in a specific job role. A renewal process is associated with certification that requires the **certificant** to obtain continued education, or in some fields pass a recertification exam, in order to retain the credential. The credential awarded by the certifier denotes that the participant possesses particular knowledge, skills, and/or competencies to practice in the profession.

■ *Certificates:* Education or training program on a specific topic for which participants receive a certificate after attendance and/or completion of the coursework. Some programs also require successful demonstration of attainment of the course objectives, such as a post-course assessment of knowledge or practical demonstration. One who completes a certificate program is known as a certificate holder. Importantly, a professional certification (or license) is usually not granted at the completion of a certificate program. There are three primary types of certificate programs: knowledge-based, curriculum-based, and certificate of completion or participation.

  ▶ *Knowledge-based certificate:* Recognizes a relatively narrow scope of specialized knowledge used in performing duties or tasks as part of a certain profession or occupation. This certificate is generally issued after the individual passes an assessment instrument. Examples include continuing education courses—generally on one topic within a broader content area—such as online courses or webinars with a quiz from ACE and other educators.

  ▶ *Curriculum-based certificate:* Issued after an individual completes a course or series of courses and passes an assessment instrument. The content of the assessment is limited to the course content and therefore may not be completely representative of professional practice. Examples include more robust curriculum-based courses, series of courses, or specialty certifications with assessments of knowledge, such as ACE specialty certifications and modality- and equipment-based courses that end with an assessment or practical demonstration.

▸ *A certificate of completion or participation:* Issued after an individual attends or participates in a particular learning event. Typically, there is no knowledge assessed prior to issuing this type of certificate. A certificate of attendance or participation is not a credential, because the recipients are not required to demonstrate competence according to professional or trade standards. Live workshops and classes issuing certificates based on course attendance and participation are common in the health and fitness industry and include ACE workshops and preconference workshops at conferences.

━━ *Licensure:* The mandatory process by which a governmental agency grants a time-limited permission to an individual to engage in a given occupation after verifying that he or she has met standardized criteria and offers title protection for those who meet the criteria

━━ *Registration:* Either the professional designation defined by a governmental entity in professional regulations or rules, or to a listing, or registry, of practitioners. Depending on the profession, there may or may not be educational, experiential, or competency-based requirements. Registration also may give a time-limited status, thereby authorizing those individuals to practice, similar to licensure. The United States Registry or Exercise Professionals (USREPS), is an internationally recognized registry of exercise professionals in the United States that is maintained by the Coalition for the Registration of Exercise Professionals (CREP). All currently ACE Certified GFIs are listed on www.USREPS.org.

DEFINING "SCOPE OF PRACTICE"

A scope of practice defines the legal range of services that professionals in a given field can provide, the settings in which those services can be provided, and the guidelines or parameters that must be followed. Many factors go into defining a scope of practice, including the education, training, and certifications or licenses required to work in a given field, the laws and organizations governing the specific profession, and the laws and organizations governing complementary professions within the same, or adjunct, field. Most laws defining a profession are determined and regulated by state regulatory agencies, including licensure. As a result, the scope of practice for licensed practitioners can vary from state to state in a given profession. In addition, most professions have organizations that serve as governing bodies within the profession that set eligibility requirements to enter educational programs or sit for certification exams, set requirements for certification to practice in the field, and establish codes for professional conduct and disciplinary procedures for professionals who break these codes.

> Many factors define a scope of practice

The laws, rules, and regulations that govern a profession are established for the protection of the public. The laws governing a GFI's scope of practice and the ramifications faced by instructors who provide services that fall outside the defined scope are detailed in Chapter 12. The eligibility and certification requirements to work within this legal scope of practice are defined by the professional organizations that offer group fitness instructor certifications. These organizations also establish codes of ethical conduct and mandate that they are upheld by certified professionals and applicants for certification in all actions related to group fitness instruction. It is crucial for practitioners in every industry to be aware of the scope of practice for their given profession to ensure that they practice within the realm of the specific education, experience, and demonstrated competency of their credential.

SCOPE OF PRACTICE FOR ACE CERTIFIED GROUP FITNESS INSTRUCTORS

The ACE Certified Group Fitness Instructor scope of practice is presented in Figure 1-2. ACE Certified Group Fitness Instructors must work within this defined scope of practice to provide effective exercise leadership for their class participants, gain and maintain support from the healthcare community, and avoid the legal ramifications of providing services outside their professional scope.

GFIs should never provide services that are outside their defined scope of practice. For example, a GFI may be asked nutrition questions by participants wanting to reduce weight and/or **body fat**. GFIs can help participants with their weight-loss goals by leading effective exercise classes that bring about positive **body composition** changes and helping them to adopt more healthful behaviors. This can include showing participants how to utilize the tools available at www.ChooseMyPlate.gov or educating them about the recommendations in the *Dietary Guidelines for Americans* to help them gain a better understanding of healthful foods and make better choices (U.S. Department of Agriculture, 2015). Participants who are looking for more detailed nutritional programming, such as specific meal plans or recommendations for nutritional supplements, should be referred to a registered dietitian, as these services are beyond the scope of practice of GFIs and are in the legal domain of services provided by registered dietitians in most states.

ACE CERTIFIED GROUP FITNESS INSTRUCTOR SCOPE OF PRACTICE

Figure 1-2
ACE Certified
Group Fitness
Instructor Scope
of Practice

The ACE Certified Group Fitness Instructor is a fitness professional who has met all requirements of the American Council on Exercise to develop and lead group fitness classes for individuals who have no apparent physical limitations or special medical needs. The ACE Certified Group Fitness Instructor realizes that group fitness instruction is a service industry focused on helping people enhance fitness and modify risk factors for disease to improve health. As members of the allied healthcare continuum with a primary focus on prevention, ACE Certified Group Fitness Instructors have a scope of practice that includes:

— Developing and leading exercise classes that are safe, effective, and appropriate for individuals who are apparently healthy or have medical clearance to exercise

— Conducting pre-class assessments of participants, and where appropriate, conducting health screenings and stratifying risk for cardiovascular disease with participants in order to determine the need for referral and identify contraindications for exercise

— Constructing group exercise classes that are appropriate for the intended audiences and goals for the class format using research-proven and published protocols

— Assisting participants in setting and achieving realistic fitness goals

— Teaching correct exercise methods and progressions through demonstration, explanation, and proper cueing and exercise leadership techniques

— Instructing class participants in how to properly monitor exercise intensity using heart rate, perceived exertion, and/or ventilatory response

— Empowering individuals to begin and adhere to their exercise programs using guidance, support, motivation, lapse-prevention strategies, and effective feedback

— Assessing the class environment by evaluating/monitoring the room and equipment before and during each class session

— Educating participants about fitness- and health-related topics to help them in adopting healthful behaviors that facilitate long-term success

— Protecting participant confidentiality according to the Health Insurance Portability and Accountability Act (HIPAA) and related regional and national laws

— Always acting with professionalism, respect, and integrity

— Recognizing what is within the scope of practice and always referring participants to other healthcare professionals when appropriate

— Being prepared for emergency situations and responding appropriately when they occur

 [THINK IT THROUGH]

How would you handle a situation in which a participant specifically asks you to make a recommendation that you know is outside your scope of practice? For example, consider a scenario in which a participant asks which medication you find more effective for post-workout soreness, ibuprofen or acetaminophen. Draft a standard response you can use in these situations.

KNOWLEDGE, SKILLS, AND ABILITIES OF THE ACE CERTIFIED GROUP FITNESS INSTRUCTOR

The ACE Group Fitness Instructor Certification is designed for health and fitness professionals wanting to provide general exercise leadership to apparently healthy individuals in a group setting. The certification program is continually evaluated to ensure that it is consistent with the most current research and industry standards. In addition, every five years a group of industry experts analyzes the specific job requirements for GFIs to update the outline of tasks, knowledge, and skills required to perform the job of group fitness instruction effectively. After being validated by several thousand ACE Certified Group Fitness Instructors, this outline is published as the ACE Group Fitness Instructor Exam Content Outline (Appendix B), which serves as the blueprint for the ACE Group Fitness Instructor Certification Exam and provides a template for candidates preparing for the exam. It is also a written job description of the knowledge, skills, and abilities required to be an effective ACE Certified Group Fitness Instructor.

PROFESSIONAL RESPONSIBILITIES AND ETHICS

The primary purpose of professional certification programs is to award credentials to individuals who meet the requirements to practice in the professional role and to protect the public from harm (e.g., physical, emotional, psychological, and financial). Professionals who earn an ACE Group Fitness Instructor Certification validate their capabilities and enhance their value to employers, class participants, and other healthcare providers. This does not happen simply because the individual has a new title. This recognition is given because the ACE credential itself upholds rigorous standards established for assessing an individual's competence in making safe and effective exercise-programming decisions. ACE has established a professional ethical code of conduct and disciplinary procedures, and ACE certifications have all received third-party accreditation from the NCCA.

To help ACE Certified Professionals understand the conduct expected from them as healthcare professionals in delivering group exercise classes and protecting the public from harm, ACE has developed the ACE Code of Ethics (Appendix A). This code of conduct serves as a guide for ethical and professional practices for all ACE Certified Professionals. This code is enforced through the ACE Professional Practices and Disciplinary Procedures (www.ACEfitness.org/getcertified/certified-code.aspx). All ACE Certified Professionals and candidates for ACE certification must be familiar with, and comply with, the ACE Code of Ethics and ACE Professional Practices and Disciplinary Procedures.

ACE CODE OF ETHICS

The ACE Code of Ethics governs the ethical and professional conduct of ACE Certified Professionals when working with clients/participants, the public, or other health and fitness professionals.

Every individual who registers for an ACE certification exam must agree to uphold the ACE Code of Ethics throughout the exam process and as a professional, should he or she earn an ACE certification. Exam candidates and ACE Certified Group Fitness Instructors must have a comprehensive understanding of the code and the consequences and public harm that can come from violating each of its principles.

CONTINUING EDUCATION VS. CERTIFICATION

Apart from accumulating hours of experience leading classes, well-qualified GFIs put an emphasis on furthering their education. Continued learning is a hallmark of excellence in any profession and group fitness is no exception, as there are numerous opportunities for health and fitness professionals to gain further knowledge in their chosen area of expertise. These opportunities are available as continuing education in the form of workshops, conference sessions, online programs, and published materials.

Often, the industry's tendency to mislabel continuing education programs as "certifications" rather than "certificates" or "specialty certificate programs" has led to confusion among certified health and fitness professionals. Certifications provide an assessment of professional competence, whereas certificates show that an individual has completed a course on a particular topic. For example, a GFI who completes a weekend workshop and receives a certificate of completion for suspension training is not certified in suspension training instruction. Instead, the GFI has advanced his or her knowledge in the area of suspension training and can now provide a new training component in his or her classes.

Continuing education workshops, such as those that offer specialty certificates, provide the GFI with new knowledge and skills, as well as the ability to offer new class modalities. Participation in these types of programs is essential for the continued career development of a certified fitness professional. However, certificate programs are not certifications and the difference between the two is an important distinction to understand.

 [APPLY WHAT YOU KNOW]

Options for Expanding Your Offerings

One way for a GFI to advance his or her career is to earn additional certifications. Professionals are encouraged to earn certifications that provide them with new areas of expertise. For example, ACE offers four NCCA-accredited certifications, each providing a different area of focus for health and fitness professionals. A GFI may consider earning the ACE Personal Trainer Certification to gain further knowledge and skills in designing and delivering safe and effective exercise programs, while also supplementing his or her group fitness income. To better serve individuals seeking to make positive lifestyle changes, including losing weight, a GFI may choose to pursue the ACE Health Coach Certification, which focuses on behavior change. For the advanced professional who would like to work specifically with clients who have special needs or are post-rehabilitation for cardiovascular, respiratory, metabolic, or musculoskeletal diseases and disorders, the ACE Medical Exercise Specialist Certification is a fitting option.

A health and fitness professional who wants to expand the services that he or she provides into another area of allied healthcare must earn the appropriate credentials to ethically and legally provide those services. This could include becoming a licensed massage therapist, earning a nutrition degree and becoming a registered dietitian, earning a master's degree in occupational therapy and becoming a an occupational therapist registered (OTR), or going to medical school and becoming a medical doctor. In all of these situations, the professional earning the new credential will advance his or her career and the services that he or she can provide, becoming an advocate for exercise and fitness training in his or her new professional arena.

SPECIALIZATION

Specialization is a great way for a health and fitness professional to become highly skilled in a particular type of training or in working with a specific population. By gaining advanced knowledge and skills in a specialized area, a GFI can enhance the services provided to participants with special needs—and hopefully attract more participants seeking these specialty services. For

Gaining knowledge and skills

example, a GFI who is interested in working with older adults might choose to complete extensive continuing education focused on teaching this population, possibly earning a specialty certificate in exercise for older adults. Once the instructor is recognized for providing safe and effective classes for older adults, he or she could more readily attract senior participants, and should be able to earn more per session when providing these lessons.

Areas of specialization should be selected by the GFI based on his or her desired career path, interests, and participant base. The area of specialization should also fall within the scope of practice, or provide the instructor with knowledge that is complementary to what he or she does within the scope of practice. For example, a course teaching techniques for manual manipulations of the shoulder would be educational, but the GFI would not be able to use the techniques learned in the course because they would fall outside the defined GFI scope of practice.

SUMMARY

Since its origins in the 1970s and 1980s, group exercise has been a mainstay in the fitness industry. With innovation in exercise equipment and programming, group fitness will continue to evolve. Successful GFIs will continue to evolve as well, as they pay heed to the standard of care and scope of practice associated with the safe and effective practice of group fitness instruction. Well-qualified GFIs hold current NCCA-accredited certifications in group fitness instruction, place an emphasis on furthering their education, and are able to discern the differences between certification, certificate courses, and continuing education.

References

Cooper, K.H. (1968). *Aerobics*. New York: M. Evans.

U.S. Department of Agriculture (2015). *2015–2020 Dietary Guidelines for Americans* (8th ed.). www.health.gov/dietaryguidelines/

Suggested Reading

The United States Registry of Exercise Professionals Mission Statement and Website http://usreps.org/Pages/default.aspx

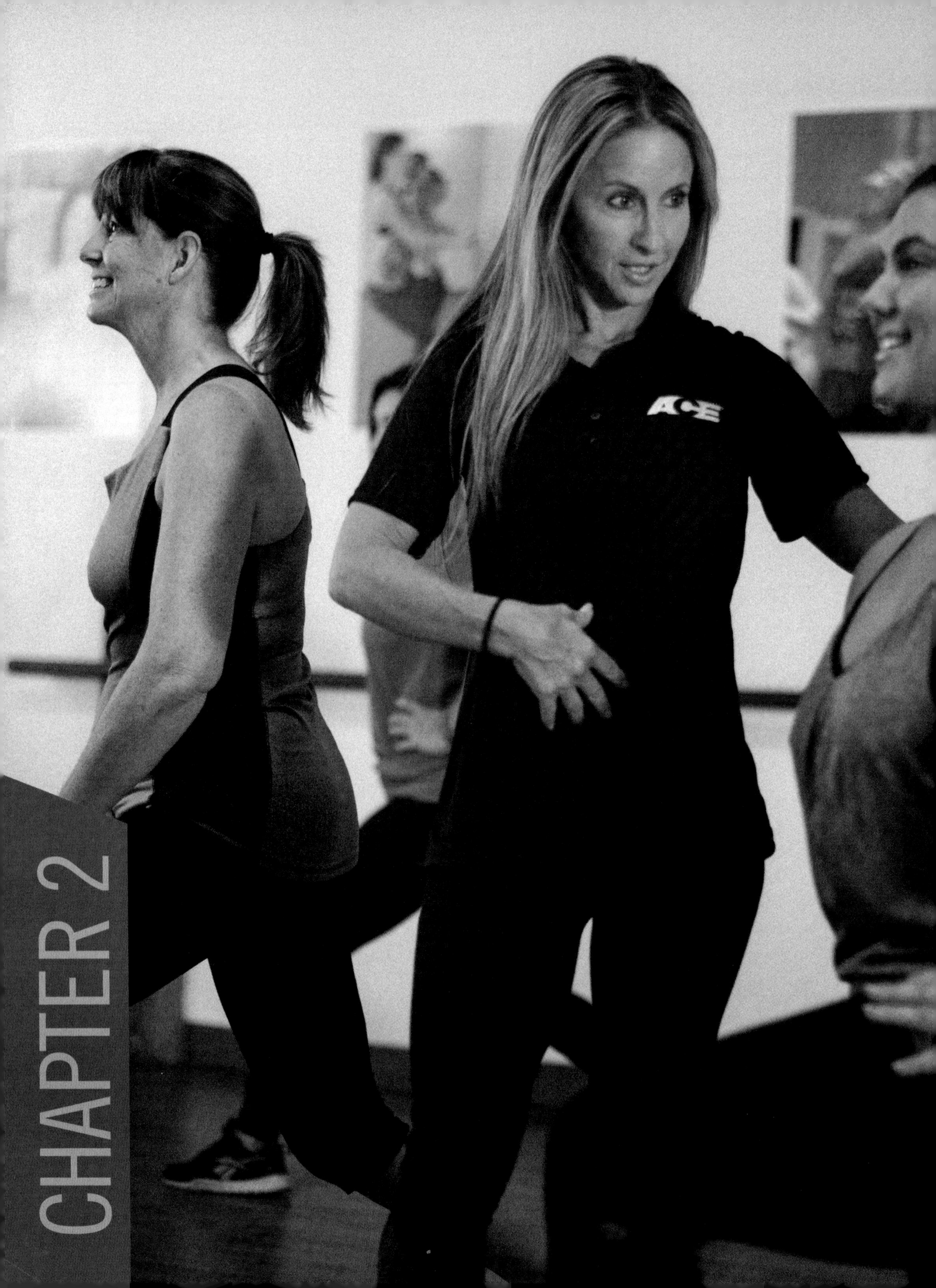

CHAPTER 2

CHAPTER 2 | GETTING TO THE CORE OF CLASS OFFERINGS

SABRENA JO

LEARNING OBJECTIVES

- Explain the difference between pre-choreographed versus freestyle methods of group fitness instruction.
- Differentiate between the basic components of most group fitness classes.
- Describe the various components of fitness, including health-based and skill-based areas.
- Explain the current guidelines for improving and maintaining cardiorespiratory fitness, muscular strength and endurance, and flexibility.
- List and briefly explain the principles of training.

Group fitness classes are usually structured to enhance participants' health-related components of fitness, such as **cardiorespiratory endurance, muscular strength** and **muscular endurance, flexibility,** and **body composition,** through movement. Health and fitness improvement, plus social engagement with others during class, are powerful tools that empower people with the ability to improve their quality of life. Although no single class structure is appropriate for every type of group fitness class, there are general formatting practices that can help to ensure a safe and effective experience for participants.

If your study program includes the ACE Learning Center, visit www.ACEfitness.org/MyACE and log in to your My ACE Account to learn more about verbal and visual cueing techniques, as well as common group fitness class formats.

GROUP FITNESS CLASS FORMATS

In general, most group fitness classes are appropriate for individuals with various fitness skills and abilities, as long as the ACE Certified Group Fitness Instructor (GFI) is capable of student-centered instruction wherein exercise modifications are offered frequently throughout the class experience.

Of course, certain group fitness classes, such as those promoting skill-specific conditioning like **plyometric** training, should ideally be attended by participants who are indeed ready for that kind of high-intensity approach to exercise. A class that is suitable for only a narrow portion of the population should be named accordingly (see Chapter 5 for more information on creating class titles). For example, a plyometric training class might be named "Jump Training EXTREME!" In this case, a deconditioned participant would read the name of that class and realize that it might not be the most appropriate option. However, GFIs should always be prepared to teach inclusive, multilevel classes in which appropriate **progressions** and **regressions** of exercises are provided (see Chapter 8), regardless of how the class is titled or described on the group fitness schedule.

CHOREOGRAPHIC METHODS

GFIs must be prepared to teach movements and exercises that together create a well-designed class experience. Delivering choreography for any cardiorespiratory-, strength-, or flexibility-focused class can take many forms, from freestyle choreography in which the class content can vary dramatically from one class to another, to different types of pre-choreographed classes, where the class content is relatively consistent from one class to the next.

Be prepared to teach and demonstrate

Many pre-choreographed classes are offered in "scripted" form, in which instructors follow a written script with music, cues, and moves all outlined from start to finish. The intent is a "performance-like" consistency of delivery and class experience, discouraging variations among instructors. From the perspective of participants, the predictability of being able to gauge their intensity more effectively is an advantage of this method, since they know the general format and can measure their own improvements over time. A disadvantage of this style is that, because instructors must follow a script, there is often little room for customizing specific progressions and regressions as appropriate for the individuals in each class.

In pre-planned class formats, instructors receive guidelines and suggestions of what a class should include. As long as instructors follow these guidelines, they can make their own individual choices from a longer list of options on such things as song selection and sequence of moves as they plan for their classes, or they can choose to implement a complete pre-choreographed class plan.

From an instructor's perspective, advantages of these pre-choreographed methods include receiving a class "in a box," from the music to the moves, that helps ensure a successful class experience. In addition, instructors receive access to a support system that often includes networks consisting of thousands of fellow instructors. A disadvantage for the GFI is the ongoing costs to receive new music and choreography, which are often offered in the form of quarterly releases.

The freestyle method of developing and delivering choreography occurs when the GFI chooses his or her own music, class design, and specific choreography. Advantages of the freestyle method include an always-changing environment that may reduce boredom for the instructor and participants. A disadvantage of this method is that participants are often unaware of what to expect from class to class, making it more challenging to improve proficiency over time because the sequence of movements constantly changes.

 [THINK IT THROUGH]

Give examples of pre-choreographed and/or pre-planned group fitness classes. Conduct a brief internet search to assist you.

BASIC COMPONENTS OF CLASS

Often, group fitness classes begin with pre-class preparation (see Chapter 7) followed by a warm-up, which includes using specific movements to prepare for the conditioning phase, or main portion of the class. These movements are performed at a low-to-moderate speed and **range of motion (ROM).** They are also designed to specifically raise internal body temperature in preparation for the activity to follow and to increase blood flow to the muscles. After the warm-up, the conditioning segment generally begins based on the goals and content of the class (e.g., cardiorespiratory exercise aimed at improving cardiorespiratory endurance or strength training aimed at working the major muscle groups).

Following the conditioning segment, a gradual cool-down, also known as the final phase, slowly lowers the **heart rate (HR)** to near pre-exercise levels. A class typically ends with a flexibility-based component that includes stretching and relaxation exercises designed to further lower HR and enhance overall flexibility.

It is important to note that not all class formats follow this exact structure. Fusion classes are an example of a type of class that may deviate from this general approach. While fusion classes can take on many different forms, they often involve blending two or more modalities, such as yoga and Pilates, together into one intertwined class experience. These hybrid classes can also pair class formats with different goals, such as 30 minutes of indoor cycling to improve cardiorespiratory endurance followed by 30 minutes of resistance training to improve muscular endurance. These classes may be combined together into one 60-minute class offering with two distinct portions, or may be offered individually as back-to-back "express" classes that are each 30 minutes in length. Regardless of format or duration of the class, GFIs should focus on providing a safe and effective movement experience that addresses the health-related components of fitness (as appropriate for the participants), as well as social engagement in order to increase participant enjoyment and ultimately enhance long-term **adherence.**

WARM-UP

There are a few common principles guiding the warm-up for any group fitness class:

- The beginning segment includes an appropriate amount of dynamic movement.
- The warm-up focuses largely on **rehearsal moves** (see Chapter 5).
- All major muscle groups (if appropriate) are addressed through dynamic ROM movements.
- Verbal directions are clear and the volume, tempo, and atmosphere created by the music, if used, are appropriate.

Appropriate Dynamic Movement

The purpose of the warm-up is to prepare the body for the more rigorous demands of the class by raising the internal temperature and enhancing **neuromuscular efficiency.** At higher body temperatures, blood flow is shunted away from the internal organs and redirected to the working muscles, and the release of oxygen to the muscles begins to increase. Because these effects allow more efficient energy production to fuel muscle contraction, one goal of an effective warm-up should be to elevate internal temperatures so that sweating occurs. Another potential outcome of a good warm-up is to enhance neuromuscular efficiency such that joint-position sense improves, joint stability is enhanced, and protective joint reflexes are developed.

Increasing body temperature has other effects that are beneficial for exercisers as well. The potential physiological benefits of the warm-up include:

- Increased metabolic rate
- Gradual redistribution of blood flow to working muscles
- Decreased muscle-relaxation time following contraction
- Increased speed and force of muscle contraction
- Increased muscle, **tendon,** and **ligament** elasticity
- Gradual increase in energy production, which limits **lactic acid** buildup
- Reduced risk of abnormal heart rhythms

Many of these physiological effects have the potential to reduce the risk of injury because they may increase neuromuscular coordination, delay **fatigue,** and make the tissues less susceptible to damage (Herman et al., 2012).

Static Stretching

To stretch or not to stretch during the warm-up to promote injury prevention is a much-debated issue, and there is no clear consensus in the scientific literature (Lewis, 2014; Herman et al., 2012). One approach is to perform an active warm-up with rehearsal moves, followed by brief stretching with a focus on the muscle groups involved in the subsequent conditioning exercises. The warm-up should contain mostly dynamic movements, but static stretches can be included if they are limited to brief periods (five to 10 seconds). GFIs should also consider the ambient environment, as cold weather may increase the amount of time needed to warm up. In addition, older adults will require additional warm-up time compared to younger individuals.

In terms of organizing a group exercise class format for the warm-up segment, begin performing large-muscle, dynamic movements and incorporate rehearsal movements. When teaching a 30-minute session, it might be preferable to save the static stretching for the end, when it may be most beneficial in terms of enhancing flexibility.

CONDITIONING SEGMENT

There are a few common principles behind the conditioning segment of most group fitness classes. For a successful class experience, a GFI should:

- Promote independence/self-responsibility
- Gradually increase intensity
- Give progression and regression options (see Chapter 8)
- Build sequences logically and progressively
- Monitor intensity using the talk test, HR, and/or **ratings of perceived exertion (RPE)**
- Incorporate a post-conditioning cool-down/stretch segment

POST-CONDITIONING COOL-DOWN

The final portion of any group fitness session that contains moderate- to vigorous-intensity work should be less intense to allow the cardiorespiratory system to recover. During this final phase, GFIs should encourage participants to slow down, keep the arms below the level of the heart, and put less effort into the movements. Using less driving music, changing tone of voice, and verbalizing the transition to the participants can create this atmosphere. Performing some static stretches at the end of this segment also works well. Participants often run off to their next commitment immediately following class, so they may risk missing important flexibility training if stretching is not included in this portion of the class format.

Stretching

It is important that GFIs lead the class through the stretching of the major muscle groups in a safe and effective manner during the final phase. Relaxation, visualization, and specific breathing techniques may be included at the end of the flexibility segment to enhance the participant experience.

GFIs should consider stretching both the muscle groups that have been the focus of the group fitness class format, as well as those muscles that are commonly tight from everyday activities. For example, after an indoor cycling class, stretching the hip flexors, quadriceps, hamstrings, calves, hips, and glutes makes sense because they are major muscles used for cycling (Figures 2-1 through 2-5). The major muscle groups people typically use during **activities of daily living (ADL)** (e.g., calves, thighs, hips, torso, back, chest, and shoulders) can also be targeted with stretching.

The American College of Sports Medicine (ACSM) guidelines suggest performing static stretches for 15 to 60 seconds,

completing two to four repetitions per muscle group, a minimum of two to three days per week (ACSM, 2014). While it is not always possible to perform four repetitions of each stretch in a group fitness class that is 60 minutes or less in duration, GFIs should incorporate at least one repetition of a stretch for each major muscle group, holding each for at least 15 to 30 seconds. However, if the GFI is leading a stretching-focused class, it would be ideal to follow ACSM's flexibility guidelines.

There are precautions for stretching that GFIs should consider. Any type of aggressive stretching that goes beyond what an individual is accustomed to can result in pain and inflammation. All types of stretching, but perhaps more specifically, ballistic (bouncing) stretching and passive overstretching, can result in injury. Research has suggested that while these types of stretches can benefit ROM in athletic populations, such as gymnasts and dancers, they may also decrease performance and increase the likelihood for pain and inflammation in clinical or nonathlete populations (Apostolopoulos et al., 2015).

Figure 2-1
Hip-flexor
stretch

Figure 2-2
Quadriceps
stretch

Figure 2-3
Hamstrings
stretch

Figure 2-4
Calf stretch

Figure 2-5
Hip/glute stretch

Passive overstretching and ballistic stretching can initiate an involuntary **stretch reflex.** Special receptors within the muscle fibers detect sudden stretches and excessive lengthening (**muscle spindles** and **Golgi tendon organs,** respectively) of the muscle (Figure 2-6). There is a complicated and continual interplay between opposing muscle groups that leads to precision of control and coordinated movement. During this interplay, if a muscle is activated by a sudden stretch or if continued overlengthening of the muscle fiber occurs, the nervous system stimulates the muscle to contract rather than lengthen and maintains the contraction to oppose the force of excessive lengthening. Simply put, if a person overstretches or bounces a stretch, the muscle may shorten to protect itself. Repeated pulling on a shortened muscle can cause either a cramp or possibly a tear—but it will not lengthen the muscle.

Figure 2-6
The stretch reflex and
autogenic inhibition

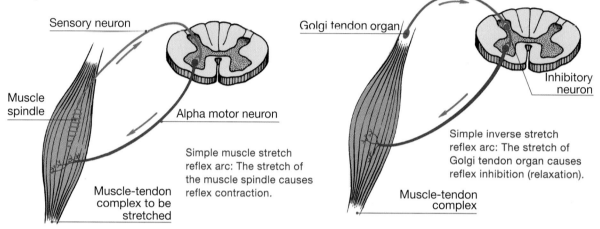

Sensory neuron

Golgi tendon organ

Muscle
spindle

Inhibitory
neuron

Alpha motor neuron

Simple muscle stretch
reflex arc: The stretch of
the muscle spindle causes
reflex contraction.

Simple inverse stretch
reflex arc: The stretch of
Golgi tendon organ causes
reflex inhibition (relaxation).

Muscle-tendon
complex to be
stretched

Muscle-tendon
complex

 **[APPLY WHAT YOU KNOW]**

Cueing a Stretch

It is important for stretching to be comfortable for participants. Encourage proper form by using cues such as "find a comfortable position where you feel gentle tension and hold; if you are shaking or if your muscles feel like rubber bands ready to snap, scale back the intensity of the stretch." Also, it is important for GFIs to model average flexibility so that participants do not imitate form they cannot comfortably or safely match. As with any other activity, it is important to progress participants appropriately. Yoga is a good example of a modality that has many advanced stretches that could be high-risk for some participants. If they are taught progressively, as is commonly done in dedicated yoga classes, the body adapts to the stretches and movements over time. However, putting advanced yoga poses into a traditional group fitness class does not allow for proper progression. Therefore, it is important that the GFI incorporate only moves that are appropriate for class participants.

Progress participants appropriately

Reminding participants of proper **posture** while stretching helps to promote overall body stability and balance, and enhances the effectiveness of the stretching experience. At least two to three concise verbal cues are needed during each stretch to make sure body positioning is optimal for an effective stretch. For example, when teaching a standing hamstrings stretch, it is important to cue to tilt the pelvis anteriorly to lengthen the hamstring muscles and to extend the knee as much as is safely possible (see Figure 2-3).

COMPONENTS OF HEALTH AND FITNESS

Physical fitness is defined as a set of measurable attributes that a person has achieved. A person who is physically fit has achieved a physiological state of well-being that allows him or her to successfully meet the demands of daily living and that provides the basis for sport performance. The most frequently cited components of physical fitness are divided into two groups: health-related attributes and skill-related attributes. The five health-related components of physical fitness are (Table 2-1):

1. cardiorespiratory endurance
2. muscular endurance
3. muscular strength
4. flexibility
5. body composition

These attributes are important to overall health, as individuals with favorable measures of these components tend to enjoy an enhanced quality of life.

Table 2-1

HEALTH-RELATED COMPONENTS OF PHYSICAL FITNESS

Cardiorespiratory endurance	The ability of the circulatory and respiratory systems to supply oxygen to working muscles during sustained physical activity
Muscular endurance	The ability of a muscle to perform repeated or sustained contractions without fatigue
Muscular strength	The ability of a muscle to exert maximal force
Flexibility	The range of motion at a joint
Body composition	The relative amounts of fat mass and fat-free mass in the body

Note: Fat mass = The actual amount of essential and non-essential fat in the body; Fat-free mass = That part of the body composition that represents everything but fat— including blood, bones, connective tissue, organs, and muscle; also called lean body mass

The skill-related components of physical fitness include (Table 2-2):

1 agility   **4** power

2 coordination   **5** reaction time

3 balance   **6** speed

Individuals who perform exercises to enhance these components typically have already achieved a certain level of conditioning through activities focused on improving the health-related components of physical fitness. Since these skills are required for the performance of most sport activities, skill-related physical-fitness components are commonly pursued by athletes who want to maintain or improve their abilities in their chosen sport. As such, the health-related components of physical fitness are considered more important to general health than are the skill-related components, which is why research on physical fitness and health primarily focuses on the health-related components.

Table 2-2

SKILL-RELATED COMPONENTS OF PHYSICAL FITNESS

Agility	The ability to rapidly and accurately change the position of the body in space
Coordination	The ability to smoothly and accurately perform complex movements
Balance	The ability to maintain equilibrium while stationary or moving
Power	The rate at which work can be performed; performing muscle contractions at high velocity
Reaction time	The amount of time elapsed between the stimulus for movement and the beginning of the movement
Speed	The ability to perform a movement within a short period of time

As the fitness industry is driven by trends, programs are continuously being created by passionate and motivated health and fitness professionals. It is important that those in the fitness industry continue to be mindful of the safety and efficacy of these programs. ACSM's guidelines on exercise programming for healthy adults can serve as a template for class design (ACSM, 2014) (Tables 2-3 and 2-4). The current guidelines include cardiorespiratory, muscular strength and endurance, flexibility, and neuromuscular (e.g., balance) exercise recommendations.

Table 2-3

AEROBIC (CARDIOVASCULAR ENDURANCE) EXERCISE EVIDENCE-BASED RECOMMENDATIONS

FITT-VP	EVIDENCE-BASED RECOMMENDATION
Frequency	≥5 days/week of moderate exercise, or ≥3 days/week of vigorous exercise, or a combination of moderate and vigorous exercise on ≥3–5 days/week is recommended
Intensity	Moderate and/or vigorous intensity is recommended for most adults. Light-to-moderate intensity exercise may be beneficial in deconditioned individuals.
Time	30–60 minutes/day of purposeful moderate exercise, or 20–60 minutes/day of vigorous exercise, or a combination of moderate and vigorous exercise per day is recommended for most adults. <20 minutes of exercise per day can be beneficial, especially in previously sedentary individuals.
Type	Regular, purposeful exercise that involves major muscle groups and is continuous and rhythmic in nature is recommended.
Volume	A target volume of ≥500–1,000 MET-minutes/week is recommended. Increasing pedometer step counts by ≥2,000 steps/day to reach a daily step count ≥7,000 steps/day is beneficial.* Exercising below these volumes may still be beneficial for individuals unable or unwilling to reach this amount of exercise.
Pattern	Exercise may be performed in one (continuous) session per day or in multiple sessions of ≥10 minutes to accumulate the desired duration and volume of exercise per day. Exercise bouts of <10 minutes may yield favorable adaptations in very deconditioned individuals.
Progression	A gradual progression of exercise volume by adjusting exercise duration, frequency, and/or intensity is reasonable until the desired exercise goal (maintenance) is attained. This approach may enhance adherence and reduce risks of musculoskeletal injury and adverse cardiac events.

*While many groups recommend 10,000 steps, the Centers for Disease Control and Prevention (CDC) recommends that adults engage in 150 minutes of moderate-intensity physical activity per week. To meet the CDC's recommendation, the average person needs to walk approximately 7,000 steps per day.

Note: FITT-VP = Frequency, intensity, time, type, volume, and pattern/progressions; MET-minutes = The product of metabolic equivalents (METs) and minutes of exercise (e.g., 5 METs x 30 minutes x 5 days = 750 MET-minutes)

Reprinted with permission from American College of Sports Medicine (2014). *ACSM's Guidelines for Exercise Testing and Prescription* (9th ed.). Philadelphia: Wolters Kluwer/Lippincott Williams & Wilkins.

Table 2-4

RESISTANCE EXERCISE EVIDENCE-BASED RECOMMENDATIONS

FITT-VP	EVIDENCE-BASED RECOMMENDATION
Frequency	Each major muscle group should be trained on 2–3 days/week.
Intensity	60–70% 1-RM (moderate-to-vigorous intensity) for novice to intermediate exercisers to improve strength
	≥80% 1-RM (vigorous-to-very vigorous intensity) for experienced strength trainers to improve strength
	40–50% 1-RM (very light-to-light intensity) for older individuals beginning exercise to improve strength
	40–50% 1-RM (very light-to-light intensity) may be beneficial for improving strength in sedentary individuals beginning a resistance-training program
	<50% 1-RM (light-to-moderate intensity) to improve muscular endurance
	20–50% 1-RM in older adults to improve power
Time	No specific duration of training has been identified for effectiveness.
Type	Resistance exercises involving each major muscle group are recommended.
	Multijoint exercises affecting more than one muscle group and targeting agonist and antagonist muscle groups are recommended for all adults.
	Single-joint exercises targeting major muscle groups may also be included in a resistance-training program, typically after performing multijoint exercise(s) for that particular muscle group.
	A variety of exercise equipment and/or body weight can be used to perform these exercises.
Repetitions	8–12 repetitions are recommended to improve strength and power in most adults.
	10–15 repetitions are effective in improving strength in middle-aged and older individuals starting exercise.
	15–20 repetitions are recommended to improve muscular endurance.
Sets	2–4 sets are recommended for most adults to improve strength and power.
	A single set of resistance exercise can be effective, especially among older and novice exercisers.
	≤2 sets are effective in improving muscular endurance.
Pattern	Rest intervals of 2–3 minutes between each set of repetitions are effective.
	A rest of ≥48 hours between sessions for any single muscle group is recommended.
Progression	A gradual progression of greater resistance, and/or more repetitions per set, and/or increasing frequency is recommended.

Note: FITT-VP = Frequency, intensity, time, type, volume, and pattern/progressions; 1-RM = One-repetition maximum

Reprinted with permission from American College of Sports Medicine (2014). *ACSM's Guidelines for Exercise Testing and Prescription* (9th ed.). Philadelphia: Wolters Kluwer/Lippincott Williams & Wilkins.

PRINCIPLES OF TRAINING

The basic training principles presented in this section apply to all forms of physical training. Successful exercise programs are the result of following established training principles from exercise science research. **Specificity, progressive overload,** and **reversibility** are general training principles of which GFIs should have a good understanding in order to provide safe and effective fitness classes.

The physiological changes caused by training are highly specific to the types of activities performed. This principle of training is called specificity. Exercise is a form of stress to which the body must overcome and adapt. Each mode of exercise places its own type of stress on the body. For example, resistance training increases strength but has little effect on cardiorespiratory endurance. Furthermore, training at a specific intensity will cause a specific conditioning outcome. For example, lifting lighter loads and performing a higher number of repetitions (low-intensity resistance training) will result in a training stimulus that favors muscular endurance, but not muscular strength.

Conversely, lifting heavier loads and performing fewer repetitions (high-intensity resistance training) will result in an increase in muscular strength, but not necessarily endurance. These low- and high-intensity weight-training examples illustrate that there is a clear relationship between intensity of exercise and duration. Namely, high-intensity exercise will be shorter in duration, whereas low-intensity exercise allows for longer duration.

Another important principle of exercise is progressive overload, which states that to improve physical fitness, the exerciser must regularly increase the demands placed on the body. The amount of overload necessary to elicit a safe and effective training response depends on the training state of the individual. A person accustomed to a **sedentary** lifestyle needs very little overload stimulus to bring about a training effect. For example, a person who has been ill or bedridden for an extended period of time may notice a sufficient training stimulus after walking 100

> ## Exercise stimulus must be gradually increased

feet. An individual who is **overweight** and deconditioned may notice strength improvements after performing resistance exercises using only his or her own body weight. However, an accomplished body builder may need to lift relatively large amounts of weight to produce an overload and stimulate a training effect. Since each individual presents a different state of physical fitness, overload must be applied specific to individual needs for intensity, frequency, and duration. Overload that is progressed properly will allow enough time for the body to adapt, thereby improving performance. An exercise stimulus must be gradually increased over time to safely elicit continued improvements.

The positive physiological effects of exercise training are reversible when individuals discontinue their exercise programs. This is called the principle of reversibility. Exercise capacity diminishes relatively rapidly, and within a few months of stopping physical activity, the improvements gained through training are lost. Furthermore, complete lack of activity, such as periods of immobility due to bed rest during sickness, causes dramatic losses in strength and bone mass. The reversibility principle demonstrates the importance of continued physical activity throughout life. In essence, "use it or lose it." Being fit as an adolescent or young adult does not provide continued benefits throughout the lifespan unless the exercise is maintained. Additionally, an exercise participant who suffers a setback and discontinues his or her fitness program for several months will have to start slowly and progress gradually if the exercise regimen is started again.

SUMMARY

Most group fitness classes should integrate some form of a warm-up, conditioning phase, and cool-down. Cardiorespiratory, resistance, and/or flexibility exercise can be included in the conditioning portion, or main body, of the workout to meet the participants' goals and the objectives of the class format. Understanding and being able to apply the variables of frequency, intensity, duration, and exercise mode as they pertain to each type of modality and/or class format will help a GFI guide participants appropriately to their goals. Additionally, having working knowledge of the general training principles of specificity, progressive overload, and reversibility is vital to designing and leading safe and effective group fitness classes.

References

American College of Sports Medicine (2014). *ACSM's Guidelines for Exercise Testing and Prescription* (9th ed.). Philadelphia: Wolters Kluwer/Lippincott Williams & Wilkins.

Apostolopoulos, N. et al. (2015). The relevance of stretch intensity and position: A systematic review. *Frontiers in Psychology,* 18, 6, 1128.

Herman, K. et al. (2012). The effectiveness of neuromuscular warm-up strategies that require no additional equipment, for preventing lower limb injuries during sports participation: A systematic review. *BMC Medicine,* 10, 75.

Lewis, J. (2014). A systematic literature review of the relationship between stretching and athletic injury prevention. *Orthopaedic Nursing,* 33, 6, 312–320.

Suggested Reading

American College of Sports Medicine (2014). *ACSM's Guidelines for Exercise Testing and Prescription* (9th ed.). Philadelphia: Wolters Kluwer/Lippincott Williams & Wilkins.

CHAPTER 3

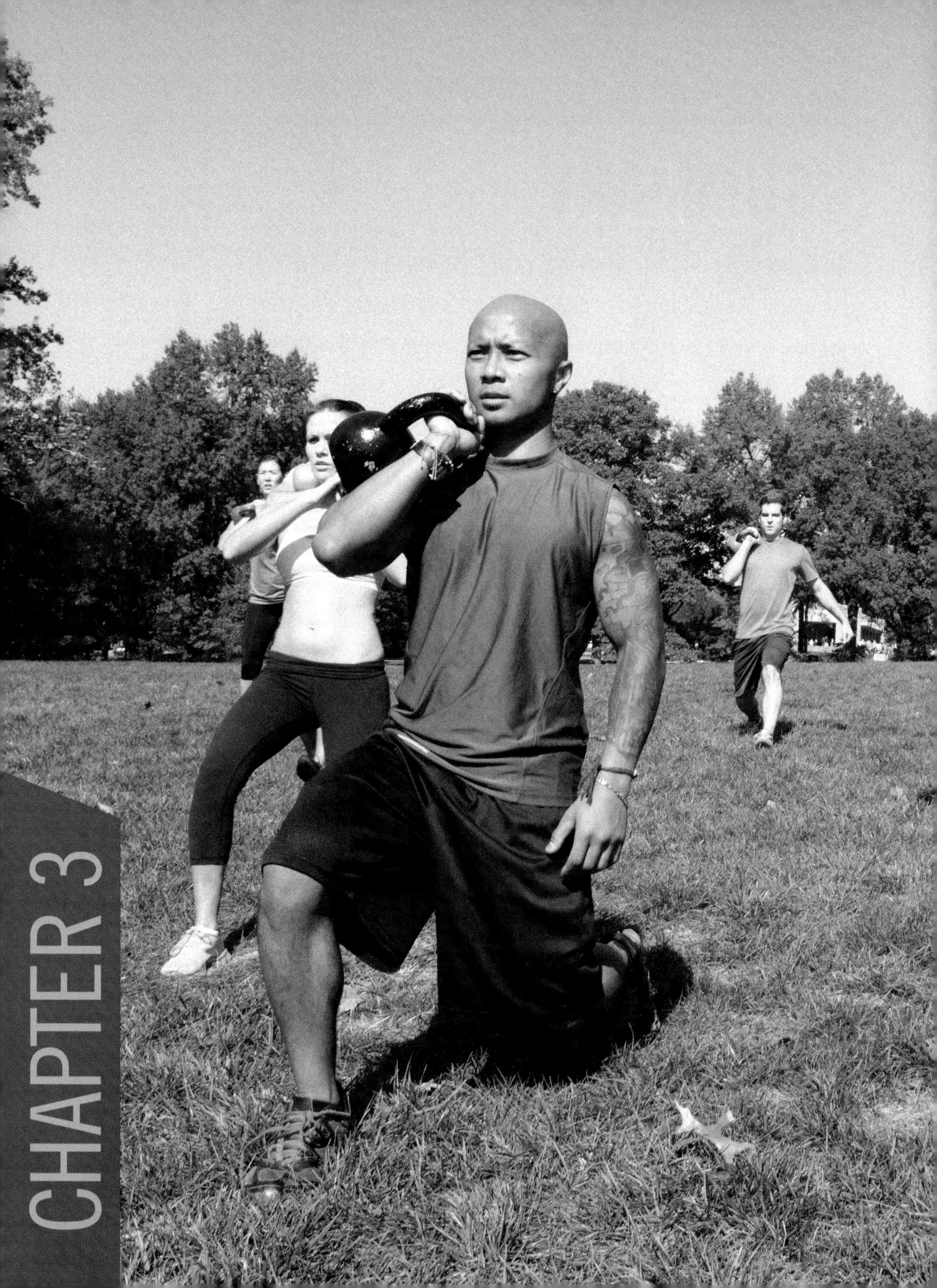

CHAPTER 3

UNDERSTANDING HUMAN MOVEMENT

SABRENA JO AND JESSICA MATTHEWS

EXERCISE BASED ON HUMAN MOVEMENT PRINCIPLES

STABILITY AND MOBILITY THROUGHOUT THE KINETIC CHAIN

MOVEMENT IN THREE PLANES

FIVE PRIMARY MOVEMENT PATTERNS

BALANCE IN GROUP EXERCISE

ENERGY PATHWAYS

THREE-ZONE INTENSITY MODEL

ACE INTEGRATED FITNESS TRAINING MODEL

ANATOMY OVERVIEW

BONES

MUSCLES

APPLIED ANATOMY

SUMMARY

LEARNING OBJECTIVES

■ Apply human movement principles to group fitness instruction.

■ Describe the three main energy pathways and how they relate to the three-zone intensity model.

■ Differentiate between the different categories and phases of the ACE Integrated Fitness Training® Model.

■ Demonstrate a basic understanding of gross anatomy, specifically bones and muscles, as required for successful exercise instruction.

■ List and briefly explain the 10 basic body positions commonly used in group fitness instruction and apply anatomical alignment concepts to each position.

In order to design and deliver cutting-edge fitness classes, ACE Certified Group Fitness Instructors (GFIs) must have a working knowledge of the human body. In addition, they must have a thorough understanding of how to practically apply general movement principles within various class formats in order to enhance the activities participants perform in the group fitness environment and in everyday life.

If your study program includes the ACE Learning Center, visit www.ACEfitness.org/MyACE and log in to your My ACE Account to learn more about anatomy and kinesiology through demonstrations of joint actions during various exercises.

EXERCISE BASED ON HUMAN MOVEMENT PRINCIPLES

The human body is designed to move and develops in response to stresses placed on its individual systems. Exercise enhances the movements and activities that people perform on a daily basis. Hence, the best way to functionally prepare the body is to train the same way in which it moves, favoring integration over isolation—that is, training movements, not solely muscles.

STABILITY AND MOBILITY THROUGHOUT THE KINETIC CHAIN

Movement is the result of muscle force, where actions at one body segment affect successive body segments along the **kinetic chain.** While an individual produces forces to move, the body must also tolerate the imposed forces of any external load, gravity pulling down on the body, and reactive forces pushing upward through the body. Consequently, the ability of an individual to move efficiently requires that his or her body possesses appropriate levels of both stability and mobility.

- **Joint stability** is the ability to maintain or control joint movement or position. It is achieved by the structures of the joints (e.g., muscles, **ligaments,** and **joint capsules**) and the neuromuscular system.
- Joint mobility is the range of uninhibited movement around a joint or body segment. It is achieved by the structures of the joints and the neuromuscular system.

While all joints demonstrate varying levels of stability and mobility, they tend to favor one over the other, depending on their function within the body (Figure 3-1). For example, while the lumbar spine demonstrates some mobility (approximately 15 degrees of rotation), it is generally stable, protecting the low back from injury. On the other hand, the thoracic spine is designed to be mobile to facilitate a variety of movements in the upper extremities. The scapulothoracic joint is a more stable joint formed by collective muscle action attaching the scapulae to the rib cage. This joint provides a solid platform for pulling and pushing movements at the glenohumeral joint and must tolerate the reactive forces transferred into the body during these movements. The foot is unique, as its level of stability varies during the gait cycle. Given its need to provide a solid platform for force production against the ground during push-off, it is stable. However, as the foot transitions from the heel strike to accepting body weight on one leg, it moves into **pronation** and forfeits some stability in exchange for increased mobility to help absorb the impact

forces. As the foot prepares to push off, the ankle moves back into **supination,** becoming more rigid and stable again to increase force transfer into motion.

MOVEMENT IN THREE PLANES

Human movement can be described as taking place in one of three **planes of motion**—the **sagittal plane, frontal plane,** and **transverse plane** (Figure 3-2). GFIs can better understand proper alignment and body mechanics as it applies to effective exercise program design when they have a good grasp on how the body moves in these three planes. While movements and positions are sometimes multiplanar, understanding each plane individually is critical to both teaching and recognizing safe and effective movement.

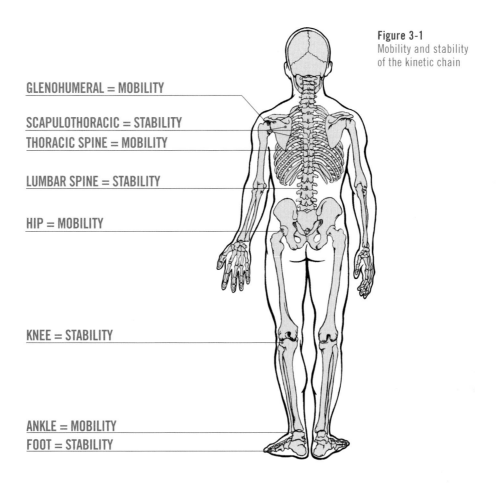

Figure 3-1
Mobility and stability
of the kinetic chain

GLENOHUMERAL = MOBILITY

SCAPULOTHORACIC = STABILITY
THORACIC SPINE = MOBILITY

LUMBAR SPINE = STABILITY

HIP = MOBILITY

KNEE = STABILITY

ANKLE = MOBILITY
FOOT = STABILITY

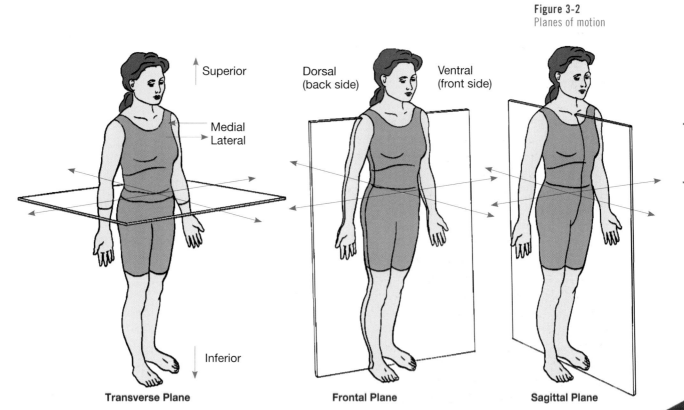

Figure 3-2
Planes of motion

Superior

Medial
Lateral

Dorsal
(back side)

Ventral
(front side)

Inferior

Transverse Plane

Frontal Plane

Sagittal Plane

Sagittal Plane

The sagittal plane separates the body into right and left halves. Forward and backward movements occur in the sagittal plane. Think of standing in a doorway and moving away from the frame forward and backward.

Possible joint actions are:

- **Flexion** (elbows, shoulders, knees, hips, and spine)
- **Extension** (elbows, shoulders, knees, hips, and spine)
- **Plantar flexion** (ankles)
- **Dorsiflexion** (ankles)

Practical application:

- Most indoor cycling classes occur in the sagittal plane. Many **supine** Pilates exercises and traditional abdominal crunches also occur in the sagittal plane, as well as many resistance-training exercises, such as squats and lunges (Figure 3-3).

Frontal Plane

The frontal plane separates the body into **anterior** and **posterior** halves. Lateral movements occur in the frontal plane. Think of moving sideways between two planes of glass while trying not to touch them.

Possible joint actions are:

- **Abduction** (shoulders and hips)
- **Adduction** (shoulders and hips)
- Lateral spinal flexion
- Ankle **eversion** and **inversion**

Figure 3-3
Movement in the sagittal plane: Lunge

Practical application:

- Many standing yoga postures, like star pose, occur in the frontal plane. Aquatic fitness exercises, like jumping jacks and tic-tocs, also occur in the frontal plane, as do common group exercise movements like the lateral lunge (Figure 3-4).

Transverse Plane

The transverse plane divides the body into upper (**superior**) and lower (**inferior**) parts. Rotational or twisting movements primarily occur in the transverse plane. Think of rotating the rib cage in one direction while the pelvis moves in the opposite direction.

Possible joint actions are:

- Rotation
- Horizontal shoulder adduction and abduction

Practical application:

- Yoga and Pilates twists occur in the transverse plane, as do abdominal/core exercises involving rotation, such as supine bicycle crunches (Figure 3-5) and seated medicine ball trunk rotations.

FIVE PRIMARY MOVEMENT PATTERNS

In addition to understanding movements in terms of the planes of motion, it is also beneficial to think of exercises in terms of their application to **activities of daily living (ADL).** Specifically, movements of everyday life can be broken down and described by five primary movements (Figure 3-6):

- Bend-and-lift (raising and lowering) movements (e.g., squatting down to pick an object off of the floor, or standing up from a chair)
- Single-leg movements (e.g., walking, lunging, or climbing stairs)
- Upper-body pushing movements (e.g., pushing open a door, putting something away on a tall shelf, or propping oneself up from a side-lying position)
- Upper-body pulling movements (e.g., opening a car door)
- Rotational movements (e.g., turning to throw something away behind you or reaching across the body to buckle a seatbelt)

GFIs should incorporate a variety of exercises into classes to help participants effectively train these important movements in order to enhance how they move both inside and outside of the group fitness environment.

Figure 3-4
Movement in the frontal plane: Lateral lunge

Figure 3-5
Movement in the transverse plane: Supine bicycle crunches

Figure 3-6
Five primary
movement patterns

Bend-and-lift movement

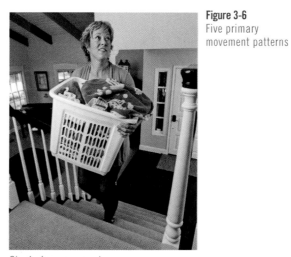

Single-leg movement

Pushing movement

Pulling movement

Rotational movement

BALANCE IN GROUP EXERCISE

As discussed in Chapter 2, a well-rounded fitness routine includes cardiorespiratory, strength, and **flexibility** exercise, as well as balance and agility training. If the goal of a class is to increase **muscular strength** and **cardiorespiratory fitness,** both of these components will be addressed within the same class format. GFIs may choose to focus on one component before the other, or elect to alternate between the two in a circuit-style format. If the goal of a class is to increase flexibility, this can either become a class in itself (such as dedicated stretching or yoga class) or specific flexibility exercises can be performed at the end of a strength, cardiorespiratory, or fusion class, as it is most effective to stretch muscles that are properly warmed and therefore more pliable.

As an instructor, it is important to understand that all participants should engage in cardiorespiratory, strength, and flexibility training. A well-rounded fitness program that incorporates these three elements reflects the concept of balance.

Overall, the principle of balance applies to group exercise in three ways:

> **Neuromuscular:**
> - Being able to stand on one leg
> - Being able to stand equally supported on both feet
> - Raising one arm or leg (or both) in the quadruped position
> - Maintaining neutral pelvic position and spinal **posture**
> - Executing exercises on an unstable surface, as appropriate
> - Raising one knee or foot off of the floor in plank position

A well-rounded fitness routine includes cardiorespiratory, strength, and flexibility exercise

> **Training:**
> - Both sides of the body (if split into right and left halves) need to be trained equally because together they connect and create a whole. This type of approach is called bilateral training. Instructors who train with a unilateral approach during cardiorespiratory moves (such as only doing mambos with the left leg, leaping only to the right, and stepping only with the right lead leg) or strength moves (such as only doing lunges with the right foot stepping forward) fail to integrate this principle of balance in their classes.
> - When GFIs teach movement patterns that utilize both sides of a given movement pattern (such as performing lunges to the right and left), it is called "transitional" and "reversible" because the movement is repeated on both sides and/or in both directions to ensure this type of balance.
> - Balance in training also means that an individual should strive to be equally balanced among the three key components of training—cardiorespiratory, strength, and flexibility training. For example, if a participant only attends indoor cycling classes, he or she should seek out additional modes of exercise that focus on muscular strength and endurance training as well, such as a group strength class that includes resistance-training exercises, especially for the upper body. Similarly, a yoga enthusiast should seek out modes of cardiorespiratory training to complement his or her yoga practice, such as dance-based fitness classes.

> **Programming:**
> - Instructors should consider opposing muscles (**agonists** and **antagonists**) as well as varying planes of motion when choosing exercises and movements for their participants.
> - As a cardiorespiratory example, always doing movement in the frontal plane with exercises like grapevines instead of sometimes incorporating marching front and back (sagittal plane) or twisting (transverse plane) would not only be boring, but would also limit the participants from experiencing exercises in all three planes of movement.
> - As a strength/endurance example, performing biceps curls in a group strength class without an exercise for the triceps (the opposing muscle group) would not be well-balanced for the muscles of the upper arm.

ENERGY PATHWAYS

The energy to move and think comes from the foods people eat and drink. **Carbohydrates** are easy for the body to break down and provide quick energy, while **fats** provide a seemingly endless supply of stored energy. **Proteins** are the building blocks of human structure and are not a primary source of energy. The body stores carbohydrates and fats in their most basic forms—**glucose** and **triglycerides,** respectively. When the body needs energy, it breaks down the chemical bonds in the stored energy, releasing **adenosine triphosphate (ATP),** the basic substance that the body uses for energy.

Exercise intensity and duration determine the fuel sources used. Generally, there is an inverse relationship between exercise intensity and duration. The more intense the workout, the less time participants are able to maintain the intensity.

When people work at extreme intensities for just seconds, they use up the small amount of **creatine phosphate** they have in the body, via the **creatine phosphate system,** or **phosphagen system,** to produce ATP. An example is sprinting as fast as possible, which people can generally sustain for only a few seconds.

When people work at hard intensities for a few minutes, they use up carbohydrate stores, via the **glycolytic anaerobic system,** which can produce ATP without oxygen. An example is doing high-intensity intervals lasting one to two minutes, and then having to recover while breathing in oxygen to replenish the muscles before continuing.

When people work at moderate and low intensities for longer than a few minutes, they use a combination of carbohydrates and fats to produce ATP for energy to move. This is accomplished via the **aerobic system,** as sufficient oxygen is present for the production of all ATP. Examples of this include swimming, most movements in cardiorespiratory classes, and stepping classes.

THREE-ZONE INTENSITY MODEL

A fairly reliable intensity marker (especially for beginning exercisers) is the ability to talk during exertion. For simplicity,

exercisers can use a three-zone model (Figure 3-7) to gauge appropriate exertion during cardiorespiratory activity, where:

- Zone 1 is low-to-moderate intensity exercise, during which the exerciser can talk comfortably.
- Zone 2 is moderate-to-vigorous intensity aerobic exercise, during which talking is a little challenging, but still possible.
- Zone 3 is vigorous to very vigorous exercise, during which the exerciser definitely cannot talk comfortably.

The three zones are separated by each participant's unique metabolic markers, known as the **first ventilatory threshold (VT1),** where talking first becomes a little challenging, and the **second ventilatory threshold (VT2),** where talking becomes very difficult and is reduced to one or two words at a time.

This simple model can be useful for GFIs in class settings as they seek to gauge the intensity at which participants are working. A GFI can simply ask participants questions and listen for responses during the conditioning portion of class. It is important to educate participants on the concept of the three-zone intensity model and how it relates to talking, as doing so may elicit more responses from participants if they know the GFI is relying on their vocal cues as a way to monitor intensity. Refer to Chapter 4 for more information on the **talk test.**

Figure 3-7
Three-zone training model

Note: VT1 = First ventilatory threshold;
VT2 = Second ventilatory threshold

ACE INTEGRATED FITNESS TRAINING MODEL

Fitness facilities face the mounting challenges associated with an aging and increasingly **overweight** population, as well as an overburdened healthcare system that is often unable to meet the need for preventive care. Health and fitness professionals, including GFIs, are seeing an influx of participants with an increasingly long list of special considerations (see Chapter 9), creating confusion as they attempt to develop group fitness classes that safely and effectively address individual needs.

To address these complex concerns, ACE created the ACE Integrated Fitness Training (ACE IFT®) Model, which provides a systematic and comprehensive approach to exercise programming to facilitate behavior change (see Chapter 6), while also improving posture, movement, flexibility, balance, core function, cardiorespiratory fitness, **muscular endurance,** and muscular strength. While the ACE IFT Model was originally developed as a tool for personal trainers, its core concepts can also be applied in the group fitness environment.

The ACE IFT Model consists of two components, each of which is then divided into four phases that run parallel to the function–health–fitness–performance continuum (Figure 3-8). **Rapport** is the foundation for success during all phases, whether the exerciser is a highly motivated fitness enthusiast or a **sedentary** adult looking to adopt more healthful habits. The primary focus of each of the four phases of the ACE IFT Model is as follows:

▬ Functional movement and resistance training
   ✔ *Phase 1: Stability and mobility training:* Correcting imbalances through training to improve joint stability and mobility prior to training movement patterns

   ✔ *Phase 2: Movement training:* Training movement patterns prior to loading those movements (i.e., body-weight exercises)
   ✔ *Phase 3: Load training:* Adding external resistance (e.g., dumbbells and medicine balls) to various movement patterns
   ✔ *Phase 4: Performance training:* Improving performance through training for power, speed, agility, and reactivity (e.g., plyometric exercises and sports conditioning drills)

▬ Cardiorespiratory training
   ✔ *Phase 1: Aerobic-base training:* Building an aerobic base to improve parameters of cardiorespiratory health
   ✔ *Phase 2: Aerobic-efficiency training:* Progressing toward improved fitness by introducing aerobic intervals to improve aerobic efficiency
   ✔ *Phase 3: Anaerobic-endurance training:* Progressing to higher levels of fitness by developing **anaerobic** endurance
   ✔ *Phase 4: Anaerobic-power training:* Improving performance by developing anaerobic power

Figure 3-8
ACE IFT Model phases and the function–health–fitness–performance continuum

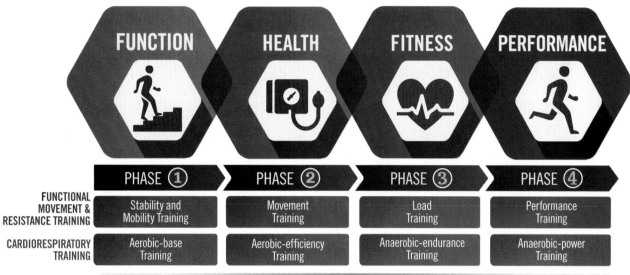

FUNCTION	HEALTH	FITNESS	PERFORMANCE

	PHASE ①	PHASE ②	PHASE ③	PHASE ④
FUNCTIONAL MOVEMENT & RESISTANCE TRAINING	Stability and Mobility Training	Movement Training	Load Training	Performance Training
CARDIORESPIRATORY TRAINING	Aerobic-base Training	Aerobic-efficiency Training	Anaerobic-endurance Training	Anaerobic-power Training

RAPPORT

Note: The phases of the ACE IFT Model are not necessarily discrete in terms of their connection to the function–health–fitness–performance continuum. Progression principles should be followed when transitioning from one phase to the next for each training component.

It is important that GFIs look at their classes and individual participants from multiple perspectives in order to keep people excited to continue exercising. Unlike personal trainers, who specifically design an exercise program for a given client, GFIs must first program for the group before offering **progressions** or **regressions** for individual participants who may be in various phases of the ACE IFT Model. The core challenge for many GFIs—whether they are novice or more experienced instructors—commonly involves finding a balance between instructing the entire group and making sure individual class participants progress appropriately and safely. For this reason, GFIs should always communicate to participants that it is their responsibility to manage their movements and work within their personal fitness levels.

One situation in which the ACE IFT Model may be applied more directly in a group setting involves the development of longer-term group programming for participants who begin a program together and progress as a group. For example, a GFI may lead a six-week boot-camp program or guide a group of new mothers through the postpartum return to exercise. In these cases, pre-participation screening can be used to classify each individual's health and fitness level, both as a baseline against which to measure future success, and as a tool to improve **motivation** and **adherence**.

ANATOMY OVERVIEW

GFIs do not need to be expert anatomists in order to teach safe and effective exercise classes. However, a basic understanding of gross **anatomy,** specifically the structure and function of bones and muscles, is required for successful exercise instruction.

BONES

Becoming familiar with the names of the major bones of the body can be helpful, as a GFI can reference them when providing verbal anatomical and alignment cues (see Chapter 8). Using the correct names of bones not only makes instructors more credible, but also helps to

truly educate participants about their bodies. Figure 3-9 illustrates the major bones of the skeletal system, while Figure 3-10 illustrates the bones of the spine.

While not an exhaustive list, Table 3-1 presents a series of practical examples of what types of cues instructors from various disciplines could use when referencing bones.

Figure 3-9
Skeletal system

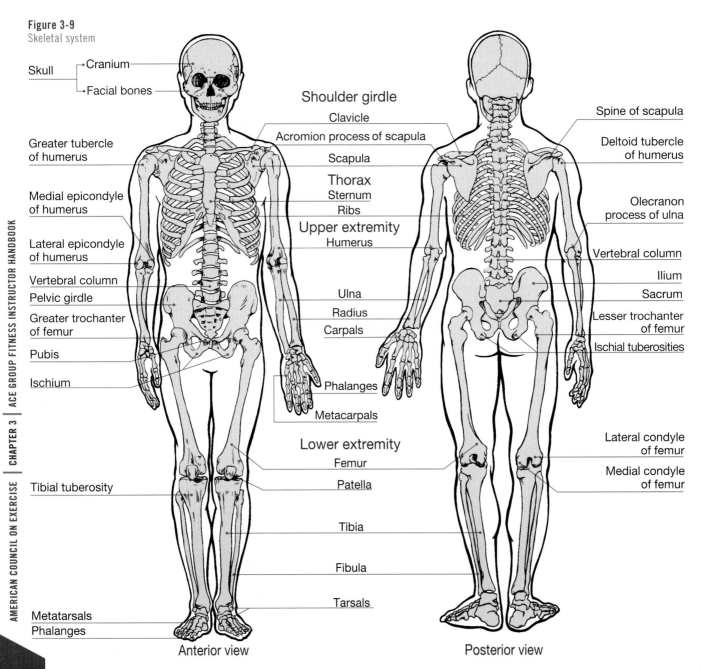

Anterior view

Posterior view

Figure 3-10
Vertebral column
(lateral view)

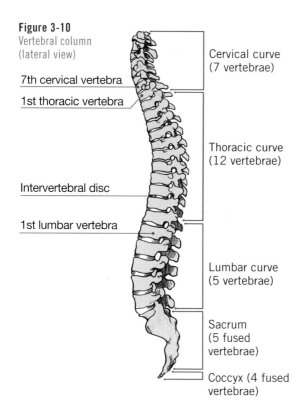

7th cervical vertebra

1st thoracic vertebra

Intervertebral disc

1st lumbar vertebra

Cervical curve
(7 vertebrae)

Thoracic curve
(12 vertebrae)

Lumbar curve
(5 vertebrae)

Sacrum
(5 fused
vertebrae)

Coccyx (4 fused
vertebrae)

Table 3-1

EXAMPLES OF ANATOMICAL CUES

DISCIPLINE	SAMPLE CUE
Cycling	"When placing the ball of your foot on the pedal to size your bike, ensure that your *patella* remains aligned with your second toe as your knee flexes slightly."
Stretching	"When lying supine in the dead bug position, make sure your *tibia* and *fibula* are parallel with the floor."
Latin-based dance	"Concentrate on moving your *pelvic girdle* up and down and from side to side as we do the merengue dance."
Yoga	"Find balance in boat pose by sitting on your *ischial tuberosities* instead of the *gluteus maximus* muscle."
Core conditioning	"When setting up the side-plank position, be sure the *radius* and *ulna* are perpendicular to the spine."
Aquatic fitness	"Keep the *humerus* stable in the water while you flex and extend the elbow for these biceps curls."

MUSCLES

In general, GFIs should know where a muscle is located and what joint or joints it crosses. Many muscles in the front, or anterior, part of the body are primarily used for pushing movements, while many muscles in the back, or posterior, part of the body are primarily used for pulling movements. When the angle between any two bones decreases, it is called joint flexion. This typically occurs as a result of a muscle pulling on its attachments and shortening. Conversely, when the angle between joints increases, it is called joint extension and is usually the result of the muscle on the flexion side of the joint lengthening while the opposing muscle on the other side of the joint pulls and shortens. The prefix "hyper" means excessive,

so **hyperflexion** occurs when a limb or part of the body is flexed beyond its normal **range of motion (ROM)**. Similarly, **hyperextension** occurs when there is movement at a joint into a position beyond the joint's normal maximal extension. Two important examples of these concepts occur at the elbows and knees. In cycling, many participants hyperextend their elbows as they prop themselves up on the handlebars, producing tension and instability throughout the core. In strength training, many participants hyperflex their knees when they squat, moving the knees forward instead of concentrating on hinging at the hips and lowering the glutes.

Figures 3-11 through 3-29 illustrate the major muscles of the body, along with their common joint actions.

Figure 3-11
Pelvic floor—Joint actions: Stabilization, support, and involvement in core bracing

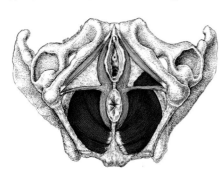

Figure 3-12
Transverse abdominis—Joint actions: Compress abdomen, drawing-in maneuver, and involvement in core bracing

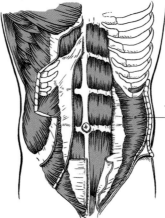

Transverse abdominis

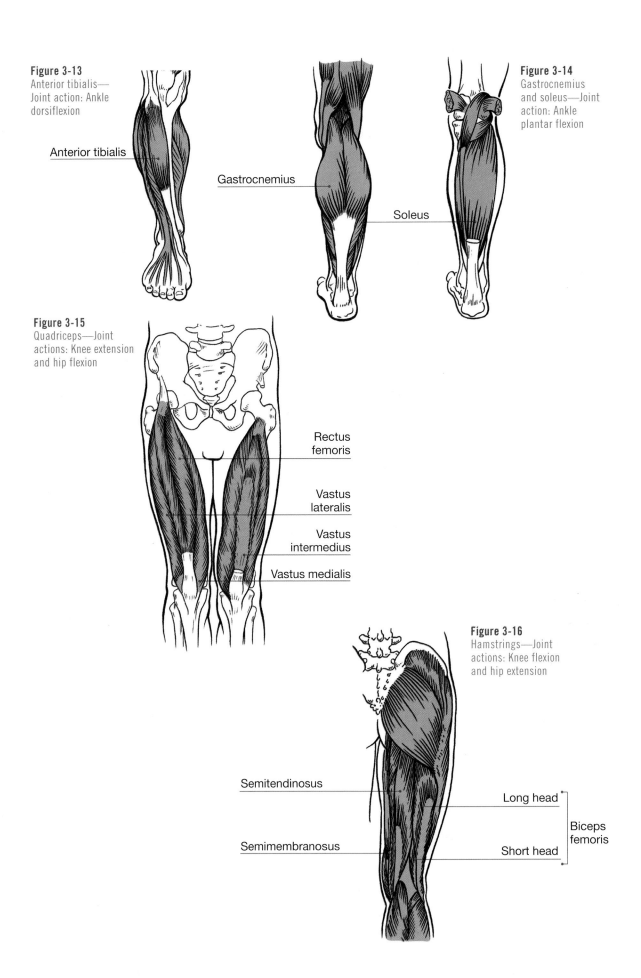

Figure 3-13
Anterior tibialis—
Joint action: Ankle
dorsiflexion

Anterior tibialis

Gastrocnemius

Figure 3-14
Gastrocnemius
and soleus—Joint
action: Ankle
plantar flexion

Soleus

Figure 3-15
Quadriceps—Joint
actions: Knee extension
and hip flexion

Rectus
femoris

Vastus
lateralis

Vastus
intermedius

Vastus medialis

Figure 3-16
Hamstrings—Joint
actions: Knee flexion
and hip extension

Semitendinosus

Semimembranosus

Long head

Short head

Biceps
femoris

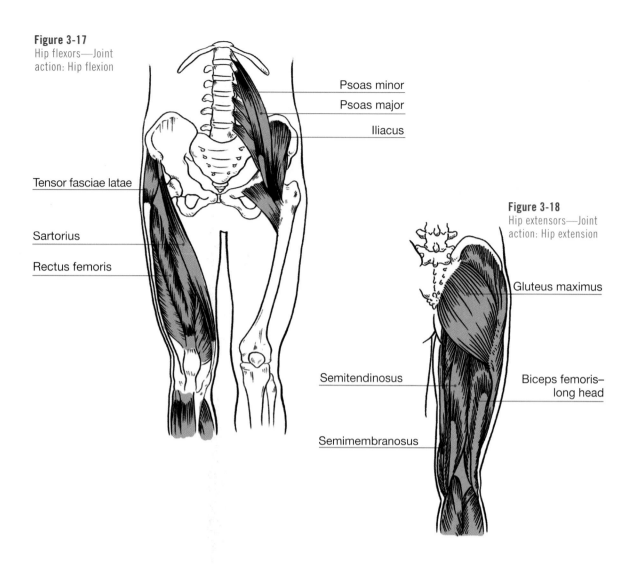

Figure 3-17
Hip flexors—Joint
action: Hip flexion

Psoas minor
Psoas major
Iliacus

Tensor fasciae latae

Sartorius

Rectus femoris

Figure 3-18
Hip extensors—Joint
action: Hip extension

Gluteus maximus

Semitendinosus

Biceps femoris–
long head

Semimembranosus

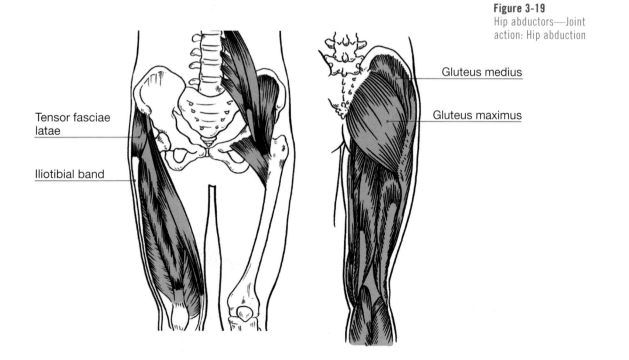

Figure 3-19
Hip abductors—Joint
action: Hip abduction

Tensor fasciae
latae

Iliotibial band

Gluteus medius

Gluteus maximus

Figure 3-20
Hip adductors—Joint
action: Hip adduction

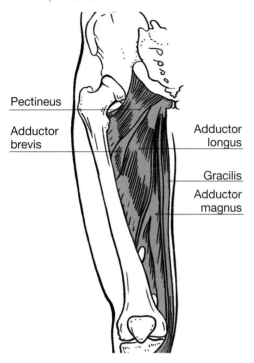

Pectineus

Adductor
brevis

Adductor
longus

Gracilis

Adductor
magnus

Figure 3-21
Rectus abdominis—Joint
action: Spinal flexion

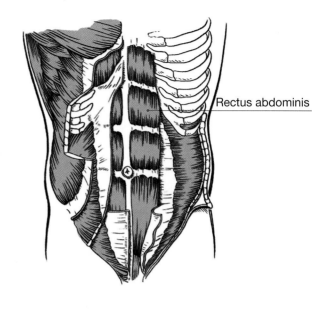

Rectus abdominis

Figure 3-22
Erector spinae—Joint
action: Spinal extension

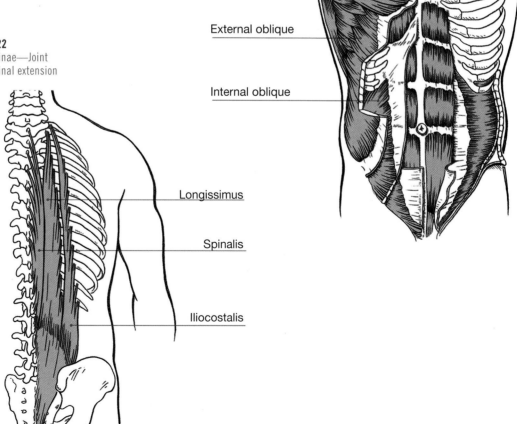

Longissimus

Spinalis

Iliocostalis

Figure 3-23
Obliques—Joint actions:
Rotation and lateral flexion

External oblique

Internal oblique

Figure 3-24
Quadratus lumborum—Joint action: Lateral flexion

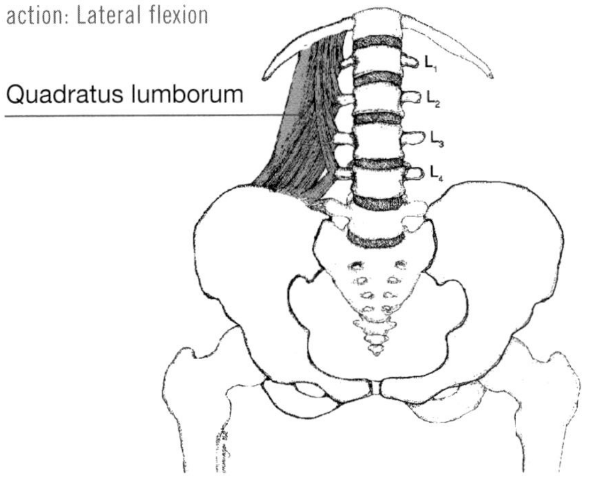

Quadratus lumborum

L₁
L₂
L₃
L₄

Figure 3-25
Pectoralis major—Joint actions: Shoulder flexion, extension, adduction, and horizontal adduction

Pectoralis major

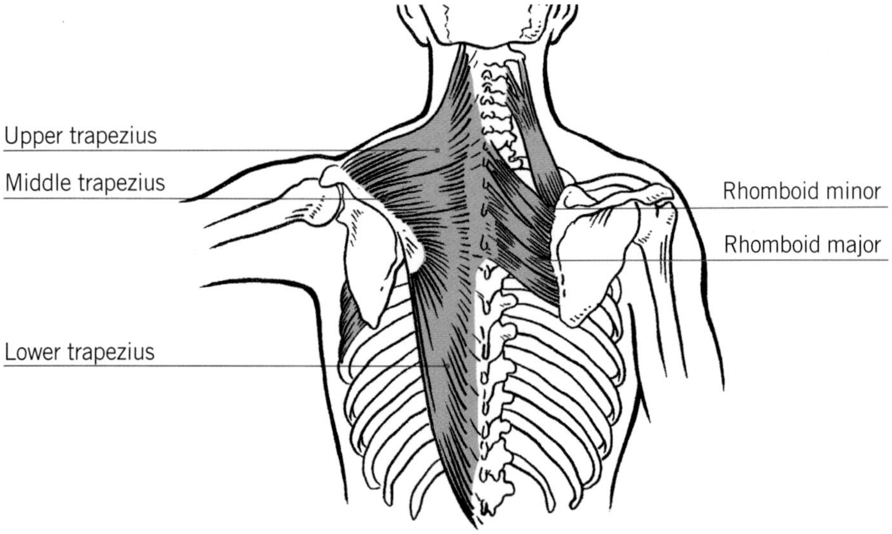

Upper trapezius
Middle trapezius

Rhomboid minor
Rhomboid major

Lower trapezius

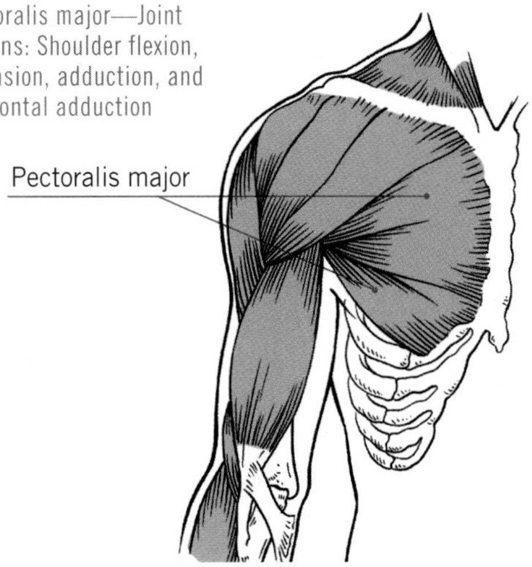

Figure 3-26
Trapezius and rhomboids—Joint actions: Upper trapezius, elevation of scapula; middle trapezius, adduction of scapula; lower trapezius, depression of scapula; rhomboids, adduction of scapula

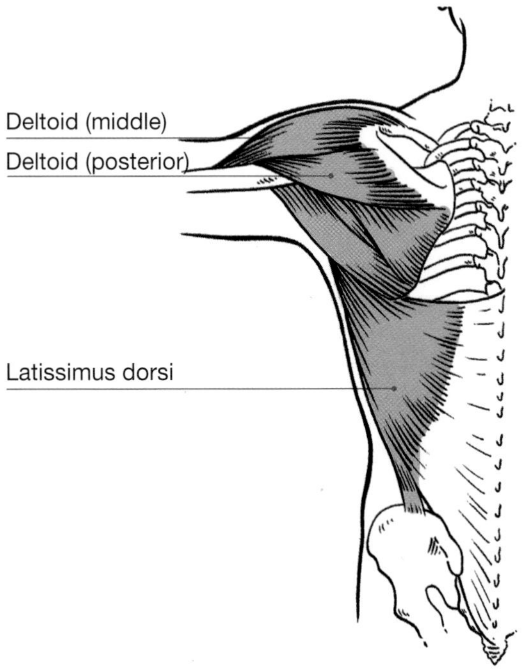

Deltoid (middle)
Deltoid (posterior)

Latissimus dorsi

Figure 3-27
Deltoids and latissimus dorsi—Joint actions: Deltoids, shoulder flexion, abduction, and horizontal adduction and abduction; Latissimus dorsi, shoulder extension, adduction, and horizontal abduction Anterior deltoid not visible from this view.

Figure 3-28
Biceps—Joint action:
Elbow flexion

Figure 3-29
Triceps—Joint action:
Elbow extension

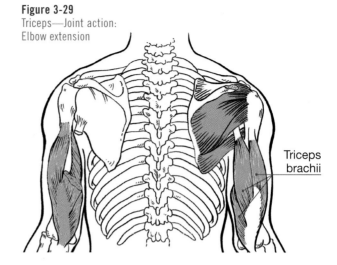

Biceps brachii

Triceps brachii

 [EXPAND YOUR KNOWLEDGE]

The Importance of Posture

The principle of balance discussed earlier also applies to general posture, as it helps one understand that neutral posture means that all of the muscles work on the body's center equally. When any muscle or muscle group pulls too strongly or becomes too tight, this can create an imbalance. Similarly, when a muscle or muscle group is too weak, it may not pull strongly enough or execute its intended movement.

A unique aspect of the trunk is how it functions as the "tunnel" through which all systems connect. The center of the core is the pelvic floor (see Figure 3-11), and core training involves a general isometric tightening of these muscles in addition to activating the transverse abdominis (see Figure 3-12), which compresses and protects the core and stabilizes the spine.

One way to describe the fitness-related function of the transverse abdominis is to think about cinching a belt around the waist, drawing in the core muscles almost as if to appear slimmer through the midsection. The technique of bracing (which involves co-contracting the core and abdominal muscles), performed in conjunction with pelvic floor maneuvers (such as Kegels), activates the core and can enhance overall core function during classes, whether they focus on cardiorespiratory, strength, or flexibility training.

Neutral posture involves an equal amount of static, isometric tension on the anterior and posterior muscles of the core. There is a natural relationship between the ribs and the hips where there is no exaggeration in either direction. The spine has seven cervical vertebrae, 12 thoracic vertebrae, five lumbar vertebrae, five fused vertebrae called the sacrum, and four fused vertebrae at the bottom, called the coccyx (see Figure 3-10).

Because the natural, aligned spine is neither straight nor flat, instructors can use the words "natural," "neutral," "aligned," "lengthened," "tall," and "proud," instead of terms that do not adequately describe the way the vertebrae should align. While some spinal curvature is natural, deviations in the spine are common and occur when someone has an exaggeration of these curves.

Faulty Posture Examples

Lordosis

When standing tall in an erect posture, all joints are in extension. When someone's pelvis tilts forward, this is called an anterior pelvic tilt and usually denotes an exaggerated lumbar curve, called **lordosis** (Figure 3-30). Often, the spinal erectors are pulling too strongly in the back, while the hip flexors are pulling too strongly in the front. Individuals most likely will need to focus on strengthening their abdominal muscles and hip extensors (gluteus maximus and hamstrings), in addition to stretching the spinal erectors and hip flexors (iliopsoas).

Kyphosis

Excessive posterior curvature of the thoracic spine—referred to as kyphosis (Figure 3-31)—is marked by rounding of the upper back, often accompanied by an anterior pelvic tilt. Somewhat similar, an increase in the rounding of the thoracic spine along with forward-head position and rounded shoulders may also be accompanied by a posterior pelvic tilt, in which the pelvis tilts backward. In both instances, individuals will likely need to strengthen the middle/lower trapezius and rhomboids that pull the shoulder blades back (see Figure 3-26), as well as strengthen the erector spinae group to increase the anterior space between the ribs and hips (see Figure 3-22). It is important to encourage stretching of the chest in addition to addressing muscular imbalances related to the respective positioning of the pelvis.

Scoliosis

When a participant's spine is an "S" shape, where the pelvis and shoulders appear uneven when looking at them from the front or back, it may be **scoliosis** (Figure 3-32). If this individual has pain and cannot assume a neutral spine position, he or she should be referred to an appropriate medical professional.

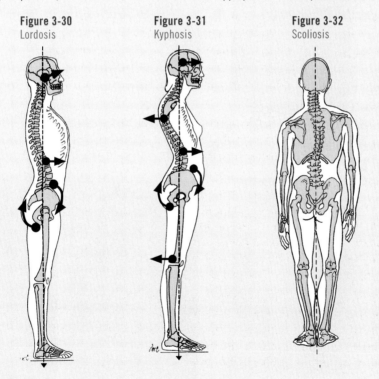

Figure 3-30
Lordosis

Figure 3-31
Kyphosis

Figure 3-32
Scoliosis

 [THINK IT THROUGH]

What specific stretches could you incorporate at the end of a sports-conditioning class to stretch the hip flexors?

APPLIED ANATOMY

The most practical way to apply the structural concepts of anatomy is to relate it to how the body moves and functions. In fitness classes, the various exercises and movements of the body can be categorized into 10 positions. GFIs must have an understanding of what neutral position of the spine both looks and feels like in each of these positions.

Instructors must also understand what the extremities, or distal body parts, both look and feel like. Figures 3-33 through 3-42 present names and cues for each of the major positions of the body. Pictured are common movements from a plethora of group fitness disciplines to illustrate some common exercises that fall within each of these categories.

Figure 3-33
Bilateral standing

Ankles under soft knees, under neutral hips; navel in; shoulders back and down and eyes forward with chin down

Examples include squats, pliés, and hinging, as well as many movements performed throughout the day, from picking things up to sitting down into a chair

Figure 3-34
Unilateral standing

Ankles under soft knees, under neutral hips; navel in; shoulders back and down and eyes forward with chin down

Examples include single-leg squats, tree pose, and lunges, as well as many movements performed throughout the day, such as climbing stairs and getting in and out of a car

Figure 3-35
Kneeling (high or low)

Knees under hips, navel in, shoulders back and down; neutral spine, head, and hips

Figure 3-36
Quadruped (hands-and-knees position)

Palms under gently flexed elbows below shoulders; knees under hips, neutral spine, head and hips, feet pointing in the same direction; fingers pointing forward

Figure 3-37
Plank

Palms under gently flexed elbows under shoulders with fingers pointing forward (for plank or triceps push-ups or toward each other for triangle push-ups); neutral spine, head, and hips; feet pointing in the same direction

Figure 3-38
Prone (lying on stomach)

Neutral spine and head usually looking to one direction; feet pointing in the same direction

Figure 3-39
Side-plank, side-lying

Neutral spine and head; supported on elbow or cradled head in arm

Figure 3-40
Supine
(lying on back)

Neutral spine, head, and hips; often at least one knee flexed to support the spine

Figure 3-41
Reverse plank

Neutral spine; short- or long-lever legs; palms or forearms on floor with fingers spread and pointing toward feet

Figure 3-42
Seated

Neutral spine; knees flexed or extended; this includes indoor cycling

SUMMARY

Understanding human movement provides one of the most practical approaches to exercise instruction available to the GFI. This chapter has provided a brief region-by-region summary of the basic anatomy and movements of the body, along with information on posture, alignment, and program-design principles associated with the ACE IFT Model. A GFI can draw on this information to design and implement specific exercises that will safely and efficiently accomplish the goals of his or her group fitness participants.

Suggested Reading

American Council on Exercise (2014). *ACE Personal Trainer Manual* (5th ed.). San Diego: American Council on Exercise.

American Council on Exercise (2012). *ACE's Essentials of Exercise Science for Fitness Professionals.* San Diego: American Council on Exercise.

Golding, L.A. (2002). *Fitness Professionals Guide to Musculoskeletal Anatomy and Human Movement.* Monterey, Calif.: Healthy Learning.

Porcari, J.P., Bryant, C.X., & Comana, F. (2015). *Exercise Physiology.* Philadelphia: F.A. Davis Company.

Introduction to Part 2:
CONSIDERATIONS, DESIGN, AND PREPARATION FOR GROUP FITNESS CLASSES

Safe, effective, and enjoyable classes are the result of diligent planning on the part of the ACE Certified Group Fitness Instructor (GFI). While great care must be taken to design intelligently structured group fitness classes, GFIs must also remain adaptable when unforeseen situations arise, such as technical issues or equipment limitations. In this section, key considerations for group fitness classes are addressed, along with practical strategies for creating memorable movement experiences.

OVER THE COURSE OF THIS PART OF THE HANDBOOK, INSTRUCTORS WILL GAIN COMPETENCY IN THE FOLLOWING FOUR AREAS:

Class considerations

Class blueprints

Memorable movement experiences

Day-of class preparation

CHAPTER 4

KEY CONSIDERATIONS FOR GROUP FITNESS CLASSES

SABRENA JO

LEARNING OBJECTIVES

- Identify ideal room characteristics, including flooring and exercise surface qualities, for group fitness classes.
- Explain appropriate strategies to ensure safe and effective group fitness classes in hot and cold environments.
- Describe exercise apparel considerations, including the use of appropriate footwear in the group fitness setting.
- Describe key equipment considerations for group fitness classes.
- Demonstrate a basic understanding of music, including volume, movement integration, and tempo considerations for group fitness classes.
- Implement various methods for monitoring cardiorespiratory intensity, as well as recognize warning signs of overexertion among class participants.

In order to create safe, effective, and enjoyable classes, ACE Certified Group Fitness Instructors (GFIs) must take into account important factors, such as the environment in which classes will take place, if and how music will be used, and how participants will monitor their exercise intensity. While a detailed blueprint will be developed after defining the purpose and objectives of the particular class format (as discussed in Chapter 5), there are general considerations GFIs should be aware of when leading any group fitness class experience.

If your study program includes the ACE Learning Center, visit www.ACEfitness.org/MyACE and log in to your My ACE Account to see the talk test in action, and to learn more about common equipment options and the various ways to use music in group fitness classes.

EXERCISE ROOM CONSIDERATIONS

Although GFIs often have minimal input in terms of the space in which they teach, instructors should strive for the following characteristics when teaching in a room or area dedicated to group fitness:

- Good ventilation, with a temperature adjustable between 65 and 85° F (18 and 29° C) for most types of class formats

- A wooden or synthetic flooring designed to absorb shock from movement and control undesirable **medial-lateral** motions of the foot

- Sufficient space for each participant to move comfortably as appropriate to meet the needs of the specific class format

- Mirrors across both the front and sides of the room for participants to be able to observe their own exercise movements and postures. Ideally, mirrors can be covered by drapes at the instructor's discretion when they prove inappropriate or a distraction.

- A raised platform for the instructor, particularly in large, "fish-bowl" style studios

- Controls for lighting, temperature, and sound connections (e.g., wireless microphone receivers and transmitters, CD player, and digital music player connection), all within easy access of the GFI's primary place of instruction

- Easy access to drinking water

- Easy and safe access to necessary cardiorespiratory and strength-training equipment for instructors and participants to use in classes, as appropriate

- In aquatic fitness classes, water temperature must be appropriate for the specific type of class, which usually

ranges from 83 to 90° F (28 to 32° C). For traditional shallow- or deep-water strength and cardiorespiratory conditioning classes, the ideal water temperature is at the lower end of this spectrum; for mind-body aquatic classes (involving less dynamic movement and travel) and for classes for special populations (such as those for individuals with **arthritis**), ideal water temperature is at the higher end of this spectrum.

FLOORING/EXERCISE SURFACE

Appropriate group fitness flooring absorbs shock to reduce the negative effects on the joints. Repeated jarring can result in stress fractures and **tendinitis.** Hardwood flooring can be suspended to provide additional shock absorption and reduce injury risk. In addition, hardwood flooring offers good traction for dynamic movements and allows for lateral movement and pivoting. Concrete is not recommended as a surface for group fitness classes, as it absorbs little shock and can be quite dangerous in the event of a fall. Carpeting is typically a poor choice for group fitness rooms, as it can catch the edge of shoes during dynamic lateral movements or pivoting, resulting in ankle **sprains** or knee injuries. In addition, carpeting is difficult to maintain hygienically and can trap bacteria and odors from the perspiration and body oils of the participants.

Outdoor classes may take exercise onto grass, sand, and hiking trails. Each surface causes concerns for participant safety. In general, natural surfaces offer good shock absorption, but may vary in terms of predictability and traction. GFIs should be aware of potential risks and choose the appropriate surface for the class format.

ENVIRONMENTAL TEMPERATURE CONSIDERATIONS

One of the many demands that sustained physical exertion places on the body is increased heat production. Working muscles produce large amounts of heat, and the body must regulate internal temperature by making adjustments in the amount of heat that is lost.

EXERCISING IN THE HEAT

Exercising in the heat poses a significant threat to individuals if they do not take adequate precautions. The danger of heat intolerance is compounded if participants are not adequately hydrated prior to starting exercise.

Considerable metabolic heat is produced during exercise. To reduce this internal heat load, blood is brought to the skin surface to be cooled. When the sweat glands secrete water onto the skin, it is evaporated (when relative humidity is low), serving to cool the underlying blood, which then returns to the interior of the body to prevent increased core temperature. If environmental conditions are favorable, these mechanisms will adequately prevent the body temperature from rising by more than about 2 to 3° F, even during intense exercise.

While exercising in the heat, however, dissipating internal body heat is more difficult, and external heat gained from the environment may significantly add to the total heat load. This results in a higher **heart rate (HR)** than normal at any level of exercise. A hot humid, environment is the most stressful environment for exercising, as it reduces the body's ability to lose heat. When the air contains a large quantity of water vapor, sweat will not evaporate readily, and since the evaporative process is the most efficient physiological mechanism for cooling the body, adequate cooling may not occur in humid conditions. Individuals become more at risk for suffering from **hyperthermia,** as exercising in a hot/humid environment produces a greater core temperature and a higher sweat rate (i.e., more fluid loss). Under these conditions, **heat exhaustion** and **heat stroke** also become dangerous possibilities.

Heat exhaustion usually develops in non-acclimatized individuals and is typically a result of inadequate circulatory adjustments to exercise coupled with fluid loss. Heat stroke is a complete failure of the heat-regulating mechanisms, with the core temperature exceeding 104° F (40° C). Both conditions require immediate medical attention. Symptoms of heat exhaustion and heat stroke, as well as appropriate responses, are presented in Table 4-1.

Table 4-1
HEAT EXHAUSTION AND HEAT STROKE

	SIGNS AND SYMPTOMS	APPROPRIATE RESPONSE
Heat Exhaustion	Weak, rapid pulse Low blood pressure Headache Nausea Dizziness General weakness Paleness Cold, clammy skin Profuse sweating	Stop exercising Move to a cool, ventilated area Lie down and elevate feet 12–18 inches (30–46 cm) Give fluids Monitor temperature
Heat Stroke	Hot, dry skin Bright red skin color Rapid, strong pulse Labored breathing Elevated body core temperature (>104° F or 40° C)	Stop exercising Remove as much clothing as feasible Try to cool the body immediately in any way possible (wet towels, ice packs/baths, fan, alcohol rubs) Give fluids Transport to emergency room immediately

 [EXPAND YOUR KNOWLEDGE]

Safety and Efficacy of Hot Yoga Classes

Research conducted on the benefits and effects of hot yoga is still in the beginning stages. A specific type of hot yoga, called Bikram yoga, provides a consistent format with which to study the body's responses to performing yoga in a heated environment. A Bikram yoga session is 90 minutes long and consists of 26 poses and two breathing exercises, all performed in a room heated to 105° F (40.6° C) with 40% relative humidity. Practitioners often find themselves absolutely drenched in perspiration by the end of a session, their yoga mats puddled with sweat. For many Bikram enthusiasts, having the mental strength and focus to overcome this type of challenge is a big part of the draw. Advocates of this extreme version of hot yoga claim improved mindfulness, flexibility, strength, muscle tone, and general fitness as a direct result of practicing this form of yoga.

The results of an ACE-sponsored study on Bikram yoga revealed that, although there are potential benefits associated with practicing this type of yoga, the potential for heat intolerance among some students, including those who may not yet be acclimated to the heat, should not be overlooked (Quandt et al., 2015). Although an extreme core temperature was not seen in all participants in the study and no signs of heat-related illness were observed, a large number of the participants reached a core temperature greater than 103° F (39.4° C), with one man exceeding 104° F (40.0° C).

> To read ACE-sponsored research on Bikram yoga, hot yoga, and other topics related to group exercise, visit www.ACEfitness.org/ACEfit/research-studies.

GFIs should keep in mind that exercising in hot and humid environments—whether inside a studio while practicing Bikram yoga or outside running during the warm months of summer—can place participants at risk for heat-related illness, especially if those individuals do not adequately hydrate before, during, and after exercise (Table 4-2). Instructors of Bikram yoga, health and fitness professionals who lead outdoor group fitness classes, and physical-activity participants who simply like breaking a sweat in hot and humid conditions should all be educated on the risks, as well as the recognition and prevention of heat-related illness. On average, it takes approximately 10 to 14 days for most healthy individuals to acclimate to engaging in physical activity in a heated environment. It is also important to offer students options to regress exercises and poses throughout the class and to encourage them to perform resting, grounding postures as needed. Not only does it take time for the body to acclimate to activity performed in hot and humid environments, proper hydration is crucial and should be encouraged throughout the duration of any exercise in the heat.

Table 4-2

FLUID-INTAKE RECOMMENDATIONS DURING EXERCISE

2 hours prior to exercise, drink 500–600 mL (17–20 oz)
Every 10–20 minutes during exercise, drink 200–300 mL (7–10 oz) or, preferably, drink based on sweat losses
Following exercise, drink 450–675 mL for every 0.5 kg body weight lost (or 16–24 oz for every pound)

Source: Casa, D.J. et al. (2000). National Athletic Trainers' Association: Position statement: Fluid replacement for athletes. *Journal of Athletic Training,* 35, 212–224.

EXERCISING IN THE COLD

The major problems encountered when exercising in the cold are associated with an excessive loss of body heat, which can result in **hypothermia** or frostbite. When the skin or blood temperature drops, mechanisms that conserve body heat and increase heat production are activated. One bodily process that occurs if other mechanisms are not sufficient in terms of preventing heat loss is shivering, which is a rapid, involuntary cycle of contraction and relaxation of skeletal muscles. Shivering can increase the body's rate of heat production by four to five times.

Cold environments can also cause a generalized vasoconstriction that can increase **blood pressure.** This may cause problems in people who are **hypertensive** or who have heart disease. Following exercise, chilling can occur quickly if the body surface is wet with sweat and heat loss continues.

The two major cold stressors are air and water. The effects of cold air are compounded by wind. As wind increases, so do convective heat loss and the rate of body cooling. Water, on the other hand, is actually more detrimental than air in terms of heat loss. In general, the body loses heat four times faster in water than it does in air of the same temperature. This rate can be increased even more if the cold water is moving around the individual (e.g., in a current) due to increased heat loss through **convection.** GFIs who teach aquatic fitness classes should understand the influences of air and water on body temperature and avoid situations where participants are exposed to undue cold stress.

GFIs can share the following tips with class participants for exercising in a cold outdoor environment.

>> Wear several layers of clothing, so that garments can be removed or replaced as needed. As exercise intensity increases, remove outer garments. Then, during periods of rest, warm-up, cool-down, or low-intensity exercise, put them back on. A head covering is also important, because considerable body heat radiates from the head.

>> Allow for adequate ventilation of sweat. Sweating during heavy exercise can soak inner garments. If **evaporation** does not readily occur, the wet garments can continue to drain the body of heat during rest periods, when retention of body heat is extremely important.

>> Select garment materials that allow the body to give off heat during exercise and retain body heat during inactive periods.

EXERCISE APPAREL CONSIDERATIONS

T he GFI should have a good understanding of the appropriate attire to wear when in instructing and participating in the specific modalities he or she will be teaching. Class participants often look to the GFI as a role model with regards to determining appropriate attire for the class format. Instructors should wear clothing that allows participants to clearly view the key movements of the body performed during the class. For example, many Pilates and yoga exercises involve subtle adjustments of the joints to correctly perform a movement. Clothing that has excess material could block the participant's view of the instructor's form, thus limiting the effectiveness of the instruction. However, care should also be taken to avoid wearing too little, as doing so could result in the GFI appearing unprofessional.

> Understand the appropriate attire to wear when instructing

In addition to wearing appropriate, properly fitted apparel, the type of material the clothing is constructed from should also be considered for both the GFI and participants. For example, cotton tends to sop up and retain moisture, whereas newer synthetic materials (e.g., polypropylene) wick away moisture. While cotton can be a good choice for exercising in the heat due to the fact that it readily soaks up sweat, for those same reasons cotton is a poor choice for exercising in the cold. Synthetic materials and synthetic blends tend to be a good choice because they allow for evaporation and keep skin dry, cool, and comfortable.

> GFIs teaching group indoor cycling classes may wish to consider format-specific attire to enhance the exercise experience. Cycling shorts with built-in padding can make sitting on the saddle more comfortable, while cycling shoes can make the ride more effective. Educating participants about these types of cycling-specific clothing can enhance **rapport** and help class participants get the most from their workouts.

Proper footwear provides good cushioning, support, and flexibility. Many group fitness formats, including step and kickboxing classes, require that the balls of the feet absorb repetitive impact during the landing and pushing-off of dynamic movements. Footwear must provide cushioning under the forefoot in addition to heel cushioning to reduce the possibility of injury to the foot from repeated impact. Lateral movement, such as shuffling or traveling side-to-side, demands support on the lateral aspect of the shoe to prevent the foot from rolling over the **base of support** and causing an ankle sprain. Running shoes are designed for forward-movement efficiency and are not appropriate for classes with excessive lateral or pivoting movements, such as dance-based fitness classes.

Various sole designs allow for good forefoot flexibility without sacrificing traction. They provide freedom of movement without slipping during cutting, stopping, or rapid changes of direction, such as in sports conditioning classes. Forefoot flexibility is also necessary for many flexibility-based classes in which full ROM is desired.

For indoor cycling, participants should wear stiff-soled or cycling shoes because soft-soled shoes flex over the pedal, which can lead to numbness, bruising, or other soft-tissue injuries such as Achilles tendinitis or calf muscle **strains.** Cycling shoes also help improve cycling-specific muscle recruitment patterns and pedaling efficiency, which may reduce **overuse injuries.**

Surface, equipment, intensity, and quality of movement determine the requirements of appropriate footwear. GFIs should be sure to evaluate the class content and adhere to any footwear guidelines indicated for different formats.

[APPLY WHAT YOU KNOW]

Educating Participants on Proper Footwear

GFIs can offer some basic guidelines to help participants make more informed decisions when purchasing appropriate footwear for physical activity. If a participant engages in a specific activity two or three times each week, such as running, walking, tennis, basketball, or a specific group fitness class format like kickboxing, he or she will want a shoe designed specifically for that sport or activity. Multipurpose shoes such as cross trainers may be a good alternative for individuals who participate in several sports or activities, such as cardiorespiratory exercise and resistance training, in a single workout. Ideally, participants should look for an athletic shoe store with a good reputation in the community. Their sales staffs are more likely to be knowledgeable about selecting appropriate shoes for the individual, considering his or her activity level and specific foot type. Some stores even offer a free gait analysis to better understand the individual's unique needs. General recommendations when purchasing footwear include the following:

— Get fitted for footwear toward the end of the day. It is not unusual for an individual's foot to increase by half a shoe size during the course of a single day. However, if an individual plans to exercise consistently at a specific time, he or she should consider getting fitted at that exact time.

— Allow a space up to the width of the index finger between the end of the longest toe and the end of the shoe. This space will accommodate foot size increases, a variety of socks, and foot movement within the shoe without hurting the toes.

— The heel of the foot should not slip out of the shoe during plantar flexion, as in walking or stepping.

— The ball of the foot should match the widest part of the shoe, and the participant should have plenty of room for the toes to wiggle without experiencing slippage in the heel.

— Shoes should not rub or pinch any area of the foot or ankle. The individual should rotate the ankles when trying on shoes, and pay attention to the sides of the feet and the top of the toes, both of which are common areas for blisters.

— The participant should wear the same weight of socks that he or she intends to use during activity. Participants should look for socks that are made with synthetic fibers such as acrylic, polyester, or Coolmax for better blister prevention.

It is also important that participants understand factors that determine when shoes need to be replaced. If they are no longer absorbing the pounding and jarring action, the individual is more likely to sustain ankle, shin, and knee injuries. Athletic shoes will lose their cushioning after three to six months of regular use [or 350 to 500 miles (~560 to 800 km) of running]. However, participants should look at the wear patterns as a good indicator for replacement. Any time the shoe appears to be wearing down unevenly, especially at the heel, it is time to replace the shoes. Additionally, if the traction on the soles of the shoes is worn flat, it is time for new shoes.

EQUIPMENT CONSIDERATIONS AND OPTIONS

The use of equipment is prevalent in group exercise classes. From steps and elastic resistance tubing to bikes and agility ladders, each piece of equipment has specific set-up, use, and/or fit requirements. To minimize the risk of injury among participants, GFIs must check equipment regularly for wear and tear and replace items when necessary (see Chapter 7). Additionally, if equipment is manufactured in various sizes, ideally all size options should be made available to accommodate participants. A GFI should also possess knowledge of specific equipment or accessories that can make a class more effective and enjoyable for participants. Even if a particular fitness facility does not currently own the equipment, the GFI can be an advocate by educating facility staff about the benefits of incorporating such items into classes. For example, yoga class participants can greatly benefit from having props such as yoga blocks, blankets, bolsters, and straps available to enable them to achieve positions that may otherwise not be accessible. Additionally, specific types of mats are better for certain modalities than others, such as yoga mats that are thin and "sticky," allowing for a better grip during standing movements compared to traditional exercise mats.

> ## Check equipment regularly for wear and tear

 [APPLY WHAT YOU KNOW]

New and Varied Equipment Options

Introducing new equipment options is an easy way to add variety to a class format. For example, if a GFI has always used hand weights and weighted bars in a group strength class, incorporating elastic resistance bands could reinvigorate the exercise experience for participants. As with new choreography and exercise ideas, equipment should not be added solely to make exercises more complex or difficult, as the training tools used should match the overall goal of the class and be suitable for the intended participants. GFIs should keep in mind that some equipment requires more in-depth training and experience prior to teaching with it (e.g., kettlebells and suspension training systems), which necessitates specific continuing education on the training tool before introducing it as an equipment option in class. Misuse of equipment can lead to injury, so it is especially important to learn the intended use, limitations, and safety precautions for all equipment.

Another consideration when deciding to incorporate equipment is the number of pieces to use in one class. It is important that each participant have appropriate space around him or her while exercising. Having too much equipment cluttered around the room poses a tripping hazard. Limiting classes to one or two pieces of resistance equipment and one prop (such as a step that serves as a bench) is generally recommend for strength-based classes. Cardiorespiratory classes, on the other hand, are typically dependent on one piece of equipment, though adding a second may be appropriate in some cases. Keep in mind that fitness equipment is not always as exciting for new members as it is for experienced participants and the GFI. For some, equipment can be intimidating, and new participants may become overwhelmed at the sight of too many training tools scattered about the room.

MUSIC

usic serves multiple purposes in group fitness classes. It provides motivation through its changing keys, lyrics, and instruments. It also can set the pace for a particular activity, such as pedaling in an indoor cycling class or moving around the room in a dance-based fitness class. Ultimately, all music chosen should contribute to, rather than detract from, the overall desired experience. Instructors who develop a mastery of music understand the importance of coupling music with cueing skills. To ensure the most professional experience, GFIs should purchase legally licensed music specifically prepared for group fitness classes, because its phrases and **beats** are consistently developed according to industry-standardized beats-per-minute (bpm) guidelines without the fluctuations and bridges that occur in music that one hears on the radio (see Chapter 12).

Asking participants about their preference for music is one option, though GFIs should strive to incorporate various music styles and genres to appeal to a wide variety of participants. Instructors often make the mistake of choosing music they find motivating for their own workouts, and while it is important that the music selected motivates the instructor, it is imperative that it motivate the participants. A student-centered instructor will make every effort to provide participants with an enjoyable and memorable movement experience. With the wide array of commercial music available, it is easy to find an assortment of appropriate options to use in class.

VOLUME

It is generally recommended that GFIs keep their music volume under 85 decibels (dB). By way of reference, normal conversations in quiet places range from 60 to 70 dB, an alarm clock ringing two feet away is about 80 dB, a chainsaw is 100 dB, and a jet plane takeoff is around 120 dB. The Occupational Safety and Health Administration (OSHA), which sets safety standards for workers, states that ear protection must be provided for workers if the noise level on the job averages 90 dB over an eight-hour period (Griest, Folmer, & Martin, 2007). Extended exposure to sound levels above 85 dB can impair and even damage a person's hearing (Chang et al., 2013). Instructors who use loud music are not only at risk of damaging their own hearing and that of their participants, but they are also much more likely to suffer from voice injury, as they find themselves having to shout over loud music, even when using a microphone (see Chapter 8). While determining decibel levels related to ambient sound was once a task reserved for the laboratory, many smartphone applications allow listeners to display the decibels of surrounding noise or music with surprising accuracy. When in doubt, a GFI should play the music at a volume at which participants can hear his or her voice clearly and easily at all times. In addition to keeping the music volume at an appropriate level to protect the hearing of class participants, audiologists recommend that instructors turn up the bass and lower the treble, since high frequencies can be more damaging than low frequencies (Price, 1990). A higher bass setting can also be beneficial for class participants who have difficulty hearing the underlying beat, because they can feel the beat through the floor reverberations.

INTEGRATING MOVEMENT AND MUSIC

As noted earlier, the use of music can be a way to motivate participants and create more overall enjoyment in the class experience. Several research studies have validated the idea that music is beneficial from a motivational standpoint (Alter et al., 2015; van der Vlist et al., 2011). Kravitz (1994) found that subjects regularly report that they believe their performance is better with music accompaniment. Moving to the beat of the music is not always necessary in a group fitness setting. However, while using music in the foreground, moving to the beat in kickboxing, step, and dance-based fitness classes, for example, is important. In classes such as boot camp, aquatic exercise, and yoga, on the other hand, music is often used in the background to help motivate or set a mood in classes.

UNDERSTANDING MUSICAL COMPONENTS AND TEMPO

Understanding the components of music is essential for any GFI. The music beat is made up of the regular pulsations that usually have an even rhythm and occur in a continuous pattern of strong and weak pulsations. Strong pulsations collectively form the **downbeat,** while weaker pulsations form the **upbeat.** A series of beats forms the underlying rhythm of a song, which is the regular pattern of sound that is heard when listening to music. A **meter** organizes beats into musical patterns or **measures,** such as four beats per measure. A measure is a group of beats formed by the regular occurrence of a heavy **accent** on the first beat or downbeat of each group. Most group fitness routines use music with a meter of 4/4 time, in which the first "4" indicates four beats per measure and the second "4" shows that the quarter note gets the beat.

When choosing music for a particular class, the first consideration is whether the music's role will be in the foreground or background. When music is in the foreground, instructors will incorporate its **tempo** (and sometimes its lyrics or general feeling) into the class. Examples of using music in the foreground include stepping to the downbeat of a musical compilation, doing dance-based movements, and performing choreographed formats. When music is in the background, instructors do not incorporate the tempo or volume as an integrated aspect of the experience. Not all classes delineate these two roles of music clearly. Classes like aquatic fitness and group indoor cycling, for example, generally include both foreground and background music. For example, during some songs, instructors ask participants to move at the rate of the music, while during others, the music is part of the background ambience.

The two main considerations when choosing music are purpose and participants. Understanding the music's purpose helps GFIs understand what types of music would be most appropriate for the objectives chosen. For example, if the purpose is steady-state training, such as in step or aquatic fitness classes, choosing music with a consistent tempo would be prudent. Alternatively, if the purpose is to introduce mindfulness and introspection, such as in a stretching or mind-body class, perhaps softer music with no beat would be appropriate. An awareness of the participants also helps provide a successful musical experience for everyone, as different populations and demographics will have preferences about both music type and volume.

Music tempo can determine the progression as well as the intensity of exercise. The tempo assists GFIs in determining a piece of music's appropriateness for a particular class. Most music specifically sold to GFIs lists the bpm for that release. Alternatively, the bpm for a song can be determined by counting the number of downbeats in 15 seconds and then multiplying by four.

Prudent instructors match music to movement, meaning that they can depart from the general standards outlined in Table 4-3, which presents the industry guidelines for music tempo *when instructors use the music in the foreground and have their participants execute all movements on the downbeat.* It is essential that GFIs choose music that safely complements the purpose of any section or class.

Table 4-3
MUSIC TEMPO FOR COMMON GROUP FITNESS MODALITIES

TEMPO (BEATS PER MINUTE)	MODALITIES
<100	Most often used for background music or slower, mind-body classes like Pilates, yoga, or stretching classes
100–122	Beginner step classes, low end of low-impact aerobics, and hip-hop classes If cycling on the beat and using pedal stroke as a measure of beats per minute, this range represents the upper limit of music tempo.
122–129	Group strength classes, advanced step classes, low-to-mid impact aerobics, some dance-based fitness classes, and aquatic fitness classes
130–160	Faster-paced movement classes, mid-to-high impact classes, some dance-based fitness classes, trampoline-based classes, and some martial arts–based classes

As safety is the most important factor regardless of whether music is used in the foreground or background, instructors matching movements to music must consider the general level of the participants, the **range of motion** required at the desired tempo, and even directional changes.

When incorporating music into the foreground of a class, seasoned instructors demonstrate music mastery, which includes demonstrating an awareness of any chosen music's organization into **musical phrases.** According to Bricker (1991), "as letters of the alphabet combine to form sentences, so beats of music combine to form measures, and measures combine to form phrases. A phrase is composed of at least two measures of music. To learn to recognize musical phrases, imagine where you would pause for breath if you were singing a song." GFIs can think of music as being composed of sentences, each with eight beats. Combine four sentences and a musical phrase results, with a total of 32 counts.

> A phrase is composed of at least two measures of music.

When creating music specifically for GFIs, most music companies make it easy for instructors to find the start of musical phrases. Adding special elements like drum rolls, vocal cues, and distinct chorus and verse sections of music all help the seasoned ear pick up the start of 32-count phrases. To guide participants in an effort to promote uniformity for direction and safety, GFIs choosing to utilize music in the foreground should teach on the downbeat whenever appropriate. Furthermore, seasoned instructors are able to not only teach on the beat, but also to cue in advance of the start of each musical phrase so that their participants can begin 32-count combinations at the start, or "top," of the musical phrases.

MONITORING INTENSITY

All group fitness formats have movements that can vary in impact and/or intensity. For example, in an indoor cycling class, a hill climb out of the saddle at a high resistance that lasts longer than three minutes is considered a higher-intensity option. This might be followed by a lower-resistance seated movement. It is the GFI's job to make sure that this increase is balanced and appropriate for the participants. It is important to take this into consideration when choosing or choreographing movement combinations and segments.

Ultimately, it is up to the GFI to choose an intensity-monitoring method that is most suitable for his or her skills and abilities, as well as one that is most practical for the class setting. Whether using **target heart rate (THR)**, the **talk test**, **ratings of perceived exertion (RPE)**, or the **dyspnea scale**, all of which are discussed in this chapter, a GFI must feel comfortable with the method so that its application is simple and easy for the participants to understand.

PROMOTING SELF-RESPONSIBILITY

Whether teaching a Pilates, indoor rowing, or boot-camp class, it is impossible to be everywhere or help everyone simultaneously. Each participant is working at a different fitness level and may also have his or her own set of goals. To help promote independence and self-responsibility, GFIs should encourage participants to work at their own pace, use the talk test, HR monitoring, or RPE check-ins, and inform them how they should be feeling throughout the class. For example, during the peak portion of the cardiorespiratory segment, let them know that they should have an increased rate of respiration. During the cool-down, remind them that they should feel their heart and breathing rates slowing down. Be as descriptive as possible about perceived exertion throughout the workout. Also, it is important to demonstrate high-, medium-, and low-intensity options to teach multilevel classes (see Chapter 8). Help participants achieve the level of effort they want to reach and continually remind them that it is up to them to select intensity based on their needs, goals, and fitness levels—the instructor cannot be solely responsible for participants' exercise intensity levels. Participants who are given autonomy often report a more positive exercise experience (Teixeira et al., 2012). It is recommended that the instructor maintain a moderate intensity most of the time, but also present other options and intensities as the need arises. Mastering this concept is the true "art" of group fitness instruction.

 [THINK IT THROUGH]

What specific cues could you provide participants to help them gauge their intensity level during the recovery segments of a **high-intensity interval training (HIIT)** class?

METHODS OF MONITORING CARDIORESPIRATORY INTENSITY

The appropriate intensity for aerobic exercise depends on several factors, including the exerciser's level of conditioning and his or her fitness goals. Beginners who have been **sedentary** should proceed with an exercise program that is low intensity for longer durations. Those who are more fit and are interested in maintaining or increasing their fitness levels can perform higher levels of intense aerobic exercise for shorter periods of time during each session.

Monitoring exercise intensity within the cardiorespiratory segment is important. Participants need to be given information regarding the purpose of monitoring HR during exercise and instruction on how to obtain a **pulse rate.** Proper instruction on how to find the pulse is the first step to monitoring intensity effectively.

The following are a few recommended sites for finding the pulse and assessing HR:

- **CAROTID PULSE:** This pulse is taken from the carotid artery just to the side of the larynx using light pressure from the fingertips of the first two fingers. Remember, never palpate both carotid arteries at the same time and always press lightly to prevent a drop in HR and/or decreased blood flow to the brain (Figure 4-1).

- **RADIAL PULSE:** This pulse is taken from the radial artery at the wrist, in line with the thumb, using the fingertips of the first two fingers (Figure 4-2).

- **TEMPORAL PULSE:** This pulse can sometimes be obtained from the left or right temple with light pressure from the fingertips of the first two fingers (Figure 4-3).

Figure 4-1
Carotid heart-rate monitoring

Figure 4-2
Radial heart-rate monitoring

Figure 4-3
Temporal heart-rate monitoring

Understanding the effective use of HR, RPE, the dyspnea scale, and the talk test is the next step in effectively monitoring exercise intensity. Some methods are preferred depending on the format. In a treadmill class or an indoor cycling class, use of HR monitors can be effective. However, in a kickboxing class, where arms and legs are moving in many different directions and against gravity, RPE might be a better choice.

GFIs should keep in mind that there is no one preferred intensity-monitoring method for all group fitness class formats or participants (Table 4-4). While some instructors have stopped using manual HR monitoring because it disrupts the flow of the class, others use HR monitors to gauge intensity. There are no hard-and-fast rules for monitoring intensity other than that it is an important responsibility of the GFI. Not monitoring intensity or failing to give constant intensity-monitoring gauges reflects an inadequate level of participant supervision and may compromise safety.

Table 4-4

RECOMMENDED METHODS OF INTENSITY MONITORING

CLASS FORMAT	INTENSITY-MONITORING METHOD
Kickboxing	RPE or talk test
Aquatic fitness	RPE or talk test
Group indoor cycling	HR or talk test
Equipment-based classes	HR, RPE, or talk test

Note: HR = Heart rate; RPE = Ratings of perceived exertion

Target Heart Rate

Cardiorespiratory training has traditionally involved **steady-state exercise** with progressions based primarily on increased duration and intensity, as noted in Chapter 2. While programs following these guidelines have shown positive results for decades, they are subject to substantial errors in training intensities, as the THRs are calculated as percentages of predicted **maximal heart rates (MHR),** which have been shown to have standard deviations of approximately 12 bpm using the long-standing equation of MHR = 220 − Age (Fox, Naughton, & Haskell, 1971), or closer to 7 bpm using newer formulas from Gellish et al. (2007) and Tanaka, Monahan, and Seals (2001).

Gellish et al.:
Maximal heart rate = 206.9 − (0.67 x Age)

Tanaka, Monahan, and Seals:
Maximal heart rate = 208 − (0.7 x Age)

Maximal Heart Rate: How Useful Is the Traditional Prediction Equation?

Two methods exist for determining MHR. The most accurate way is to directly measure the MHR with an **electrocardiogram (ECG)** monitoring device during a graded exercise test. The other way is to estimate MHR by using a simple prediction equation or formula. In 1971, the formula "220 − Age" was introduced and was widely accepted by the health and fitness community (Fox, Naughton, & Haskell, 1971). However, the validity of the formula has come under attack for several reasons. The subjects used in the study to determine the formula were not representative of the general population. In addition, even if the prediction equation did represent a reasonable average MHR, a significant percentage of individuals will deviate substantially from the average value for any given age. In fact, standard deviations of plus or minus 10 to 20 bpm have been observed. Consequently, basing a participant's exercise intensity (i.e., THR) on a potentially inaccurate estimation of MHR can be problematic. When the THR is based on an estimated MHR, it should be used in conjunction with RPE (see Table 4-5, page 71). GFIs should instruct participants to decrease the intensity of the exercise experience if they report a high level of perceived exertion, even if their THR has not been achieved.

This error in predicted MHR becomes amplified when this value is used to calculate THR ranges for cardiorespiratory exercise as either a direct percentage of MHR (as is represented on HR training zone charts commonly seen on in fitness facilities) or using the Karvonen formula, which uses MHR and **resting heart rate (RHR)** to first calculate **heart-rate reserve (HRR),** then calculate THR as a percentage of HRR.

KARVONEN FORMULA

Heart-rate reserve = Maximal heart rate − Resting heart rate

Target heart rate = (Heart-rate reserve x % intensity) + Resting heart rate

Another option to assist in determining exercise intensity is called HR **telemetry.** In this method, the exerciser wears an electronic HR monitor strapped to his or her chest during the workout that transmits HR to a wristwatch. HR telemetry is especially convenient in group fitness classes that rely heavily on the individual participant's HR as a measure of intensity and progression throughout the class. The use of HR monitors is common in indoor cycling and treadmill-based classes, but the devices can be used in most other aerobic-based group fitness classes as well.

If the HR is too fast (greater than 90% MHR), the participant should be instructed to slow down. If the HR is below 55% MHR, and the participant is capable of greater exercise intensity, he or she should be encouraged to pick up the pace. It is important to keep in mind, however, that HR monitoring devices can produce erratic readings in addition to the standard deviations in determining MHR, as noted previously. It is advisable to use RPE and physical observation along with electronic HR monitoring technology to ensure the exerciser's intensity stays within an acceptable range.

Talk Test

Approaches that use a relative percent of predicted MHR, HRR, or even predicted $\dot{V}O_2max$ or $\dot{V}O_2reserve$ $(\dot{V}O_2R),$ are essentially flawed, as they do not take into account the individual's metabolic responses to exercise. Instead, exercise experiences can be tailored to each participant's unique metabolic markers by identifying and using the participant's HR at the **first ventilatory threshold (VT1)** and **second ventilatory threshold (VT2)** (see Chapter 3). There are many different exercise intensity markers that can be used to delineate moderate- from vigorous-intensity exercise, or vigorous from very vigorous (anaerobic) exercise. However, HR at VT1 and VT2, the talk test, and RPE using the Borg 6 to 20 scale or the 0 to 10 category ratio scale are the recommended methods, as they are more accurate and enable more effective intensity monitoring among individual participants.

The talk test takes into account an exerciser's ability to breathe and talk during a workout. If a person can comfortably answer a question during exercise while still feeling like he or she is getting a good workout, it is likely that the activity being performed is appropriate for cardiorespiratory conditioning. The talk test is especially useful for beginners who are learning to pace themselves by monitoring their bodily responses to exercise. For those with higher fitness levels, the use of the talk test may not be appropriate.

A GFI can conduct the talk test on participants by simply asking them questions and listening for responses during the conditioning portion of class. Ideally, the responses of the participants should be in the form of sentences, rather than one-word statements, such as "fine" or "okay." For example, a GFI could ask a participant to describe how he or she is feeling and the participant could respond by saying, "I feel like I'm working pretty hard." If the exerciser can string those words together in a sentence without stopping and gasping for air, he or she is probably working at an appropriate intensity. Of course, this method is not always reliable, since many participants may feel uncomfortable speaking out and responding to the instructor in class. However, educating the class on the concept of the talk test might elicit more responses from participants if they know the GFI is using their vocal cues as a gauge for intensity.

Ratings of Perceived Exertion

Another method for measuring exercise intensity is by assigning a numerical value to subjective feelings of exercise exertion. Known as the RPE scale, this method, developed by Dr. Gunnar Borg, takes into account all that the exerciser is perceiving in terms of **fatigue,** including psychological, musculoskeletal, and environmental factors. RPE correlates well with physiological factors associated with exercise, such as HR, breathing rate, oxygen use, and overall fatigue. Table 4-5 lists two commonly used rating scales. For the RPE method of monitoring exercise intensity, the participant uses a scale to assign a rating to his or her physical effort.

Table 4-5

RATINGS OF PERCEIVED EXERTION (RPE)

RPE	CATEGORY RATIO SCALE
6	0 Nothing at all
7 Very, very light	0.5 Very, very weak
8	1 Very weak
9 Very light	2 Weak
10	3 Moderate
11 Fairly light	4 Somewhat strong
12	5 Strong
13 Somewhat hard	6
14	7 Very strong
15 Hard	8
16	9
17 Very hard	10 Very, very strong
18	* Maximal
19 Very, very hard	
20	

Source: Adapted from American College of Sports Medicine (2014). *ACSM's Guidelines for Exercise Testing and Prescription* (9th ed.). Philadelphia: Wolters Kluwer/Lippincott Williams & Wilkins.

When using the Borg 6 to 20 scale, an RPE of 12 to 13 (somewhat hard) corresponds to approximately 55 to 69% of MHR, whereas a rating of 15 to 16 (hard) corresponds to about 90% of MHR. Thus, individuals who train in the RPE range of 12 to 16 achieve the most efficient path to increased aerobic fitness.

In the group fitness class setting, explaining the Borg 6 to 20 RPE scale to participants is usually difficult. A GFI who uses the 0 to 10 category ratio scale, rather than the 6 to 20 scale, as a means to incorporate RPE into the class setting will probably fare better in educating the participants about the use of RPE. An appropriate range of intensity for increasing cardiorespiratory fitness within the 0 to 10 scale is between 3 (moderate) and 5 (strong).

Another, perhaps more practical, way to use RPE is to simply instruct the participants to use words instead of numbers to evaluate how hard they are working. For example, a GFI could explain prior to the conditioning portion of class that participants should gauge their intensities by feelings that correspond to the words "just noticeable," "light," "hard," and "maximal." An appropriate perception of intensity, using these words as indicators, would range somewhere between *light* and *hard*, whereas *just noticeable* and *maximal* are (depending on the class) intensities to avoid.

Dyspnea Scale

When a deconditioned person attempts to exercise vigorously, he or she can experience **dyspnea** (difficult and labored breathing). Individuals who have pulmonary conditions, such as **asthma** and **emphysema,** also can experience problems with breathing during exercise. GFIs should observe their class participants for signs of difficulty with breathing so that the participants can be coached to reduce their exercise intensities if dyspnea occurs.

Participants can be taught the dyspnea scale to gauge the appropriateness of breathing performance during class. It is normal for participants engaging in cardiorespiratory exercise to experience mild and even moderate difficulty breathing, but those suffering from severe difficulty should be instructed to stop exercising and breathe deeply to recover from intense exercise.

DYSPNEA SCALE

The dyspnea scale is a subjective score that reflects the relative difficulty of breathing as perceived by the participant during physical activity.

+1 Mild, noticeable to the exerciser, but not to an observer

+2 Mild, some difficulty that is noticeable to an observer

+3 Moderate difficulty, participant can continue to exercise

+4 Severe difficulty, participant must stop exercising

 **[APPLY WHAT YOU KNOW]**

Teaching Participants to Monitor Their Intensity

Monitoring exercise intensity during group fitness classes is a skill that GFIs must be able to teach to their participants, as the responsibility for exercising within an appropriate range of intensity ultimately rests with the participant. This concept should be explained by the GFI at the beginning of each class. It is important for the class to understand that while the GFI will do his or her best to provide a safe and effective exercise experience, each individual participant must gauge the intensity of his or her true effort and adjust performance accordingly.

It is helpful to explain to the participants at the beginning of class the physical sensations that are normal with various intensities of exercise and how to adjust performance, if necessary. For example, a GFI could announce, "At different points during class, we will check the intensity of our effort. I will ask you to think about how hard you are working. You should reflect on how fast you are breathing and how fatigued you feel at the moment the question is asked. Those of you who are wearing HR monitors and who are aware of your THR range can check your monitor while simultaneously taking an inventory of how you feel. If you feel like you're working too hard (at a level that cannot be sustained), I will show you how to reduce the intensity of what we are doing at that time. If you feel as if you're not working hard enough, I'll show you how to increase the challenge."

It is advisable to perform intensity-monitoring checks several times during the workout. An intensity check can be as simple as taking 10 seconds to ask the participants how they feel. At the very least, an intensity check should be performed during a relatively high-intensity point of the cardiorespiratory conditioning portion of the class, and again after the cardiorespiratory cool-down portion of class. It is important for the GFI and each participant to acknowledge that the intensity of effort was elevated at the appropriate times during class and that it was decreased prior to the conclusion of class.

AWARENESS OF WARNING SIGNS

Sometimes, even while using intensity-monitoring strategies, participants can overexert themselves during a group fitness class. A competent GFI will be able to recognize cues or warning signs that necessitate the lowering of intensities for individual participants or the class as a whole.

The first, and perhaps most obvious, warning sign that a GFI is likely to observe when a participant is working too vigorously is a breakdown in proper form and exercise execution. For example, an individual who is beginning to fatigue during a step-training class might not be able set his or her foot completely on top of the bench, resulting in the heel hanging off the platform. This increases the risk of tripping and poses a hazard to the participant and the individuals around him or her. Another situation that would illustrate compromised form due to overexertion is a participant getting fatigued while performing a bench press exercise in a group strength-training class. Excessive arching of the back, shoulder elevation, and locking the elbows at the top of the repetition to rest would indicate that the exerciser has reached muscular fatigue of the chest, shoulders, and triceps.

In either of these examples, it would be appropriate for the GFI to recommend a reduction in the intensity of the exercise. In most cases, it is adequate for a GFI to make a general statement to the entire class about proper execution of the exercise and how to reduce the intensity through modifications if the participants find themselves exhibiting poor form. Sometimes, however, it might be necessary for the GFI to approach a participant and use specific, corrective feedback if the exerciser continues to risk injury by performing movements incorrectly (see Chapter 10).

Other warning signs that could indicate a need for reducing exercise intensity include labored breathing, excessive sweating, and dizziness. A GFI should recommend to participants who are experiencing these symptoms to stop exercising and lightly march in place until the symptoms subside. As the HR lowers and the breathing becomes more normal, the participant can attempt to continue at a new lower intensity. However, it might be necessary to discontinue the exercise session if the symptoms do not improve. More severe signs, such as chest pain or discomfort, heart palpitations, or severe musculoskeletal pain, indicate the need for immediate cessation of exercise and possibly the activation of the emergency medical system (EMS). Refer to Chapter 11 for more information.

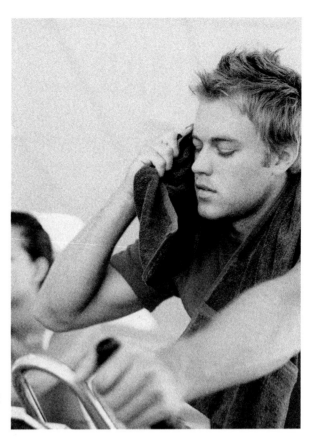

Recognize cues or warning signs that necessitate the lowering of intensities

SUMMARY

In order to safely and effectively lead group fitness classes, it is imperative that GFIs be well-versed in selecting appropriate equipment, understanding environmental factors, utilizing music, and employing methods for monitoring intensity. During classes, instructors must be able to recognize warning signs of participants who may be overexerting themselves in order to mitigate the potential for injury. Successfully leading participants through various fitness class formats requires a solid understanding of the general considerations presented in this chapter.

References

Alter, D.A. et al. (2015). Synchronized personalized music audio-playlists to improve adherence to physical activity among patients participating in a structured exercise program: A proof-of-principle feasibility study. *Sports Medicine - Open,* 1, 1, 23. DOI: 10.1186/s40798-015-0017-9

American College of Sports Medicine (2014). *ACSM's Guidelines for Exercise Testing and Prescription* (9th ed.). Philadelphia: Wolters Kluwer/Lippincott Williams & Wilkins.

Bricker, K. (1991). Music 101. *IDEA Today,* 3, 55–57.

Casa, D.J. et al. (2000). National Athletic Trainers' Association: Position statement: Fluid replacement for athletes. *Journal of Athletic Training,* 35, 212–224.

Chang, H. et al. (2013). Effects of blood flow to the prefrontal cortex on high-intensity exercise combined with high-decibel music. *Journal of Exercise Nutrition and Biochemistry,* 17, 4, 115–122.

Fox III, S.M., Naughton, J.P., & Haskell, W.L. (1971). Physical activity and the prevention of coronary heart disease. *Annals of Clinical Research,* 3, 404–432.

Gellish, R.L. et al. (2007). Longitudinal modeling of the relationship between age and maximal heart rate. *Medicine & Science in Sports & Exercise,* 39, 5, 822–829.

Griest, S.E., Folmer, R.L., & Martin, W.H. (2007). Effectiveness of dangerous decibels: A school-based hearing loss prevention program. *American Journal of Audiology,* 16, S165–S181.

Kravitz, L. (1994). The effects of music on exercise. *IDEA Today,* October, 56–61.

Price, J. (1990). Hear today, gone tomorrow? *IDEA Today,* 5, 54–57.

Quandt, E. et al. (2015). *ACE Study Examines Effects of Bikram Yoga on Core Body Temps.* www.acefitness.org/acefit/expert-insight-article/47/5384/ace-study-examines-effects-of-bikram-yoga-on/

Tanaka, H., Monahan, K.D., & Seals, D.R. (2001). Age-predicted maximal heart revisited. *Journal of the American College of Cardiology,* 37, 153–156.

Teixiera, P.J. et al. (2012). Exercise, physical activity, and self-determination theory: A systematic review. *International Journal of Behavioral Nutrition and Physical Activity,* 9, 78.

van der Vlist, B. et al. (2011). Using interactive music to guide and motivate users during aerobic exercising. *Applied Psychophysiology Biofeedback,* 36, 2, 135–145. DOI: 10.1007/s10484-011-9149-y

Suggested Reading

Armstrong, L.E. et al. (2007). Exertional heat illness during training and competition. *Medicine & Science in Sports & Exercise,* 39, 3, 556–572. DOI: 10.1249/MSS.0b013e31802fa199

Karageorghis, C.I. & Priest, D-L. (2012). Music in the exercise domain: A review and synthesis (Part I). *International Review of Sport and Exercise Psychology,* 5, 1, 44–66.

Karageorghis, C.I. & Priest, D-L. (2012). Music in the exercise domain: A review and synthesis (Part II). *International Review of Sport and Exercise Psychology,* 5, 1, 67–84.

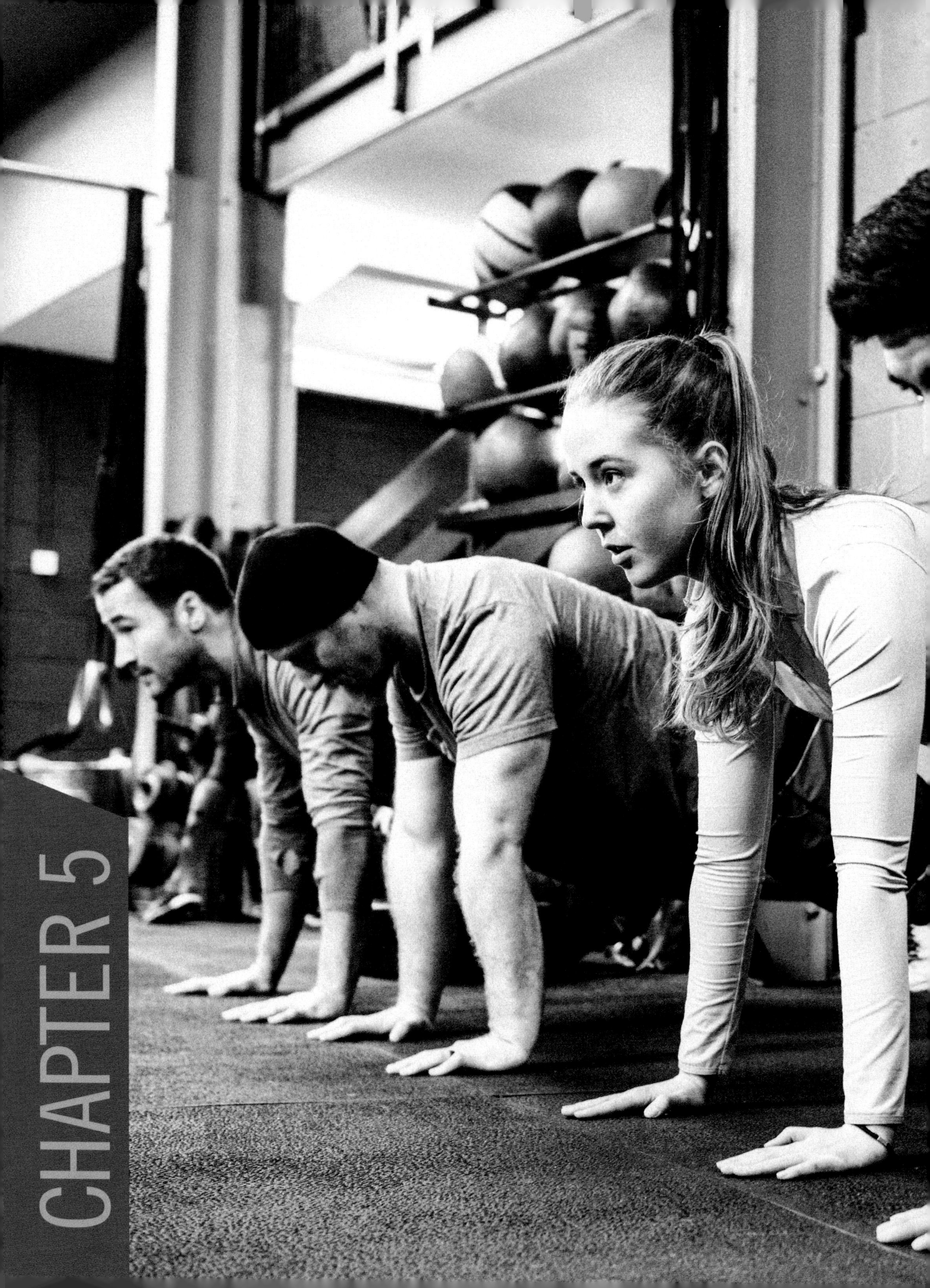

CHAPTER 5

CHAPTER 5 | DESIGNING A CLASS BLUEPRINT

JESSICA MATTHEWS

LEARNING OBJECTIVES

- ■ Define class purpose and objectives.
- ■ Apply knowledge of exercise science to the three core components of a group fitness class.
- ■ Evaluate movements and exercises to determine safety and effectiveness.
- ■ Explain the importance of rehearsal moves.
- ■ Design intelligently structured and sequenced classes.

The safest and most effective group fitness experiences are well-planned, applying the most up-to-date exercise science—related principles in a practical and thoughtful way. From identifying the purpose and objectives of a class to evaluating specific movements and exercises, an ACE Certified Group Fitness Instructor (GFI) must be well-versed in constructing classes in which the success and safety of the student is always a top priority. This chapter discusses key considerations for designing a comprehensive, logically structured group fitness class plan.

If your study program includes the ACE Learning Center, visit www.ACEfitness.org/MyACE and log in to your My ACE Account for a video showing practical examples of progressions, regressions, and rehearsal moves and their use in group fitness classes.

SYSTEMATIC CLASS DESIGN

The difference between truly amazing classes and mediocre ones boils down to proper planning. While some aspects of an experience cannot always be controlled, such as mishaps with audio equipment, the GFI should make it a point to plan as many aspects of the class experience as possible, including devising back-up plans should unexpected issues arise (see Chapter 7). The newer the instructor, the more important it is that the class design be written out and thoroughly practiced. Effective GFIs begin this systematic planning process by first identifying the overall goal of the class and the intended outcomes for participants. Considering this important information first will allow for more informed decisions regarding specific movements, exercises, and instructional techniques that will be needed to accomplish the established class objectives.

> Identify the overall goal of the class

CLASS PURPOSE

In order to best serve class participants, the GFI should have a strong understanding of the goal of the specific class he or she intends to teach, as well as an idea of the type of participants who will most likely attend. Beginning the planning process by identifying the broader focus of what the class intends to accomplish will prove instrumental in designing a well-organized class blueprint. For example, the primary goal of an indoor cycling class may be to improve participants' cardiorespiratory endurance, whereas the intent of a restorative yoga class may be to reduce stress and promote relaxation. Regardless of the format the GFI is teaching, identifying the overall emphasis of the class will provide a framework for determining specific learning objectives.

[APPLY WHAT YOU KNOW]

Class Titles

Properly naming a class not only proves helpful in attracting individuals for whom the class format would be most appropriate, but it can also aid in managing participant expectations by providing insight into what they can anticipate during the class experience. Many GFIs will teach classes in gyms and studios that already have set class titles and descriptions, and/or will lead pre-choreographed classes with specifically branded names (see Chapter 2). However, some GFIs will be asked to craft their own class titles, especially if being hired for the primary purpose of bringing a new class format to a facility. Care and consideration should be taken when deciding how to most appropriately title a new class offering. For example, while an all-encompassing class name like "Senior Fitness" aptly states who the class is for, what exactly is being offered to participants is less clear (Williams, 2002). A class title such as "Chairobics for Active Agers" may be a more suitable option, as it, (1) clearly and concisely denotes who the class is primarily intended for and (2) it creatively, yet descriptively, expresses what participants can expect during the class, which is to perform chair-based exercises to improve fitness.

ESTABLISHING OBJECTIVES

With the general goal for the class established, a GFI should construct specific learning objectives that appropriately capture the knowledge and skills that participants should be able to exhibit following instruction (University of New Mexico, 2005). The class objectives can encompass all three domains of learning, as discussed in Chapter 8. Examples of common class objectives include:

- *Indoor cycling class:* Participants will be able to demonstrate the three hand positions and identify the foundational movements that correspond with each.

- *Dance-based fitness class:* Participants will be able to perform a basic salsa step.

- *Yoga class:* Participants will be able to explain two different ways to use a yoga block to perform crow pose (bakasana).

One option for creating an even more compelling and focused class experience is to establish a specific theme. The theme can be thought of as a central focus point that the GFI would like participants to see as a common thread weaving through the entire class (Biscontini, 2011). While setting a theme is not an essential component of the class blueprint, it can assist in ensuring that class objectives are successfully met while creating a more memorable movement experience for participants, as discussed further in Chapter 6.

DESIGNING A CLASS PLAN

Once the class objectives have been established, the next step in systematic class design is to consider what major movements, skills, and exercises are necessary to accomplish the objectives for any participant. Often seen as a "cheat sheet," a class blueprint helps the GFI prepare for, plan, and practice the core components of the class, applying the most up-to-date evidence-based information to ensure safe and effective movement experiences for participants (Figure 5-1).

Figure 5-1
Group fitness class blueprint planning sheet

Class title: _____

Class purpose and objectives: _____

Primary audience: _____

Class duration: _____

Class theme: _____

General format: _____

Equipment: _____

Music: _____

Warm-up

Duration	Moves (with progressions/regressions)	Purpose

Conditioning phase

Duration	Moves (with progressions/regressions)	Purpose

Cool-down

Duration	Moves (with progressions/regressions)	Purpose

Visit www.ACEfitness.org/GFIresources to download an expanded version of this sample group fitness class blueprint template.

WARM-UP CONSIDERATIONS

As discussed in Chapter 2, the warm-up is a period of lighter exercise preceding the conditioning phase of the exercise bout. A more efficient, effective, and engaging class experience starts with a dynamic warm-up that properly prepares the body for the activity to come. While there is not one "right" way to warm up, there are some general guidelines and key considerations GFIs should keep in mind when planning this important component of the group fitness class experience.

Ideally, the warm-up should last at least five to 10 minutes, beginning with low-to-moderate intensity exercise or activity that gradually increases in intensity. Depending on what is planned during the conditioning phase, the warm-up should be adjusted accordingly. For example, if planning a **high-intensity interval training (HIIT)** class, the latter portion of the warm-up could include some brief higher-intensity exercise to prepare participants for the intense elements they will experience later on in the class. As a general principle, the harder the conditioning phase, the more extensive the warm-up should be. However, the warm-up should not be so demanding that it creates **fatigue** that would reduce performance.

An extended warm-up may also be needed when leading classes such as dance-based and aquatic fitness classes geared toward specific demographics of participants, such as active agers and/or deconditioned individuals. Refer to Chapter 9 for detailed information on developing inclusive class experiences that serve various populations of participants.

Exercises to Enhance Stability and Mobility

A well-rounded warm-up routine can help decrease the risk of developing overuse injuries by addressing underlying muscle imbalances and enhancing quality of movements to be performed during the main portion of class, whether the focus is cardiorespiratory, strength, or a combination of the two. When it comes to preventing injury, ensuring adequate joint **mobility** is a must. As discussed in Chapter 3, the body is a **kinetic chain** comprised of certain joints that tend to favor **stability**—such as the scapulothoracic region and lumbar spine—as well as joints that favor mobility—such as the ankles, hips, thoracic spine, and shoulders. To help participants develop more effective movement patterns, the GFI should develop a dynamic warm-up that focuses on establishing adequate mobility specifically in these four areas.

[APPLY WHAT YOU KNOW]

Warm-up Ideas to Enhance Stability and Mobility

While there are many movement and exercise options, a dynamic warm-up should be designed in a way that best serves the needs of the class participants while supporting the overall purpose and objectives of the class format. The following are sample exercise ideas that focus on enhancing joint stability and mobility as outlined in phase 1 of the functional movement and resistance training component of the ACE Integrated Fitness Training® (ACE IFT®) Model (see Chapter 3):

- *Cat/camel:* To promote thoracic spine mobility (Figure 5-2)
- *Birddog:* To enhance stability of the lumbar spine (Figure 5-3)
- *I, Y, W, O formations:* To improve shoulder stability and mobility (Figure 5-4)
- *Glute bridge:* To enhance hip mobility (Figure 5-5)
- *Kneeling prisoner rotations:* To improve thoracic spine mobility (Figure 5-6)
- *Standing ankle mobilization:* To promote ankle mobility (Figure 5-7)
- *Arm circles and standing diagonals:* To improve shoulder mobility (Figures 5-8 and 5-9)

Figure 5-2
Cat/camel

Figure 5-3
Birddog

Figure 5-4
I, Y, W, O, formations

I formation

W formation

Y formation

O formation

Figure 5-5
Glute bridge

Single-leg glute bridge progression

Figure 5-6
Kneeling
prisoner
rotations

Figure 5-7
Standing ankle mobilization

Figure 5-8
Arm circles

Figure 5-9
Standing diagonals

Rehearsal Moves

Participants may become frustrated in a group fitness class when they find themselves unable to perform the movements and exercises effectively. For this reason, it is important that **rehearsal moves** be incorporated throughout the warm-up, preparing participants mentally and physically for the challenges of the workout ahead. Rehearsal moves are defined as movements that are similar to, but less intense than, the movements that participants will execute during the conditioning phase of class. The concept of rehearsal moves relates to the principle of **specificity** (see Chapter 2), which states that the body adapts specifically to whatever demands are placed on it. Rehearsal moves make up a large part of the warm-up, as their purpose is to prepare the body from a neuromuscular standpoint, as introducing new movement patterns in the warm-up will assist with activating associated **motor units.**

Examples of rehearsal moves include teaching participants how to adjust hand positioning and rise slowly out of the saddle for a brief hill climb in an indoor cycling class, incorporating basic body-weight exercises at a low-to-moderate intensity to prepare for loaded movements later on in a group strength-training class, or practicing a side kick slowly with music at half-tempo during a kickboxing class warm-up before performing the move as part of the routine at a higher intensity level.

In order to successfully perform movements, participants must be provided with the opportunity to practice. Giving participants the opportunity to practice a new exercise or skill will not only enhance their ability to execute the movements safely and more efficiently, but it will also provide them with a greater sense of success and accomplishment, which in turn can enhance overall exercise **adherence.**

CONDITIONING CONSIDERATIONS

Functional movements, such as squats and lunges, are not only staple exercises in many group fitness class formats, but also movements that participants use in everyday life, from rising out of a chair to walking and climbing up stairs. Incorporating exercises that mimic the five primary movement patterns, as outlined in phase 2 of the functional movement and resistance training component of the ACE IFT Model (see Chapter 3), can help create a class experience that enhances participants' overall functionality, both inside and outside of the group fitness environment.

With this integrated approach to exercise, GFIs should incorporate multijoint movements that train the body to function as one continuous unit, which better mimics participants' **activities of daily living (ADL).** Multijoint movements also help to burn additional calories, given that more muscle groups are working simultaneously compared to when performing isolated, single-joint exercises. This movement-based approach should also include multiplanar training, in which exercises and movement patterns are performed in all three **planes of motion** (See Figures 3-3, 3-4, and 3-5, pages 36–37).

A GFI should consider the primary audience of his or her class and make exercise decisions accordingly. For example, if leading a class primarily designed for deconditioned participants, it may be most appropriate to incorporate movements performed in a supported position using a bench or chair, focusing on one joint moving in one plane of motion. In time, the movements incorporated in the class can ultimately be progressed to more unsupported, free standing, multijoint exercises moving in multiple planes of motion in order to more closely mimic ADL.

[APPLY WHAT YOU KNOW]

Exercise Evaluation

As discussed in Chapter 4, learning how to choose the appropriate exercises is among the most important tasks performed by GFIs. Having both an understanding of exercise science and a specific framework in which to initially judge all exercises will prove valuable in the class-planning process. GFIs should consider physiological, biomechanical, and psychological factors for any exercise or movement pattern. To this end, an **exercise evaluation** can be done for each movement in class to determine its effectiveness and safety.

> # GFIs should consider physiological, biomechanical, and psychological factors

Exercise-evaluation Criteria

1. What is the objective of this exercise?

- Is the goal cardiorespiratory-, strength-, or flexibility-based, or a combination of two or more health- or skill-related components of physical fitness?

- Am I trying to teach an isolated or integrated movement?

- How does this movement or skill enhance the participants' ability to perform ADL and improve overall functionality?

2. What muscle(s) are being worked during the exercise or skill?

- Which joint actions (and other movements) must be performed to achieve the objective safely?

- When using equipment, is the appropriate muscle(s) being sufficiently and safely challenged?

- When using body weight as resistance, is the body positioned appropriately against gravity?

3. Do the benefits of the exercise outweigh the potential risks?

- Does the exercise commence from a point of stability and add mobility as appropriate within a safe **range of motion (ROM)**?

4. Can this movement or skill be scaled to various ability levels?

- Who are my participants?

- Am I prepared to offer **progressions** and **regressions** to ensure the success of all individuals?

The ability to evaluate the effectiveness and safety of exercises will improve as a GFI learns more about functional anatomy and the many factors that can affect efficient human movement. Using the exercise-evaluation criteria helps instructors get into the habit of exploring their understanding of exercise specificity, joint actions and biomechanics, safety, and progressions and regressions. Working through the analysis requires thought, time, and practice at the onset, but with continued use this work will eventually become second nature.

 Visit www.ACEfitness.org/GFIresources to download an exercise-evaluation checklist you can use while designing your classes.

[EXPAND YOUR KNOWLEDGE]

Considerations for Utilizing Weighted Vests in Cardio-based Classes

Adding external load to a workout increases the total mass that must be moved, so it seems logical that wearing a weighted vest would be beneficial with regards to boosting the physiological demands of a workout for participants. However, for GFIs considering incorporating weighted vests into cardio-based classes (e.g., indoor cycling, step, and treadmill-based classes) it is important to look to the science to properly evaluate how and when to utilize this type of training tool:

— Wearing a weighted vest to increase exercise intensity appears to be an effective approach depending on the magnitude of the load. Most experts, however, recommend that vests not exceed 5 to 10% of the participant's body weight to help ensure safety and comfort (Rantalainen, Ruotsalainen, & Virmavirta, 2012).

— The metabolic impact of wearing a weighted vest is greatest in activities requiring a significant component of vertical work (e.g., step classes or inclined walking or running in treadmill-based classes).

— If teaching an indoor cycling class with many standing hill climbs, calorie expenditure appears to be relatively similar with or without the use of a weighted vest when the vests worn are at 5 to 10% of participant's body weight (Kravitz, 2013).

— Weighted vests are preferred over hand weights in classes such as step, as the use of hand weights during cardiorespiratory conditioning classes may place undue stress on arm and shoulder muscles and the wrist and elbow joints.

To read ACE-sponsored research on weighted vests and other topics related to group exercise, visit www.ACEfitness.org/ACEfit/research-studies.

Scaling Exercise Intensity

In order to ensure the safety, success, enjoyment, and effectiveness of the fitness experience for participants, GFIs must be prepared to offer scaled variations of the exercises and movements included in the class. In order to accommodate individuals at different ability levels, GFIs must understand how to decrease the intensity or complexity of a skill (known as a regression) as well as how to increase the intensity or complexity of a skill (known as a progression). A regression of an exercise may include decreasing **lever** length by lowering the hands to the hips, as opposed to reaching the arms overhead. A progression of an exercise may include transitioning from a tandem, or heel-to-toe, stance to a single-leg stance to more effectively challenge balance. Appropriate progression and regression options should be included within the class blueprint in order to ensure the GFI is adequately prepared to lead inclusive movement experiences. Refer to Chapter 8 for specific strategies for teaching multilevel classes.

 [THINK IT THROUGH]

When designing a group strength class, you decide to include dumbbell front squats within the conditioning phase. In what ways could you scale the exercise intensity to ensure the safety and success of all participants by offering both more accessible and more challenging exercise options?

COOL-DOWN CONSIDERATIONS

Just as it is important to gradually increase core body temperature and **heart rate** during the warm-up portion of a class, it is critical to gradually decrease the intensity of exercise during the cool-down, or conclusion of class. The cool-down should be of approximately the same duration and intensity as the warm-up (i.e., five to 10 minutes of low-to-moderate intensity activity). This will allow ample time within the class to allow participants' heart rates to gradually lower and their bodies to comfortably and safely transition to a diminished level of work. An active cool-down also helps remove metabolic waste from the muscles so that it can be metabolized by other tissues. Walking at a reduced speed and incline during the final phase of a treadmill-based class is an example of an effective strategy used to gradually decrease the intensity of the class experience. GFIs should take care to avoid abruptly stopping intense exercise, which can cause blood to pool in the lower extremities and lead to dizziness and even fainting post-workout, especially in individuals who may have compromised cardiovascular health.

Myofascial Release and Stretching

In addition to generally decreasing the overall intensity of the class experience, GFIs may wish to consider incorporating **self–myofascial release (SMR)** as part of the cool-down if equipment such as foam rollers are available. Myofascial release is a technique that applies pressure to tight, restricted areas of **fascia** and underlying muscle tissue in an attempt to relieve tension and improve flexibility. Tender areas of soft tissues, known as trigger points or adhesions, can be diminished by applying pressure (myofascial release) to relieve tension, increase blood flow, and improve tissue density, followed by static stretching of the tight areas to address tissue length and enhance joint ROM.

Performing flexibility exercises when muscles are warm following cardiorespiratory or resistance training may prove to be most effective [American College of Sports Medicine (ACSM), 2014]. The exact stretches incorporated into the cool-down can vary depending on a number of factors, including the class format, intensity of the movements, and exercises included in the conditioning phase. Refer to Chapter 2 for examples of targeted stretches a GFI may wish to incorporate at the end of an indoor cycling class.

[APPLY WHAT YOU KNOW]

Incorporating Foam Rolling into Group Fitness Classes

If choosing to incorporate myofascial release as part of the class cool-down, GFIs may choose to use foam rollers where participants control their own intensity and duration or pressure. A common technique is to instruct participants to perform small, continuous, back-and-forth movements on a foam roller, covering an area of 2 to 6 inches (5 to 15 cm). Once a tender spot is located, participants should be instructed to maintain back-and-forth pressure over the region for 20 to 30 seconds. The GFI should advise participants to ease into foam rolling gradually, given the discomfort that comes with exerting pressure on an already tender area of the body. At the conclusion of class, SMR should focus on addressing all major muscles worked during the movement experience. Figure 5-10 depicts several examples of myofascial release techniques for targeting major muscles of the lower body, including the gluteals, quadriceps, and hamstrings.

Figure 5-10
Myofascial release using a foam roller

Myofascial release for gluteals/external rotators

Myofascial release for the quadriceps

Myofascial release for the hamstrings

INTELLIGENTLY STRUCTURED
AND SEQUENCED CLASSES

A GFI must take great care in designing intelligently structured and sequenced group fitness class experiences. In addition to selecting exercises and movements that complement and balance each other, he or she must be able to apply principles of exercise science to make smart decisions regarding how to order exercises, structure work-to-recovery ratios, and seamlessly transition from one movement to the next to minimize risk of injury among participants and ensure that learning objectives are successfully met.

DETERMINING EXERCISE ORDER

Determining exercise selection and order is a complex process in which there is not a one-size-fits-all approach. As noted earlier, it is important that the GFI incorporate rehearsal moves within the warm-up to prepare for exercises and skills later in the class, as well as utilize the exercise-evaluation criteria when determining which specific movements best serve participants and meet the overall purpose and objectives of the class. Within the conditioning phase of a group strength, boot camp, or HIIT class, GFIs may choose to have participants perform primary exercises first, such as multijoint linear exercises like squats, lunges, and shoulder presses. These exercises can then be followed by assisted exercises, such as lateral raises, biceps curls, and chest flys, which are single-joint rotary exercises that

involve smaller muscle groups. The multijoint to single-joint approach is thought to be prudent from a safety standpoint to help prevent any undue consequences of muscle fatigue at the end of a workout (Simao et al., 2010).

If power-type, explosive exercises—such as **plyometrics**—and heavy strength-training exercises are incorporated into a class, these should be performed at the beginning of the workout after an appropriate warm-up, when energy and concentration levels are highest and fatigue level is lowest. Performing these exercises later in a workout when higher levels of fatigue may increase the risk of injury.

Based on a review of the available research, it is clear that the chief determining factors for exercise ordering should be the goal and intended outcomes of the class, as well as the movement-pattern needs of the participants (Simao et al., 2012).

Research Highlights on Exercise Ordering

While ACSM (2014) recommends resistance exercise–based classes and programs focus on performing multijoint exercises first before performing single-joint exercises targeting major muscles, some studies have shown that this is not always an absolute rule. Simao et al. (2012) summarized various training studies investigating the chronic effect on exercise order and concluded that exercise order does not always have to proceed according to the conventional large-muscle-group to small-muscle-group sequence. The most important determinant of exercise order should be the movement patterns most in need of improvement.

Gentil et al. (2007) investigated the effects of the pre-exhaustion technique, which involves performing a single-joint exercise immediately before a multijoint exercise (e.g., performing a set of chest flys immediately before performing a set of bench press). This was compared to the reverse order, in which the multijoint exercise was performed immediately before the single-joint exercise. The study found that the number of exercise repetitions performed was always greater for a specific exercise when that particular exercise was completed first. The researchers concluded that the exercise that is of most importance to the overall goals or objectives should be placed at the beginning of the conditioning phase of the class, regardless of whether the exercise is a multijoint or single-joint exercise.

Mindful Transitions

In order to create a cohesive class experience, GFIs should not only consider the ordering of exercises, but also the transitions between the movements. While transitioning techniques can vary (see Chapter 10), GFIs should be mindful to avoid quick changes in body positioning when sequencing exercises and transitioning between movements, in order to maximize safety and enhance the overall class flow. Abrupt changes to posture, especially during intense exercise, can produce significant changes in **blood pressure. Orthostatic hypotension**—also known as **postural hypotension**—is defined as a sharp drop in blood pressure often caused by transitioning from a **supine** or seated position to standing, resulting in dizziness or even loss of consciousness. GFIs should carefully and intelligently sequence movements and transitions to avoid extreme and rapid changes in body position.

WORK-TO-RECOVERY RATIOS

Interval-based classes continue to grow in popularity in the group fitness environment. From aquatic classes to outdoor boot camps, many GFIs are utilizing this approach to exercise in structuring their class experiences. Aerobic interval training generally involves bouts of **steady-state exercise** performed at higher intensities for sustained periods (typically a minimum of three minutes), followed by a return to lower aerobic intensities for the recovery interval (Bacon et al., 2013). It is extremely important that when designing an interval-based class plan, GFIs ensure an adequate work-to-recovery ratio. Intervals often utilize exercise-to-recovery ratios between 1:2 and 1:1. An example of a 1:1 exercise-to-recovery ratio involves performing a four-minute steady-state bout followed by a four-minute recovery period at a lower intensity.

With a desire among many participants to "exercise smarter, not longer," express classes have been added to many group fitness class schedules (see Chapter 2). Due to the condensed timeframe of these classes, GFIs may opt to include higher-intensity intervals, in which the duration of the work interval will often range between 15 and 60 seconds. The recovery interval in these higher-intensity classes should still be equal to, or longer than, the work interval.

[APPLY WHAT YOU KNOW]

Designing an Interval-based Treadmill Class Using the ACE IFT Model

Using the ACE IFT Model as a guide, GFIs can plan safe, effective, and enjoyable interval-based treadmill classes. As noted in Chapter 3, phase 2 of the cardiorespiratory training component of the ACE IFT Model focuses on improving participants' aerobic efficiency by incorporating aerobic intervals into the class design and using **ratings of perceived exertion (RPE)** to assess intensity level. One way in which this could be done within the conditioning phase of class is to include aerobic intervals in a 1:2 work-to-recovery ratio, in which participants perform a "work" interval at a RPE of 6 on the 0 to 10 scale for 60 seconds at an increased speed, followed by a recovery interval of 120 seconds at an RPE of 3 to 4 at a decreased speed. The duration of the class will then dictate how many interval bouts can be performed, while still ensuring ample time is allocated for an appropriate warm-up and cool-down.

A BALANCED APPROACH TO EXERCISES

Each muscle in the body performs specific functions. A muscle that creates a major movement at a joint is referred to as the **agonist,** or **prime mover,** and the muscle on the opposite side of the joint is referred to as an **antagonist,** or opposing muscle. This type of functional pairing of muscles is found throughout the body. For example, the quadriceps muscle group in the front of the thigh produces knee **extension,** whereas on the opposite side of the joint the hamstrings—the antagonist muscles—produce knee **flexion.** In order to ensure proper postural alignment in the body, opposing muscle groups have a mutually respectful relationship, in which they maintain an adequate degree of pull on either side of a joint and share essential information from the nervous system. This enables the joint to move freely and with equal efficiency in all directions. However, when imbalances in this relationship occur, deviations to posture and faulty movement patterns can result, placing abnormal loading and excessive stress on various structures and joints within the body.

To enhance participants' movement quality both inside and outside of the group fitness environment, GFIs can create balance in terms of the muscle groups used and the movement patterns performed when designing class experiences. For example, in a group strength class, instructors should strive to train all major muscle groups equally. GFIs may choose to structure the class sequence to alternate targeting joint agonists and antagonists (e.g., biceps and triceps) or to alternate movement patterns, such as pushing and pulling movements. Another approach a GFI may take to creating a class experience that targets all major muscles is to design a circuit that alternates between upper- and lower-extremity exercises within the class.

Even when a class has a specific focus or theme, it is important to provide participants with a well-rounded experience. For example, in a core-conditioning class, GFIs should not only include exercises to strengthen the muscles on the front side of the body (e.g., rectus abdominis and obliques), but also exercises that target the muscles on the back of the body (e.g., erector spinae) and the deep musculature of the core that helps enhance stability of the lumbar spine (e.g., transverse abdominis).

 [THINK IT THROUGH]

When teaching a dance-based fitness class, what movements could you incorporate into the class sequence to create balance between opposing muscle groups in the body? When evaluating exercises, be sure to consider the joint actions that are taking place, as well as the muscles that are producing the movements (see Chapter 3).

SUMMARY

Designing an effective group fitness class blueprint requires an application of exercise science–related principles in an intelligently structured manner. From selecting appropriate exercises to determining how to appropriately order movements within each of the three core components of the class plan, a successful GFI dedicates time to appropriately planning and thoroughly practicing the class plan he or she designs.

References

American College of Sports Medicine (2014). *ACSM's Guidelines for Exercise Testing and Prescription* (9th ed.). Philadelphia: Wolters Kluwer/Lippincott Williams & Wilkins.

Bacon, A.P. et al. (2013). $\dot{V}O_2$max trainability and high intensity interval training in humans: A meta-analysis. *PLoS One*, 8, 9, e73182. DOI: 10.1371/journal.pone.0073182.

Biscontini, L. (2011). *Cream Rises: Excellence in Private and Group Fitness Education.* New York: FG2000.

Gentil, P. et al. (2007). Effects of exercise order on upper-body muscle activation and exercise performance. *Journal of Strength and Conditioning Research,* 21, 4, 1082–1086.

Kravitz, L. et al. (2013). *ACE-sponsored Research: The Metabolic Cost of Weighted Vests during Standing Cycling.* www.acefitness.org/prosourcearticle/3472/ace-sponsored-research-the-metabolic-cost-of/

Rantalainen, T., Ruotsalainen, I., & Virmavirta, M. (2012). Effect of weighted vest suit worn during daily activities on running speed, jumping power, and agility in young men. *Journal of Strength and Conditioning Research,* 26, 11, 3030–3035.

Simao, R. et al. (2012). Exercise order in resistance training. *Sports Medicine,* 42, 3, 251–265.

Simao, R. et al. (2010). Influence of exercise order on maximum strength and muscle thickness in untrained men. *Journal of Sports Science and Medicine,* 9, 1–7.

University of New Mexico School of Medicine, Teacher & Educational Development (2005). *Effective Use of Performance Objectives for Learning and Assessment.* http://ccoe.rbhs.rutgers.edu/forms/EffectiveUseofLearningObjectives.pdf

Williams, A. (2002). What older adults want. *IDEA Fitness Edge,* 2003, 5.

Suggested Reading

American Council on Exercise (2012). *ACE's Essentials of Exercise Science for Fitness Professionals.* San Diego: American Council on Exercise.

CHAPTER 6

CREATING MEMORABLE MOVEMENT EXPERIENCES

JESSICA MATTHEWS

FACTORS INFLUENCING PARTICIPATION AND ADHERENCE

PERSONAL ATTRIBUTES

ENVIRONMENTAL FACTORS

PHYSICAL-ACTIVITY FACTORS

UNDERSTANDING BEHAVIOR CHANGE

ESTABLISHING RAPPORT

EFFECTIVE COMMUNICATION STRATEGIES

TRANSTHEORETICAL MODEL OF BEHAVIORAL CHANGE

UNDERSTANDING MOTIVATION

STRATEGIES FOR ENHANCING SUCCESS

CONSIDERATIONS FOR CLASS EXPERIENCES

CREATING A THEME

OPENING AND CLOSING STATEMENTS

CULTIVATING COMMUNITY

TEAM COHESIVENESS

RECRUITING AND RETAINING PARTICIPANTS

SUMMARY

LEARNING OBJECTIVES

- ▓ Identify factors that influence exercise adherence.
- ▓ Define rapport and apply strategies for effectively connecting with participants.
- ▓ List and describe the five stages of behavioral change.
- ▓ Explain the difference between extrinsic and intrinsic motivation.
- ▓ Instruct participants on how to formulate SMART goals.
- ▓ Create and deliver powerful opening and closing statements.

Exceptional ACE Certified Group Fitness Instructors (GFIs) not only instruct classes, but also serve as leaders and coaches who empower participants to develop a positive association with exercise by experiencing physical activity in enjoyable and meaningful ways. While it is imperative for a GFI to possess skill in safely and effectively cueing movements, as covered in Chapter 8, he or she must also be well-versed in the art of constructing memorable movement experiences in order to reach and retain participants. From building **rapport** with participants and understanding the basics of behavior change, to implementing strategies that enhance **motivation**, improve **adherence**, and develop group camaraderie, the GFI can create a positive and inclusive environment in which all participants can thrive.

If your study program includes the ACE Learning Center, visit www.ACEfitness.org/MyACE and log in to your My ACE Account to learn more about creating themes and using positive and inclusive language in group fitness classes.

FACTORS INFLUENCING PARTICIPATION AND ADHERENCE

Much research has examined the factors related to physical-activity participation, including an understanding of potential determinants for physical activity, which are those factors that influence a person's decision to engage in exercise behavior. The potential determinants for physical activity can be broken down into three categories (Dishman & Buckworth, 1997):

 Personal attributes    Environmental factors    Physical-activity factors

GFIs should have a general understanding of these factors in order to better address the challenges participants may face with regards to attending group fitness classes.

PERSONAL ATTRIBUTES

Demographics

Adherence to physical-activity programs has proven to be consistently related to education, income, age, and gender [Centers for Disease Control (CDC), 2013]. Specifically, lower levels of activity are seen with increasing age, fewer years of education, and low income. Age, however, has been shown to be unrelated to adherence levels when examined in supervised exercise settings, such as the group fitness environment. This is of importance to GFIs who lead structured movement-based classes, because when exercise sessions are conducted under the guidance of health and fitness professionals, adherence levels are increased among participants of various ages (Lowry et al., 2013; Dorgo et al., 2011).

Health Status

Individuals who suffer from chronic illness, such as **diabetes** and heart disease, typically exercise less than those who are apparently healthy (Newsom et al., 2012). While physical limitations might be a mitigating factor, it is likely that the misconception that individuals with **chronic diseases** should not exercise plays a role in the reduced physical-activity levels. As a GFI, it is important to create an environment in which all participants are able to engage in exercise safely and successfully, through the incorporation of **progressions** and **regressions** of exercises and a general understanding of the needs of various participants. See Chapter 9 for more information on creating inclusive class experiences.

Activity History

Arguably one of the most important and influential personal attribute variables is activity history. In supervised exercise programs, past program participation is the most reliable predictor of current participation. This relationship between past participation and current participation is consistent regardless of gender, obesity, and **coronary heart disease** status (Dishman & Buckworth, 1997). Therefore, it is important that GFIs take time to get to know participants as part of the onsite pre-class preparation (see Chapter 7) in order to garner activity history information from participants while also developing rapport.

Psychological Traits

General personality tendencies and psychological traits among participants, while often difficult to define and measure, can influence adherence to physical activity. For example, self-motivation, which is reflective of one's ability to set goals, monitor progress, and self-reinforce, has been shown to have a positive relationship with physical-activity adherence (Dishman, 1982).

Knowledge, Attitudes, and Beliefs

Individuals have a wide variety of knowledge, attitudes, and beliefs about starting and continuing with a consistent routine of physical activity. Modifying the way a participant thinks and feels about exercise has been shown to influence his or her intentions regarding being active. **Health** perception has been linked to adherence, as individuals who perceive their health to be poor are unlikely to start or adhere to an activity program. Furthermore, if they do participate, it will likely be at an extremely low intensity and frequency (Dishman & Buckworth, 1997). The use of appropriate teaching techniques (see Chapter 8), self-monitoring methods (see Chapter 4), and the effective communication strategies discussed on page 99 can prove helpful in positively influencing how a participant feels about attending group fitness classes.

ENVIRONMENTAL FACTORS

Access to Facilities

The location of a fitness facility influences participant adherence. When facilities are conveniently located near a person's home or work, the individual is more likely to adhere to physical activity. Specifically, when facility access is measured objectively (i.e., true access and availability of a facility), it is a consistent predictor of physical-activity behavior, such that people with greater access are more likely to be physically active than people with less access (Humpel, Owen, & Leslie, 2002). GFIs should ask their participants about access issues and understand how convenient or inconvenient it is for each individual to reach the facility during the specific day and time of the class he or she is teaching. If a GFI finds that an individual is struggling to regularly attend class due to factors such as distance of the facility from home or work, traffic conditions during that time, and/or a varying work schedule, the instructor should discuss alternative class options with the participant that will enable him or her to attend class more consistently, even if the other class option is taught by another instructor.

Time

Lack of time is the most common reason individuals provide for not exercising and for dropping out of an exercise program, as people perceive that they simply do not have time to be physically active (Brownson et al., 2001). The perception of not having enough time to exercise is likely a reflection of not being interested in or enjoying the activity, or not being committed to the activity program. GFIs can

help shift participant perception of time availability through the use of strategies such as goal setting, as discussed on page 103. If an individual considers health and physical activity top priorities, he or she will find—or make—the time to be active.

Social Support

Social support from family and friends is an important predictor of physical-activity behavior (Fraser & Spink, 2002). It is difficult for an individual to maintain an exercise program if he or she does not have support at home. When support is broken down into specific types, support from a spouse is shown to be an important and reliable predictor of program adherence. Social support is a critical topic that GFIs should discuss with the class, and instructors should be proactive in creating and establishing a support network for participants by building group camaraderie within the class, as discussed on page 107.

PHYSICAL-ACTIVITY FACTORS

Intensity

The drop-out rate in vigorous-intensity exercise programs is almost twice as high as in moderate-intensity programs. Additionally, when people are able to choose the type of activity they engage in, six times as many women and more than twice as many men choose to start moderate-intensity programs than vigorous-intensity programs. These results are true regardless of whether intensity is measured physiologically, such as by percentage of **heart-rate reserve,** or psychologically, such as by **ratings of perceived exertion (RPE)** (Sallis et al., 1986).

Injury

There is a reliable relationship between physical activity and injury, such that the higher the level of physical activity, the higher the risk for developing an activity-related injury (Knapik et al., 2011). Injuries that occur as a result of program participation are directly related to program dropout. Therefore, it is imperative that GFIs take as many steps as possible to mitigate the potential for injury (see Chapter 11).

> Location of a fitness facility influences adherence

UNDERSTANDING BEHAVIOR CHANGE

n order to create impactful group fitness experiences, GFIs must have a strong understanding of the foundational components associated with adopting and adhering to healthful behaviors such as physical activity. From learning how to establish meaningful relationships with participants by using effective communication strategies, to understanding a participant's readiness for change and the specific strategies that will help ensure ongoing success and motivation, GFIs must be well-versed in more than just selecting exercises and building movement sequences.

ESTABLISHING RAPPORT

When attending a group fitness class for the first time or taking a class taught by a new instructor, participants may have feelings of insecurity and apprehension. A GFI can help combat these feelings of uncertainty by developing rapport with individuals. Rapport can be defined as a relationship of trust and mutual understanding. While rapport is ongoing and will continue to grow throughout the relationship between instructor and participant, GFIs should take great care to set the foundation for rapport when first meeting new participants. This is done through positive and thoughtful interactions rooted in **empathy,** which involves attempting to understand what the other person is feeling and experiencing demonstrated through an

attitude of caring and concern (Egan, 2013). When GFIs use strategies such as **active listening,** clear communication, and professionalism, participants can feel confident and a bit more at ease knowing that their needs are understood and their involvement in class is valued.

Learning Names

While it can be challenging to get to know each participant individually given constantly changing classes of often 30 or more people, GFIs should make it a point to learn as many participant names as possible to further assist in the rapport-building process. Using names before class when greeting participants, during class while offering positive **feedback,** as well as after class to provide praise for a job well done can help GFIs commit names to memory while creating strong, lasting relationships with participants. GFIs may also wish to consider using ice-breaker activities at the start of each class (see Chapter 7) to personally become acquainted with new participants while also allowing individuals in the class to get to know one another.

EFFECTIVE COMMUNICATION STRATEGIES

Empathy and rapport evolve over time from good communication between the GFI and participants. Research suggests that the time spent establishing a good working relationship enhances adherence (Ryan et al., 2011). The capabilities of the GFI, including his or her knowledge and skills, are only important to participants if they feel that the GFI truly cares about their success and enjoyment in the class.

In order to communicate effectively with participants, GFIs must encode and decode messages accurately through active listening. Essential components of active listening include, but are not limited to, asking **open-ended questions** at appropriate times and using nonverbal communication techniques such as body language to appropriately demonstrate attentiveness, empathy, and genuine concern.

Verbal Skills

When engaging in discussion with a participant, a GFI can utilize several different approaches to demonstrate good listening in response to information provided. These verbal skills include:

▬ *Open-ended questions:* Open-ended questions commonly begin with the words "what," "why," and "how." This type of questioning technique is useful in opening a conversation with a participant, learning more details about what is being communicated, developing a better understanding of the participant's views, or simply keeping the conversation going.

▬ *Reflective listening:* This approach helps the GFI empathize, reflect, and clarify the main points and feelings a participant is expressing.

▬ *Summarizing:* At appropriate points in the conversation, the GFI should try to synthesize what he or she has heard in one or two concise sentences, helping to keep the topic of the conversation focused and on track.

▬ *Encouragement:* GFIs should occasionally use short words or phrases, such as "good point" and "well said" to demonstrate to the participant that what is being said is being followed. GFIs should use encouraging phrases sparingly as to avoid excessive interruptions.

Nonverbal Skills

While the words spoken verbally during a class are important, they only constitute a small portion of the complete message that participants receive. Mehrabian (1971) noted that when communicating a message, 7% of the message is comprised of spoken words, 38% is related to tone of voice, and an astonishing 55% consists of body language. Nonverbal skills that convey genuine care, concern, and undivided attention include:

▬ *Facial expressions:* Friendliness, warmth, and happiness are easily conveyed through facial expressions. As GFIs engage with participants, their faces should display the concern, thoughtfulness, and/or enjoyment they are feeling.

▬ *Eye contact:* Direct, yet friendly eye contact demonstrates that the participant is valued by the GFI. Instructors should make it a point to make eye contact with individuals while leading a class and also when speaking one-on-one with participants before or after class.

▬ *Body language:* An open, well-balanced, erect body position conveys confidence and symbolizes professional expertise. Keeping arms uncrossed and facing directly toward the participant indicates that the GFI is receptive to, and interested in, engaging in discussion.

 [THINK IT THROUGH]

Practice these verbal and nonverbal skills when conversing casually with friends and family members. Afterwards, think of ways in which you can incorporate these active listening strategies into your interactions with participants before, during, and after your classes.

[APPLY WHAT YOU KNOW]

Increasing Your Cultural Competence

The concept of **cultural competence** refers to the ability to communicate and work effectively with people from different cultures. GFIs can increase their cultural competence in several ways, beginning by first acknowledging their own biases that may hinder their ability to respectfully and positively interact with people of various ethnic backgrounds, ages, sexual orientations, physical-ability levels, socioeconomic levels, and other diversity factors. For example, a GFI may mistakenly assume that all older adults are frail and will be unable to keep up in class, or that participants at a lower level of fitness are lazy or less motivated than those who are well-conditioned. Identifying these misconceptions and addressing them by learning more about participants' beliefs, attitudes, and lifestyles through the use of effective listening skills will help ensure that each participant is treated with the dignity and respect he or she deserves.

TRANSTHEORETICAL MODEL OF BEHAVIORAL CHANGE

An important factor in the successful adoption of any routine of physical activity is the individual's readiness to make a change. This individual readiness for change is the focus of a well-accepted theory examining health behaviors called the **transtheoretical model of behavioral change (TTM)** (Prochaska & DiClemente, 1984). More commonly called the **stages-of-change model,** the TTM is important for GFIs to understand when promoting group fitness participation.

The TTM is made up of the five stages of behavioral change. These stages can be related to any health behavior, but in the exercise context the stages are as follows:

■ The first stage is the **precontemplation** stage, during which individuals are **sedentary** and are not currently considering engaging an activity program. These individuals do not see activity as relevant in their lives, and may even discount the importance or practicality of being physically active.

■ The next stage is the **contemplation** stage. People in the contemplation stage are still sedentary, but they are starting to consider activity as important and have begun to identify the implications of being inactive.

■ The **preparation** stage is marked by some physical activity, as individuals are mentally and physically preparing to adopt an activity program. Activity during the preparation stage may be a sporadic walk, or even a periodic visit to the gym, but it is inconsistent. People in

the preparation stage are getting ready to adopt and live an active lifestyle.

■ Next is the **action** stage. During this stage, people engage in regular physical activity, but have been doing so for less than six months.

■ The final stage is the **maintenance** stage. This stage is marked by regular physical-activity participation for longer than six months.

Many participants in group fitness classes will be in the preparation stage of change, and their motivation and self-confidence may be quite fragile. Individuals in this stage of change need plenty of support and reassurance in the form of positive feedback that they are doing well in the class. Ongoing feedback is also important for participants in the action stage, as even though they have regularly participated in physical activity, they have been doing so for less than six months and need continued positive reinforcement to ensure long-term adherence.

GFIs will also occasionally encounter individuals in the contemplation stage of change, such as a currently sedentary individual who comes in to tour the facility to gather information about the types of classes offered. The GFI should make it a point to emphasize the fun and social aspects of exercising in the group fitness environment and extend an invitation to the individual to attend a group fitness class, such as by providing a free guest pass or information about an upcoming open house that will feature demo classes.

Table 6-1 presents the goal of each stage of change, as well as effective interventions that can be utilized to help advance an individual to the next stage of change.

Table 6-1

TRANSTHEORETICAL MODEL OF BEHAVIORAL CHANGE

STAGE OF CHANGE	GOAL	STRATEGIES
Precontemplation	Increase awareness of the risks of being inactive and the benefits of engaging in physical activity; encourage them to start thinking about change.	Provide information about the risks of being inactive and the benefits of being active. Provide information from multiple sources (e.g., news, posters, pamphlets, and general health-promotion material). Validate that making a change is their decision.
Contemplation	Get involved in some type of activity with basic structured direction.	Provide opportunities to ask questions and to express apprehensions. Provide information about different types of activity options, fitness facilities, programs, and classes. Offer invitations to become more active (e.g., free trial pass or discounted classes).
Preparation	Regularly participate in structure physical activity.	Provide continued support and positive feedback. Assist in identifying social support and establishing personal goals. Encourage small steps toward building self-efficacy.
Action	Maintain regular physical activity as a habit through motivation and adherence.	Provide continued support and feedback. Increase awareness of inevitable lapses and bolster self-efficacy in coping with lapses. Reiterate long-term benefits of adherence.
Maintenance	Maintain continued interest in activity, avoiding boredom or burnout.	Reinforce the need to transition from external to internal rewards. Encourage program variety. Identify early signs of staleness to prevent burnout.

Building Self-efficacy

An important component of the TTM is **self-efficacy,** which refers to the belief in one's own capabilities to successfully execute necessary courses of action, such as engaging in an exercise program (McAuley & Blissmer, 2000). An individual's self-efficacy is related to whether he or she will participate in activity, and a person's participation in activity in turn influences his or her self-efficacy level. Therefore, self-efficacy is both a determinant of behavior as well as an outcome of behavior change.

There is also a relationship between self-efficacy and stage of behavioral change, as individuals in the precontemplation and contemplation stages of change have significantly lower levels of self-efficacy than those in the action or maintenance stages. One of the most powerful predictors of self-efficacy is past performance experience. Therefore, participants with little to no exercise experience will have lower self-efficacy regarding their ability to engage in a consistent routine of physical activity. In light of this, GFIs should focus on creating positive, meaningful, inclusive classes in which all participants experience feelings of success and accomplishment.

Decisional Balance

Another important aspect of TTM is decisional balance, which refers to the numbers of pros and cons an individual perceives regarding adopting and/or maintaining an activity program. Individuals in the precontemplation and contemplation stages of change perceive more cons related to being regularly physically active (e.g., time, sore muscles, cost, and boredom) than pros. It is important to note that newcomers to exercise may not be accustomed to the feeling of increased breathing, heart rate, and sweating associated with physical activity. Therefore, GFIs should acknowledge these minor discomforts associated with exercise and reassure participants that they are normal responses and should be expected. GFIs should then focus on emphasizing the wide variety of benefits of being physically active. Incorporating verbal and nonverbal cues that emphasize enjoyment of movement and feelings of accomplishment will help participants experience a greater sense of satisfaction during each class, which over time can help individuals identify more pros than cons associated with regular physical activity.

In addition to being aware of the discomforts participants who are new to exercise may experience, GFIs must also be able to recognize the warning signs of potential injuries and emergency situations that warrant immediate attention. Instructors may find it helpful to regularly check in with participants throughout the class, asking them how they are feeling. Participants can respond verbally or nonverbally (i.e., thumbs up or down). Instructors can also incorporate specific methods for monitoring intensity (e.g., RPE and talk test). Refer to Chapter 9 for detailed information on the signs and symptoms that warrant activation of emergency medical services (EMS).

UNDERSTANDING MOTIVATION

Motivation is a complex topic, but one that directly relates to long-term adherence to physical activity. Many adults depend on some amount of **extrinsic motivation,** which is defined as motivation that comes from external sources outside of oneself. Extrinsic rewards can be of particular importance during the early stages of exercise adoption to offer an incentive while working toward boosting self-efficacy. Inexpensive rewards, such as a water bottle or free class, as well as praise from friends or members of the facility staff, can help motivate participants to attend classes consistently. Fitness "challenges" can also provide rewards for different levels of participation by offering alternative prizes for a variety of achievements, attracting both the novice exerciser and the long-term group fitness participant.

Intrinsic Motivation

In order to boost self-efficacy and ensure long-term adherence to exercise, GFIs should strive to maximize enjoyment and engagement among participants in an effort to enhance **intrinsic motivation.** To be intrinsically motivated, in an exercise context, means that a participant is engaged in physical activity for the inherent pleasure and experience that comes from the engagement itself. Such involvement in an activity is associated with positive attitudes and emotions (e.g., happiness, relaxation, and freedom), as well as persistence when faced with barriers.

> GFIs can help create optimal conditions for building intrinsic motivation

GFIs can help create optimal conditions for building the intrinsic motivation of participants by offering opportunities to experience movement success by incorporating appropriate progressions, regressions, and teaching strategies; providing consistent, clear feedback (see Chapter 10); and creating an environment that provides a unique and memorable experience with exercise, as discussed on pages 104–105. Participants who enjoy the experience are likely to continue coming to class and remain involved in a consistent exercise program.

STRATEGIES FOR ENHANCING SUCCESS

As participants progress through the stages of change and develop greater intrinsic motivation, it is important that GFIs employ strategies to help ensure their ongoing success and enjoyment with physical activity. Instructors should provide participants with guidance regarding how to establish and refine realistic health and fitness goals, while also preparing them for inevitable **lapses** and setbacks in group fitness participation.

Goal Setting

When an individual joins a group fitness class, it is important that he or she take the time to develop realistic, flexible, and individualized short-term goals that build off of the objectives of the class (see Chapter 5). Realistic goals are important to not only avoid injury, but also to help maintain interest and manage expectations.

GFIs can teach participants goal-setting strategies by applying the **SMART goal** guidelines. This catchy acronym includes the key components for developing effective goals. Goals should be:

SPECIFIC	**MEASURABLE**	**ATTAINABLE**	**RELEVANT**	**TIME-BOUND**
What will you do, when, where, and with whom?	How will you know when you have reached your goals?	Can you really do this? Can you do it at this time?	Are your goals relevant to your particular interests, needs, and abilities?	How soon, how often, and for how long?
Example: Instead of "I will go to the gym for a workout," a more specific goal may be, "I will go to FitWell gym with my wife for a cycling class on Monday, Wednesday, and Friday at 6:30 p.m. after work."	*Example:* Instead of "I will exercise at a moderate intensity today," a more measurable goal may be, "I will row at an RPE of 6 for 10 minutes."	*Example:* Instead of "I will do a three-minute plank," a more attainable goal may be "I will perform a plank with proper form for 30 seconds."	*Example:* Instead of "I will train to run a marathon in under three hours," a more relevant goal may be "I will increase the amount of physical activity I do by going to a boot-camp class twice per week."	*Example:* Instead of "I will lose at least 10% of my body weight in an effort to improve my appearance," a time-bound goal may be "I will lose 20 pounds in the next four months at a reasonable rate of 1 to 2 pounds per week."

Goals can be specific to the exercise process, such as attending a certain number of classes in the coming weeks or supplementing group fitness classes with physical activity performed outside of the gym. Participants can also choose to set goals related to making new friends or developing a new social network. It is useful to encourage goals related to enjoyment and pleasure from moving and being active rather than only focus on physical goals such as weight loss.

Preparing for Setbacks

It is important that participants realize there will be times when they will not be able to attend class, such as during vacations, holidays, or times of increased work or family obligations. How lapses in an exercise routine are handled determines if they will be temporary or permanent.

When participants must miss a regular class, GFIs should encourage them to engage in physical activity outside of the group fitness environment, such as by performing home-based exercises and/or engaging in other modes of physical activity, such as walking, swimming, or hiking, perhaps with a friend, family member, or coworker. When a participant successfully exercises on his or her own, the foundation for long-term exercise adherence is reinforced.

 **[APPLY WHAT YOU KNOW]**

Addressing a Defeatist Attitude

In addition to letting participants know that missing a class is a realistic probability, GFIs should also encourage participants to predict and prepare for lapses in their normal exercise routines whenever possible so that these occurrences will likely not be as disruptive. While not all situations can be anticipated (e.g., family crises and illnesses), if a lapse is viewed as a challenge that can be overcome rather than as a failure that cannot be rectified, adherence is more likely to be maintained.

GFIs should make participants aware of the defeatist attitude that often accompanies the belief that once a physical-activity program is disrupted, total **relapse** or dropout is inevitable. Instead, instructors should encourage individuals to view exercise as a process during which there will undoubtedly be times that they will be less active than others. Rather than view missing a class as a sign of failure, participants can remain flexible in their approach to leading an active lifestyle, making attempts to either attend the next feasible class or to exercise on their own outside of the group fitness environment in a way which they find enjoyable.

CONSIDERATIONS FOR CLASS EXPERIENCES

While all GFIs teach classes, outstanding instructors take the planning and instructional process one step further in order to create experiences. From establishing specific themes and incorporating elements such as visualization, to developing opening and closing statements constructed using positive and inclusive language, GFIs have the ability to create meaningful and memorable classes for participants by considering a few additional components designed to enhance the class blueprint.

CREATING A THEME

One way in which to create a group fitness experience is to establish a central theme for the day's class. The theme should emphasize a specific aspect of the experience that the GFI would like to make the focal point for participants (Biscontini, 2011). Themes not only offer the opportunity for participants to learn something new, but also provide a more cohesive class experience by weaving a common thread consistently from start to finish. Themes can focus on increasing **kinesthetic awareness** (e.g., utilizing a theme of posture in an aquatic fitness class); targeting a specific area of the body (e.g., a core-themed suspension training class); introducing a philosophical concept (e.g., a gratitude-themed yoga class); emphasizing a specific event or time of year (e.g., a Halloween-themed cycling class); or even highlighting a particular time period or musical genre [e.g., an 80s themed **high-intensity interval training (HIIT)** class], just to name a few.

While there are countless themes from which to choose, GFIs should consider selecting a theme that fits the specific class format they are teaching, while also resonating with the needs, expectations, and preferences of class participants, as well as with the GFI him- or herself. For example, a heart chakra theme might be a feasible option for a yoga class in which back-bending postures are appropriate for participants and the instructor is well-versed in the seven chakras. However, this particular theme would likely not resonate well with participants in a group strength class in which the instructor is unfamiliar with the seven chakras and the purpose of the class is to increase muscular strength and endurance.

GFIs should take time to brainstorm a list of themes for the classes they currently teach, and then choose one specific theme they feel most comfortable presenting that will resonate well with participants. From there, instructors can identify at least three specific ways in which the theme will be emphasized throughout the class. In order for a theme to be most impactful, it should be clearly stated at the start of the class as well as evident throughout the entire experience, which includes being reiterated at the end of the class.

Music and Other Considerations

In order to ensure a well-developed theme that is of value to participants, GFIs should take time to carefully consider a variety of elements that will be used to convey the theme during the class experience. These elements may include the particular music used, the exact orientation of participants in the room, or the inclusion of specific keywords within verbal cues. When selecting music, GFIs should be mindful of the specific content of each song, including lyrics, if applicable. Instructors should also consider crafting a list of keywords that help bring the theme to life.

Another way in which GFIs can emphasize a theme is to incorporate quiet or silent relaxation segments, guided imagery, creative visualization, or storytelling, especially during times within the class when participants are most receptive (i.e., the last few minutes of class). The exact structure of these components should be determined based on what best supports the specific theme as well as the class format and participants.

 [EXPAND YOUR KNOWLEDGE]

Creating Compelling Experiences Using the Five Senses

Lawrence Biscontini (2011) suggests that GFIs can create compelling experiences for participants by considering each of the five senses when designing classes.

- *Hearing:* Biscontini recommends choosing music that complements the experience in a thematic way and using either silence or music so that it adds to, rather than detracts from, the overall experience. He also recommends devising creative new ways in which to phrase verbal cues that are commonly given.

- *Smell:* GFIs may wish to use aromatherapy to complement a particular class, when appropriate. For example, lavender is a scent associated with relaxation and may be appropriate to use during the final phase of a yoga class while participants are lying quietly in a supine position. Biscontini recommends always announcing when and how aromatherapy will be used in order for participants to have an opportunity to discretely convey whether or not they would prefer aromatherapy spray to be used in their space.

- *Taste:* Biscontini uses the sense of taste both literally and figuratively during a class. For a literal use, he may offer small mint candies to participants when in a seated position in a mind-body class to help reinforce a specific breathing technique, such as cooling breath. The figurative interpretation involves creating experiences that are in good taste, featuring inclusive language and positive feedback.

- *Sight:* GFIs may use their attire, the lighting, and/or the class environment to create a pleasing aesthetic. Biscontini personally tries establishing a connection between traditional color and his clothing, such as wearing black apparel when teaching a tai chi class.

- *Touch:* GFIs can provide physical touch to participants, with permission, to help them achieve a posture or movement (see Chapter 8). In another sense, Biscontini suggests that through personal and inspirational anecdotes as well as a focus on body, mind, and spirit, GFIs can "touch" participants in an emotional way.

OPENING AND CLOSING STATEMENTS

The beginning and ending of a class are crucial for success and for creating a noteworthy experience. The first and last five minutes of a class experience tend to be the most memorable for class participants. Therefore, Biscontini (2011) recommends utilizing formal, memorized, and well-rehearsed opening and closing statements to define the purpose of a class, set a professional tone, and bring the class to an inspirational conclusion.

Opening statements generally include a salutation and personal introduction, an expression of gratitude to participants for attending, acknowledgment of new and familiar faces, a statement regarding class purpose and learning objectives, reference to equipment and specific exercises that will be explored, and ways to monitor intensity and tailor movements, as well as the introduction of the day's theme to inspire individuals to stay for the entire experience. GFIs may also choose to incorporate some form of an ice-breaker activity to better acquaint participants with one another.

Closing statements generally include a reiteration of the class purpose, a reference to the theme of the experience, insight as to how what was covered in class applies in a meaningful way outside of the group fitness environment, a heartfelt thank you to participants for attending, and a compelling reason why they should return to a future class (e.g., divulging an exciting theme for an upcoming dance-based fitness class).

Positive and Inclusive Language

In both the opening and closing statements, as well as throughout the class experience, GFIs should make it a point to use positive and inclusive language that supports participants and appropriately conveys the theme. GFIs should also provide participants with ample and ongoing positive reinforcement and individual praise. Feedback that is specific and relevant to the participant is known to be a powerful reinforcement (see Chapter 10).

 [APPLY WHAT YOU KNOW]

Managing Participant Expectations

As noted in Chapter 5, establishing a class purpose is essential when designing a group fitness class. As part of the class experience, it is important that GFIs communicate the purpose so that participants are well aware of what to expect during the class. For example, if a GFI is teaching a class titled "Boot Camp," it is valuable for the instructor to address at the start of class what the specific purpose and objectives are and how he or she will personally be approaching the class format, from the specific equipment used to the types of exercises and movements featured. Doing this will help better manage expectations, especially among those participants who may have preconceived notions about what the class will or will not entail based on their past experiences in classes of a similar nature.

CULTIVATING COMMUNITY

It is particularly important for class members to feel a sense of cohesiveness. Research shows that individuals who have strong beliefs about the cohesiveness of their class attend more fitness classes, are less likely to drop out, are more likely to enjoy physical activity, and have high self-efficacy toward physical activity (Estabrooks, 2000). Group cohesion starts when participants gather around a shared task. Learning a new routine as a group or working to meet class objectives will enhance this type of group cohesion. As participants become satisfied with their accomplishments, social cohesion increases. The social support and reinforcement for exercise developed through group interactions is powerful and should not be overlooked.

TEAM COHESIVENESS

Community is created through connections, and when participants feel connected to a facility, they attend classes more frequently. This sense of community, which is a selling point of the facility, is due in large part to the teamwork among the group fitness staff.

A staff that communicates and works together produces a great environment and sense of community. When instructors take one another's classes and/or suggest that participants check out another instructor's class, individuals take note. A facility truly becomes a place of connection when participants feel like the focus is placed on them having positive experiences and becoming more active by attending a wide variety of class offerings within the facility, rather than GFIs competing for class numbers. When participants feel that they are valued and supported, they become more vested in the facility, and in turn become more loyal members and class participants.

RECRUITING AND RETAINING PARTICIPANTS

In addition to creating dynamic and memorable class experiences and positively collaborating with fellow instructors, GFIs can utilize technology to further recruit and retain participants. Through the use of well-branded social media channels and websites, participants can choose to connect with GFIs outside of the group fitness environment. From encouraging individuals to opt in to email lists, follow the facility on social media platforms, and review monthly e-newsletters, there are many ways in which GFIs can leverage additional "touch points" through which to engage participants and further develop rapport.

 [THINK IT THROUGH]

Social support is a driving factor for exercise adoption and long-term adherence. As a GFI, what strategies can you use to ensure each participant in a class has some type of social support?

SUMMARY

An outstanding GFI is one who possesses skill in designing and leading safe and effective classes while also demonstrating a thorough understanding of how to connect with participants in a meaningful way. Through the use effective communication strategies rooted in behavioral science and additional considerations beyond what is outlined in the basic class blueprint, GFIs can create unique and memorable movement experiences that ensure participant success and enhance motivation and adherence.

References

Biscontini, L. (2011). *Cream Rises: Excellence in Private and Group Fitness Education.* New York: FG2000.

Brownson, R.C. et al. (2001). Environmental and policy determinants of physical activity in the United States. *American Journal of Public Health,* 91, 12, 1995–2003.

Centers for Disease Control and Prevention (2013). Adult participation in aerobic and muscle-strengthening physical activities— United States, 2011. *Morbidity and Mortality Weekly Report,* 62, 17, 326–330.

Dishman, R.K. (1982). Compliance/adherence in health-related exercise. *Health Psychology,* 1, 237–267.

Dishman, R.K. & Buckworth, J. (1997). Adherence to physical activity. In: Morgan, W.P. (Ed.). *Physical Activity & Mental Health* (pp. 63–80). Washington, D.C.: Taylor & Frances.

Dorgo, S. et al. (2011). Comparing the effectiveness of peer mentoring and student mentoring in a 35-week fitness program for older adults. *Archives of Gerontology & Geriatrics,* 52, 3, 344–349.

Egan, G. (2013). *The Skilled Helper: A Problem-Management and Opportunity-Development Approach to Helping* (10th ed.). Pacific Grove, Calif.: Brooks/Cole.

Estabrooks, P.A. (2000). Sustaining exercise participation through group cohesion. *Exercise and Sport Sciences Reviews,* 28, 63–67.

Fraser, S.N & Spink, K.S. (2002). Examining the role of social support and group cohesion in exercise compliance. *Journal of Behavioral Medicine,* 25, 3, 233–249.

Humpel, N., Owen, N., & Leslie, E. (2002). Environmental factors associated with adults' participation in physical activity. *American Journal of Preventive Medicine,* 22, 3, 188–199.

Knapik J.J. et al. (2011). Association between ambulatory physical activity and injuries during United States Army basic combat training. *Journal of Physical Activity and Health,* 8, 496–502.

Lowry, R. et al. (2013). Obesity and other correlates of physical activity and sedentary injuries among U.S. high school students. *Journal of Obesity.* DOI: 10.1155/2013/276318.

McAuley, E. & Blissmer, B. (2000). Self-efficacy determinants and consequences of behavior. *Exercise & Sport Sciences Reviews,* 28, 2, 85–88.

Mehrabian, A. (1971). *Silent Messages.* Belmont, Calif.: Wadsworth.

Newsom, J.T. et al. (2012). Health behavior change following chronic illness in middle and later life. *The Journals of Gerontology,* 67B, 3, 279–288.

Prochaska, J.O. & DiClemente, C.C. (1984). *The Transtheoretical Approach: Crossing Traditional Boundaries of Therapy.* Homewood, Ill.: Dow Jones/Irwin.

Ryan, R.M. et al. (2011). Motivation and autonomy in counseling, psychotherapy, and behavior change: A look at theory and practice. *The Counseling Psychologist,* 39, 2, 193–260.

Sallis, J.F. et al. (1986). Predictors of adoption and maintenance of physical activity in a community sample. *Preventive Medicine,* 15, 331–341.

Suggested Reading

American Council on Exercise (2014). *Coaching Behavior Change.* San Diego: American Council on Exercise.

American Council on Exercise (2013). *ACE Health Coach Manual.* San Diego: American Council on Exercise.

Bandura, A. (1986). *Social Foundations of Thought and Action: A Social Cognitive Theory.* Englewood Cliffs, N.J.: Prentice-Hall.

Dishman, R.K. (1994). *Advances in Exercise Adherence.* Champaign, Ill.: Human Kinetics.

Duncan, T.E. & McAuley, E. (1993). Social support and efficacy cognitions in exercise adherence: A latent growth curve analysis. *Journal of Behavioral Medicine,* 16, 199–218.

Hagger, M.S. & Chatzisarantis, N. (2007). *Intrinsic Motivation and Self-Determination in Exercise and Sport.* Champaign, Ill.: Human Kinetics.

Uchino, B. (2004). *Social Support and Physical Health: Understanding the Health Consequences of Relationships.* New Haven, Conn.: Yale University Press.

CHAPTER 7

CHAPTER 7

DAY-OF PREPARATION FOR CLASSES

SHANNAN LYNCH

LEARNING OBJECTIVES

- Demonstrate leadership qualities by preparing for classes and arriving organized and outfitted to teach.
- Identify and address potential hazards related to equipment and environment.
- Demonstrate correct set-up of music and equipment.
- Modify positioning of participants and equipment to ensure class safety.
- Gather pertinent information about participants and orient newcomers.
- Respond to equipment failures and malfunctions.
- Address frequently asked questions from participants.

Chapters 5 and 6 discuss two core competencies of an ACE Certified Group Fitness Instructor (GFI)—designing the blueprint of a class and creating a memorable experience. Characteristics such as attitude and personality are among the motivating factors that affect **adherence**. Other qualifying traits of an ideal GFI are professionalism and the ability to adapt and overcome. From orienting new students to teaching class "a cappella" due to a malfunctioning audio system, a GFI must demonstrate professionalism by diffusing unpredictable situations and devising creative ways to adjust to conditions that are less than ideal. This chapter covers day-of class considerations and offers suggestions for immediate onsite solutions to potential setbacks.

If your study program includes the ACE Learning Center, visit www.ACEfitness.org/MyACE and log in to your My ACE Account to learn more about day-of preparation for group fitness classes.

LEADERSHIP QUALITIES

Teaching group fitness classes is a rewarding experience because GFIs serve as agents of change, facilitating activities that improve both physical health and state of mind. Leadership abilities and first impressions affect participants' perception of the type of class they are about to experience. It is often thought that leadership is an innate trait, but leadership skills can be developed even by those not considered "born leaders" (Fox, Rejeski, & Gauvin, 2000). Some of the qualities of a GFI that produce an effective, adherence-boosting class experience include punctuality, dependability, professionalism, and dedication.

PUNCTUALITY AND DEPENDABILITY

GFIs must assure participants that each class will start and end on time. A class that starts late or does not end as scheduled is disruptive to both participants and other group fitness classes. As such, GFIs should plan on arriving at least 15 minutes early to greet participants and ensure a punctual class start. Additionally, participants like to know that their regular instructor, not a parade of substitutes, will be there consistently to lead their fitness experience. Whenever possible, absences should be planned in advance, allowing substitutes to be scheduled accordingly and participants to be well informed of changes.

PROFESSIONALISM

All participants should be treated with respect. Gossiping about class members or fellow instructors is inappropriate and should not occur in the group fitness environment. Negative comments about other class formats or fitness brands adversely affect the fitness industry and diminish the credibility of a GFI. Remember, all facility staff members are on the same team and have the same goal—to improve exercise adherence and instill excitement and enjoyment for exercise among class participants.

As a team player, a GFI will often offer to substitute classes for other instructors when needed. Teaching another GFI's regular class is always an adjustment for everyone. However, the substituting GFI should teach the class as if it were his or her own, offering the same level of service and attention

he or she would give to regular classes. A GFI should always refrain from language, opinions, or actions that may undermine the regular instructor.

Professionalism extends beyond communication to also include choice of attire. Although a GFI may wish to be stylish by following popular fashion trends, it is not professional to be dressed in a provocative manner when leading group fitness classes, as doing so can make participants feel uncomfortable. See Chapter 4 for additional information on appropriate class attire.

DEDICATION

Part of being an effective leader involves ongoing dedication to one's work. Participants will often approach GFIs before and after class with health- and fitness-related questions (see pages 121–122). Obtaining and maintaining a professional certification demonstrates commitment to one's profession and enables a GFI to best serve class participants. Additionally, efforts should be made on a continual basis to keep fitness classes diverse, fun, and enjoyable for participants. This means GFIs must continually seek out continuing education opportunities to keep up with the latest exercise trends and to obtain science-based information to appropriately address questions participants may have on health-related topics (see Chapter 12). GFIs should use discretion when referring participants to the internet (and help them identify the more credible sites) and refer them to healthcare providers when the topic is beyond a GFI's **scope of practice.**

INITIAL ONSITE PROCEDURES AND RESPONSIBILITIES

As mentioned previously, arrival time is very important. GFIs should make a practice of arriving early to class to complete pre-class responsibilities, communicate with participants, and set the atmosphere for the experience to follow. Turning on music and adjusting the lighting and temperature (if possible) to complement the format sets the tone for the class. In the event a GFI does arrive late to class, he or she should turn on the music and get the class warming up while assessing the room and equipment set-up for any safety hazards, adjusting participants' set-up as needed. A GFI should strive to employ the following best practices at the beginning of each class to create a safe, enjoyable, and successful experience for participants.

ROOM/EXERCISE AREA ASSESSMENT

Upon arrival, the GFI should let the front desk/facility operator know he or she is present on site. If there are no standard facility practices in place pertaining to instructor arrival, a simple wave or hello is sufficient. This verifies the GFI has arrived, which is helpful in case there are facility-related issues that the staff needs to notify the instructor about, and it also gives everyone peace of mind that the class will start on time.

Next, unless there is a class currently taking place in the group fitness room/space, the GFI should enter the room to check the temperature and lighting and identify any immediate hazards such as leaks or electrical problems, notifying staff immediately if any are observed. If it is not possible to enter the room, the GFI should wait outside the room to ensure he or she is the first person to enter the room once access is possible. If the class is outdoors, the GFI should be mindful of any hazards in the proximity of the movement area, especially objects that cannot be moved. Marking holes, roots, or wet areas with cones is highly recommended.

SET UP MUSIC AND EQUIPMENT

After the room/space assessment, if using music the GFI should check the pitch position, volume, treble, and bass controls of both the sound system and microphone to guarantee the most appropriate experience for all. Chapter 4 provides additional information on appropriate music volume.

Any exercise equipment that does not appear to be functioning properly or that has obvious signs of deterioration should be removed from the group fitness space or locked in a secure location that is not accessible by participants. If removing the equipment is not an option because it is too large (e.g., indoor cycling bike, Pilates reformer, or rebounder), a clearly visible sign should be placed on the equipment that alerts the participants that the equipment is out of order and could result in injury if used in its present condition. The policies of each fitness facility typically dictate the responsibilities of the staff regarding placing signage on faulty equipment. The GFI must fully understand those policies and notify the appropriate staff member, if necessary, to place the signage on the equipment prior to the start of class. Failure to remove broken, defective, or malfunctioning equipment increases a facility's **liability** exposure and places the establishment at risk for **negligence** claims and lawsuits (see Chapter 12). Allegations could arise from any of the following (Eickhoff-Shemek, Herbert, & Connaughton, 2009):

- Purchasing substandard or defective equipment
- Improper assembly
- Inadequate spacing between equipment units per the manufacturer's standards
- Failure to maintain equipment per the manufacturer's standards
- Failure to remove or replace defective equipment
- Failure to keep equipment clean
- Failure to provide appropriate instruction and adequate supervision

It is also the responsibility of the GFI to follow up with the appropriate staff member regarding the status of the malfunctioning equipment to find out if the piece will be repaired or replaced. Reporting equipment issues to staff ahead of class time can help prevent capacity issues such as having one less stability ball available for use.

Common equipment issues include:

- Chipped dumbbells or barbells
- Torn or peeling rubber strip on step platforms
- Tears in resistance tubes
- Broken pedal clips, stripped knobs, or saddle upholstery damage on indoor cycle bikes
- Deflated or damaged stability balls, or other inflatable equipment options
- Torn yoga mats
- Damaged flotation devices or aquatic dumbbells
- Torn or fraying suspension straps
- Broken springs on Pilates apparatus or rebounders

Lastly, any technical equipment required to effectively teach a class (e.g., microphone or sound system) should be checked for proper functioning prior to starting each class. Often, facilities will have backup equipment and batteries for situations when technical problems arise. The GFI should know if these backup items exist, as well as how to access and use them when necessary.

ARRANGEMENT AND POSITIONING OF PARTICIPANTS

The arrangement and positioning of participants is important for a couple of reasons, depending on the class format. First, regardless of the arrangement used, consider the spacing needs for the class and ensure the arrangement is appropriate and safe for the class. In formats that rely on instructor demonstration, participants' positions need to be arranged so that everyone can see the front of the room and the instructor. A stagger arrangement is suggested for these formats, especially when teaching larger groups (Figure 7-1). A stagger arrangement can take on a curved shape as well, such as in aquatics, indoor cycling, dance-based, and yoga classes.

Figure 7-1
Stagger arrangement

For circuit classes with stations, large Pilates reformer classes, mat/floor-based classes, or partner classes, two parallel rows work well (Figure 7-2). The distance between the two rows depends on the personal space needed for each participant. This arrangement allows the GFI to walk up and down the row to supervise the class.

Some instructors like a circle arrangement for active older adults, youth, circuit training, and boot-camp classes (Figure 7-3). It makes supervision simple and encourages a sense of community.

Some GFIs prefer everyone in a horizontal line, provided the class size allows, so they can see everyone's movement and coordination pattern in a synchronized fashion from all angles (Figure 7-4). Kettlebell, suspension training, barre, and small- to moderate-sized reformer classes are a few examples of when this arrangement may be applied.

Figure 7-2
Parallel lines

Instructor often walking around

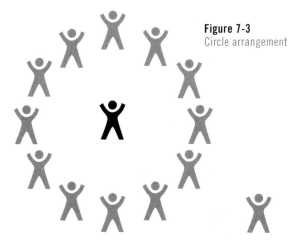

Figure 7-3
Circle arrangement

Figure 7-4
Horizontal line

ESTABLISH AND ADJUST EQUIPMENT SET-UP

For classes that require a dedicated space for each participant (e.g., step or group strength classes), instructors should orient their equipment as soon as possible to provide a visual example for how everyone should position their equipment. As a safety practice, the GFI should suggest that participants keep their equipment to the right side of their personal space so that they and neighboring participants always know where the equipment is—"right is right!" For circuit classes that rely on stations, the GFI should set out the equipment, or at least supervise the set-up to ensure equipment is positioned safety.

Proper equipment set-up is important to ensure each participant is comfortable on the equipment. Discomfort could affect the participants' **self-efficacy** and overall experience (Hu et al., 2007). Common set-up hazards include:

- Improper bike fit
- Incorrectly stacking step platforms atop risers
- Unfastened barbell clips
- Unstable suspension strap anchor
- Placing equipment on unleveled surfaces
- Incorrect foot bar, headrest, carriage, and tower set-up on reformers (and other Pilates apparatus such as cadillacs and chairs)
- Bench pop-pins not fastened or secured

The GFI should set up suspension trainers to ensure straps are adjusted properly and that the anchor point is sturdy and stable. Pilates instructors who teach classes using apparatus should be formally trained to do so, and should personally check all springs, straps, and moving parts prior to class. Adjusting bike fit for every participant in an indoor cycling class is rarely necessary, but new riders should be oriented and educated about proper bike fit. While it is highly recommended that GFIs obtain instructor training through organizations that specialize in indoor cycling, basic knowledge of bike set-up is helpful.

Indoor Cycling Bike Fit

GFIs should know the critical steps to ensure comfort, proper and safe **biomechanics,** and efficient pedaling (Figure 7-5). The standard steps for proper bike fit are:

- Adjust the resistance knob so there is a small amount of resistance on the flywheel.

- For saddle height, ask the rider to stand beside the bike facing the handlebars and lift his or her leg to bring the hip and knee to 90 degrees. Position the saddle to match the height of the thigh/lap. Adjust the saddle accordingly and fasten the pop-pins and knobs.

- Ask the rider to mount the bike by placing his or her hands on the handlebars, stepping over the frame to straddle the bike, and then placing the foot into the pedal basket or clips and lifting up onto the saddle. He or she is ready for the next step once the second foot is positioned on the pedal.

- To ensure saddle height is appropriate, the knee should be at 25 to 35 degrees of flexion when the foot is at the bottom of the pedal stroke (6 o'clock position). If the rider is rocking side to side while pedaling (because it is too high), or if the knee is over-flexed (because it is too low), make adjustments to the saddle height.

- For the seat fore and aft adjustment, ask the rider to position the pedals at the 3 and 9 o'clock positions. The saddle position is correct when the rider's knee cap is directly above and in line with the pedal spindle (the bolt that is screwed through the pedal) and he or she can hold a slight bend in the elbow with the hands on the handlebars (when seated, riders should not reach out toward the tips of the handlebars because that section of the handlebars is for standing movements only).

- Ask the rider to pedal to check the saddle height one more time.

- For the handlebar adjustment, a beginner's handlebars should be adjusted to the same height as the saddle or higher. Experienced riders may prefer a handlebar height that is lower than the saddle.

- If the bike has a handlebar fore and aft adjustment, a rider can make even finer adjustments for his or her arm reach. Simply slide the handlebars fore or aft to find a comfortable position. The elbows should not be locked.

Make sure all pop-pins, knobs, and sliders are fastened and that the rider understands how to stop the flywheel and safely dismount the bike. Again, GFIs are strongly encouraged to seek modality-specific continuing education before teaching formats such as indoor cycling to learn proper technique, safety protocols, teaching methods, and discipline-specific knowledge.

Figure 7-5
Proper bike fit

KNOW YOUR AUDIENCE

Establishing **rapport** with individuals before the official class commences by welcoming new and returning participants is a GFI's first opportunity to make a great impression. This period can be used to investigate what participants like most and least about particular classes as well as offer an opportunity for the GFI to learn about any specific limitations or considerations individual participants may have. Aside from the standard welcome greeting, GFIs can learn quite of bit of information by asking a few different participants at the beginning of each class some key questions, such as:

> » *"What brings you here today?"*
> » *"Do you have any limitations that may affect your exercise performance?"*
> » *"Have you ever participated in a Pilates class before?"*
> » *"Thank you for regularly coming to my yoga class. What motivates you to be here every Monday morning?"*
> » *"Remember when you first started class, you performed push-ups on your knees and now you can complete 15 push-ups on the toes? May I share your progress with the class?"*
> » *"Would you like to see new exercises for a particular muscle group today? If so, which areas?"*

Asking different participants a few questions each week will give GFIs information about participants' readiness to learn, prior experience, and level of motivation—all factors that affect the way adults learn and how a GFI modifies his or her teaching methods (see Chapter 10).

Acquainting participants at the beginning of class with one another is the first step toward creating a community. "Class cliques" may develop as a consequence of regular participants who form relationships, but GFIs can mitigate this by introducing new participants to regular class goers and identifying a commonality between them (Fable, 2015). One tactic that helps break the ice at the beginning of class is to ask everyone to introduce themselves to the person on his or her right and left and share what brings him or her to class. Overall, getting to know the audience and building community embodies excellent customer service (see Chapter 6).

PRE-CLASS EVALUATION

In addition to social interaction, with experience GFIs can become proficient at using on-the-spot indicators to assess class needs prior to each session. There are three on-the-spot indicators that can be used to gauge participants' potential limitations and alert the instructor to the type of exercise **progressions** and **regressions** he or she may need to provide during the class. These indicators are:

▬ *Age*—While not always the case, some participants may have age-associated limitations that require the GFI to offer appropriate regression options for the movements and exercises included in the class.

▬ *Posture*—Poor posture is associated with some muscles being tight and others being weak. This imbalance makes proper movement execution increasingly difficult and increases the importance of providing regression options to accommodate limited **range of motion.**

▬ *New participation*—New participants require increased attention and should be watched closely during class to ensure safety and success. The more frequently an individual attends classes, the less instruction he or she will need over time to understand how to modify movements and execute them with proper form.

ADAPTING TO UNEXPECTED SITUATIONS

Adapting to and overcoming unexpected situations comes with the territory of leading a class. It is not uncommon for a GFI to arrive with a well-planned class only to find factors outside of his or her control hamper the class plan. A GFI's ability to utilize his or her training and devise solutions with minimal resources is the mark of a professional.

Devise solutions with minimal resources

LACK OF EQUIPMENT

Broken or out-of-order equipment can affect a participant's ability to participate in a class. Damaged equipment in an indoor cycling, Pilates reformer, suspension training, rebounder, or other class format that requires a dedicated unit per participant may leave participants feeling like they are not being accommodated. When lack of equipment is an issue, participants may either have to share equipment and/or the GFI has to adjust the class plan to best serve all individuals.

If possible, a GFI should consider these solutions:

— Teach without equipment in order to make equipment available to another participant.

— Pair participants for partner-based exercises when equipment is limited and must be shared. For example,

if there are extreme bike shortages during an indoor cycling class, alternate drills. For instance, as one participant performs a drill on the bike, his or her partner performs body-weight exercises, after which they switch roles. Splitting the class into two groups helps to keep instruction manageable for the GFI while ensuring every participant experiences an effective workout.

— Change the set-up in a group strength class to a circuit-style format, arranging stations around the room using specific equipment.

— When teaching outdoor classes, always have a backup plan ready in case the class has to be moved indoors due to inclement weather.

— Design a "no equipment needed" class in case room or equipment availability changes without notice.

TECHNICAL DIFFICULTIES

Technical difficulties can transpire at any time during class, but in most situations the GFI will know if the stereo, lighting, or other audio/visual aids are not working before a class begins. During class, instructors may be faced with abrupt technical difficulties that may interrupt instruction. In any case, GFIs must be resourceful and ready to deal with worst-case scenarios related to technical malfunctions.

Consider these troubleshooting solutions:

▬ Bring extra batteries for the microphone.

▬ Always have a back-up music option. In the event a facility's sound system may not be updated for portable electronic devices (e.g., iPod, MP3 player, or iPhone), it may be helpful to also have music saved on a CD. Alternatively, because of advances in technology, many facilities may now only have the option to play music from a portable electronic device, so GFIs should plan on having music also available digitally. Additionally, to avoid having portable electronic devices lose battery power during class, ensure that any device being used is fully charged. If using a mobile phone to access the class playlist, switch the device into airplane mode to avoid disruptions to the music in the event of an incoming call or text message.

▬ If the lights are not dimming for classes meant for darker settings (e.g., yoga), ask participants to close their eyes at times and incorporate more imagery and mindfulness cues. Of course, safety must always be a top priority, so use common sense before asking participants to close their eyes.

▬ If the lights do not turn on, do not teach movement-based classes in a dim room. If possible, move outdoors or offer to teach a different format that limits movement (e.g., mat Pilates, core conditioning, and restorative yoga).

▬ When visual aids are not functioning properly in indoor cycling or circuit-based classes, focus on motivational cueing and emphasize technique.

▬ If the music is not working, shift the focus to mental training. Keep participants' minds engaged with shorter intervals and purpose-driven drills (e.g., "for 60 seconds, do as many push-ups as possible," or "for 90 seconds, bring your intensity to a 7 on a scale of 1 to 10"), using imagery or corrective cueing along the way.

▬ For GFIs who teach classes that are dependent on music, invest in a back-up portable speaker that connects to portable electronic devices.

 [APPLY WHAT YOU KNOW]

What's in Your Duffle Bag?

Every GFI has essential items and tricks of the trade that they stow in their gym bags for every class they teach. In many cases, GFIs bring extra gear to ensure participants are comfortable, while also being prepared for unexpected situations that might arise. Below is a list of "must haves" from seasoned GFIs:

- ✔ First-aid kit: critical for outdoor classes
- ✔ Extra batteries for microphone
- ✔ Sports drink: in case someone experiences low blood sugar or **dehydration**
- ✔ Extra bottle of water
- ✔ Hair ties, bobby pins, and safety pins
- ✔ Headbands: to hold loose headsets in place
- ✔ Extra CDs and a back-up portable electronic device in case an iPod is not working

- ✔ A/V cords to connect portable devices (e.g., HDMI, auxiliary cable, and charger)
- ✔ Windscreens
- ✔ Mints
- ✔ Snacks (e.g., protein bar and nuts)
- ✔ Towels (one small hand towel and one larger bath towel)

- ✔ Dry change of clothes, including an extra pair of socks
- ✔ Deodorant
- ✔ Wet wipes and/or hand sanitizer
- ✔ Essential oils or light aromatherapy mist

 Visit www.ACEfitness.org/GFIresources to download a checklist you can use while packing your own duffle bag.

FREQUENTLY ASKED QUESTIONS

One of the most rewarding aspects of teaching group fitness is the connections one makes over the course of a career. GFIs get to meet a wide variety of people, each with his or her own unique goal and motivation for exercising. Over time, some participants entrust and confide in their instructors, often inquiring about various health- and fitness-related topics. The following are some examples of common questions that may arise, along with suggested answers to help ensure GFIs are able to best support their participants while remaining within their professional scope of practice.

Q: *"I'm dealing with some shoulder issues today. What can I do?"*

A: "First, be sure to listen to your body. If raising your arms overhead is uncomfortable, watch and listen for my cues to explore alternative exercise options. As always, feel free to omit any movements that do not feel good to you today. If you find that you are experiencing pain, please visit your doctor as soon as possible to assess what might be causing the issue."

Q: *"I tend to have some knee troubles from time to time. What should I do in class today?"*

A: "While every individual's body is different, some general tips to enhance comfort and safety during class include reducing the depth of your squats and lunges and hinging your hips to initiate these movements. I will also be offering alternative options for each lower-body exercise in class today and encourage you to choose an option that feels best in your body."

Q: *"How can I tone my triceps and get rid of the arm flab?"*

A: "The idea that we can burn off fat from a specific part of the body by selectively exercising that area of the body only is known as spot reduction, and studies show it is not effective. Research suggests that regular exercise, which includes both cardio and resistance training, in conjunction with a sensible diet is the only way to truly eliminate excess body fat. However, there are some science-supported exercises that can be incorporated into your workout routine to effectively strengthen the triceps, such as triangle push-ups and triceps kickbacks. Would you like me to show you how to perform each exercise with proper form?"

Q: *"What should I be eating after class?"*

A: "If you do not have any specific dietary restrictions, some people find great results eating or drinking a snack that contains a blend of protein and fast-digesting carbohydrates within about 30 minutes post-workout. A handful of nuts and dried fruit, or an apple with peanut butter are some examples of snacks that can provide fast, well-balanced nutrition."

Q: *"What kind of shoes should I wear for dance-based fitness classes?"*

A: "Consider investing in shoes that have lateral support and little to no tread on the sole. You want to be able to pivot and change directions quickly without placing undue stress on the joints, but you also want support on both sides of your foot, which may protect your ankle."

Q: *"The bike seat really hurts. What can I do to make the ride more comfortable?"*

A: "First, let me check your bike fit before next class to see if I can make any adjustments to improve comfort. When sitting on the saddle, you want to make sure the biggest part of your butt is on the biggest part of the saddle. Another option is to buy a gel seat cover, which adds cushioning, or to wear cycling-specific shorts that have built-in padding. The saddle is always a little uncomfortable at first, but over time it becomes more comfortable, provided your set-up is correct."

Q: *"I've been working out every day for a month and I've only lost 5 pounds. What can I do to lose more weight?"*

A: "It's great that you have been so committed to your fitness routine, which is an important component when it comes to weight loss. However, there are other things to consider in addition to the work that you do in class, such as a healthful diet of nutrient-dense food, and incorporating more movement into your day outside of the gym. Keep in mind that research shows the rate for safe, long-term weight loss is 1 to 2 pounds per week, so you are already making great progress toward your goal."

⚙ [THINK IT THROUGH]

After class, a participant confides in you that she is trying to lose weight for an upcoming wedding. She shares that a friend of hers has lost a significant amount of weight following an extremely low-carb diet, and asks if you think limiting carbohydrates is a good way for her to lose weight too. As a GFI, how can you respond to this participant's question in a way that offers practical, evidence-based guidance while also ensuring you remain within your scope of practice? Hint: Use Appendix C to assist you in crafting your response.

SUMMARY

Successfully teaching group fitness classes requires knowing how to adapt and overcome potentially stressful situations while maintaining composure and a positive attitude. Coming prepared and ready to adjust the plan at a moment's notice is an important part of demonstrating professionalism as a GFI. When participants see a GFI who can troubleshoot, problem-solve, assist, place others before themselves, and make a potentially unpleasant situation pleasant, it sets a good example for the types of people the fitness industry develops and employs.

References

Eickhoff-Shemek, J.M, Herbert, D.L, & Connaughton, D.P. (2009). *Risk Management for Health/Fitness Professionals: Legal Issues and Strategie*s. Philadelphia: Wolters Kluwer/Lippincott Williams & Wilkins.

Fable, S. (2015). How to deal with class cliques. *IDEA Fitness Journal*, 12, 5.

Fox, L.D., Rejeski, W.J., & Gauvin, L. (2000). Effects of leadership style and group dynamics on enjoyment of physical activity. *American Journal of Health Promotion,* 14, 5, 277–283.

Hu, L. et al. (2007). Effects of self-efficacy on physical activity enjoyment in college-aged women. *International Journal of Behavioral Medicine*, 14, 2, 92–96.

Suggested Reading

American Council on Exercise (2014). *Coaching Behavior Change*. San Diego: American Council on Exercise.

Eickhoff-Shemek, J.M, Herbert, D.L, & Connaughton, D.P. (2009). *Risk Management for Health/Fitness Professionals: Legal Issues and Strategies.* Philadelphia: Wolters Kluwer/Lippincott Williams & Wilkins.

IDEA Health and Fitness Association (2011). IDEA code of ethics: Group fitness instructors. *IDEA Fitness Journal,* 9, 6.

Mad Dogg Athletics (2015). *Spinning Instructor Manual* (2nd ed.). Venice, Calif.: Mad Dogg Athletics.

PART 3

Introduction to Part 3:

ELEMENTS OF LEADING GROUP FITNESS CLASSES

At the heart of group fitness instruction lies the ability to effectively lead participants of various ability levels through a safe and enjoyable exercise experience. ACE Certified Group Fitness Instructors (GFIs) must not only be well-versed in instructional strategies for different types of learners, but they also must be keen observers and be able to adapt teaching methods as needed in order to ensure cohesive and inclusive classes.

OVER THE COURSE OF THIS PART OF THE HANDBOOK, INSTRUCTORS WILL GAIN COMPETENCY IN THE FOLLOWING THREE AREAS:

| How to lead group fitness classes | Creating inclusive classes for all participants | Strategies for enhancing instruction |

CHAPTER 8

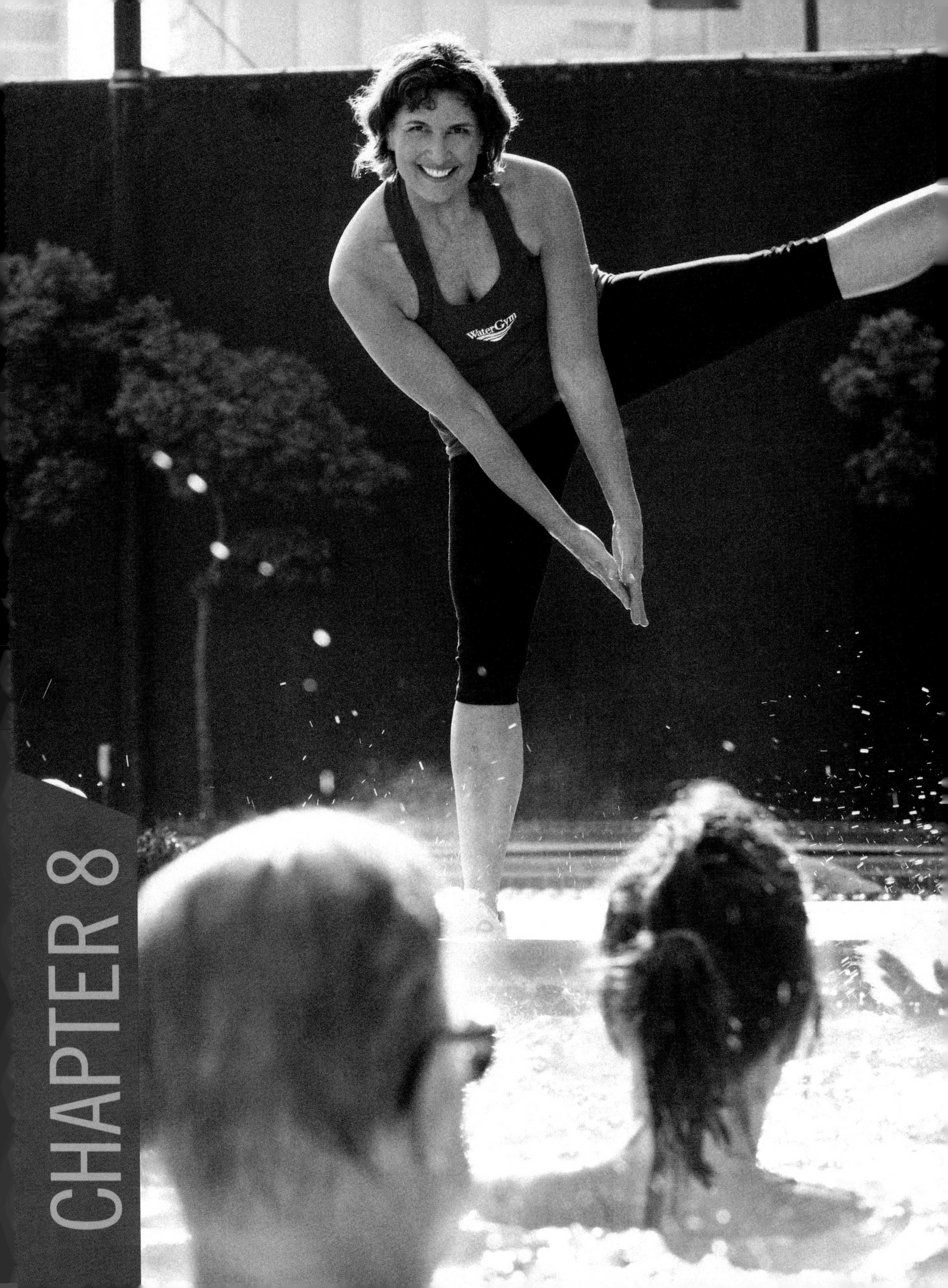

CHAPTER 8

LEADING GROUP FITNESS CLASSES

JESSICA MATTHEWS

PARTICIPANT LEARNING STYLES
VERBAL LEARNERS
VISUAL LEARNERS
KINESTHETIC LEARNERS

INSTRUCTIONAL FOCUS
COMMAND STYLE OF TEACHING
PRACTICE STYLE OF TEACHING
SELF-CHECK STYLE OF TEACHING

DOMAINS OF LEARNING
COGNITIVE DOMAIN
AFFECTIVE DOMAIN
PSYCHOMOTOR DOMAIN

STAGES OF LEARNING
COGNITIVE STAGE OF LEARNING
ASSOCIATIVE STAGE OF LEARNING
AUTONOMOUS STAGE OF LEARNING

TEACHING STRATEGIES
SLOW-TO-FAST/HALF-TIME
REPETITION-REDUCTION
PART-TO-WHOLE/ADD-IN
SIMPLE-TO-COMPLEX/LAYERING

TEACHING MULTILEVEL CLASSES

SUMMARY

LEARNING OBJECTIVES

■ Describe the three participant learning styles and apply effective cueing techniques for each.
■ List and briefly explain the three stages of learning.
■ Differentiate between styles of teaching.
■ Explain and apply effective teaching strategies.
■ Design appropriate progressions and regressions of movements.

As educators, ACE Certified Group Fitness Instructors (GFIs) effectively impart knowledge to participants using a variety of research-supported teaching strategies rooted in a firm understanding of learning styles and domains. At the heart of group fitness instruction is **cueing,** which involves delivering information to participants to empower them to experience movement success, both inside and outside of the group fitness environment. Effective cueing allows GFIs to lead safe, effective, motivational, and cohesive class experiences for participants of all ability levels.

If your study program includes the ACE Learning Center, visit www.ACEfitness.org/MyACE and log in to your My ACE Account to learn more about the use of mirroring and matching techniques and three-dimensional cueing in group fitness classes.

PARTICIPANT LEARNING STYLES

The manner in which cues are delivered in a group fitness class is based on the three ways people learn. While most participants can use all three techniques to varying degrees and assimilate a range of different types of cues, most learners tend to favor one particular instructional method as their preferred way to obtain information.

VERBAL LEARNERS

A verbal learner needs to *hear* specific cues. To create the most successful experience possible for this type of learner, GFIs should ensure that verbal cues are specific and succinct. Non-specific cues, such as "go this way," or "try this now," do not clearly convey what the participant is being asked to do. Instead, descriptive, yet concise cues should be used to specify immediate movement, such as "four knees on the right." Verbal cues should also be anticipatory, meaning they must be heard and understood immediately before movement becomes imminent. When cueing to music, GFIs should provide cues at least four counts before movement is initiated. When not using music, a few moments should be given to allow participants to process instructions before the movement begins. In most group fitness classes, counting down (e.g., "4-3-2") as opposed to counting up will help participants know how many movements remain before a change ensues.

 [APPLY WHAT YOU KNOW]

Voice Care Tips

A GFI must take care to protect his or her voice to ensure that verbal cues can be delivered safely, properly, and consistently from class to class. Employing the following tips can help minimize the potential for vocal injuries and issues (IDEA, 2001):

- Project from the diaphragm regardless of whether or not a microphone is being used.
- Speak at a normal volume when using a microphone.
- Avoid frequent coughing, which can stress the voice box (larynx).
- Avoid cueing at biomechanically inopportune times (e.g., in positions that constrict the vocal tract, such as when performing push-ups). It is preferable to give cues before the exercise is executed or to walk around during such verbal cueing.
- Keep music at a decibel level that does not require shouting over the music (see Chapter 4).
- Take small, frequent sips of water to keep the larynx lubricated.

VISUAL LEARNERS

A visual learner needs to *see* specific cues. To create the most successful experience for this type of learner, GFIs should focus on incorporating appropriate body language and gestures that allow participants to understand the desired movement. For example, when targeting a specific muscle group, such as the triceps, a GFI may choose to palpate the area (in this case, the back of the upper arm) in addition to providing appropriate technique-related cues to convey to participants what part of the body is being worked during the exercise.

When instructing participants to move, GFIs should point to the direction that matches the cued words. For example, if giving the verbal cue "lunge right," the instructor should also outstretch his or her arm and point to the right, giving participants a visual cue regarding in what direction to move. Additionally, to indicate the number of repetitions remaining of an exercise, a GFI should hold up a specific number using his or her fingers in addition to counting down verbally.

Without words, GFIs can also convey crucial instructions to participants by incorporating Aerobic Q-signs (Webb, 1989), as shown in Figure 8-1.

WATCH ME

HOLD/STAY

FROM THE TOP

Figure 8-1
Aerobic Q-signs

Source: Webb, T. (1989). Aerobic Q-signs. *IDEA Today,* 10, 30–31.

FORWARD/BACKWARD

DIRECTION 2-4-8

SINGLE/DOUBLE

Visual cueing not only assists visual learners and participants whose primary language may be different from that of the GFI, but it also helps create a successful experience for persons who are hearing impaired. Oliva (1988) promotes visual cues based on the principles of Visual-Gestural Communication and American Sign Language (Figure 8-2). Oliva maintains that visual cues must be "visually logical" and clearly visible to participants. For example, GFIs can indicate lower-body moves such as marching on the right by patting the thigh of the lead leg.

Figure 8-2
Visual cues for exercise classes

Source: Oliva, G.A. (1988). *Visual Cues for Exercise Classes.* Washington, D.C.: Gallaudet University.

LEAD LEG

STAY IN PLACE

SHIFT TO FACE THIS DIRECTION

MARCH IN PLACE

HOLD THIS POSITION
AND CHANGE NOTHING

OR, WHICH CAN BE USED TO SHOW EITHER
A PROGRESSION OR A REGRESSION

BREATHE EXCLUSIVELY
THROUGH THE NOSE

BREATHE THROUGH THE
MOUTH ON EXHALATION

"ONE THUMB UP" OFFERS POSITIVE
REINFORCEMENT AND PRAISE

Considerations for Delivering Visual Cues

In order to effectively provide visual cues to participants, a GFI must consider the orientation he or she will use when delivering information and evaluate the pros and cons associated with it. If teaching in a room with a mirror, a GFI may choose to face the mirror when cueing, observing participants' movements in the reflection. An advantage of facing the mirror is that this positioning gives the participants an easy understanding of movement orientations and directions, allowing participants to follow the GFI exactly as he or she moves. A disadvantage to this approach is that the personal connection with each participant diminishes because instructors can only make indirect eye contact through the reflection in the mirror.

An advantage to standing facing participants with one's back to the mirror or front wall is that this position allows the GFI to build **rapport** with participants through direct eye contact. It also allows participants to see the front of the instructor's body more clearly with no reflection. A disadvantage of facing the class, however, is that participants often have difficulty understanding how to follow an instructor cueing "reach the right arm," if the GFI is reaching with his or her right arm (which would be to the participants' left).

One solution to reducing this confusion is to use a technique known as **mirroring**. An example of mirroring is when the GFI, positioned facing toward participants, moves his or her left arm while calling out to the participants to move their right arm. This enables the participants to see a mirror image of the move they are being cued to perform. However, mirroring is a skill that can be difficult to learn. Therefore, the GFI must thoroughly practice this technique before using it in a class.

> Use a technique known as mirroring

KINESTHETIC LEARNERS

A kinesthetic learner needs to *feel* specific cues. To create the most successful experience for this type of learner, GFIs should get in the habit of utilizing cues that offer participants an element of sensation. This can be done through utilizing words such as "sense," "imagine," "pretend," and "feel," in which the GFI strives to convey where and how a sensation should be felt and/or when a mental component of visualization may be appropriate. For example, when a GFI is cueing the triangle pose during a yoga class, he or she might say to participants "imagine your body is pinned between two sheets of glass" to help create an appropriate mental image of proper body positioning in the posture.

Kinesthetic learners may also find value in being provided with a subtle touch by the GFI that helps them better experience the movement or exercise. However, it is imperative that GFIs always ask for and receive permission from participants before offering any type of physical touch or assist. Instead of physically touching a participant to assist with form and alignment, a GFI may opt to instead cue participants to the solution, placing an open hand near the participant and instructing the participant to move his or her body toward it (Biscontini, 2011). More details regarding how to provide participants with valuable **feedback** using this technique can be found in Chapter 10.

> Utilize cues that offer participants an element of sensation

 **[APPLY WHAT YOU KNOW]**

Asking for Permission to Provide Cues and Feedback Through Hands-on Assists

One way in which a GFI can broach the subject of providing cues and feedback through hands-on assists is to ask for permission from the group as a whole at the beginning of a group fitness class. For example, during a yoga class the subject of physical touch can be addressed at the start of the practice when participants have privacy in an eyes-closed posture, such as extended child's pose. The GFI may offer a blanket statement to the group, such as "Today I will be offering gentle hands-on assists to help further explore alignment and sensation with each pose. If you prefer that I offer feedback in a way that does not involve physical touch, simply flip both palms to the sky to let me know, and I will certainly honor your personal space throughout the class."

It is also important when teaching a discipline such as yoga in a fitness center that the GFI be familiar with the facility's policy regarding hands-on assists, as many gyms do not allow instructors to provide physical touch whatsoever for fear of legal action (McCarthy, 2012).

 [EXPAND YOUR KNOWLEDGE]

Types of Effective Cues

In group fitness classes, a great deal of information needs to be communicated in a relatively short amount of time. Therefore, GFIs must condense cues and deliver multiple pieces of information simultaneously, all while addressing the three learning styles. The best cuers are both efficient (able to get the job done in a very short amount of time) and efficacious (able to get the job done well). While each of these is possible alone, the goal is for a GFI to accomplish both simultaneously. Biscontini (2011) recommends the following types of **three-dimensional cueing** that can be offered during a group fitness class:

— *Breathing:* Cues that indicate the best breathing technique to match the discipline, exercise, or movement series, and can indicate both *when* (e.g., on which phase of a movement to inhale or exhale) and *how* to breathe (e.g., in through the nose and out through the mouth)

— *Rhythm:* Cues that indicate the pace at which the movements or exercise will occur

— *Anatomical:* Cues that reference the body to enhance **kinesthetic awareness** and inform participants which muscles are active during an exercise or movement pattern

— *Numerical:* Cues that tell participants how many repetitions of an exercise or movement series will be performed in total or how many remain, and allow participants to gauge their intensity accordingly. This may include rhythm cueing.

— *Directional:* Cues that tell participants where a movement will be taking place in relation to the classroom space and their own bodies

— *Safety:* Cues that emphasize proper execution of the movement or exercise to minimize the risk of injury

— *Motivational:* Cues that are directed toward the group or individual exercisers to encourage positive reinforcement

— *Alignment:* Cues that include exercise set-up, general posture, and awareness of body dynamics before and during a movement

— *Spatial:* Cues that reference areas of the body, equipment set-up around the body, and/or the body's orientation to the equipment and/or the group fitness space

— *Humorous:* Cues that are designed to create an enjoyable, entertaining, yet educational experience in which participants feel comfortable

INSTRUCTIONAL FOCUS

While Chapter 5 helps GFIs decide *what* to teach (i.e., appropriate exercises and general sequencing of movements), this is only half of the challenge. GFIs must also explore *how* to teach each movement, which is one of the most exciting aspects of group fitness instruction. Mosston (2001) discusses several different teaching styles that have direct application to the group fitness environment.

COMMAND STYLE OF TEACHING

An instructor using the **command style of teaching** makes all decisions about posture, rhythm, and duration, seeking imitation by all participants. The effect created is one of uniformity, but without proper planning this could result in a less than inclusive class experience for participants of varying ability levels.

The command style has traditionally been the most commonly used style of teaching in group fitness classes, as some GFIs find this style particularly well-suited to warming up, cooling down (final phase), and introducing new movements or exercises where the point is for everyone to follow uniformly. Effective leaders using the command style are able to follow the gist of a standardized script (such as those required in **pre-choreographed classes**) while still offering **progressions** and **regressions** to create a successful experience for all.

PRACTICE STYLE OF TEACHING

The **practice style of teaching** provides opportunities for individualization and one-on-one instructor feedback for participants while still effectively leading a group experience. While all participants are working on the same task, such as performing as many push-ups as possible during a one-minute round within a **high-intensity interval training (HIIT)** class, the GFI encourages everyone to choose his or her own intensity level to guarantee individual success. The effect created is one of nurturing and support by providing participants the freedom to discover what works best for them via practice. An advantage of this style of instruction is that it allows instructors to walk around and interact because they do not need to remain stationary in front of the room, as is often done when using the command style approach.

It is important for GFIs to move around the room in order to effectively instruct all participants. To observe participants from different angles and to offer physical assists and/or specific feedback on form, a GFI should consider demonstrating a movement for several repetitions, then observe and coach form, interacting in a more meaningful way with participants. Instructors should keep in mind that when teaching classes, the focus is on providing the best experience possible for participants, as opposed to personally getting in a good workout.

SELF-CHECK STYLE OF TEACHING

The **self-check style of teaching** relies on participants to provide their own feedback. Participants perform a given task and then view or record the results, comparing their performance against given criteria or past performances. Instructors who emphasize **target heart rate** or **recovery heart rate** to their participants, or who opt to utilize other intensity-gauging measures such as **ratings of perceived exertion (RPE)** or the **talk test,** may choose to incorporate this style into their classes. For equipment-based classes that utilize options such as rowers, treadmills, or indoor cycling bikes with electronic consoles, the information displayed can be invaluable for instructors who use the self-check style.

DOMAINS OF LEARNING

During every class, a GFI must be able to quickly ascertain the group's abilities, strengths, and weaknesses. By the end of the warm-up, the instructor must decide which types of cues and what exercise intensity level will prove most appropriate and effective for the participants present. By understanding the learning process and being familiar with strategies that facilitate the teaching of **motor skills,** the GFI will be better able to educate participants.

Magill (2000) defines learning as an "internal change in the individual that is inferred from a relatively permanent improvement in performance of the individual as a result of practice." It is important that GFIs understand the difference between performing and teaching. When performing, a GFI leads participants through safe movement by having them mimic the movements of the instructor in a follow-the-leader type approach. In true teaching, however, the GFI imparts knowledge on the participants, and they in turn demonstrate the aforementioned "internal change" toward "permanent improvement" as they begin to learn and practice new behaviors and movement patterns. Over time, these new skills become ones that participants can reproduce independently in life. GFIs who truly teach are able to get their participants to learn new things about their bodies and demonstrate movement patterns with less variability

over time, thus indicating that the learning experience is taking place. Learning takes place in three levels of human behavior—cognitive, affective, and psychomotor—all of which have direct application to the field of group fitness instruction.

COGNITIVE DOMAIN

The **cognitive domain** describes the brain's ability to gather and retain information and knowledge. This includes skills such as counting out movements as well as remembering patterns of **choreography.** Training the cognitive domain within a fitness program in which participants are challenged to understand and apply knowledge positively affects **motivation** and exercise compliance among participants. Therefore, GFIs should incorporate some elements of education into their classes (Casey, Benson, & MacDonald, 2004).

AFFECTIVE DOMAIN

The **affective domain** describes emotional behaviors, beliefs, and attitudes. Overall feelings regarding health and motivational attitudes in general will shape a person's feelings about exercise. GFIs hold the potential to help participants develop positive attitudes about physical activity by enhancing how they receive, respond to, and ultimately value the physical movements produced both in class and in everyday life (Wilson, 2001). GFIs can serve as role models who positively influence the affective domain of their participants. Refer to Chapter 6 for more on creating a compelling movement experience.

PSYCHOMOTOR DOMAIN

Finally, the **psychomotor domain** refers to those activities requiring movement. Learning new motor skills forms the basic foundation of most group fitness classes. While most instructors pay careful attention to the psychomotor domain as they design classes, by considering elements such as physical abilities, fundamental movements, and skilled movements, a well-rounded GFI emphasizes all three domains of learning to provide a more comprehensive approach to instruction.

 [APPLY WHAT YOU KNOW]

Heightening Participants' Kinesthetic Awareness

GFIs teach participants in an attempt to bring about an independent change in behavior or thought in each individual. That said, the goal and priority of a GFI as an educator should be to teach in such a way as to empower participants to independently execute moves with proper form. Keeping this in mind will help GFIs become the best communicators they can be in order to encourage individuals to understand how to take responsibility for their own form and body mechanics, and transfer those skills to activities outside of class. To help participants gain kinesthetic awareness and improve how they perform in the group fitness environment, as well as in everyday life when performing **activities of daily living (ADL),** GFIs can incorporate alignment and movement cues into each segment of a group fitness class.

For example, if a student in class demonstrates good alignment when performing a hip hinge, the participant is not only moving safely, but he or she will also move more effectively when transitioning into in-class exercises such as squats or lunges. However, if this participant hinges with incorrect form at home, such as with a rounded spine when bending down to pick up his or her child, then the participant is not reaping the benefits of the quality of movement discussed and demonstrated in class since he or she has not changed behavior and body mechanics in everyday life. An effective teaching strategy is to educate participants about the purpose of movements not just for class, but for enjoyment and success in ADL.

To assist students in successful movement both inside and outside of the class, the GFI can impart knowledge and skills that make them more aware of how they position their bodies in space, which is known as **spatial awareness.** When instructing new movements, the GFI may opt to reference body parts in relation to other body parts or surroundings in the room. For example, when standing, the GFI may begin by establishing stability in the body using a "ground up" approach, bringing heightened attention to the position of the feet, and then move up the body using the metaphor of building a house with a firm foundation. In other positions, instructors may commence with other body parts. For example, in the quadruped position, an instructor may begin cueing by saying "come down to hands and knees to find a position where the torso is parallel to the floor with wrists below shoulders and knees below hips."

STAGES OF LEARNING

Understanding the three stages of learning helps GFIs gain an appreciation for their participants in a deeper way. The traditional Fitts and Posner model (1967) explains the three stages of learning for motor skills: cognitive, associative, and autonomous. GFIs must take into consideration the learning stages of participants in order to create the most successful experience possible. The more successful participants feel, the more motivated they become. Refer to Chapter 6 for detailed information on improving both motivation and **adherence.**

COGNITIVE STAGE OF LEARNING

Within the **cognitive stage of learning,** movements are new to the participant, who acts as a novice. Errors and imperfect form may be the norm. An example of this occurs the first time a group does grapevines together at a particular music speed. Many participants struggle with the skill itself, the direction, and the coordination of timing the movement with the music.

ASSOCIATIVE STAGE OF LEARNING

The next stage, the **associative stage of learning,** includes improvements in the basic fundamentals of the skills. In this stage, the majority of participants are able to grapevine back and forth with the music and can concentrate on occasional cues from the instructor to improve performance.

AUTONOMOUS STAGE OF LEARNING

During the **autonomous stage of learning,** the skill becomes automatic or habitual. Learners can perform without following an instructor and can detect their own errors. In a group fitness setting, participants react automatically with music, direction, and movement upon hearing the instructor's cue: "Four grapevines left."

 [THINK IT THROUGH]

When performing push-ups, what movement errors might be observed in a participant who is in the cognitive stage of learning?

Mindful Instruction

Instructors must be aware of all participants in a group fitness class at all times. Though there are sometimes exceptions, often the most experienced, intense, and comfortable participants (those in the autonomous stage of learning) tend to congregate toward the front of the room. Such participants are usually able to do all skills that the GFI cues, often opting for ways in which to increase the intensity of exercises throughout the class experience.

Participants with average skill levels (i.e., those in the associative stage of learning) often congregate toward the center of the room and are able to do most skills the GFI cues, often seeking ways in which to refine their form to enhance movement execution.

Newer and more timid students (i.e., those in the cognitive stage of learning) often will congregate toward the rear of the room. These participants will often benefit from exploring ways in which to make exercises less intense while learning the fundamental skills of the class.

Ultimately, when leading group fitness classes, instructors must teach so that all class participants experience success. To do this, GFIs should consider leading classes with the following saying in mind: *Have an ear for the front row, an eye for the middle row, and a heart for the back row.*

> # Have an ear for the front row, an eye for the middle row, and a heart for the back row

[EXPAND YOUR KNOWLEDGE]

The Importance of Feedback

GFIs who give individual feedback show that they care for the true progress of their participants. Wlodkowski (2008) defines feedback as information that learners receive about the quality of their performance on a given task. Feedback, while important across all stages of learning, is of the utmost importance during the associative stage of learning, in which participants are working toward skill mastery and are able to process efficient and effective cues offered to help improve performance.

— First, instructors should point out something positive the individual is doing.

— Second, they should mention the needed correction, known as the **performance standard** of the movement or exercise.

— Third, instructors should point out an additional positive feedback point, usually offering positive reinforcement on the immediate correction.

For example, a GFI notices that a participant's shoulders are elevated when performing standing biceps curls. A sample script could be, "Great job keeping your spine extended and chest lifted (positive point). To better challenge the muscles we're working, keep the shoulders down away from the ears (performance standard). With that small change, notice how much less tension you now feel in the shoulders (positive reinforcement)." Refer to Chapter 10 for additional strategies on providing feedback.

TEACHING STRATEGIES

One of the most important aspects of group fitness instruction is taking the appropriate steps to ensure the movements and exercises included in the class are delivered in a safe and effective manner. An instructor must not only acknowledge the limitations of participants within the various stages of learning, but he or she must also understand how to appropriately break down and build up movement patterns to ensure all participants experience success.

> Ensure all participants experience success

SLOW-TO-FAST/HALF-TIME

When using the **slow-to-fast teaching strategy,** instructors introduce movement patterns so that participants are first performing them slower than the desired speed. This often includes a rhythmic variation, as instructors use the **half-time** of the music. When introducing a grapevine to exercisers for the first time, a GFI may move more slowly so that a grapevine that typically uses four counts of music instead uses eight counts. Since this strategy may reduce exercise intensity, GFIs should minimize using this approach for extended periods of time during the peak of the conditioning segment of class.

REPETITION-REDUCTION

The **repetition-reduction teaching strategy** involves reducing the number of repetitions that make up a movement sequence. An instructor may have participants execute four alternating grapevines followed by eight alternating hamstring curls. This could then be reduced to two alternating grapevines and four alternating hamstring curls, and eventually again be reduced to one grapevine and two alternating hamstring curls.

PART-TO-WHOLE/ADD-IN

A GFI using the **part-to-whole teaching strategy,** which is also called the **add-in strategy,** breaks down skills and teaches movement in isolation before integration. Commencing with movements in their simplest form, the instructor teaches sections of a move, followed by the performance of an isolated movement. For example, an instructor teaching a squat and biceps curl combination may begin with either the arm or leg movements until he or she observes mastery by the majority of participants. Once participants have mastered each component, the instructor then demonstrates how to combine the movements to become more functional, teaching either the **concentric** or **eccentric** phase of elbow flexion with the downward or upward phase of the squat, as desired.

SIMPLE-TO-COMPLEX/LAYERING

When using the **simple-to-complex teaching strategy,** which is an advanced teaching strategy that is sometimes called **layering,** instead of separating movement patterns into sections, the instructor will reduce all complexity options to the lowest common denominator and engage the class in movement. Next, the GFI adds layers of complexity onto these movements. For example, consider the performance of a grapevine and two alternating step-touches for a total of eight counts. In this method, the instructor engages all participants in this pattern from the start. While engaging everyone in repetition for proficiency, the instructor offers additional options, which could include leaping to the side twice instead of the grapevine and a full 360-degree pivot with hamstring curls in place of the step-touches. Generally, the available variables for layering additional complexity involve changes in direction, rhythm, and lever length.

 [APPLY WHAT YOU KNOW]

Layering Choreography

The freestyle method of delivering choreography, discussed in Chapter 2, most often involves linear progression, in which an instructor lines up movements lacking combinations. Newer instructors often find the linear-progression method easier because they only have to change one aspect of movement at a time, and never need to create repeating sequences or patterns. The method is simple: one skill at a time.

For example:

━━━ *Base movement:* Four alternating knee lifts in place (eight counts of music)

━━━ *Add arms:* Four bilateral elbow flexions (eight counts of music)

━━━ *Add direction:* Travel forward (eight counts of music); travel backward (eight counts of music)

Ready to move on? Change the skills:

━━━ *Change the legs:* Eight alternating hamstring curls with same arm movements (16 counts of music)

━━━ *Change the arms:* Clapping hands while moving front and back (16 counts of music)

Instructors may also choose to gradually incorporate other changes following the DRILLS acronym (see page 140), such as manipulating the rhythm of how the movements are executed. Half-time may prove an ideal teaching strategy to demonstrate a more complex movement pattern slowly at first, before adding the challenge of **double-time. Syncopation** occurs in a grapevine when, instead of the normal four-count grapevine, instructors hold the first lead leg for two counts ("1, 2") and then rush the rest of the movement with counts ("and 3, 4"), in which case the traveling leg crosses behind the lead leg quickly (on count "and") and the movement returns to normal (on counts "3, 4").

Copeland (1991) suggests considering, at the very least, a combination of freestyle and repeating choreography. "There are many advantages to using repeating patterns in your choreography. The human mind instinctively arranges events into patterns, which allow the mind to relax and easily anticipate what will happen next. This repetition allows participants to commit to the movement more fully and to maintain a steady-state workout."

Ultimately, all methods and teaching strategies are available to instructors when developing choreography, and GFIs should consider instructing movement patterns using a combination of teaching strategies. Observant instructors continuously monitor their participants to see which techniques work best for which groups, and teach using the methods that guarantee the highest rate of success for all.

TEACHING MULTILEVEL CLASSES

While it would be easier to instruct participants who all possess the same fitness aptitude, almost every group fitness class brings an assortment of students at different ability levels. Effective GFIs, therefore, must be able to create progressions and regressions so that all participants can explore any movement within the class and experience success. When increasing the difficulty, complexity, or intensity of a movement (progression) or decreasing the difficulty, complexity, or intensity of a movement (regression), it is the skill that is labeled as opposed to the individual, creating a more supportive and accepting environment for participants to learn and thrive.

Among the ways to create progressions and regressions of movements are the following considerations, which form the acronym DRILLS:

Direction

Rhythm, range of motion, resistance, repetitions

Intensity, impact

Lever **L**ength

Stability

Learning how to manipulate each of these variables will help all participants master the movements that are most appropriate for them. For example, if a participant needs a regression when performing a single-leg squat with hands on hips, the GFI can cue to place both feet on the ground hip-width apart for greater stability through a broader base of support, thereby reducing the intensity of the movement. For a participant in the same class needing a progression, the GFI could provide the option for participants to raise the arms overhead, increasing the lever length, thereby providing more intensity and challenge to the movement.

Improper execution can increase the risk for injury in a group fitness class. Large participant-to-instructor ratios make individual attention difficult and participants can often repeat movements incorrectly numerous times without correction, leading to injury. The best defense against movement error is to offer progressions and regressions, and to explain methods for self-evaluation. Refer to Chapter 12 for the legal and professional responsibilities of a GFI to provide adequate and proper instruction.

SUMMARY

A successful GFI has a firm understanding of the various ways in which participants learn while also being well-versed in how to adapt instructional methods accordingly to ensure that the needs of participants are safely and effectively met. The knowledge and skills that GFIs impart on participants by delivering high-quality educational experiences enables individuals to experience movement success both inside and outside of the group fitness environment.

References

Biscontini, L. (2011). *Cream Rises: Excellence in Private and Group Fitness Education.* New York: FG2000.

Casey, A., Benson, H., & MacDonald, A. (2004). *Mind Your Heart: A Mind/Body Approach to Stress Management Exercise and Nutrition for Heart Health.* New York: Free Press.

Copeland, C. (1991). Smooth moves. *IDEA Today,* 6, 34–38.

Fitts, P.M. & Posner, M.I. (1967). *Human Performance.* Belmont, Calif: Brooks/Cole.

IDEA Health & Fitness Association (2001). *Injury Prevention for Fitness Instructors.* San Diego: IDEA Health & Fitness Association.

Magill, R.A. (2000). *Motor Learning* (6th ed.). New York: McGraw-Hill.

McCarthy, S. (2012). *Transformation Teaching Through Yoga Adjustments: Adjustments and Strategies to Build a Thriving and Sustainable Yoga Career.* San Diego: Yoga Namastacy.

Mosston, M. (2001). *Teaching Physical Education* (5th ed.). San Francisco: Benjamin Cummings.

Oliva, G.A. (1988). *Visual Cues for Exercise Classes.* Washington, D.C.: Gallaudet University.

Webb, T. (1989). Aerobic Q-signs. *IDEA Today,* 10, 30–31.

Wilson, L.O. (2015). *Three Domains of Learning: Cognitive, Affective and Psychomotor.* http://thesecondprinciple.com/instructional-design/threedomainsoflearning/.

Wlodkowski, R.J. (2008). *Enhancing Adult Motivation to Learn* (3rd ed.). San Francisco: Jossey-Bass.

Suggested Reading

Ayers, S.F. & Sariscsany, M. (Eds.) (2011). *Physical Education for Lifelong Fitness* (3rd ed.). Champaign, Ill.: Human Kinetics.

Biscontini, L. (2011). Cueing in three dimensions. *IDEA Pilates Today,* 2, 1.

Kennedy-Armbruster, C. & Yoke, M.M. (2014). *Methods of Group Exercise Instruction* (3rd ed.). Champaign, Ill.: Human Kinetics.

Long, J. et al. (1998). Voice problems and risk factors among aerobic instructors. *Journal of Voice,* 12, 2, 197–207.

Popowych, K. (2005). Cuing beyond counting. *IDEA Fitness Journal,* 2, 4.

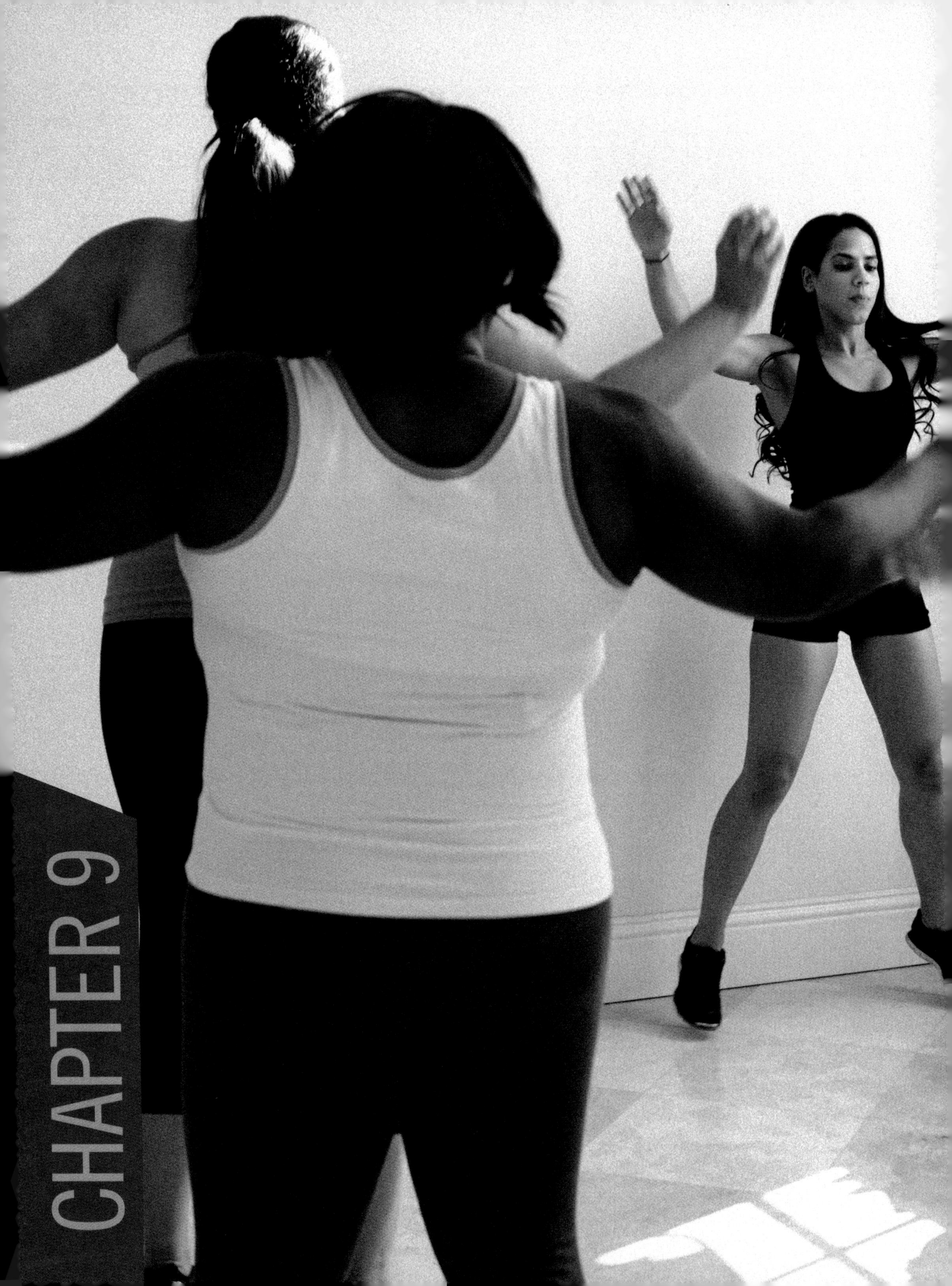

CHAPTER 9

CHAPTER 9

FOSTERING INCLUSIVE EXPERIENCES

SHANNAN LYNCH

PRE-PARTICIPATION SCREENING

CARDIAC CONDITIONS

CORONARY HEART DISEASE

HYPERTENSION

EXERCISE CONSIDERATIONS FOR PARTICIPANTS WITH CARDIAC CONDITIONS

PULMONARY CONDITIONS

ASTHMA

EXERCISE CONSIDERATIONS FOR PARTICIPANTS WITH ASTHMA

ARTHRITIS

OSTEOARTHRITIS

EXERCISE CONSIDERATIONS FOR PARTICIPANTS WITH OSTEOARTHRITIS

DIABETES MELLITUS

TYPE 1 DIABETES

TYPE 2 DIABETES

EXERCISE CONSIDERATIONS FOR PARTICIPANTS WITH DIABETES

LOW-BACK PAIN

EXERCISE CONSIDERATIONS FOR PARTICIPANTS WITH LOW-BACK PAIN

SPECIAL POPULATIONS

OLDER ADULTS

YOUTH

PRENATAL AND POSTPARTUM PARTICIPANTS

EFFECTS OF COMMON MEDICATIONS ON HEART-RATE RESPONSE

SUMMARY

LEARNING OBJECTIVES

▪ Explain how common chronic conditions, such as coronary heart disease, asthma, arthritis, and diabetes, may influence participation in group fitness classes.

▪ Identify and apply appropriate movement regressions and other exercise considerations to ensure a safe and effective class experience for all participants.

▪ Demonstrate appropriate exercises to enhance low-back health.

▪ Describe how common medications affect heart-rate response.

ACE Certified Group Fitness Instructors (GFIs) regularly encounter participants with specific needs and health considerations when leading various group fitness class formats. While screening for health concerns is not typically the responsibility of a GFI, it is important to understand how these chronic conditions may influence a participant's ability to perform physical activity.

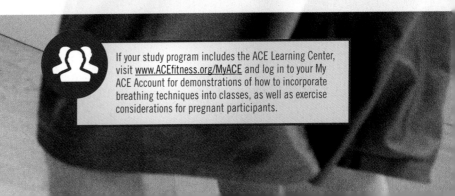

If your study program includes the ACE Learning Center, visit www.ACEfitness.org/MyACE and log in to your My ACE Account for demonstrations of how to incorporate breathing techniques into classes, as well as exercise considerations for pregnant participants.

PRE-PARTICIPATION SCREENING

Pre-participation screening forms are health-history documents that are typically collected at the initiation of enrollment to a fitness facility or a defined group fitness program, along with **informed consent** and a release of **liability** waiver. It is the responsibility of the facility/business operator to determine if medical evaluation by a physician is warranted prior to an individual participating in physical activity based on the health-related information provided on his or her pre-participation forms.

While most GFIs do not have access to participant health-history information, instructors should assume that some participants may have known or unknown medical conditions that could impact their exercise experience. In 2012, about 50% of all adults suffered from one or more chronic health conditions (Ward, Schiller, & Goodman, 2014).

As a general rule for GFIs who are directly responsible for collecting pre-participation forms, it is prudent, from both a professional and legal perspective, to obtain a medical clearance for all participants with an identified chronic disease, disability, or injury, even if clearance is not explicitly recommended in established physical-activity guidelines.

Looking for on-the-spot indicators before the start of class, such as age, posture, and first-time participation, can provide insight into what modifications or teaching methods may be needed during class (see Chapters 7 and 8). It is important to note that anticipating potential modifications and safety considerations based on age and body weight is not an example of bias, because these are known risk factors for chronic diseases [American College of Sports Medicine (ACSM), 2014a; ACSM, 2014b]. GFIs should be sensitive toward participants and not make obvious judgments, but rather use the power of observation during class, as discussed in Chapter 10, to provide appropriate **progressions, regressions,** and additional coaching cues to ensure the safety and effectiveness of the exercise experience. Health and fitness professionals, including GFIs, are important members of the allied health continuum, as physically fit individuals are 25 to 50% less likely to develop high-risk diseases such as heart disease and **type 2 diabetes** (Kraemer et al., 2002; Hartung & Rangel, 1981).

 [APPLY WHAT YOU KNOW]

Making Participant Privacy a Priority

It is not uncommon for class participants to share confidential information, such as medical conditions or health concerns, with a GFI through conversation before or after class. In addition, some GFIs may directly collect health-history information prior to the start of specific programs, such as a six-week boot-camp program. GFIs should maintain a level of security for each participant's personal information. Failure to do so could prove detrimental for the participant and the participant–instructor relationship, and is in violation of the ACE Code of Ethics (see Appendix A) as well as state and federal privacy laws.

To help prevent violations of participant privacy, ACE GFIs should become familiar with, and adhere to, the **Health Insurance Portability and Accountability Act (HIPAA),** which addresses the use and disclosure of individuals' protected health information. By following HIPAA regulations, GFIs can maintain the confidentiality of each participant's protected health information according to the same rules that govern most healthcare professions. More details about participant privacy and keeping participants' protected health information secure can be found in Chapter 12.

CARDIAC CONDITIONS

Cardiovascular disease (CVD) refers to any disease that affects the cardiovascular system, principally cardiac disease, vascular diseases of the brain and kidney, and **peripheral arterial disease.** Risk factors for CVD include **hypertension** and blood **lipid** disorders. Specific mechanisms, treatments, considerations, and exercise programming for each condition are beyond the **scope of practice**

> It is important for the GFI to learn general information about CVD

of a GFI. It is important, however, for the GFI to learn general information about CVD to ensure safety and inclusiveness for all participants.

CORONARY HEART DISEASE

A common subset of CVD is **coronary heart disease (CHD).** CHD results from the development of **atherosclerosis** in the coronary arteries, which involves the hardening and accumulation of lipid-rich plaques within the walls of the arteries that supply the **myocardium** (the muscle of the heart). Over time, the coronary arterial walls narrow, blocking the flow of blood and oxygen (**ischemia**), and, if left untreated, can lead to a **myocardial infarction (MI), stroke,** or **peripheral heart disease.** CHD is the most common cause of sudden death, and the most common cause of death in people over 65 years old. Men are 10 times more likely to develop CHD than women [Centers for Disease Control and Prevention (CDC), 2013].

HYPERTENSION

Hypertension, or high **blood pressure (BP),** is defined as a **systolic blood pressure (SBP)** >140 mmHg and/or a **diastolic blood pressure (DBP)** of >90 mmHg (Fields et al., 2004; Chobanian et al., 2003). According to these criteria, approximately 1 billion individuals worldwide have hypertension [Go et al., 2013; World Health Organization (WHO), 2010)], and the incidence increases with age, with approximately 70% of Americans over the age of 75 having hypertension (Fleg et al., 2013).

The nervous system acts like telephone lines between the brain and the **baroreceptors,** constantly forwarding signals to adjust and maintain a BP that is commensurate with the current demands on the body. When BP is too low, there is not enough force to push blood through the vessels quickly enough to reach the organs and tissues in need of oxygen and **nutrients.** When BP is chronically too high, that constant force pushing against the arterial walls can be damaging, not only to the arteries but to other organs as well. This constant stress on the arterial walls promotes chronic inflammatory responses that are involved in the plaque accumulation and narrowing of arteries (Woolard & Geissmann, 2010). More pressure is required to shunt blood through narrow arteries, thereby creating a vicious cycle of abuse on numerous systems in the body, including the source of the force—the heart.

Hypertension is classified based on severity of the condition. Table 9-1 lists BP classifications for adults 18 and older.

EXERCISE CONSIDERATIONS FOR PARTICIPANTS WITH CARDIAC CONDITIONS

GFIs should keep the following general exercise guidelines in mind when instructing participants with known CVD or risk factors for CVD:

- Emphasize the importance of self-monitoring exercise intensity (see Chapter 4).
- Avoid abruptly changing from lying down or seated to standing, which can elicit **orthostatic hypotension** (i.e., a rapid drop in BP), causing dizziness. Gradually changing positions is recommended (see Chapter 5).
- Avoid performing the **Valsalva maneuver.**
- Avoid performing **isometric** exercise, which elicits a significant rise in BP.

Table 9-1

CLASSIFICATION OF BLOOD PRESSURE FOR ADULTS AGE 18 AND OLDER*

CATEGORY	SYSTOLIC (mmHg)		DIASTOLIC (mmHg)
Normal[†]	<120	and	<80
Prehypertension	120–139	or	80–89
Hypertension[‡]			
Stage 1	140–159	or	90–99
Stage 2	≥160	or	≥100

* Not taking antihypertensive drugs and not acutely ill. When systolic and diastolic blood pressures fall into different categories, the higher category should be selected to classify the individual's blood pressure status. For example, 140/82 mmHg should be classified as stage 1 hypertension, and 154/102 mmHg should be classified as stage 2 hypertension. In addition to classifying stages of hypertension on the basis of average blood pressure levels, clinicians should specify presence or absence of target organ disease and additional risk factors. This specificity is important for risk classification and treatment.

[†] Normal blood pressure with respect to cardiovascular risk is below 120/80 mmHg. However, unusually low readings should be evaluated for clinical significance.

[‡] Based on the average of two or more readings taken at each of two or more visits after an initial screening.

Source: Chobanian, A.V. et al. (2003). *JNC 7 Express: The Seventh Report of the Joint National Committee on Prevention, Detection, Evaluation, and Treatment of High Blood Pressure. NIH Publication No. 03-5233.* Washington, D.C.: National Institutes of Health & National Heart, Lung, and Blood Institute.

PULMONARY CONDITIONS

Pulmonary diseases and disorders can be debilitating for some exercisers because they can affect the ability to progress exercise intensity, and sometimes physical activity itself can instigate the onset of symptoms. **Asthma** and **chronic obstructive pulmonary disease (COPD)** are the most common pulmonary conditions, affecting more than 25 million and 6.8 million Americans, respectively. Children comprise over 25% of asthma suffers in the United States (CDC, 2014a). Exercise is strongly recommended for pulmonary rehabilitation and management because it helps individuals overcome the psychological and cognitive comorbidities that may accompany these conditions (Paz-Diaz et al., 2007; Ries et al., 2007).

Regardless of the type of pulmonary disease, the goals of physical activity for people with pulmonary conditions include improved exercise tolerance and performance; alleviation of the magnitude of **dyspnea**; improved state of mind, emotional state, and quality of life; enhanced ability to perform **activities of daily living (ADL)**; improved gas exchange in the lungs and circulatory system; and improved mechanical efficiency of the anatomical structures involved in breathing (i.e., lungs, diaphragm, and inspiratory muscles).

ASTHMA

Asthma is a chronic inflammatory disorder of the airways that causes airflow obstruction characterized by varying degrees of difficulty breathing, wheezing, coughing, and chest tightness. Asthma symptoms can present at any time during the human lifecycle, although the onset typically begins in childhood. In some individuals, exercise and physical activity can induce an asthmatic response, which is referred to as **exercise-induced asthma (EIA)** (ACSM, 2014b).

Since ventilatory rate increases during higher-intensity exercise, the risk for experiencing EIA grows during vigorous exercise [**ratings of perceived exertion (RPE)** ≥16 on the 6 to 20 scale]. However, low- to moderate-intensity aerobic conditioning improves one's tolerance to exercise by reducing the ventilatory requirement for any given activity, or simply, by improving one's breathing efficiency (National Asthma Education and Prevention Program, 2007). People with well-controlled, managed asthma and EIA can engage in regular physical activity as outlined for the general population (ACSM, 2014a).

Participants with a pulmonary disease should be educated by their physicians about the early signs and symptoms of pulmonary distress and have a written action plan to guide self-management. A written action plan includes emergency phone numbers and actions to take based on symptoms. This is a document that should be written by the participant and his or her physician so the physician can prescribe the appropriate medications and doses to take according to symptom severity, and so the participant can realize what symptoms require emergency medical services. Participants with asthma should carry rescue medication at all times, especially during outdoor exercise. Participants with pulmonary diseases who are beginning or restarting an exercise program may be hesitant to increase their intensity, but their confidence should increase as they adapt to training and build **self-efficacy** with each successful session. Setbacks are expected, but as long as they become comfortable with their action plan, occasional episodes should not be a permanent deterrent to exercise. Table 9-2 provides steps for managing an asthma attack should symptoms occur.

Table 9-2

STEPS FOR MANAGING AN ASTHMA ATTACK

The time to address an asthma episode is when the symptoms (e.g., coughing, wheezing, chest tightness, and difficulty breathing) first appear.

REST AND RELAX

- At the first sign of breathing difficulties, the person should STOP and rest for at least 10 minutes.
- Make the person feel comfortable and relaxed.

TAKE MEDICATION

- Make sure the prescribed medicine is available and that the person understands how to correctly take the medicine (inhalers require practice).

DRINK WARM LIQUID

- Have the person drink slowly.
- Do not allow the person to ingest cold drinks.

EMERGENCY CARE

- If you have any doubts about the severity of the attack, get medical help immediately.
- If the person's lips or fingernails are turning blue or if he or she exhibits shallow breathing and is focusing all attention on breathing, get medical help immediately.

EXERCISE CONSIDERATIONS FOR PARTICIPANTS WITH ASTHMA

Despite the physiological challenges associated with pulmonary diseases, well-designed and effectively implemented exercise programs can help minimize pulmonary distress symptoms and exacerbations. GFIs should keep the following general exercise guidelines in mind when instructing participants with asthma:

- If pulmonary exacerbations arise before or during exercise, physical activity should be limited until symptoms subside.
- Encourage individuals to utilize an extended warm-up and cool-down.
- Emphasize hydration before, during, and after exercise (to keep airways moist).
- Diaphragmatic or pursed-lip breathing may be beneficial.
- Use RPE and the **dyspnea scale** to monitor exercise intensity (see Chapter 4).
- Limit exposure to cold, polluted, or high-allergen environments.

 [APPLY WHAT YOU KNOW]

Breathing Techniques

Pursed-Lip Breathing

Pursed-lip breathing has been shown to increase tidal volume and reduce respiratory rate in individuals with asthma. The following pursed-lip breathing technique can be used to ease shortness of breath:

- Relax the neck and shoulder muscles.
- Breathe in for two seconds through the nose, keeping the mouth closed.
- Breathe out for four seconds through pursed lips. If this is too long, simply have participants breathe out for twice as long as they breathe in.

Diaphragmatic Breathing

Diaphragmatic breathing can be used to help asthma sufferers improve breathing capacity.

- From the **supine** position, have the participants place one hand on the abdomen and one hand on the chest.
- Teach the participant to inspire with maximal outward movement of the abdomen.
- Once the participant is comfortable in the supine position, he or she can perform the technique in sitting and standing positions.

 [THINK IT THROUGH]

When teaching a yoga class, what specific breathing techniques could you incorporate that would be beneficial for participants with asthma?

ARTHRITIS

Arthritis is a degenerative joint disease and a leading cause of disability, affecting more than 50 million adults in the United States. By 2030, prevalence is estimated to be 67 million (CDC, 2010). More than 100 arthritic diseases or chronic conditions have been identified, with the most common types being **osteoarthritis (OA)** and **rheumatoid arthritis (RA)** (ACSM, 2014b). The structural changes and symptoms associated with arthritis can lead to activity limitations, making it a contributing factor to the progression of comorbidities such as diabetes, **obesity,** and heart disease (CDC, 2010).

OSTEOARTHRITIS

OA accounts for approximately 85% of all arthritis cases. It is a disease characterized as a degeneration of **synovial fluid,** which over time progresses into a loss of **articular cartilage** and the underlying **subchondral bone.** Articular cartilage provides a protective barrier between bony structures, but it does not have pain receptors. Thus, when cartilage degrades, the bone-on-bone interactions are very painful. Moreover, cartilage has no blood supply, which prevents injured or degraded cartilage from healing (Figure 9-1). Weight-bearing joints of the lower extremity, such as the knee, hip, and lumbar spine, as well as the wrist are most commonly afflicted. Primary symptoms include localized joint pain, stiffness, a reduction of **range of motion (ROM),** and **atrophy** of the surrounding muscles (Arthritis Foundation, 2014).

Figure 9-1

Injured or degraded cartilage causes painful bone-on-bone interactions affecting mobility, range of motion, and overall function and performance.

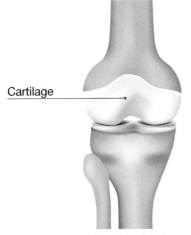

Cartilage

Healthy joint

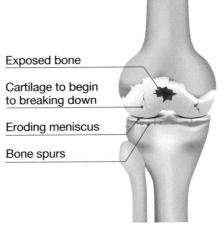

Exposed bone

Cartilage to begin to breaking down

Eroding meniscus

Bone spurs

Osteoarthritis

EXERCISE CONSIDERATIONS FOR PARTICIPANTS WITH OSTEOARTHRITIS

Due to the decrease in physical mobility in individuals with OA, muscle atrophy, ROM limitations, and loss of function are major concerns. Exercise is considered an important component of management for individuals with OA, as it helps to preserve muscle tissue, improve ROM, improve cardiovascular fitness, and maintain a healthy body weight. GFIs should keep the following general exercise guidelines in mind when instructing participants with OA:

- Avoid vigorous exercise during acute flare-ups and periods of inflammation. However, gentle ROM exercises are appropriate during these periods.
- Stop exercise if joint pain is too severe.
- Explain that a small amount of joint and/or muscle discomfort during exercise is normal, and that it does not necessarily mean that damage has occurred to the joints. However, reduce volume and intensity if pain is present at higher levels two hours after the exercise session than before the session.
- Perform an adequate warm-up (five to 10 minutes) to ensure joint lubrication and increased elasticity of tissues.
- Start with light aerobic exercise to increase systemic blood flow and body temperature.
- **Dynamic flexibility** exercises should be performed to enhance tissue elasticity and further increase joint lubrication (see Chapter 5).
- Perform an adequate cool-down, gently taking the joints through their ROM.
- Water temperatures for aquatic exercise should be between 83 and 88° F (28–31° C) to help relax muscles and reduce pain.
- Start with bilateral exercises and advance to unilateral exercises once strength and technique have been established.
- Perform activation exercises to target specific areas (e.g., knees and hips) during the warm-up and body of the class.

DIABETES MELLITUS

Diabetes mellitus is one of the most debilitating conditions affecting the U.S. population, ranking as the seventh leading cause of death in the U.S. [American Diabetes Association (ADA), 2015]. Diabetes is often linked to a number of chronic diseases and disabilities, including CVD, hypertension, stroke, amputations, blindness, and kidney failure (CDC, 2014b). Diabetes is a broadly applied term used to denote a complex group of syndromes that result in a disturbance in the utilization of **glucose.**

In 2012, 29.1 million Americans, or 9.3% of the population, had diabetes (ADA, 2015). Approximately, 1.7 million new cases are diagnosed each year, and 86 million Americans were diagnosed with **prediabetes** in 2012—an astonishing 9% increase since 2010. Prediabetes is diagnosed when eight-hour fasting blood glucose levels range between 100 mg/dL and 125 mg/dL. After an eight-hour fast, a glucose level of 126 mg/dL or higher delineates the cutoff for diabetes (ADA, 2015; ACSM, 2014b).

There are two principal types of diabetes. **Type 1 diabetes** is an autoimmune disease caused by the destruction of pancreatic cells that produce the body's **insulin** (Tsai et al., 2006). Type 2 diabetes results from **insulin resistance** combined with defective insulin secretion (Parchman, Romero, & Pugh, 2006).

TYPE 1 DIABETES

Type 1 diabetes is a serious medical condition that can result in death if not properly treated. A person with this condition must take regular amounts of insulin to sustain a safe amount of glucose in the blood. When insulin is not taken, blood glucose can reach 1,000 mg/dL or higher (normal range after an eight-hour fast is less than 100 mg/dL) and cause the person to go into a diabetic coma. Individuals with type 1 diabetes are insulin-dependent, meaning they must receive periodic doses of insulin. Some people with type 1 diabetes wear an insulin pump that is connected to a catheter under the skin, or they periodically self-administer insulin shots.

TYPE 2 DIABETES

Type 2 diabetes is the most common form of diabetes, affecting over 90 to 95% of all individuals with diabetes. It typically occurs in adults who are **overweight** and is characterized by insulin resistance—a reduced sensitivity of insulin target cells to available insulin, resulting in increased glucose in the blood. Unfortunately, increasing numbers of children are being diagnosed with type 2 diabetes, making the term "adult-onset diabetes" no longer accurate. Unlike those with type 1 diabetes, people with type 2 diabetes are not always prescribed insulin treatment.

EXERCISE CONSIDERATIONS FOR PARTICIPANTS WITH DIABETES

Exercise can have a significant effect on lowering blood glucose for all participants, and is an essential component of treatment for persons with type 1 and type 2 diabetes. People with type 1 and type 2 diabetes are also encouraged to exercise to gain other benefits such as a reduction in body fat, cardiovascular health improvement, and stress reduction, all of which improve overall health and well-being.

Proper timing of medication administration and nutrient consumption, as well as measuring blood glucose levels before and after exercise, are necessary for safe participation. Consuming too many calories before exercise and/or not enough insulin can cause **hyperglycemia** during exercise, due to excess glucose from the food recently consumed and **fatty acids** and glycogen being converted into glucose during exercise, adding to circulating blood glucose levels. **Hypoglycemia** is a dangerous scenario, especially for those with type 1 diabetes, and is defined as a blood glucose level lower than 70 mg/dL (ACSM,

2014b). It can result from low pre-exercise blood glucose levels, too much pre-exercise insulin, or not enough glucose consumption during long-duration physical activity.

People with diabetes should test their blood glucose levels prior to activity; if levels are below 100 mg/dL, they should consume a small carbohydrate snack prior to activity, such as juice or other fast-absorbing carbohydrates, such as a banana. Ideally, participants should adhere to an eating schedule that includes a balance of protein, fats, and low–**glycemic index (GI)** carbohydrates to maintain normal blood glucose levels. Hydration before, during, and after exercise is also very important for participants with diabetes. In fact, one of the classic signs of early hypoglycemia is extreme hunger and/or thirst. In addition, it is prudent to avoid high-intensity activity when blood glucose levels trend toward low levels. Table 9-3 lists the early and late symptoms of an insulin reaction and details how a GFI should best respond if it does occur. This is discussed further in Chapter 11.

Table 9-3
INSULIN REACTION (HYPOGLYCEMIA)

EARLY SYMPTOMS	LATE SYMPTOMS
Anxiety, uneasiness	Double vision
Irritability	Sweating, palpitations
Extreme hunger	Nausea
Confusion	Loss of motor coordination
Headaches	Pale, moist skin
Insomnia	Strong, rapid pulse
	Convulsions
	Loss of consciousness
	Coma

HELPING A PARTICIPANT WHO IS HAVING AN INSULIN REACTION

- Stop the activity immediately.
- Have the person sit down and check his or her blood glucose level.
- Have the participant drink orange juice or some other rapidly absorbing carbohydrate.
- Allow the individual to sit quietly and wait for a response.
- When the participant feels better, check the blood glucose level again.
- If the blood glucose level is above 100 mg/dL and the participant feels better, resume activity.
- Check blood glucose level after 15 to 30 minutes to reassure that levels are within a safe range.
- Do not allow the participant to leave the facility until blood glucose levels are within a normal range.
- If the participant does not improve, seek medical attention immediately.

Source: Rimmer, J.H. (1994). *Fitness and Rehabilitation Programs for Special Populations.* Dubuque, Iowa: WCB McGraw-Hill.

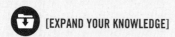 **[EXPAND YOUR KNOWLEDGE]**

Understanding the Glycemic Index

GI values are based on the blood glucose response to a given food item. High-GI foods break down rapidly, causing a large glucose spike, while low-GI foods are digested more slowly and cause a smaller increase in blood glucose. Table 9-4 provides examples of low-, medium-, and high-GI foods.

Table 9-4

GLYCEMIC INDEX (GI) OF VARIOUS FOODS

HIGH GI ≥70	MEDIUM GI 56–69	LOW GI ≤55
White bread	Rye bread	Pumpernickel bread
Corn Flakes	Shredded Wheat	All Bran
Graham crackers	Ice cream	Plain yogurt
Dried fruit	Blueberries	Strawberries
Instant white rice	Refined pasta	Oatmeal

Regular exercise helps reduce CVD and cardiometabolic risk factors, such as mild to moderate hypertension, insulin action and resistance, and glucose metabolism. Also, regular exercise favorably affects the psychological and cognitive health of individuals with diabetes. Table 9-5 provides general guidelines and safety tips for working with participants with diabetes.

Table 9-5

GENERAL GUIDELINES AND SAFETY TIPS FOR PERSONS WITH DIABETES

Regulating blood glucose levels requires optimal timing of exercise periods in relation to meals and insulin dosage.
Aim to keep blood glucose levels between 100 and 200 mg/dL one to two hours after a meal.
Exercise can have a significant effect on insulin reduction (American Diabetes Association, 2006). Some experts note that insulin may need to be reduced by 10 to 50% when starting an exercise program (Wallberg-Henriksson, 1992)*.
If blood glucose levels are lower than 100 mg/dL, have the person consume a rapidly absorbing carbohydrate to increase blood glucose.
If blood glucose is greater than 300 mg/dL before exercise (some doctors may recommend that exercise not be initiated at blood glucose levels greater than 250 mg/dL), make sure that insulin or the oral hypoglycemic agent has been taken. In some circumstances, participants with a high blood glucose level (>300 mg/dL) may lower it to a safe enough level to exercise by drinking water.
No participant should be allowed to exercise if his or her blood glucose level does not fall to a safe range before exercise.
Teach participants to check their feet periodically to avoid foot ulcers. If an ulcer is found, have the person consult with his or her physician immediately for proper treatment. Foot ulcers can worsen and cause major problems if left untreated.
Check blood glucose at the end of the exercise session to make sure that the person does not become hypoglycemic. This could happen very quickly, particularly after high-intensity or long-duration activities or when the person is not accustomed to understanding how the body reacts to exercise.
Make sure the participant is well hydrated and drinking water frequently during the exercise class. Be especially cautious in hot environments, as blood glucose can be impacted by dehydration, and the sweating response of diabetics may be impaired, limiting their thermoregulatory abilities.
Participants with diabetes need to take care of their feet due to possible complications with neuropathy. They should look for cuts, blisters, and signs of infection. Good, comfortable shoes are very important and barefoot exercise is not recommended for most people suffering from neuropathy in the feet. If cuts or signs of infection are present, participants should wear socks in yoga and Pilates classes to avoid the spread or contraction of infection.

*A change in insulin or oral hypoglycemic medication should only be made on the recommendation of a participant's physician.

LOW-BACK PAIN

Low-back pain (LBP) is a non-specific symptom that affects people for a number of reasons, including mechanical problems, excess body weight, injuries, and chronic diseases. Exercise is considered one of the cornerstones of both prevention and treatment of LBP. Aerobic exercise and exercises designed to enhance lumbar spine stability should be performed on a regular basis, and movement mechanics should be emphasized (see Chapter 5). Maintaining and improving muscle balance across the joints is also particularly important for people with musculoskeletal conditions.

EXERCISE CONSIDERATIONS FOR PARTICIPANTS WITH LOW-BACK PAIN

GFIs should keep the following general exercise guidelines in mind when instructing participants with chronic LBP:

- Individuals with LBP, or a history of LBP, should consult with a physician and get specific recommendations for exercise.
- Adequately warm up and cool down before and after each class.
- Always be aware of proper form (exercising in front of a mirror may help).
- Avoid working through pain.
- Always maintain neutral posture and an erect torso during any movements.
- Avoid forward-head positions in which the chin is tilted up.
- When leaning forward to lift or lower an object, always hinge at the hips and bend the knees.
- Avoid hyperextending the spine in an unsupported position.
- Avoid extreme ROM, excessive spinal **flexion** under load, and abrupt twisting movements.

[APPLY WHAT YOU KNOW]

Daily Routine for Enhancing Low-back Health

Because of the high prevalence of low-back pain, GFIs should consider incorporating the movements presented in Figures 9-2 through 9-5 as part of a core conditioning class or during the cool-down segment of other group fitness classes. The following exercises will spare the spine, enhance the muscle challenge, and enhance the motor control system to ensure that spine stability is maintained in all other activities. Keep in mind that these are only examples of well-designed exercises and may not be for everyone—the initial challenge may or may not be appropriate for every individual, nor will the progression be the same for all participants. These are simply examples to challenge the muscles of the torso (McGill, 2007).

Figure 9-2
Cat-camel
The routine should begin with the cat-camel motion exercise (spine flexion-extension cycles) to reduce spine viscosity (internal resistance and friction) and "floss" the nerve roots as they outlet at each lumbar level. Note that the cat-camel is intended as a motion exercise—not a stretch—so the emphasis is on motion rather than "pushing" at the end ranges of flexion and extension. Five to eight cycles have shown to be sufficient to reduce most viscous-frictional stresses.

Cat position

Camel position

Figure 9-3
Modified curl-up
The cat-camel motion exercise is followed by anterior abdominal exercises, in this case the curl-up. Keep the lumbar spine in a neutral position. One knee is flexed but the other leg is straight to lock the pelvis–lumbar spine and minimize the loss of a neutral lumbar posture. Have participants alternate the bent leg (right to left) midway through the repetitions.

Figure 9-4
Birddog
The extensor program consists of leg extensions and the "birddog." In general, these isometric holds should last no longer than seven to eight seconds given evidence from near infrared spectroscopy indicating rapid loss of available oxygen in the torso muscles when contracting at these levels; short relaxation of the muscle restores oxygen. The evidence supports building endurance with increased repetitions rather than extending "hold time."

Figure 9-5
Side bridge
The lateral muscles of the torso (i.e., quadratus lumborum and abdominal obliques) are important for optimal stability, and are targeted with the side bridge exercise. The exercise involves bridging the torso between the elbow and the knees. Once this is mastered and well-tolerated, the challenge is increased by bridging using the elbow and the feet. It is important when performing the side bridge exercise to maintain a neutral neck and spine position and not let the hips rotate forward.

Side bridge

Progression

SPECIAL POPULATIONS

OLDER ADULTS

Older adults may face debilitating health problems that affect them physically, psychologically, and socially. A GFI can motivate older adults to perform exercises as a way of improving function, but also as a means of improving the ability to live an emotionally satisfying life. Exercise programs for older adults should include the same components as those for younger people, with an emphasis on functional capacity, mobility, balance, strength and power development, and bone health. Strength and power training are relevant for older adults to reduce the rate of age-related **sarcopenia,** which is associated with falls and diminished functional capacity (ACSM, 2009).

Exercise Considerations for Older Adults

GFIs should observe the fitness level, mobility limitations, and self-efficacy levels of all class participants, especially older adults. In doing so, a GFI will be able to identify the best approach for maximizing participants' ability and willingness to commit to a lifestyle that includes regular exercise.

Older adults generally suffer losses to multiple senses that impact balance and, consequently, movement efficiency and motor control. Balance, therefore, is the foundational skill to all programming, as it enhances physical performance and contributes to improving the **cognitive domain** and **affective domain,** and building self-efficacy and self-confidence. Core conditioning is a critical component of balance training and must therefore be considered a prerequisite to effective training. High-velocity power training has been shown to elicit meaningful changes in muscle force production, peak power, and contractile speed,

and can safely be undertaken with proper instruction and supervision, once adequate base fitness is established. High-velocity power training may help improve overall performance and quality of life (Henwood & Taaffe, 2005).

GFIs should keep the following general exercise guidelines in mind when instructing older adult participants:

- Ask participants at the beginning of class if they have any limitations they would like to share with the instructor.
- Perform an extended warm-up and cool-down (10 minutes each), and include activation exercises such as those presented in the "Daily Routine for Enhancing Low-back Health."
- Incorporate exercises and movement patterns participants can replicate on their own at home or elsewhere to remain active when they cannot participate in class.

- Due to possible physical limitations or orthostatic BP changes, be mindful of older adults' ability to move quickly from the floor to seated or standing positions.
- Barefoot balance training, such as in yoga or Pilates classes, can be helpful for improving **proprioception** and tactile response. However, older adults with diabetes or pre-existing podiatric or orthopedic conditions should not train in bare feet unless endorsed by their healthcare provider.
- Monitor intensity using the dyspnea scale or the RPE scale.
- Select music that is appealing to this generation if teaching a dedicated class for older adults. Be mindful of the music and microphone volume, as well as tempo.
- For outdoor formats, such as boot-camp classes that involve running or relay races, allow older adults to complete shorter distances, or offer stationary options such as toe taps on a curb, modified jumping jacks, or step-ups on a stable surface, such as a bench.
- For agility exercises, dedicate a specific "lane" in the area for less complex coordination and agility exercises—even walking backward can be a coordination challenge for some older adults.

- If using resistance tubes or bands, coach participants to control the **eccentric** phase, as rapidly "snapping" during the lowering phase can impose excessive **shear forces** on the elbow joint.
- Include cognitive exercises, such as catching a tennis ball with one hand, "Simon says," or boxing with target and mitts to improve reaction time and cognitive function.

Older adults who are frail and possess severe functional and mobility limitations are typically beyond the scope of a GFI (and not likely to participate in programs designed for the general population).

 [EXPAND YOUR KNOWLEDGE]

Exercise Considerations for Participants with Osteoporosis

Osteoporosis a condition characterized by very low bone mass, diagnosed by a bone mass density of more than 2.5 standard deviations below the average peak value for normal adults (ACSM, 2014b). Osteoporosis and low bone mineral density afflicts more than 50 million Americans (National Osteoporosis Foundation, 2015). The clinical significance of osteoporosis in adults is attributed to increased susceptibility to bone fractures, particularly in older adults, who are prone to **osteoporotic fractures** from falling or injuring themselves by performing ADL such as bending over or lifting objects. Osteoporotic fractures are low-trauma injuries, meaning they occur from a standing height or lower. Overall, the risks for osteoporotic fractures in aging adults are staggering—one in three women and one in five men will suffer from an osteoporotic fracture after the age of 50 years. These statistics are comparable to the risk of developing CVD (ACSM, 2014b). The short- and long-term consequences of osteoporotic fractures are associated with severe disability, immobility, decreased functional status, poor quality of life, negative self-esteem, and mortality (Harvey et al., 2006; U.S. Department of Health & Human Services, 2004).

Weight-bearing cardiorespiratory exercise and resistance training are both beneficial for building and maintaining bone mineral density. Group fitness classes that incorporate these types of activities include, but are not limited to, group strength, dance-based fitness, step training, and treadmill-based classes.

YOUTH

The needs of youth differ from those of adults in that their growth status is an indicator of health. Lack of regular exercise could impact functional development and skeletal and muscular growth. In addition, inactive lifestyles could lead to obesity, which has become an epidemic among today's youth (Riner & Sabath, 2009). Sadly, this trend continues to worsen and children are being diagnosed with lifestyle-related conditions that were once distinctive to adults, such as type 2 diabetes and hypertension. Most children above the age of 10 years are not meeting the recommended physical-activity guidelines, further magnifying the need for public health movements aimed toward youth fitness programs.

Exercise Considerations for Youth

GFIs should keep the following general exercise guidelines in mind when instructing youth participants:

- Children's thermoregulatory systems are not as mature as adults. Compared to adults, children have a higher body surface–to–mass ratio, and need to devote a large proportion of their **cardiac output** to the skin surface instead of the core in hot conditions. All of these factors contribute to the way children cool their bodies—through dry heat dissipation (they sweat less)—whereas adults cool via **evaporation** (Falk & Dotan, 2008). This mechanism allows children to conserve water better than adults. Since children sweat less, caution should be taken when exercising in hot, humid environments because **heat exhaustion** can occur quickly if their core temperatures rise faster than their dissipation rate (see Chapter 4).
- For children, **maximal heart rate (MHR)** is much higher than in the adult population, and is generally 200 to 205 bpm (Riner & Sabath, 2009).
- BP responses during exercise are similar among youth and adults, although SBP changes during exercises tend to be lower in children.
- RPE may be a way to measure exercise intensity for youth over eight years of age, but younger children may not have the cognitive skills to use the RPE scale accurately and consistently. "Easy" and "hard" may be the extent of their communication.
- For children, muscle-mass increases occurring during growth lead to increased **muscular strength.**

Before the onset of puberty, muscular strength can be improved similarly in both males and females through resistance training, whereas during puberty, maturation and **testosterone** levels increase muscle size and strength more significantly among males (Riner & Sabath, 2009).

- Gamify exercise sessions (e.g., relay races, scavenger hunts, or dance competitions) and encourage children to use their imaginations when exercising, such as by performing animal-inspired yoga poses to increase **adherence.**
- Supervise appropriately and use light-weight equipment for safety (e.g., medicine and athletic balls, resistance tubing and bands, suspension straps, stability balls, light dumbbells, gliding discs, sand bags, and resistance balls).
- There is no evidence that resistance training stunts growth. Therefore, encouraging safe strength-training practices early will instill good habits for the future. Setting up strength circuits in a circle is an effective way to supervise and coach a group of youth.

PRENATAL AND POSTPARTUM PARTICIPANTS

The potential benefits of a well-designed prenatal exercise program are numerous. Women who exercise during pregnancy have better cardiorespiratory and muscular fitness; reduced **fatigue** thresholds; lower resting heart rates; higher $\dot{V}O_2max$; and reduced rates of urinary incontinence, low-back pain, **deep vein thrombosis,** pregnancy-induced hypertension, **diastasis recti**, nausea, Caesarean section (C-section), **anxiety,** heartburn, insomnia, leg cramps, and symptoms of **depression** (Lamina & Agbanusi, 2013; Nascimento, Surita, & Cecatti, 2012; Hall & Brody, 2010; Yeo et al., 2000).

In terms of fetal health, there is no relationship between mothers who exercise during pregnancy and reduction in birth weight or preterm pregnancies. However, factors such as **ambient temperature** and nutrient availability during exercise can potentially harm the fetus. Therefore, exercising in temperature-controlled areas and eating a snack prior to exercising will promote a safe, healthy exercise experience for mother and baby.

Physical changes during pregnancy may limit some women's ability to exercise. On average, women gain between 25 and 40 pounds (11 to 18 kg), imposing additional stress on the joints of the back, pelvis, hips, and legs. Over the course of gestation, the mother's growing belly will move upward and out, displacing her **center of gravity** and resulting in low-back discomfort and changes in balance and coordination. Women are also more flexible during pregnancy due to an increase in **relaxin,** a hormone that relaxes ligaments and soft tissues in preparation for childbirth. The combination of joint **laxity** and altered balance and coordination can increase the risk of falls and injuries during pregnancy. Therefore, exercising in a controlled environment with few new situations that require novel or intense physical negotiation and motor skill is ideal.

Exercise Considerations for Pregnant Participants

GFIs should learn basic knowledge about the special needs of pregnant women and provide modifications when necessary. The American College of Obstetricians and Gynecologists (ACOG) recommends that pregnant women engage in moderate-intensity exercise for at least 30 minutes on most, if not all, days of the week (ACOG, 2002). The U.S. Department of Health & Human Services (2008) states that healthy pregnant women should get at least 150 minutes per week of moderate-intensity aerobic exercise. *Note:* ACOG's 2002 guidelines were reaffirmed by the organization in 2009.

GFIs should keep the following general exercise guidelines in mind when instructing participants who are currently pregnant:

- Reduce intensity, duration, and frequency over the course of pregnancy if activity is not well tolerated.
- Use the RPE scale if not familiar with HR monitors. Choose a comfortable intensity (e.g., RPE of 9 to 13 on the 6 to 20 scale).
- Incorporate exercises for postural muscles (e.g., thighs, hips, trunk, and shoulders).
- Avoid the following exercises:
  - ✔ Repetitive jumping, hopping, skipping, or bouncing
  - ✔ Deep knee bends, full sit-ups, double-leg raises, and straight-leg toe touches
- After the first trimester, supine and **prone** exercise positions should be avoided. Prolonged exercise in the supine position (>5 minutes) should be discouraged because it pulls blood away from the fetus, depriving it of oxygen. Replace supine positions with semirecumbent and side-lying positions, and replace prone positions with an all-fours position or an elbows-and-knees position.
- Avoid long periods of standing and do not lock out the knees.
- Avoid hot and humid environments.
- Utilize an extended warm-up and cool-down.
- In outdoor or treadmill-based classes, walking and running should occur on a flat surface to reduce the risk of falling.
- Heat dissipation is important throughout pregnancy, so adequate hydration and appropriate clothing are key considerations (see Chapter 4).
- Some women may need a snack prior to exercise to help avoid hypoglycemia.

 [THINK IT THROUGH]

When teaching a group strength class that includes several participants who are pregnant, what alternative exercise options could you suggest in lieu of a supine abdominal strengthening exercise such as bicycle crunches?

Exercise Considerations for Postpartum Participants

Recovery time post-delivery is individualized, and women who had C-section deliveries require more recovery time. Once the obstetrician authorizes a return to physical activity, the first few months will be devoted to gradually improving maternal fitness, which may include weight loss, restoring pre-pregnancy cardiovascular and muscular performance, and regaining a sense of control.

GFIs should keep the following general exercise guidelines in mind when instructing postpartum participants who have been cleared to resume exercise:

- Start slowly, and gradually increase intensity and duration of exercise.
- Avoid excessive fatigue and dehydration (good hydration is important for milk production if nursing).
- Wear a supportive bra.
- Cease activity if unusual pain is experienced.
- Cease activity and seek medical attention if bright red vaginal bleeding occurs that is heavier than a normal menstrual period.
- Women who have had C-section deliveries will need extra time before performing abdominal exercises.

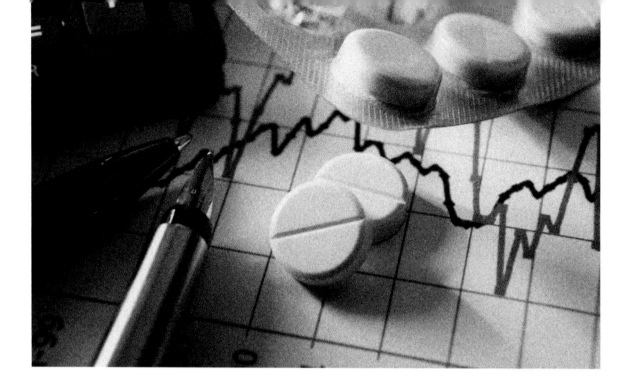

EFFECTS OF COMMON MEDICATIONS ON HEART-RATE RESPONSE

P rescription medication use is an important consideration when addressing a participant's response to exercise. Substances can alter the biochemistry of the body, which can affect an individual's physiological response to exercise. Moreover, dose response can influence the magnitude of the affects as well. Table 9-6 lists common medication categories and their effects on HR response.

In a group fitness setting, the topic may arise if a participant reports unpredicted or unexpected HR responses during exercise. If this occurs, the GFI can ask the participant if he or she is taking any medications or using other substances, and refer to this section for more information based on the participant's reply. GFIs should not attempt to diagnose or provide medical advice, but they should use the information in Table 9-6 to make recommendations on how participants can better monitor their intensity if they are taking medication that alters their exercising HR. Any participant taking a prescription medication that could potentially alter his or her physiological response to exercise should obtain a physician's clearance for physical activity prior to participation.

 [APPLY WHAT YOU KNOW]

Intensity Monitoring for Participants Taking Beta Blockers

Beta blockers are commonly prescribed for various cardiovascular disorders, hypertension, and other disorders. This type of medication reduces resting, exercise, and maximal heart rates. Consequently, beta blockers may not allow exercisers to reach **target heart rate (THR)** based on age-predicted MHR. As such participants should use RPE to monitor intensity.

Table 9-6

EFFECTS OF MEDICATION ON HEART-RATE (HR) RESPONSE

MEDICATIONS	RESTING HR	EXERCISING HR	MAXIMAL EXERCISING HR	COMMENTS
Beta blockers	↓	↓	↓	Dose-related response
Diuretics	←→	←→	←→	
Other antihypertensives	↑, ←→, or ↓	↑, ←→, or ↓	Usually ←→	Many antihypertensive medications are used. Some may decrease, a few may increase, and others do not affect heart rates. Some exhibit dose-related responses.
Calcium-channel blockers	↑, ←→, or ↓	↑, ←→, or ↓	Usually ←→	Variable and dose-related responses
Antihistamines	←→	←→	←→	
Cold medications: without sympathomimetic activity (SA)	←→	←→	←→	
with SA	←→ or ↑	←→ or ↑	←→	
Tranquilizers	←→, or if anxiety reducing may ↓	←→	←→	
Antidepressants and some antipsychotic medications	←→ or ↑	←→	←→	
Alcohol	←→ or ↑	←→ or ↑	←→	Exercise prohibited while under the influence; effects of alcohol on coordination increase possibility of injuries
Diet Pills: with SA	↑ or ←→	↑ or ←→	←→	Discourage as a poor approach to weight loss; acceptable only with physician's written approval
containing amphetamines	↑	↑	←→	
without SA or amphetamine	←→	←→	←→	
Caffeine	←→ or ↑	←→ or ↑	←→	
Nicotine	←→ or ↑	←→ or ↑	←→	Discourage smoking; suggest lower target heart rate and exercise intensity for smokers

↑ = increase   ←→ = no significant change   ↓ = decrease

Note: Many medications are prescribed for conditions that do not require clearance. Do not forget other indicators of exercise intensity (e.g., participant's appearance and ratings of perceived exertion).

SUMMARY

An increased focus on health and fitness for special populations and those suffering from chronic diseases means that more people within these groups will seek the instruction of knowledgeable health and fitness professionals, including GFIs. Instructors must increase their awareness and apply their knowledge of the unique physical, physiological, cognitive, and emotional needs among these populations. To foster an inclusive environment, GFIs need to design classes that are physically feasible for virtually everyone and encourage gradual progression as well as appropriate regressions as needed.

References

American College of Obstetricians and Gynecologists (2002). *ACOG Committee Opinion #267: Exercise During Pregnancy and the Postpartum Period.* Washington, D.C.: American College of Obstetricians and Gynecologists.

American College of Sports Medicine (2014a). *ACSM's Guidelines for Exercise Testing and Prescription* (9th ed.). Philadelphia: Wolters Kluwer/Lippincott Williams & Wilkins.

American College of Sports Medicine (2014b). *Resource Manual for Guidelines for Exercise Testing and Prescription* (7th ed.). Philadelphia: Wolters Kluwer/Lippincott Williams & Wilkins.

American College of Sports Medicine (2009). American College of Sports Medicine position stand: Progression models in resistance training for healthy adults. *Medicine & Science in Sport & Exercise,* 41, 3, 687–708.

American Diabetes Association (2015). *Diabetes Statistics: National Diabetes Statistics Report 2014.* www.diabetes.org/diabetes-basics/statistics/

American Diabetes Association (2006). *Complete Guide to Diabetes* (4th ed.). New York: Bantam Press.

Arthritis Foundation (2014). *Understanding Arthritis.* www.arthritis.org/about-arthritis/understanding-arthritis/

Centers for Disease Control and Prevention (2014a). Summary Health Statistics for U.S. Adults: National Health Interview Survey, 2012. *Vital and Health Statistics,* 10, 260. www.cdc.gov/nchs/data/series/sr_10/sr10_260.pdf

Centers for Disease Control and Prevention (2014b). *National Diabetes Statistics Report: Estimates of Diabetes and Its*

Burden in the United States. Atlanta, Ga.: U.S. Department of Health & Human Services. www.cdc.gov/diabetes/pubs/statsreport14/national-diabetes-report-web.pdf

Centers for Disease Control and Prevention (2013). Surveillance for certain health behaviors among states and selected local areas—United States, 2010. *Morbidity and Mortality Weekly Report: Surveillance Summaries,* 62, 1–247.

Centers for Disease Control and Prevention (2010). Prevalence of doctor-diagnosed arthritis and arthritis-attributable activity limitation—United States, 2007–2009. *Morbidity and Mortality Weekly Report,* 59, 39, 1261–1265.

Chobanian, A.V. et al. (2003). *JNC 7 Express: The Seventh Report of the Joint National Committee on Prevention, Detection, Evaluation, and Treatment of High Blood Pressure. NIH Publication No. 03-5233.* Washington, D.C.: National Institutes of Health & National Heart, Lung, and Blood Institute.

Falk, B. & Dotan, R. (2008). Children's thermoregulation during exercise in the heat: A revisit. *Applied Physiology, Nutrition and Metabolism,* 33, 2, 420–427.

Fields, L.E. et al. (2004). The burden of adult hypertension in the United States 1999 to 2000: A rising tide. *Hypertension,* 44, 4, 398–404.

Fleg, J.L. et al. (2013). Secondary prevention of atherosclerotic cardiovascular disease in older adults: A scientific statement from the American Heart Association. *Circulation,* DOI: 10.1161/01.cir.0000436752.99896.22

Go, A.S. et al. (2013). Heart disease and stroke statistics—2014 update: A report from the American Heart Association. *Circulation,* DOI:10.1161/01.cir.0000441139.02102.80

Hall, C. & Brody, L. (2010). *Therapeutic Exercise: Moving Toward Function* (3rd ed.). Philadelphia: Wolters Kluwer/Lippincott Williams & Wilkins.

Hartung, G.H. & Rangel, R. (1981). Exercise training in post-myocardial infarction patients: comparison of results with high risk coronary and post-bypass patients. *Archives of Physical Medicine and Rehabilitation,* 62, 4, 147–150.

Harvey, N. et al. (2006). The epidemiology of osteoporosis. In: Lane, N.E. & Sambrook, P. *Osteoporosis and the Osteoporosis of Rheumatic Diseases: A Companion to Rheumatology.* St. Louis, Mo.: Mosby: 1–13.

Henwood, T.R. & Taaffe, D.R. (2005). Improved physical performance in older adults undertaking a short-term programme of high-velocity resistance training. *Gerontology,* 51, 108–115.

Kraemer, W.J. et al. (2002) American College of Sports Medicine position stand: Progression models in resistance training for health adults. *Medicine & Science in Sports & Exercise,* 34, 2, 364–380.

Lamina, S. & Agbanusi, E.C. (2013). Effect of aerobic exercise training on material weight gain in pregnancy: A meta-analysis of randomized controlled trials. *Ethiopian Journal of Health Sciences,* 23, 1 59–64.

McGill, S.M. (2007). *Low Back Disorders* (2nd ed.). Champaign, Ill.: Human Kinetics.

Nascimento, S.L., Surita, F.G., & Cecatti, J.G. (2012). Physical exercise during pregnancy: A systematic review. *Current Opinion in Obstetrics & Gynecology,* 24, 6, 387–394.

National Asthma Education and Prevention Program (2007). *Expert Panel Report 3: Guidelines for the Diagnosis and Management of Asthma.* Bethesda, Md.: U.S. Department of Health & Human Services, Public Health Service, National Institutes of Health, National Heart, Lung, and Blood Institute; NIH publication number 08-4051.

National Osteoporosis Foundation (2015). *What Is Osteoporosis?* http://nof.org/articles/7

Parchman. M.L., Romero, R.L., & Pugh, J.A. (2006). Encounters by patients with type 2 diabetes—complex and demanding: An observational study. *Annals of Family Medicine*, 4, 40–45.

Paz-Diaz, H. et al. (2007). Pulmonary rehabilitation improves depression, anxiety, dyspnea and health status in patients with COPD. *American Journal of Physical Medicine & Rehabilitation*, 86, 1, 30–36.

Ries, A.L. et al. (2007). Pulmonary Rehabilitation: Joint ACCP/AACVPR Evidence-Based Clinical Practice Guidelines. *Chest,* 131, 5, 4S–42S.

Rimmer, J.H. (1994). *Fitness and Rehabilitation Programs for Special Populations.* Dubuque, Iowa: WCB McGraw-Hill.

Riner, W.F. & Sabath, R.J. (2009) Physical activity for children and youth. In: Durstine, J.L et al. (Eds). *ACSM's Exercise Management for Persons with Chronic Diseases and Disabilities* (3rd ed.) Champaign, Ill.: Human Kinetics.

Tsai, E.B. et al. (2006). The rise and fall of insulin secretion in type 1 diabetes mellitus. *Diabetologia,* 49, 261–270.

U.S. Department of Health & Human Services (2008). *Physical Activity Guidelines for Americans.* www.health.gov/paguidelines/

U.S. Department of Health & Human Services (2004). *Bone Health and Osteoporosis: A Report of the Surgeon General.* Rockville, Md.: U.S. Department of Health & Human Services, Office of the Surgeon General. www.ncbi.nlm.nih.gov/books/NBK45513/

Wallberg-Henriksson, H. (1992). Exercise and diabetes mellitus. In: Holloszy, J.O. (Ed.) *Exercise and Sport Sciences Reviews,* Vol. 20, 339–368. Baltimore, Md.: Williams & Wilkins.

Ward, B.W., Schiller, J.S., & Goodman, R.A. (2014). Multiple chronic conditions among US adults: A 2012 update. *Preventing Chronic Disease,* 11, 130389. http://dx.doi.org/10.5888/pcd11.130389

Woollard, K.J. & Geissmann, F. (2010). Monocytes in atherosclerosis: Subsets and functions. *National Review of Cardiology,* 7, 2, 77–86. www.ncbi.nlm.nih.gov/pmc/articles/PMC2813241/

World Health Organization (2010). *Global Status Report on Non-Communicable Diseases.* Geneva, Switzerland: World Health Organization.

Yeo, S. et al. (2000). Effect of exercise on blood pressure in pregnant women with a history of gestational hypertensive disorders. *Journal of Reproductive Medicine*, 45, 4, 293–298.

Suggested Reading

Centers for Disease Control and Prevention (2015). *How Much Physical Activity Do Children Need?* www.cdc.gov/physicalactivity/basics/children/

Delgado, J., Barranco, P., & Quirce, S. (2008). Obesity and asthma. *Journal of Investigational Allergology and Clinical Immunology,* 18, 6, 420–425.

Jensen, M.D. et al. (2013). AHA/ACC/TOS guideline for the management of overweight and obesity in adults: A report of the American College of Cardiology/American Heart Association. *Circulation,* DOI: 10.1161/01.cir.0000437739.71477.ee

Juel, CT-B. et al. (2012). Asthma and obesity: Does weight loss improve asthma control? A systematic review. *Journal of Asthma and Allergy,* 5, 21–26.

CHAPTER 10

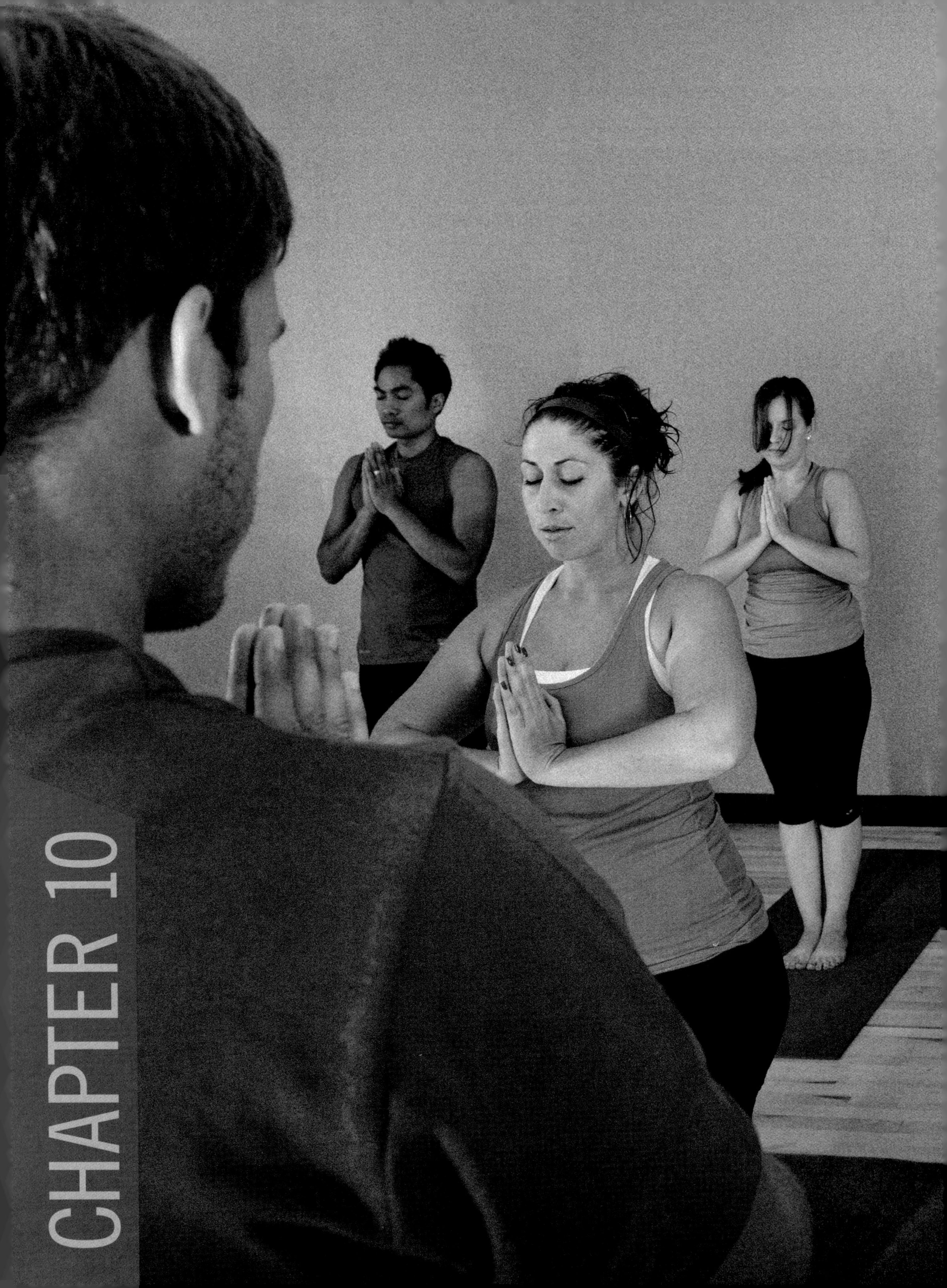

CHAPTER 10

STRATEGIES FOR ENHANCING INSTRUCTION

SHANNAN LYNCH

LEARNING OBJECTIVES

- Modify teaching style and method to meet the needs of class participants.
- Educate participants about class goals and benefits, as well as general exercise science–based information pertaining to the class format.
- Solicit meaningful feedback and incorporate information to enhance teaching strategies.
- Analyze performance and progress and provide feedback accordingly.
- Resolve conflicts or incidents with professionalism.
- Implement strategies to avoid instructor burnout.

Chapters 6 and 8 discuss effective communication strategies, teaching techniques, and various learning styles (i.e., verbal, visual, and kinesthetic). Considering that transfer of learning is highly variable across individuals and that factors such as demographics, cultural background, fitness experience, level of mastery, and personality can affect one's experience and success, this chapter is dedicated to equipping ACE Certified Group Fitness Instructors (GFIs) with strategies to enhance instruction and learning within a group fitness environment.

If your study program includes the ACE Learning Center, visit www.ACEfitness.org/MyACE and log in to your My ACE Account for tips on how to enhance instruction through the proper use of transitions and cueing to the solution.

TEACHING STYLES AND METHODS

The teaching strategies and techniques introduced in Chapter 8 lay the groundwork for becoming an effective leader. How GFIs practically apply and adapt this information is what creates a dynamic learning environment. Understanding how to modify, deliver, and adjust teaching methods is key not only to meeting participant needs, but also to ensuring performance success and minimizing the risk of injury.

Understanding how to modify, deliver, and adjust

TEACHING STYLES

Teaching **pedagogy** is interdisciplinary because it applies to all subject matter and forms the basis of knowledge acquisition and application. The way one learns to tie his or her shoes is the same way one learns to cut hair or perform a choreographed dance. Learning to teach human movement is complex because the learner must possess the motor skills necessary to execute the movements, memorize the steps or sequence, understand how an exercise is supposed to look and feel, and have the body awareness to perform movements correctly and repeatedly. The success of the movement not only depends on the aforementioned skills, but also on the participants' ability to physiologically keep up with the demands of learning. Additionally, GFIs must possess the ability to build **rapport** (see Chapter 6) as well as provide effective instructions that are as clear and concise as possible. Mastery evolves over time, but becoming familiar with various approaches to teaching and understanding how to apply this knowledge in a group fitness environment is a start toward developing one's instructional abilities.

TEACHING METHODOLOGY

In Chapter 8, various teaching methods were presented to provide new GFIs with some tools of the trade to develop their teaching style and practices. Regardless of the teaching style chosen, there are a few methodological tenets that apply to any group fitness setting. These principles include set-up, execution, **transitions, cueing**, and **rhythm**.

Set-up

Set-up entails naming the exercise and positioning the equipment (when applicable) or body for the exercise or movement—this is the "start" position. This could mean calling out the next move in a dance-based or cardio kickboxing class (e.g., grapevine, mambo, upper cut, or "bob 'n' weave"), naming a specific exercise in a group strength training class such as a single-leg deadlift, or calling out a series of exercises such as the "side kick series" in Pilates. Naming the movement, exercise, or series gives participants a few key words to anticipate the equipment set-up and execution.

 [APPLY WHAT YOU KNOW]

Providing Movement Education

In addition to naming the exercise and the starting positions, GFIs should also educate participants about the differences between body positions and movement techniques during the set-up. For example, in preparing for a dumbbell lateral raise, the GFI may share that a straight-arm lateral raise is more challenging than a bent-arm lateral raise due to the fact that the **lever** is longer in the straight-arm variation. Additional information about **progression** and **regression** options empowers individuals to choose movements and exercises that they feel best serve them and their personal fitness experience.

Execution

Execution involves performing the movement or exercise through the full **range of motion (ROM)** with correct technique and form. In a dance-based class, the exact performance of certain movements may be somewhat open to interpretation. However, in a strength-based class, proper execution of technical movements such as a chest press or squat should be coached with direct cues. Only the words that impact the outcome should be spoken—this is called using economy of words. Execution cues should be clear and concise to improve participants' recall in future classes. By the fourth or fifth time participants hear a familiar term, they should know what it means. See page 170 for additional information about cueing.

 [APPLY WHAT YOU KNOW]

Integrating Learning Styles Through Cueing

In understanding that participants have various learning styles, GFIs should strive to effectively integrate visual, verbal, and kinesthetic cues to coach participants through the execution of exercises. For example, during a push-up, a GFI can visually demonstrate the exercise along with the class, while providing a few verbal execution cues during the movement ("bend the elbows, allowing them to flare out slightly; your upper and lower body move as one") and a quick kinesthetic cue ("brace your core, pretending that you are about to be punched in the stomach"). Adding brief learning opportunities, such as identifying target muscle groups and benefits, improves the overall experience and the GFI's credibility.

Consider feedback from previous classes to personalize the workout or improve the experience. For example, some participants may prefer that a GFI teach with his or her back to the class, while others may prefer he or she face the class. In this instance, the GFI would teach the exercises from both perspectives, switching positions periodically.

Transitions

Flowing to the next exercise maintains motion and connects one exercise to the next. This is important for rhythm-based formats that place an emphasis on arm or leg leads, and proper transitions can also prevent injury. For example, in an indoor cycling class, it is a safe practice to keep at least one hand on the handlebars when transitioning between the seated and standing positions. A GFI can incorporate this safety rule by first setting up the transition verbally by saying, "one hand on the bars at all times," and then demonstrate the motion during the transition as a visual cue.

Transitioning techniques can take on a few forms, and relevance depends upon the format. Three common ways to transition movements are **matching**, **mending**, and **patching** (Khai-Cronin, Ganulin, & Metzo, 2013).

Matching: Where one exercise ends, another starts. Examples: A barbell front squat followed by an overhead press, or a grapevine followed by single-leg hamstring curls

Mending: Stringing two exercises/movements together. Examples: Incorporating thrusters (a squat and overhead press in unison) into a group strength class, or, in cardio kickboxing, a right knee and left uppercut performed simultaneously

Patching: Performing an additional movement between two exercises or movements for a seamless transition. Examples: Burpees (a push-up, knees tuck in to stand, and jump—the knee tucks are the patch component) or, in mat Pilates, to transition from the 100 to the Roll Up, the participant pulls his or her knees into the chest to patch the two exercises together

Cueing

The key to cueing is using as few words as possible to deliver directions and desired outcomes. There is an appropriate time to cue depending on the format. For rhythm-based formats, the GFI must cue ahead of the movement. In other formats, such as group strength classes, the instructor can provide corrective cues during the exercise. Regardless of format, there are some standard guidelines for cueing:

- Provide no more than one corrective action at a time and choose the most critical. For example, during a deadlift, if one participant is rounding his or her back and another is holding the bar too wide (non-critical), cue the participants to maintain an extended, neutral spine— "draw your shoulders back, imagining you're balancing a glass of water on your upper back." GFIs should strive to ensure gross movement errors are addressed first before refining other aspects of form and technique.

- Form and corrective cues should be sequential, often starting from the trunk/core (**proximal** stability) then moving to the extremities (**distal** mobility), unless the gross errors are critically apparent in a specific area of the body. For many exercises, setting up and later evaluating movements may be done from "the ground up."

- Cues should be positive and solution-based. Refrain from words such as "don't" and "no" and build your vocabulary to cue what to do, as opposed to what not to do (see page 174). Filler words such as "the next exercise is" or "next you're going to…" should be removed as well, allowing for more direct cues.

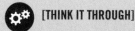 **[THINK IT THROUGH]**

Imagine you are leading a group strength class and are teaching reverse lunges to participants. As you look around the room, you notice that many participants are performing the exercise with incorrect form. Script out how you would clearly and concisely provide feedback to participants in the form of positive cues that are free of filler words.

Rhythm

Rhythm exists in any format, regardless of whether if it is a choreographed class or not. Rhythm is defined as the **tempo** of the movement. Tempo in choreographed classes depends on the music's beats per minute (bpm) or the instructor's cueing. In some strength-based classes, rhythm can manipulate the cadence, which can affect **overload.** For example, when performing a biceps curl, a GFI may choose a 1-count **concentric** movement (flexing the elbows, lifting the dumbbells) to a 3-count **eccentric** movement (extending the elbows, lowering the weights down to the starting position). In classes that play music as a background motivator, as opposed to being a component of the program or class, rhythm is still a factor because music provokes emotion and **motivation** and helps keep exercises in motion, enhancing skill acquisition. For example, when teaching a new exercise, the rhythm of the music can be used to break down the steps or beat of the movement, provided the tempo is at an appropriate speed.

Rhythm is not exclusive to music

Rhythm, however, is not exclusive to music. GFIs can speak the rhythm of the movement or exercise to better meet the needs of verbal learners who are trying to execute the movement but are having trouble mastering the timing and motor patterns of the skill.

EDUCATING GROUP FITNESS PARTICIPANTS

Participant education is just as important as form and technique. While personal trainers and other health and fitness professionals commonly work one-on-one with clients and provide individualized education based on their clients' personalized program design and unique abilities, needs, and goals, GFIs must educate groups of participants all at once. As a result, education typically caters to the general population while being mindful of participants' needs, goals, and limitations.

> GFIs educate groups of participants all at once

While GFIs do not have the benefit of understanding each participant's background as thoroughly as a personal trainer might, it is important to stay abreast of a variety of exercise science subjects that will enable the GFI to educate participants in a meaningful way during each class.

STRATEGIES FOR CLASS EDUCATION

To enhance the effectiveness of instruction, GFIs must deliver clear and concise information, using only a few moments to deliver the most important points, while also ensuring the content is not too technical. Remember, a good instructor does not show off what he or she knows, and what others do not. Instead, a good teacher inspires others. Keeping this in mind, there are three primary strategies for educating group fitness participants.

Triple F: Form, Function, and Fit

This strategy educates participants on the benefits of performing the exercise with proper technique and form, and goes into greater detail about target muscles and function. The following example features a GFI teaching participants how to perform a body-weight squat:

- *Form:* "Stand with feet hip-width apart to create a solid base of support. Keeping the core engaged, initiate the movement by hinging at the hips."

- *Function:* "Since squats are a movement pattern that we perform frequently in our everyday lives, they serve the very functional purpose of training the body to move more efficiently both inside and outside of the gym. For example, bracing the core helps to stabilize the lumbar spine, reducing the potential for developing low-back issues later down the road."

- *Fit (target muscles):* "This is a multijoint exercise involving multiple muscles. It primarily targets the quadriceps, hamstrings, and glutes."

Performance

This strategy solely focuses on the performance benefits of an exercise or class. Consider these examples (Hall, 2014):

- *Hammer curl versus biceps curl:* "In hammer curls, your forearms are neutral, so you're not using the biceps brachii to their full potential. In a traditional biceps curl, your forearms supinate to turn the palms forward. This position activates the biceps brachii more effectively."

- *Body-weight lunge:* "Lunges are transferable to activities of daily living. For example, consider climbing steps, getting up off the floor, or getting in and out of your car. Body-weight lunges help you master your own body weight so you can perform these activities efficiently."

Health Benefits

Educating participants on the behavioral and health aspects of exercise can help bridge the gap between fitness and wellness by building participants' awareness about their health and overall well-being. Consider these examples:

- *Exercise intensity:* "If you're new to indoor cycling and you haven't been consistently exercising, keep your intensity between a 3 and 4 on the **ratings of perceived exertion (RPE)** scale for today" (pointing to the RPE poster). This helps acquaint newer participants with what low-to-moderate intensity exercise feels like, allowing them to monitor their own effort appropriately. (See Chapter 4 for more information on proper use of the RPE scale.)

- *Mood:* At the beginning of class, ask participants to acknowledge their current state of mind or mood. At the end of class, ask the question again. They should make a mental note of their pre- and post-exercise mood and track how many times in 30 days they left a workout feeling better. Although the GFI is not providing explicit information or knowledge, he or she is teaching mindfulness and acknowledging some of the behavioral benefits of exercise.

- *Sedentary work environments:* "If you work behind a desk, these next four yoga poses can also be performed at your desk to help improve posture."

ANALYZING PERFORMANCE AND PROVIDING FEEDBACK

When analyzing performance in a group setting, GFIs should always commence with an evaluation of the stability of their participants before introducing mobilization exercises. Establishing proper standing or floor-based postures is key to avoiding injury and promoting benefits. Ultimately, teaching techniques—including corrective teaching skills—help empower participants to improve in each class so that, over time, their movement integrity enhances independently.

> Empower participants to improve

When making corrections, the following tips will assist instructors in creating positive experiences for all participants (Biscontini, 2011):

- Instructors should cue to the solution, not to the problem. Instead of saying "don't let the knees lock out," for example, cueing to "keep a slight bend in the knees at all times" offers a more positive approach. Eliminating the ubiquitous word "don't" from the GFI's vocabulary will help ensure a more positive experience for all participants.

- When making corrections, use the following three steps. First, cue verbally to the solution in a general sense. For example, "Be sure to keep that chest lifted!" Second, if that does not resolve the issue, GFIs can gently call attention to the specific individual and concern if immediate safety is involved. For example, "Nancy, that's great lower-body form; be sure to keep the chest lifted!" Third, if a kinesthetic intervention is needed because neither of the first two steps prove successful, GFIs should approach the participant, offering guidance as to where he or she should move—away from potential injury and toward correction. For example, a GFI can approach the participant at his or her eye level and say, "Nancy, I'm placing my palms on either side of your elbows; gently guide your elbows toward my palms." In this way, instructors avoid the issue of having to touch the participants directly because, in teaching **kinesthetic awareness,** participants take responsibility for positioning their bodies in space, and learn to move away from misalignment and toward correct form.

When having to reorganize a movement to guarantee success for more participants, use "progressions" and "regressions" instead of "modifications," which can be nonspecific and perceived as negative. A regression offers an exerciser ways to decrease intensity or complexity, while a progression increases one or both of those elements. Offering "level 1" and "level 3" movements while teaching to the intermediate intensity of "level 2" allows all exercisers to feel successful. GFIs may want to avoid the terms "beginner," "intermediate," and "advanced," since these adjectives do not always appropriately identify difficulty.

Offering specific and immediate feedback always takes a bit more thought and time, but signifies a seasoned instructor who is able to spot good form and verbalize it. Instead of cueing "Good job, Rebecca," for example, an instructor may cue specifically what the participant is doing so well. Stating both what is good and why it merits mention constitutes effective and appropriate feedback. For example, saying "Great work hinging at the hips to initiate the squat (performance standard), your lower back thanks you (rationale)" may take a moment more to verbalize, but incorporates all of the components of effective cueing.

ANALYZING INTENSITY AND MONITORING PROGRESS

As discussed in Chapter 4, both instructors and participants must monitor exercise intensity. Whether using **target heart rate,** RPE, talk test, or another intensity-monitoring technique, GFIs should establish at the beginning of class which methods participants can use to gauge their intensity. Participants must also learn to take responsibility for monitoring their own intensity via the formats that the GFI offers. When offering intensity options, GFIs should try to create a non-competitive environment, reminding all exercisers to move at an intensity that is appropriate for them instead of comparing their workout to that of other participants.

GFIs should seek to create experiences of empowerment every time they teach. To achieve this goal, they should evaluate the objectives of the class periodically to verify congruence between the class purpose and the participants. If a participant is not showing progress, an instructor can problem-solve to determine if unrealistic goals exist, or if another issue must be corrected. When instructors show that they care about each participant, this encourages long-term participation in group fitness classes.

Ultimately, GFIs must stay abreast of the changing standards, guidelines, and trends in an industry that evolves quickly. Maintaining a familiarity with this information is key when dealing with the health and safety of the many participants together in one class.

Specific and immediate feedback always takes a bit more thought and time

PROVIDING FEEDBACK

Providing participants with information about their progress and performance in a group fitness class is one of the most important roles of a GFI. This information is known as feedback. Learning is limited without feedback, because if participants are unable to effectively gauge how they are doing, they will be unaware of how, when, and why to make adjustments and refine behaviors.

Feedback can be either intrinsic or extrinsic, and both are important for enhancing learning and increasing motivation. **Extrinsic feedback** is the reinforcement, error correction, and encouragement that GFIs provide participants. **Intrinsic feedback** is information that participants provide themselves based on their own sensory systems (i.e., what they feel, see, or hear). While extrinsic feedback plays an important role in the exercise environment, long-term program **adherence** is dependent on the participant's ability to provide his or her own feedback. It is important for GFIs to also balance the amount of feedback provided. As participant motivation, **self-efficacy,** and ability develop, GFIs should taper off the amount of external feedback provided, allowing participants more opportunities to provide themselves feedback.

While general motivational comments (i.e., "good job") during a class can help keep participants engaged, specific feedback serves an important role in terms of motivation because it provides a guide to participants of how they are doing. The type of feedback that provides information on progress can be referred to as **knowledge of results.** Without it, persistence suffers and people may give up. Feedback also helps in the goal-setting process. Both intrinsic and extrinsic feedback can contribute to knowledge of results and provide information about progress toward goal attainment. Whether a participant is achieving goals and experiencing success or is falling short of desired performance levels, GFIs can help the participant use the feedback to adjust and reestablish goals for continued motivation and program participation (Coker, Fischman, & Oxendine, 2005).

Observational Assessments

One of the most powerful instructional strategies that can be used by a GFI is to observe participants while they are performing a movement and then provide feedback based on those observations. Each participant's posture, exercise form and technique, and tolerance to **fatigue** should be monitored by the GFI throughout the class.

Posture and Movement

Since all movement is based on a person's posture, a GFI should be able to recognize the important characteristics associated with proper spinal alignment and good overall posture. The following points represent what a GFI should look for when assessing a participant's standing posture.

Lateral view (Figure 10-1a):

> » The head should be suspended (not pushed back or dropped forward) with the ears in line with the shoulders, shoulders over hips, hips over knees, and knees over ankles.
>
> » Participants must maintain the three natural curves of the spine. A decrease or increase in the spinal curvature changes the amount of compression the spine can withstand. The hips can be tucked slightly, particularly for individuals with exaggerated lumbar **lordosis,** pregnant women, and participants with large, protruding abdominal areas.
>
> » The knees should be unlocked or soft. Hyperextended knees shift the pelvis, contributing to an increased low-back curve and back strain, along with decreased blood flow to and from the legs.

Visit www.ACEfitness.org/GFIresources to download a checklist you can use while observing a participant's alignment and posture.

Anterior and posterior views (Figures 10-1b and 10-1c):

> » The feet should be shoulder-width apart with the weight evenly distributed. Excessive foot **pronation** or **supination** could lead to musculoskeletal injuries if a participant performs high volumes of exercise with poor foot mechanics. Any individual who complains of joint pain in the ankles, knees, hips, or back should consult his or her healthcare provider, especially if he or she exhibits high arches (excessive supination) or flat feet (excessive pronation).
>
> » There should be overall symmetry between the two sides of the body with no visible lateral shifting or leaning to one side.

Anterior view (Figure 10-1b):

> » The arms should hang with equal spaces between each arm and the torso and the hands should hang such that only the thumbs and index fingers are visible (i.e., no knuckles should be visible from the **anterior** view). Hands that hang with the knuckles facing forward indicate an imbalance of the muscles of the shoulder and/or forearm.
>
> » The kneecaps (patellae) should be oriented forward without deviation inward or outward (internal or external rotation, respectively). A patella that appears rotated inward or outward is an indication of a potential muscular imbalance or structural deviation of the hips and/or foot/ankle complex.

Figure 10-1
Assessing a participant's posture

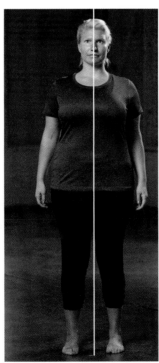
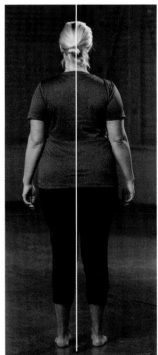

a. Lateral view

b. Anterior view

c. Posterior view

Form and Technique

While it certainly is not the responsibility of the GFI to conduct individual postural assessments and design restorative exercise programs for participants, knowledge of ideal postural alignment is crucial for understanding proper exercise technique. A GFI can cue participants to maintain correct posture throughout the exercise class with statements such as, "Keep your shoulders down and your knees slightly bent while we do this exercise."

Muscular imbalances are often found around the hips, trunk, and shoulder girdle due to prolonged sitting throughout the day. Giving participants in group fitness classes an opportunity to work those joints through their intended ROMs while simultaneously promoting adequate strength and flexibility of the joints' associated structures, is one way to help them improve posture.

Generally, a participant's exercise technique should adhere to a few basic guidelines:

- Controlled, purposeful movements require more muscle involvement, and thus protect the joints better than quick, uncontrolled movements. This is true during both resistance-training exercise and cardiorespiratory exercise.

- The availability of specific amounts of weight in group strength classes is often limited, resulting in some participants lifting loads that are too light for advancing muscular fitness. In these situations, it is important to cue the participant to focus even more on the muscular contraction being performed to move the weight rather than increasing the velocity of the lift. In classes that promote momentum training, such as in kettlebell classes, it is essential for a GFI to have the proper knowledge and training to correctly instruct technique.

> Always demonstrate good posture

- In load-bearing cardiorespiratory classes, such as traditional aerobics and step classes, participants should be cued to control the descent of the lower extremity as it makes contact with the ground (or step) surface by making as little noise as possible with the feet. This practice will ensure a thoughtful impact with the ground and result in muscular deceleration forces that attenuate much of the **ground reaction forces** that could affect the body's joints. Coaching a participant to "land quietly" or to "be light on your feet" are helpful cues.

- Regardless of the exercise being performed, participants should be coached to always demonstrate good posture. This typically means that the spine and pelvis should maintain their neutral, or ideal, positions through a mild contraction or bracing of the core musculature, and the knees should remain slightly bent.

SOLICITING AND INCORPORATING MEANINGFUL FEEDBACK

Personal and career development is important in any industry. A GFI's class is a reflection of his or her personality, breadth of knowledge, and passion. Accepting feedback is one of the best ways to develop one's craft. Along with education and experience, feedback from participants, supervisors, and colleagues can help shape one's personal "brand" and enhance marketability.

FEEDBACK FROM PARTICIPANTS

Some participants will be brutally honest, while others may be more passive with their feedback. There will be feedback to which an instructor can immediately adjust, while other times the instructor may need to report feedback to their supervisors to resolve. Common comments that a GFI can respond to may include touch techniques, music or microphone volume, audibility of the instructor's cues, music selection, exercise variety, need for progressions or regressions, and use of fans in the room. Feedback a GFI may need to forward to supervisors include temperature of the room, lack of equipment, equipment quality and cleanliness, crowdedness, odors (in the room or from other participants), complaints about other instructors, or class schedule (formats and times).

In circumstances when the GFI can adapt and respond to a participant's feedback, he or she should make immediate changes during class or in the next class depending on when the feedback is received. For example, be sure to check the volume of the music and microphone and adjust as needed, avoid touching participants without permission, utilize music from a variety of genres, cool the room by using fans, if needed, and avoid using foul language or making remarks regarding sensitive subjects (e.g., politics). GFIs may need to confide in veteran instructors or seek out additional resources to best accommodate participants who require additional modifications or request variety. Part of the job is realizing that the workout is for the participants, and that satisfied participants are more likely to adhere to a regular fitness routine, reducing attrition rate. If a participant has a question that a GFI cannot readily answer, the GFI should agree to have an answer for the next class or refer the participant to someone who can answer the specific question(s).

> Satisfied participants are more likely to adhere

Some participants may not want to approach the GFI in class to provide feedback. Some ways GFIs can overcome this include offering an email address or communication channel through social media, suggesting that participants leave feedback with the front desk or facility supervisor, and periodically handing out surveys to be completed anonymously.

FEEDBACK FROM SUPERVISORS

Most group fitness managers perform periodic evaluations of their instructors, which typically include verification of credentials and continuing education, as well as a practical in-class appraisal. Occasionally, supervisors may ask for participants' feedback as well. Following the evaluation, the GFI and supervisor meet to review the GFI's performance. Supervisors will offer constructive feedback and provide advice on implementing that feedback moving forward. Some GFIs may receive feedback about their professional conduct, attire, or failure to adhere to format or facility guidelines. This type of feedback should be corrected

immediately. Performance evaluations are conducted in almost all fields of business, as they are a normal and valuable part of professional development. Group fitness instruction is a very soft science, meaning there are very few absolutes and more than one way to successfully lead group fitness classes.

FEEDBACK FROM COLLEAGUES

Soliciting feedback from colleagues is a great way to receive constructive feedback outside of evaluation periods. Moreover, this is an opportunity to seek advice and industry guidance from other practicing professionals. Bear in mind that constructive criticism is not exclusive to new instructors, as the fitness industry is always evolving and new techniques and standards emerge continuously. Attending other instructors' classes and even observing people speak, present, and teach outside of the fitness industry are also beneficial in terms of enhancing one's instructional abilities.

RESOLVING CONFLICTS

Although group fitness classes are typically a positive environment, when a group of people convene, no matter the purpose or setting, conflicts can arise. From disruptive participants and lack of equipment, to arguments over someone's favorite spot in the room, conflicts can arise when least expected. Peer mediation and fostering a respectful environment are just some of the qualities a GFI will need to master.

MATERIAL ISSUES

- *Lack of equipment:* If equipment availability is an issue, GFIs should be prepared to lead the class without using any equipment so that participants may use all available equipment items. If this does not alleviate the problem, participants may need to share equipment or the GFI might have to change the format to a circuit or interval-based class so less equipment is needed (refer to Chapter 7).

- *Location preferences in the room:* If two participants are arguing over the same spot or piece of equipment (e.g., bike) in the room, the GFI should institute a first come, first served rule. Moving forward, politely make this announcement at the beginning of each class so that all participants are aware.

- *Music:* Music selection ties into the feedback section, but some branded formats require instructors to use specific music. If this is the

case and someone does not like the music, explain that it is a requirement to teach the format and that a new set of songs will be launched soon. Most branded formats have a customer service email or phone number that participants can use, which is something GFIs may choose to share with participants as well.

NON-MATERIAL ISSUES

Partner exercises: Some classes call for partner exercises. This can be uncomfortable for some participants since there may be body contact with another person, or some participants may be shy. First, the class description on the schedule should clearly indicate it is a partner-based class. Before the start of class, the GFI should announce, "If you would like to partner with someone, please do so now. If you would like me to help you find a partner, please come to the front of the room."

Odors: If body odor from another person is an issue, this can create conflict because participants may not wish to partner with, or set up near, that person. This can be a difficult situation due to cultural or gender differences. If a GFI is not comfortable addressing the issue with the participant, he or she should notify a supervisor. If the GFI does choose to resolve the conflict, it is a good idea to first try to indirectly address the issue to the entire class, "Everyone, please be mindful of others around you and wash your gym clothes and bathe in between workouts. I know we're all busy, but personal hygiene can affect other

participants' class experiences." If this approach does not resolve the issue, politely address the individual directly without other participants around or ask a supervisor to do so.

Interpersonal issues between participants: Interpersonal issues can arise in class, especially if the class is held at a community-based, corporate, or school facility where participants know each other and may have issues outside of the group fitness class. If arguments arise due to interpersonal conflicts, the GFI should ask participants to refrain from talking or respectfully ask them to leave the room. If unforeseen conflicts arise, such as a participant becoming irate because the person in front of him or her keeps obstructing the view of the mirror, suggest the participant move to an alternative location in the room and return his or her attention back to class.

HARASSMENT OR THREATS

Any complaints about harassment or threats from other participants or facility members must be reported to management or the facility operator immediately. This is not just a conflict; it is a potential violation or criminal act. Refer to Chapter 11 for incident-reporting guidelines.

Overall, a GFI should act as the "quiet professional," resolving any issues as quickly as possible without becoming emotional or drawing too much attention to the conflict. Resuming class and maintaining a positive environment is the goal when faced with unforeseen challenges.

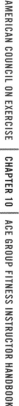

AVOIDING INSTRUCTOR BURNOUT

Teaching fitness classes demands mental and physical energy, which can result in mental burnout and/or **overtraining** over time. Symptoms of overtraining may include sleep loss, elevated resting heart rate, fatigue, and changes in weight. Burnout symptoms may include disinterest in exercise and teaching classes, lack of motivation, poor class preparation, and **depression.** Many health and fitness professionals will experience this phenomenon to some degree at some point in their careers. The following are strategies designed to help the GFI remain engaged and enthusiastic about his or her craft:

- Talk with other GFIs about how to prevent or address burnout.

- Take a vacation to relax and recharge, both physically and mentally.

- Switch classes with another GFI to have exposure to new students.

- Learn a new class modality.

- If possible, hone other teaching skills such as imagery or the use of informative cueing to minimize the amount of time physically demonstrating in unison with the class (e.g., instruct off the bike during an indoor cycling class or lead a yoga class without physically performing all of the poses along with the group).

- Attend classes as a participant or engage in activities outside of the gym, such as hiking or road cycling (provided symptoms of overtraining are not present).

SUMMARY

Teaching group fitness classes extends beyond just leading exercises and emulating ideal form and technique; GFIs need to transfer knowledge. To do this effectively, GFIs must develop and adopt diverse teaching methods to meet the needs of participants. This is accomplished by incorporating various instructional styles and understanding how the elements of effective cueing foster a successful environment, improve exercise adherence, and enhance self-efficacy.

References

Biscontini, L. (2011). *Cream Rises: Excellence in Private and Group Fitness Education.* New York: FG2000.

Coker, C.A., Fischman, M.G., & Oxendine, J.B. (2005). Motor skill learning for effective coaching and performance. In: Williams, J.M. (Ed.) *Applied Sport Psychology: Personal Growth to Peak Performance.* New York: McGraw-Hill.

Hall, S. (2014). *Basic Biomechanics* (7th ed.). New York: McGraw-Hill.

Khai-Cronin, A., Ganulin, D., & Metzo, V. (2003). *Level 1 Introduction to Kettlebell Lifting Instructor Course Manual.* New York: Kettlebell Concepts, Inc.

Suggested Reading

American Council on Exercise (2012). *ACE's Essentials of Exercise Science for Fitness Professionals.* San Diego: American Council on Exercise.

PART 4

Introduction to Part 4:
PROFESSIONAL AND LEGAL CONSIDERATIONS

Ensuring a safe exercise experience for participants is the primary responsibility of an ACE Certified Group Fitness Instructor (GFI). This includes effectively delivering well-designed multilevel classes, as discussed in previous chapters, as well as appropriately responding to incidents and emergency situations that may arise. GFIs must develop a firm understanding of the professional responsibilities and legal guidelines that ultimately will guide their actions as a leader of group-based movement experiences.

OVER THE COURSE OF THIS PART OF THE HANDBOOK, INSTRUCTORS WILL GAIN COMPETENCY IN THE FOLLOWING TWO AREAS:

Ensuring participant safety

Legal and professional responsibilities

CHAPTER 11 | MAKING PARTICIPANT SAFETY A PRIORITY

SHANNAN LYNCH

LEARNING OBJECTIVES

■ Describe the common injuries and acute illnesses that could occur in a group fitness setting.

■ Explain the major risk factors that could increase a participant's incidence of injury or acute illness.

■ Understand how to prevent and manage common injuries and acute illnesses within the group fitness instructor's scope of practice, and when to activate emergency medical services.

Healthy lifestyle habits, such as regular exercise, are associated with numerous benefits and long-term health and wellness outcomes. While the benefits of consistent exercise outweigh the potential risks, health and fitness professionals must be aware of the possible exercise-related injuries, signs and symptoms of exercise intolerance, and how to respond to injuries or **acute** illnesses that may occur in group fitness classes.

If your study program includes the ACE Learning Center, visit www.ACEfitness.org/MyACE and log in to your My ACE Account to learn more about how to respond to medical emergencies in group fitness settings.

RECOGNIZING WARNING SIGNS

ACE Certified Group Fitness Instructors (GFIs) should be able to recognize the observable signs and symptoms that indicate the safety of class participants may be compromised. In the event a participant does sustain an injury or presents signs or symptoms of illness, GFIs must possess the confidence and skillset to respond to emergencies within their **scope of practice.**

Recognizing the warning signs of **overexertion,** illness, or injury is paramount when leading any fitness class, especially if some participants have health limitations or are newer to exercise. Overexertion is defined as pushing oneself past the point of volitional control or exceeding the limits of one's abilities. This typically occurs when the energy systems are taxed beyond tolerable levels. Symptoms may include nausea, dizziness, loss of strength, poor and/or unsafe form and technique, vomiting, and in extreme cases **rhabdomyolysis.**

While not as serious as overexertion, exercise **fatigue** should also be monitored by the GFI. Because the most obvious sign of fatigue is improper exercise technique, GFIs should teach participants that the inability to continue performing an exercise correctly is an indication that they need to modify the movement. Executing any exercise with improper form could reinforce poor technique, increasing the likelihood that it will occur again in the future.

[APPLY WHAT YOU KNOW]

The "Instructor's Eye"

Group fitness programs are typically scheduled with the intent to offer a variety of different exercise classes that might appeal to a large portion of the facility members. In this sense, most schedules are created with apparently healthy individuals in mind and not necessarily those with unique health concerns and needs. Therefore, a GFI must conduct a quick "screening" of participants that often comes in the form of asking them if they are aware of the type or intensity level of the class. Individuals with health limitations will often approach a GFI to inquire about the format of the class and to let the instructor know of their concerns. However, a GFI cannot rely on participants always informing them of their health issues. In addition to asking class participants if they are aware of the physical requirements of the workout and if they have any questions about modifications, the GFI should intently watch for warning signs of exhaustion or injury throughout the class. Experience helps instructors develop the "instructor's eye" for recognizing improper mechanics, erroneous movement patterns, and signs of overexertion. Demonstrating the most basic movement first and then providing progressive options will accommodate most participants (see Chapter 8). Remember, the goal is to provide a safe and effective experience for everyone that yields results and healthy habits.

COMMON INJURIES AND MEDICAL EMERGENCIES

Exercise-related injuries can range from acute (abrupt) to **chronic** (ongoing). The key is to learn the characteristics of the most common injuries and illnesses a GFI could encounter in class, and understand the classic signs and symptoms of serious medical events. A sign is defined as an objective, observable indicator, such as loss of coordination, blue lips, or heavy coughing. A symptom, on the other hand, is a sensory indicator that a participant feels, such as dizziness or nausea. Knowing basic injury and illness management and when to activate emergency medical services (EMS) is within the scope of practice of a GFI and imperative to ensuring participant safety.

Activating EMS should be reserved for life-threatening situations. For all other conditions, GFIs should respond within the scope of practice they learned in **cardiopulmonary resuscitation (CPR), automated external defibrillator (AED),** and first-aid training. ACE requires all GFIs to successfully complete CPR and AED training and encourages first-aid training prior to taking the ACE Group Fitness Instructor Certification Exam. Once certified, GFIs must maintain current CPR/AED certification in order to renew their certification every two years.*

> Understand the classic signs and symptoms

The following sections list some of the most common injuries and acute illnesses a GFI may be faced with over the course of his or her career. Keep in mind this is not an exhaustive, detailed list of conditions, but rather is intended to reflect potential signs of exercise intolerance, injuries, and medical events that could occur in group fitness classes. In many cases, a GFI will not be able to ascertain the specific ailment (unless he or she has medical training and licensure within this scope), but recognizing the difference between life-threatening and non-life-threatening situations is vital for participant safety.

 [EXPAND YOUR KNOWLEDGE]

Acute vs. Chronic Injuries

An abrupt onset of injury or medical emergency, such as twisting an ankle or choking on gum, presents immediate symptoms of distress and is categorized as an acute injury. Chronic injuries, illnesses, or medical conditions, such as **tennis elbow** or **diabetes mellitus**, are ongoing. Sometimes an acute injury can progress into a chronic injury, such as slipping on a wet surface and consequently suffering from a low-back injury leading to chronic back pain. See Chapter 9 for more information on chronic conditions.

*Obtaining and maintaining AED certification is only applicable to regions that allow non-healthcare providers to practice life-saving maneuvers. The American Council on Exercise does not supersede regional or federal laws on this statute. Therefore, this AED requirement will be waived for GFIs who live in regions that prohibit non-healthcare professionals from using AEDs.

MUSCULOSKELETAL INJURIES

Acute musculoskeletal injuries present complex challenges for GFIs, as they can interfere with an individual's ability to participate in exercise and present emergency situations that escalate very quickly, requiring the GFI to remain calm and act swiftly. Table 11-1 highlights several musculoskeletal injuries with which GFIs should be familiar.

Table 11-1

ACUTE MUSCULOSKELETAL INJURIES

INJURY	DESCRIPTION	SIGNS AND/OR SYMPTOMS	ACTIVATE EMS?
Sprain	Tearing or overstretching of a ligament and/or connective tissue. The lateral ankle and anterior cruciate ligament (ACL) of the knee are common sprains.	Swelling, pain, joint instability, immobility, and possible discoloration	Possibly, if the person is not able to move to safety and there are no other means to move the person (e.g., along an outdoor trail).
Strain	Tearing or overstretching of a muscle or tendon. Shoulders and hamstrings are common locations for strains.	Pain, local tenderness, possible discoloration, and loss of strength and range of motion (ROM)	Possibly, if the person is not able to move to safety and there are no other means to move the person (e.g., along an outdoor trail)
Compound fracture	Bone fracture resulting in an open wound	Bony protrusion, bleeding, and possible shock	Yes, especially if there is heavy bleeding
Contusion	A bruise formed from an acute, traumatic blow to the body	Soft tissue hemorrhage, hematoma, and restricted ROM	Possibly, if the person sustains a blow to the head or possible internal bleeding

Sources: American College of Sports Medicine (2014a). *ACSM's Guidelines for Exercise Testing and Prescription* (9th ed.). Philadelphia: Wolters Kluwer/ Lippincott Williams & Wilkins; American Council on Exercise (2014). *ACE Personal Trainer Manual* (5th ed.). San Diego: American Council on Exercise; Prentice, W.E. (2012). *Essentials of Athletic Injury Management* (9th ed.). New York: McGraw-Hill.

Chronic Musculoskeletal Conditions

Some participants may approach a GFI for advice about a condition that is exacerbated by exercise; however, diagnosing or treating medical conditions is outside the scope of a GFI. Because instructors can provide options and modifications to help participants perform pain-free exercise, it is important for the GFI to have general knowledge of several common chronic conditions (Table 11-2).

If pain persists with a particular exercise, GFIs may recommend a modified or different movement, alternative positioning of the body, single-joint movements, or referral for medical evaluation for more severe or ongoing ailments. For example, a participant who struggles with **carpal tunnel syndrome** can avoid placing the wrist in extreme **flexion** or **extension** by adopting a neutral wrist position throughout all upper-body exercises.

Table 11-2

COMMON CHRONIC CONDITIONS

CONDITION	DESCRIPTION	SIGNS AND/OR SYMPTOMS
Tendinitis	Inflammation of a tendon due to overuse	Tenderness, localized or dispersed pain, and loss of strength
Bursitis	Inflammation of a bursa sac near a tendon or joint	Swelling, pain, and some loss of function
Plantar fasciitis	Inflammation of the plantar surface of the foot	Pain and tightness under the foot that may worsen with weight bearing
Shin splints (medial tibial stress syndrome)	Pain or inflammation of the soft tissue(s) along the shin bone from repetitive loading	Bone and soft-tissue tenderness, and pain during and after activity
Iliotibial (IT) band friction syndrome	Inflammatory overuse condition in which the IT band (connective tissue) rubs against the lateral femoral epicondyle (outside of the knee)	Pain, burning, or tightness during running, cycling, or multidirectional movements along the lower outside of the knee
Patellofemoral pain syndrome	Lateral deviation of the patella during knee extension that causes painful contact between the patella and femur	Tenderness, pain, swelling, and discomfort during activity
Impingements	When a muscle, tendon, or nerve pinches between bony structures; common areas are the shoulder and the spine	Local pain and tenderness, burning sensation, loss of range of motion and mobility, and muscle weakness
Low-back pain	Condition resulting from an acute injury or multiple events of microtrauma causing joint or muscle pain	Pain, especially during sudden flexion, extension, or rotation; muscle weakness; and loss of function

CARDIORESPIRATORY EMERGENCIES

Cardiorespiratory emergencies, in which a participant is experiencing difficulty breathing or may not be breathing at all, require immediate activation of EMS. GFIs should be familiar with the signs and symptoms of the conditions outlined in Table 11-3 and be prepared to take action should one of these emergency situations arise.

Table 11-3

CARDIORESPIRATORY EMERGENCIES

CONDITION	DESCRIPTION	SIGNS AND/OR SYMPTOMS	ACTIVATE EMS?
Heart attack	Caused by an obstruction or blockage of blood flow to the heart	Pain in the chest, arms, back, neck, or jaw; labored or difficulty breathing; nausea; anxiety; lightheadedness; sweating; fatigue; and syncope	Yes
Asthma attack	Swelling, inflammation or narrowing of the airways that inhibits breathing	Wheezing, coughing, and pain and/or tightness in the chest and neck; dyspnea; panic; and pale face	Yes, if the person is not able to relieve the symptoms with medication and especially if breathing becomes labored or the person loses consciousness
Choking	When an object obstructs the airway	Coughing, loss of speech, pale or blueish skin, and syncope	Yes, and you can always call off the EMS if the object is dislodged

Sources: American College of Sports Medicine (2014a). *ACSM's Guidelines for Exercise Testing and Prescription* (9th ed.). Philadelphia: Wolters Kluwer/ Lippincott Williams & Wilkins; American Council on Exercise (2014). *ACE Personal Trainer Manual* (5th ed.). San Diego: American Council on Exercise; Prentice, W.E. (2012). *Essentials of Athletic Injury Management* (9th ed.). New York: McGraw-Hill.

CEREBROVASCULAR EMERGENCIES

Cerebrovascular emergencies such as strokes, **seizures,** and concussions can be serious and life-threatening. Table 11-4 provides an overview of the common signs and symptoms that should prompt the GFI to activate EMS.

Table 11-4

CEREBROVASCULAR EMERGENCIES

CONDITION	DESCRIPTION	SIGNS AND/OR SYMPTOMS	ACTIVATE EMS?
Stroke	Cerebrovascular emergency caused by a lack of blood supply and oxygen to the brain	Numbness in the arms, legs, or face; confusion; trouble speaking; dizziness; loss of vision, balance, or coordination; drooping on one side of the face; and loss of consciousness	Yes
Concussion	Impairment of neural function as a result of a direct blow to the head	Shock, blurred vision, sensitivity to light, sleep disturbance, and amnesia. Moderate to severe cases can result in loss of consciousness.	Yes
Seizures	Changes in brain activity that can cause mild to severe convulsions	Convulsions, syncope, loss of coordination, clenching of the jaw, and loss of bladder and/or bowel function	Yes

Sources: American College of Sports Medicine (2014a). *ACSM's Guidelines for Exercise Testing and Prescription* (9th ed.). Philadelphia: Wolters Kluwer/ Lippincott Williams & Wilkins; American Council on Exercise (2014). *ACE Personal Trainer Manual* (5th ed.). San Diego: American Council on Exercise; Prentice, W.E. (2012). *Essentials of Athletic Injury Management* (9th ed.). New York: McGraw-Hill.

METABOLIC EMERGENCIES

Low blood sugar attributed to the physiological and effects of exercise, known as exercise-induced **hypoglycemia,** can occur in group fitness class participants. Signs and symptoms may include dizziness, confusion, hunger, headache, pale skin, sweating, anxiety, weakness, and poor coordination. At the onset of these symptoms, participants should stop activity and check **glucose** levels if possible, then obtain treatment as soon as possible (e.g., medication, juice, or glucose tabs). EMS may need to be activated if these symptoms worsen.

For participants with diabetes, dangerously low blood sugar levels can result in **diabetic shock** (see Chapter 9), characterized by worsening of the signs and symptoms of hypoglycemia with possible loss of consciousness. EMS should be activated immediately if diabetic shock occurs. GFIs should never try to give an unconscious participant anything by mouth (e.g., sugar), as doing so could comprise the individual's airway.

ENVIRONMENTAL EMERGENCIES

Exercising under extreme environmental conditions can add significant stress to the cardiovascular and thermoregulatory systems. GFIs should take special precautions under these conditions and should be aware of the signs and symptoms of heat- and cold-related illnesses (Table 11-5).

Table 11-5

ENVIRONMENTAL EMERGENCIES

CONDITION	DESCRIPTION	SIGNS AND/OR SYMPTOMS	ACTIVE EMS?
Heat cramps	Muscle spasms in the arms, legs, and stomach due to loss of electrolytes and fluids	Painful cramps, loss of strength, thirst, and dehydration	No, but medical attention may be necessary if vomiting or nausea occur
Heat exhaustion	Heat-related illness attributed to hot, humid temperatures and the loss of electrolytes and fluids	Weak, rapid pulse; low blood pressure; fatigue; headache; dizziness; weakness; cold, clammy skin; profuse sweating; dehydration; elevated core temperature	Possibly, if symptoms progress and participant's temperature is not decreasing
Heat stroke	Medical emergency and the most serious heat-related illness resulting from overexposure to heat	Hot, dry skin; red skin color; rapid pulse; anxiety; irritability; dyspnea; dehydration; elevated core temperature (>104° F/40° C); syncope	Yes
Hypothermia	A drop in body temperature below 97° F/40°C.	Shivering, tingling, numbness in fingers and toes, and burning feeling in nose and ears. Extreme exposure can result in fatigue, lethargy, and possible cardiac arrest.	Possibly, if symptoms progress to extreme exposure symptoms, or if participant's temperature is not rising

SOFT-TISSUE INJURIES

Wounds such as **lacerations** (cuts), **punctures** (holes), **avulsions** (skin tearing off), and **abrasions** (scrapes) are injuries that result from an acute trauma to the skin. Signs and symptoms may include bleeding, pain, and exposure of bone, soft tissue, and, in extreme cases, internal organs. If the injury results in heavy, uncontrolled bleeding, EMS should be activated immediately.

PREGNANCY-RELATED EMERGENCIES

While there numerous benefits associated with exercising during pregnancy, including reduced prenatal discomforts, faster recovery from labor, and reduced incidence of postpartum **depression,** there are potential risks of which GFIs should be aware. Due to the fact that pregnant woman have lower fasting blood glucose levels than non-pregnant women and also utilize **carbohydrates** during exercise at a greater rate [American College of Obstetricians and Gynecologists (ACOG), 2002], they are more likely to become hypoglycemic as a result of the heightened physiological demands. If pregnant participants experience signs and symptoms of hypoglycemia such as dizziness, confusion, hunger, headache, pale skin, weakness, and poor coordination, EMS may need to be activated if symptoms do not subside. Pregnant participants who experience hypoglycemic events should be sure to consume food and/or drinks containing easily digestible sugar sources (e.g., fruit or juice) as soon as possible and to contact their healthcare providers. *Note:* ACOG's 2002 guidelines were reaffirmed by the organization in 2009.

> They are more likely to become hypoglycemic

Pregnancy-related emergencies that require immediate activation of EMS include both labor and miscarriage. Miscarriage is the spontaneous loss of pregnancy in which bleeding, extreme cramping, inability to stand, nausea, vomiting, and dizziness may occur.

 [EXPAND YOUR KNOWLEDGE]

Recognizing Exercise Dependence

While the GFI wants to encourage regular exercise participation, it is important to recognize the signs of **exercise dependence** or addiction that may occur in a participants who take the habit of exercise to the extreme. An accepted definition of exercise dependence is when the commitment to exercise assumes a higher priority than other personal commitments (i.e., work and family). Signs and symptoms of exercise dependence/addiction include weight loss in a very short period of time (~10 to 15% of body weight), extreme guilt for missing a workout, compulsive and excessive exercise even when sick or injured, hair loss, dry skin, and dizziness. If the GFI suspects a participant is exercising to excess, it is important that the matter be dealt with directly with the participant, using forethought and sensitivity. However, the activation of EMS may be necessary if a participant's condition progresses to the point that he or she loses consciousness.

 [THINK IT THROUGH]

Apart from the physical aspects of injury, many exercisers struggle with the emotions brought on by healthcare provider recommendations to temporarily reduce or eliminate exercise, especially if they were regularly active prior to the injury. As such, some participants might try to convince you to allow them to participate in a class before their injuries have gone through the appropriate stages of healing, or prior to medical clearance for physical activity. How would you handle someone who requests that you step outside your professional scope of practice and allow him or her to participate in your class before he or she has been cleared for exercise?

INCIDENT MANAGEMENT AND EMERGENCY RESPONSE

Acute injuries need to be handled quickly, but with caution, as participant safety is paramount. A GFI should apply the first aid and emergency response actions learned from their primary emergency training, and refer the participant to an appropriate healthcare provider when an injury is serious enough (e.g., an individual who is unable to walk after twisting an ankle during agility exercises or who feels sudden shoulder pain and weakness after swinging a kettlebell). Injuries that result in heavy bleeding, airway obstruction, labored or loss of breathing, symptoms of **shock,** or unconsciousness are scenarios that necessitate immediate activation of EMS. If an acute injury occurs, early intervention often includes medical management. The acronym RICE (rest or restricted activity, ice, compression, and elevation) describes a safe early-intervention strategy for many acute injuries. In the following example, an ankle injury has taken place (Kaminski et al., 2013).

R	I	C	E
REST OR RESTRICTED ACTIVITY	**ICE**	**COMPRESSION**	**ELEVATION**
Avoid weight-bearing activity until cleared by the physician	Should be applied every hour for 10 to 20 minutes until the tendency for swelling has passed	Involves placing a compression wrap on the area to minimize local swelling	Of the ankle 6 to 10 inches above the level of the heart will also help control swelling. This is done to reduce hemorrhage, inflammation, swelling, and pain.

Maintaining a clean environment is important to minimize the risk of spreading bloodborne pathogens or other bodily fluids that could spread disease or cause infection. First-aid training is highly recommended for GFIs to educate themselves about wound care, precautions to avoid exposure and transmission of diseases, and how to secure the area until emergency services arrive. Such training may even be required in order to work at certain facilities. ACE believes organizations such as the American Red Cross and the American Heart Association possess core competency in this category. Accordingly, CPR, AED, and first-aid training are not delivered in this handbook, and GFIs must complete these trainings through a reputable provider of their choosing.

 **[EXPAND YOUR KNOWLEDGE]**

To Ice or Not to Ice?

Icing, or **cryotherapy,** is a longstanding practice as a first-line treatment for acute soft-tissue injuries. Despite its widespread application, research to support a specific protocol for icing is limited.

Several studies have found that the data to substantiate evidence-based guidelines for icing was lacking and much of what they found was anecdotal (Bleakley et al., 2006; Bleakley, McDonough, & MacAuley, 2004; Hubbard, Aronson, & Denegar, 2004). Hubbard and Denegar (2004) also reviewed cryotherapy outcomes on soft-tissue injury and resolved that cryotherapy seems to be an effective analgesic, but more studies need to be conducted that investigate the efficacy of specific protocols to gain a better understanding of reliable treatment methods. Interestingly, several researchers have conducted studies to compare icing versus no icing and found no differences in pain, swelling, ROM, weight-bearing ability, or function (Laba, 1989; Sloan, Hain, & Pownall, 1989).

While additional icing research is needed, the application of ice appears to be relatively safe and effective for managing acute soft-tissue injury and post-operative pain, and to reduce inflammation. Current recommendations include intermittent (i.e., 10 minutes of ice, 10 minutes no ice, and 10 minutes of ice) or 20 continuous minutes of icing every two hours for the first 24 hours following acute injury. In some situations, healthcare providers may recommend up to 72 hours for continued relief of acute symptoms.

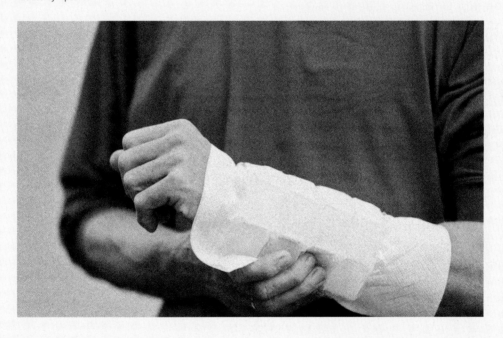

ACTIVATING EMS

Managing life-threatening situations—such as loss of consciousness, obstruction of the airway, impaired breathing or circulation, convulsions, severe bleeding, or apparent shock—takes precedence over all other injuries. A GFI's first reaction in a critical situation is to activate EMS and then assess what emergency care can be rendered, such as CPR, defibrillation with an AED, or locating the victim's medication (e.g., inhaler). In some cases, rescue services will provide emergency care directions over the phone until the medics arrive.

It is appropriate for a GFI to call in any other emergency if he or she is unsure. However, a GFI should not call if there is *not* a true emergency, as doing so can delay response time to true emergencies. For non-emergencies, call the appropriate agency or the emergency contact listed in the participant's file. CPR, AED, and first-aid certifications provide training and education to understand the various circumstances and courses of action to take during a medical emergency.

Remember that the diagnosis and treatment of injuries is outside the scope of practice of a GFI.

Accident Reporting

Regardless of the safety measures provided, some injuries are going to occur on occasion during fitness activities. When someone is injured, it is necessary for the GFI to file an accident report at the facility. Accident reports should include the following information:

- Name, address, and phone number of the injured person
- Time, date, and place of the accident
- A brief description of the part of the body affected and the nature of the injury (e.g., "cut on the right hand")
- A description and model number of any equipment involved
- A reference to any instruction given and the type of supervision in force at the time of the injury
- A brief, factual description of how the injury occurred (no opinions as to cause or fault)
- Names, addresses, and phone numbers of any witnesses
- A brief statement of actions taken at the time of the injury (e.g., first aid given, physician referral, or ambulance called)
- Signatures of the supervisor and the injured person

Accident reports should be kept for several years, depending on the statute of limitations in each state or country. If the person was injured in a formal class setting, it may also be helpful to file a class outline or lesson plan with the accident report. In addition, a yearly review of injuries can be helpful in reducing accidents causing injuries to participants.

>> If a GFI collects medical information about a participant following an incident or accident, the victim's information must be kept confidential and only shared with management or medical providers. The **Health Insurance Portability and Accountability Act (HIPAA)** of 1996 is a federal law that protects a victim's privacy by putting the individual in control of who has access to his or her health and medical records. Therefore, accident and incident reporting documents must be stored in a locked area. See Chapter 12 for more information on participant confidentiality.

STRATEGIES FOR PREVENTING COMMON INJURIES

I t can be a challenging task to create an environment in which participants can achieve their varied fitness goals, while also addressing each of the participant's individual needs to ensure everyone's safety. Doing so requires knowledge of the factors associated with injuries, methods for prevention, and appropriate modifications for specific limitations.

The injury-related responsibilities of GFIs are to:

1 Prevent injury by carefully planning and delivering every exercise class

2 Provide regressions for participants with movement limitations

3 Address injuries that may occur during a class

Execution of these responsibilities is challenging because participants attending a group fitness class have a wide variety of exercise goals, backgrounds, and physical strengths or limitations. It is the job of a GFI to encourage participants to work within their own individual limits and to inform them that they ultimately have control over their workout intensity. The instructor is there for the participants' workout, not his or her own, and should appropriately set the intensity of the class by example. It is important to remember that the risk of a musculoskeletal injury occurring or being aggravated is always present during exercise. Therefore, a primary objective for a GFI is to provide a safe environment for all participants.

With new class formats constantly being introduced into group fitness schedules, ranging from yoga and martial arts to group strength training and **high-intensity interval training,** GFIs must be able to manage risks and provide modifications for participants with limitations. Success is dependent on understanding musculoskeletal injuries, their causes, and contraindications for participation.

Obtaining pre-screening questionnaires and **informed consent** forms generally falls under the responsibility of the facility operators (see Chapter 12). Additionally, some participants may require a medical clearance based upon pre-existing conditions and contraindications. Once these guidelines are met, the GFI can proceed with leading a group fitness class that is appropriate for a diverse group of participants.

RISK FACTORS AND PREVENTION

The risk of in-class injuries and medical emergencies can be higher when the environment poses extrinsic risk factors, or if one or more participants possesses intrinsic factors. GFIs can help reduce or mitigate these risks by eliminating some of the extrinsic factors, as introduced in Chapter 4, and provide modifications for those who may possess intrinsic factors.

Tables 11-6 and 11-7 provide an overview of the most common group fitness–related intrinsic and extrinsic factors and how a GFI can respond and reduce the risks when possible.

Table 11-6

INTRINSIC RISK FACTORS IN GROUP FITNESS

INTRINSIC	GFI PREVENTION/COURSE OF ACTION
Pre-existing injuries, ailments, and conditions (including age and any of the conditions described in Table 11-2)	Provide regressions to reduce range of motion (ROM), intensity, complexity, and duration of exercise. Offer exercises that do not involve the affected body part(s) and avoid ballistic exercises. Participants with known cardiovascular, pulmonary, or metabolic conditions should obtain a physician's consent prior to activity.
Unhealthy body composition	Suggest lower-impact exercises and demonstrate basic movements before progressing intensity and complexity. If an eating disorder or exercise addiction is suspected, a GFI should confront the participant with sensitivity and provide professional guidance about healthy exercise habits and body weight, and refer him or her to a healthcare provider.
Deconditioned	Suggest fewer repetitions and sets, and shorter exercise bouts. Provide ratings of perceived exertion (RPE) periodically so participants are aware of what a particular interval or exercise should "feel" like. Offer options for active recovery and coach participants to focus on quality of movement and exercise technique.
Strength or flexibility imbalances	Limit ROM by reducing the amount of joint movement required to achieve the exercises(s). Begin with dynamic flexibility movements and end with static stretches. Offer yoga blocks, bolsters, and stretch straps for support. . The goal is to perform the exercises pain-free.

Table 11-7

EXTRINSIC RISK FACTORS IN GROUP FITNESS

EXTRINSIC	GFI RESPONSE/COURSE OF ACTION
Complexity, intensity, speed, and type of movement	Beginners and deconditioned participants should master the foundational exercise layers before advancing to movements that demand more coordination, speed, metabolic conditioning, and developed technique. GFIs should always demonstrate the foundational layers first, and then provide advanced progressions.
Number of repetitions and sets	Performing exercises or movements beyond one's ability poses risks for improper form, poor technique, and injury. Suggest lighter loads or alternate exercises to allow active recovery.
Surface	Perform lateral movements cautiously on carpet or uneven surfaces. Harder surfaces are ideal for group fitness classes (see Chapter 4).
Footwear	Running shoes lack lateral support, but many group fitness classes incorporate running; therefore, a hybrid shoe, such as a cross-trainer, is suitable for short distances. For dance classes, participants should wear shoes with lateral support and minimal tread on the sole. Barefoot dancing, running, or cross-training is only advisable provided one has progressed into barefoot training and is free of preexisting conditions that are contraindicated for barefoot exercise (e.g., diabetic neuropathy, athletes' foot, or a history of ankle or foot injury).
Fatigue	Suggest fluid breaks, create active recovery opportunities by targeting different energy systems, or discontinue the activity for the day. Fatigue affects neural activation, and therefore can affect coordination, balance, speed, and acuity.
Equipment	Use equipment according to the manufacturer's instructions. Building homemade equipment for public use is not advisable because the quality, safety, and applicability of the unit has not been validated or deemed reliable by authoritative safety testing organizations.
Climate/temperature	Clothing should be breathable while providing protection from the elements. Participants who show signs of heat illness or hypothermia should stop exercising and seek medical treatment if signs and symptoms do not subside. Exercise indoors on days with extreme temperatures or humidity. Hot, humid rooms, such as in hot yoga, can be contraindicated for some populations. Anyone considering exercising in a hot environment needs to allow time to gradually acclimate. Fluid replacement is critical for every participant.
Altitude	The only way to acclimate to altitude is to ascend slowly. Oxygen may be indicated for exercisers who present symptoms of altitude sickness.
Air quality	Areas with high pollution or allergens can affect one's cardiorespiratory response to exercise. The U.S. Environmental Protection Agency posts alerts and information about air quality in hundreds of U.S. and Canadian cities. Avoid outdoor exercise on high alert days. www.airnow.gov

MINIMIZING RISK THROUGH INSTRUCTIONAL STRATEGIES

Symptoms of many musculoskeletal injuries or wounds include pain, swelling, loss of motion and strength, reduced functional capacity, and bleeding. These symptoms are present in various degrees and combinations in most injuries. Acute injuries are the result of an immediate trauma. Chronic injuries are developed gradually from repeated stress over time. As covered in this chapter, both types of injuries can be caused by any number of factors, including footwear, flooring or exercise surface, equipment, movement execution, class intensity, and frequency of participation. Other factors, such as teaching techniques and the inclusion of a proper warm-up and cool-down, are discussed in previous chapters.

Preventing or managing injuries within the scope of a GFI can be summarized by a few key concepts and guidelines (Anderson & Parr, 2012; Prentice, 2012):

- Limit motion and stretching to a pain-free range and intensity.
- Gradually increase the intensity of activity and volume (load x repetitions).
- Focus on technique and proper form.
- Avoid extreme ROM.
    - ✔ Assess the appropriateness of jumping, especially box jumps and other plyometric-type techniques with high loads. Load **closed-kinetic-chain exercises,** such as squats and lunges, according to the tolerance of the joints (including the back). Avoid excessive flexion for knee injuries.
    - ✔ Teach overhead-activity modifications, such as avoiding full extension of the arms and positioning the shoulders more toward the front of the body (i.e., in the **scapular plane,** where the shoulder is positioned between the **sagittal plane** and the **frontal plane,** approximately 30 degrees anterior to the frontal plane (Figure 11-1).
- Check equipment for proper fit. Repetitive movements, like cycling, can cause inflammation of the soft tissues if the equipment is improperly fit to the exerciser.

Figure 11-1
Shoulder press in the scapular plane, which lies 30 degrees anterior to the frontal plane

UNDERSTANDING FACILITY
POLICIES AND PROCEDURES

While some emergency situations are unavoidable, the best approach is to be prepared. The AHA and American College of Sports Medicine (ACSM) publish guidelines for fitness facilities that involve pre-screening members, having adequate staffing, and establishing emergency policies. A fitness facility can take the following steps to minimize the risk of injuries (ACSM, 2014b; Balady et al., 1998):

▬ Fitness staff should hold current certifications accredited by the National Commission for Certifying Agencies (NCCA) or equivalent in their specialty areas (e.g., personal training, group fitness instruction, or lifeguarding). If a staff member works with special population groups such as seniors, youth, or prenatal or postpartum women, additional training for working safely and effectively with that population is recommended.

▬ Record and track all employees' CPR, AED, first aid, and fitness certification information including the issuing organization, issue date, certification number, and expiration date.

▬ Many states now have laws that require health clubs to have at least one AED on the premises. Visit the Sudden Cardiac Arrest Foundation's website www.sca-aware.org/aed-laws for an updated listing.

▬ Facilities should screen new members to identify those at high risk for cardiovascular events by using a simple screening questionnaire such as the **Physical Activity Readiness Questionnaire (PAR-Q)** (Figure 11-2). Collecting and maintaining this information is typically outside the scope of a GFI, but it is important to understand the significance and necessity of this information. The PAR-Q can help to identify high-risk individuals who need medical referral or require modifications to their exercise programs. This tool can also help identify the need for additional qualified staff members if there are a number of high-risk participants (ACSM, 2014b; Balady et al., 1998).

▬ Fitness facilities should establish a method of notifying participants about the risk of injury associated with exercise, such as having new members sign informed consent forms. Additionally, fitness facilities should have participants complete medical screening forms and obtain medical clearance when necessary, as determined by the participant's risk stratification (ACSM, 2014b).

The club should take responsibility for minimizing any additional risks by ensuring the following (ACSM, 2014b; Balady et al., 1998):

▬ Adequate staffing and supervision

▬ Cleanliness and clear walkways

▬ Adequate lighting

▬ Nonslip surfaces around showers and pools

▬ Caution signs for wet floors and other hazards (for example, "No Diving" signs at the shallow end of the pool)

▬ Regular maintenance and repair of equipment

▬ A clean drinking water supply

▬ Fire/smoke alarms installed

▬ Limiting the number of people in the building and in group fitness classes to avoid overcrowding

▬ First-aid kits that are kept in convenient locations and assigned to someone to restock on a regular basis

▬ Phones that can be easily accessed with emergency numbers posted nearby

▬ Establishing and practicing an emergency action plan that includes what documentation should be kept, the location of emergency equipment (first-aid kits, AEDs, how to use the land lines, emergency exits, and accessible emergency routes).

Figure 11-2
Physical Activity Readiness
Questionnaire (PAR-Q)

Physical Activity Readiness
Questionnaire - PAR-Q
(revised 2002)

PAR-Q & YOU

(A Questionnaire for People Aged 15 to 69)

Regular physical activity is fun and healthy, and increasingly more people are starting to become more active every day. Being more active is very safe for most people. However, some people should check with their doctor before they start becoming much more physically active.

If you are planning to become much more physically active than you are now, start by answering the seven questions in the box below. If you are between the ages of 15 and 69, the PAR-Q will tell you if you should check with your doctor before you start. If you are over 69 years of age, and you are not used to being very active, check with your doctor.

Common sense is your best guide when you answer these questions. Please read the questions carefully and answer each one honestly: check YES or NO.

YES	NO		
☐	☐	**1.**	**Has your doctor ever said that you have a heart condition <u>and</u> that you should only do physical activity recommended by a doctor?**
☐	☐	**2.**	**Do you feel pain in your chest when you do physical activity?**
☐	☐	**3.**	**In the past month, have you had chest pain when you were not doing physical activity?**
☐	☐	**4.**	**Do you lose your balance because of dizziness or do you ever lose consciousness?**
☐	☐	**5.**	**Do you have a bone or joint problem (for example, back, knee or hip) that could be made worse by a change in your physical activity?**
☐	☐	**6.**	**Is your doctor currently prescribing drugs (for example, water pills) for your blood pressure or heart condition?**
☐	☐	**7.**	**Do you know of <u>any other reason</u> why you should not do physical activity?**

If
you
answered

YES to one or more questions

Talk with your doctor by phone or in person BEFORE you start becoming much more physically active or BEFORE you have a fitness appraisal. Tell your doctor about the PAR-Q and which questions you answered YES.

- You may be able to do any activity you want — as long as you start slowly and build up gradually. Or, you may need to restrict your activities to those which are safe for you. Talk with your doctor about the kinds of activities you wish to participate in and follow his/her advice.
- Find out which community programs are safe and helpful for you.

NO to all questions

If you answered NO honestly to <u>all</u> PAR-Q questions, you can be reasonably sure that you can:
- start becoming much more physically active – begin slowly and build up gradually. This is the safest and easiest way to go.
- take part in a fitness appraisal – this is an excellent way to determine your basic fitness so that you can plan the best way for you to live actively. It is also highly recommended that you have your blood pressure evaluated. If your reading is over 144/94, talk with your doctor before you start becoming much more physically active.

DELAY BECOMING MUCH MORE ACTIVE:
- if you are not feeling well because of a temporary illness such as a cold or a fever – wait until you feel better; or
- if you are or may be pregnant – talk to your doctor before you start becoming more active.

PLEASE NOTE: If your health changes so that you then answer YES to any of the above questions, tell your fitness or health professional. Ask whether you should change your physical activity plan.

<u>Informed Use of the PAR-Q</u>: The Canadian Society for Exercise Physiology, Health Canada, and their agents assume no liability for persons who undertake physical activity, and if in doubt after completing this questionnaire, consult your doctor prior to physical activity.

No changes permitted. You are encouraged to photocopy the PAR-Q but only if you use the entire form.

NOTE: If the PAR-Q is being given to a person before he or she participates in a physical activity program or a fitness appraisal, this section may be used for legal or administrative purposes.

"I have read, understood and completed this questionnaire. Any questions I had were answered to my full satisfaction."

NAME _____

SIGNATURE _____ DATE_____

SIGNATURE OF PARENT _____ WITNESS _____
or GUARDIAN (for participants under the age of majority)

Note: This physical activity clearance is valid for a maximum of 12 months from the date it is completed and becomes invalid if your condition changes so that you would answer YES to any of the seven questions.

© Canadian Society for Exercise Physiology www.csep.ca/forms

SUMMARY

GFIs have several responsibilities regarding musculoskeletal injuries. They must:

1. Prevent injury by carefully planning and delivering every exercise class
2. Provide regressions for participants with injury limitations
3. Respond to injuries that may occur during a movement

Success is dependent on knowing the factors associated with injuries, methods for prevention, and contraindications and appropriate modifications. Providing modifications for all participants based on their needs is difficult but essential to ensure an outstanding exercise experience for everyone.

Fitness facilities can better serve their members and avoid possible emergency situations by having a risk-management plan, having an AED available, and maintaining a well-stocked first-aid kit. Although the diagnosis and treatment of injuries is outside the scope of practice for GFIs, all health and fitness professionals should have knowledge and understanding of possible medical emergencies that can arise during group fitness classes. GFIs should learn to recognize medical emergencies and know when it is necessary to activate EMS.

References

American College of Obstetricians and Gynecologists (2002). Exercise during pregnancy and the postpartum period, ACOG Committee Opinion No. 276. *Obstetrics and Gynecology*, 99, 171–173.

American College of Sports Medicine (2014a). *ACSM's Guidelines for Exercise Testing and Prescription* (9th ed.). Philadelphia: Wolters Kluwer/Lippincott Williams & Wilkins.

American College of Sports Medicine (2014b). *ACSM's Resource Manual for Guidelines for Exercise Testing and Prescription* (7th ed.). Philadelphia: Wolters Kluwer/Lippincott Williams & Wilkins.

American Council on Exercise (2014). *ACE Personal Trainer Manual* (5th ed.). San Diego: American Council on Exercise.

Anderson, M.K. & Parr, G.P. (2012). *Foundations of Athletic Training: Prevention, Assessment, and Management* (5th ed.). Philadelphia: Wolters Kluwer/Lippincott Williams & Wilkins.

Balady, G.J. et al. (1998). AHA/ACSM Scientific Statement: Recommendations for cardiovascular screening, staffing, and emergency policies at health/fitness facilities: A Joint Position Statement by the American College of Sports Medicine and the American Heart Association. *Circulation*, 97, 2283–2293.

Bleakley, C.M., McDonough, S.M., & MacAuley, D.C. (2004). The use of ice in the treatment of acute soft-tissue injury: A systematic review of randomized controlled trials. *American Journal of Sports Medicine*, 32, 1, 251–261.

Bleakley, C.M. et al. (2006). Cryotherapy for acute ankle sprains: A randomised controlled study of two different icing protocols. *British Journal of Sports Medicine*, 40, 8, 700–705.

Hubbard, T.J., Aronson, S.L., & Denegar, C.R. (2004). Does cryotherapy hasten return to participation? A systematic review. *Journal of Athletic Training*, 39, 1, 88–94.

Hubbard, T.J. & Denegar, C.R. (2004). Does cryotherapy improve outcomes with soft tissue injury? *Journal of Athletic Training*, 39, 3, 278–279.

Kaminski, T.W. et al. (2013). National Athletic Trainers' Association position statement: Conservative management and prevention of ankle sprains in athletes. *Journal of Athletic Training*, 48, 4, 528–545. DOI: 10.4085/1062-6050-48.4.02

Laba, E. (1989). Clinical evaluation of ice therapy for acute ankle sprain injuries. *New Zealand Journal of Physiotherapy*, 17, 7–9.

Prentice, W.E. (2012). *Essentials of Athletic Injury Management* (9th ed.). New York: McGraw-Hill.

Sloan, J.P., Hain, R., & Pownall, R. (1989). Clinical benefits of early cold therapy in accident and emergency following ankle sprain. *Archives of Emergency Medicine*, 6, 1, 1–6.

CHAPTER 12

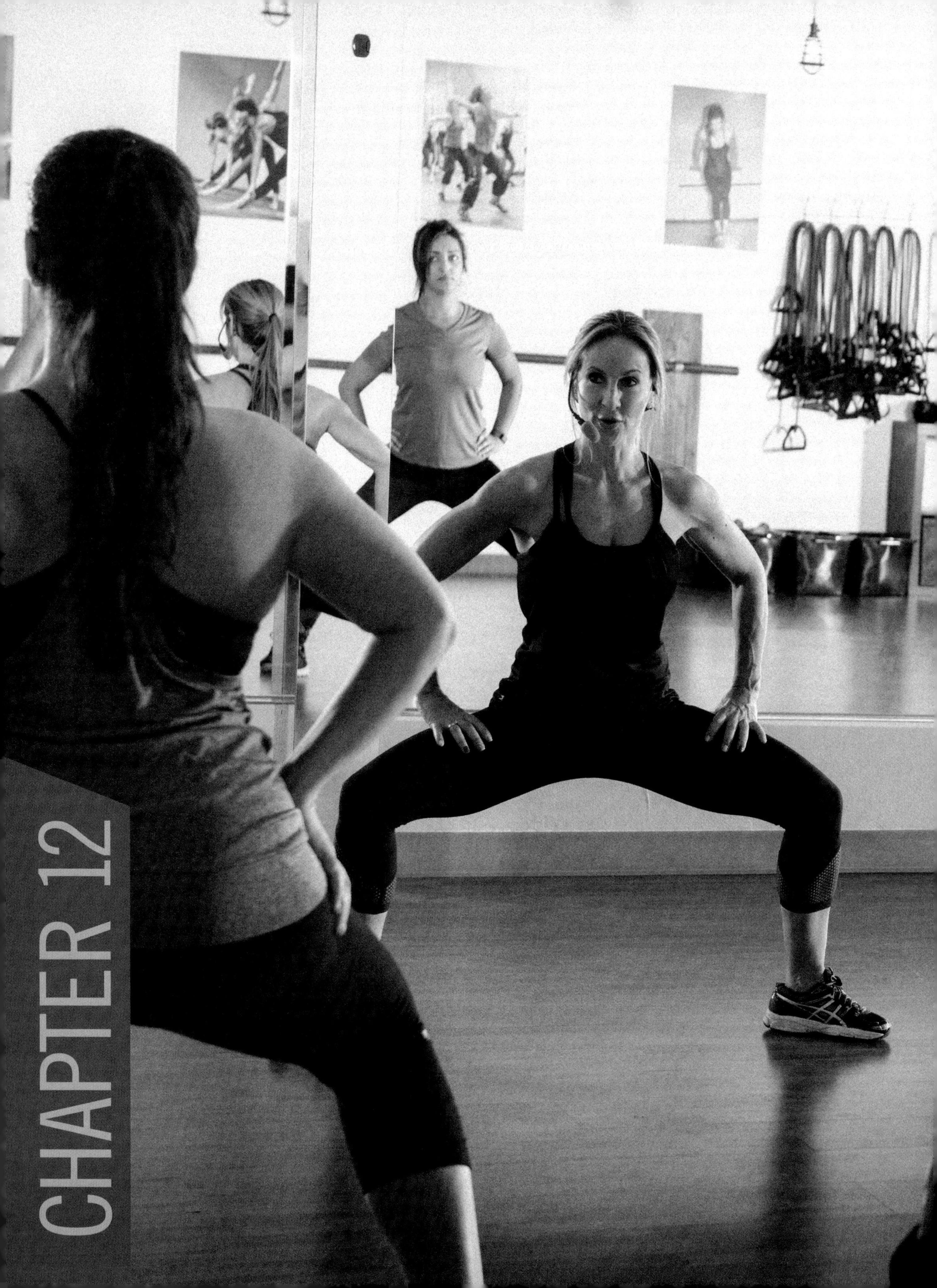

CHAPTER 12

LEGAL GUIDELINES AND PROFESSIONAL RESPONSIBILITIES

MARK NAGEL

LEARNING OBJECTIVES

■ Identify ways to stay current through ongoing education and training in order to safely and effectively instruct participants.

■ Understand important legal terms—including liability, negligence, standard of care, copyright, and trademarks—and how each relates to a career in the fitness industry.

■ List and describe a group fitness instructor's responsibilities related to health screening, instruction, supervision, facilities, and equipment.

■ Explain the appropriate use of legal forms, including waivers, informed consents, and agreements to participate.

■ Describe the differences between an independent contractor and employee.

In order to provide safe and effective classes in which both participants and the instructor are protected legally, ACE Certified Group Fitness Instructors (GFIs) must understand the fundamental professional and business-related concerns that pertain to the group fitness environment. This chapter offers guidance to help instructors navigate the legal aspects of a career in the health and fitness industry.

If your study program includes the ACE Learning Center, visit www.ACEfitness.org/MyACE and log in to your My ACE Account for an overview of legal considerations, including the use of shared space, music copyright considerations, and best practices for using social media.

PROFESSIONAL CONDUCT

The decision to pursue certification as a GFI is an important step in being a recognized and respected professional in the field of health and fitness. Those who earn the ACE Group Fitness Instructor Certification demonstrate competency in designing and delivering safe, effective, and engaging fitness class experiences that enhance the general well-being and movement abilities of class participants. While the newly certified GFI has proven his or her ability to appropriately apply broad-based knowledge of various subjects in a variety of practical situations, this credential should be viewed

> Ongoing education and training are both necessary and required

as the foundation of professional development. Ongoing education and training are both necessary and required, as is a thorough understanding of one's professional boundaries and **scope of practice** in order to protect and best serve participants.

CONTINUING EDUCATION

GFIs are encouraged to pursue continuing education in areas of personal interest as well as those that best serve the needs of participants (see Chapter 1). Factors that should be considered when evaluating continuing education courses include identifying courses with level-appropriate content, selecting educational opportunities that are offered in a preferred learning format (e.g., live workshop or home study course), verifying that the instructor has the appropriate qualifications to teach the course, learning if the course is ACE-approved or will have to be petitioned for continuing education credits (CECs), and determining if the education provided is within the GFI's scope of practice.

While completing continuing education in more than one area of interest can be beneficial in terms of diversifying the GFI's career path options, focusing on a specific modality (e.g., indoor cycling) or participant demographic (e.g., older adults) can prove helpful in establishing the GFI as a recognized and sought-after expert in a given discipline.

BEST PRACTICES FOR STAYING CURRENT ON RESEARCH AND GUIDELINES

The dynamic nature of the health and fitness industry requires professionals to maintain an understanding of the latest research and professional standards and guidelines, and how they impact the design and delivery of movement-based classes. To stay abreast of the most current information and best practices, GFIs must make time to regularly review a variety of credible industry resources such as professional journals, position statements, guidelines from leading professional organizations [e.g., United States Department of Agriculture (USDA) and American College of Obstetricians and Gynecologists (ACOG)], and trade and lay periodicals. GFIs should also attend professional meetings, conferences, and workshops, and complete web-based courses and online educational offerings (e.g., webinars) whenever possible.

REFERRALS

GFIs must have a clear understanding of their professional qualifications and boundaries (see Chapter 1), and always refer participants who require services and guidance outside of their scope of practice to the appropriate qualified fitness, medical, or health professionals. It is most prudent for GFIs to network and develop **rapport** with other health professionals in their local area first before referring participants, as doing so demonstrates a strong commitment to the safety and well-being of participants while also conveying great respect for the expertise and services of these important professionals, many of whom may provide reciprocal referrals. GFIs must also be well-versed in the scope of practice of various professionals in order to ensure referrals are appropriate so that participants are promptly provided with the attention and care that they need. Knowing both when and how to refer participants enhances the GFI's credibility, while also providing clarity about the services and information the GFI does and does not have the legal right to offer.

[EXPAND YOUR KNOWLEDGE]

Developing a Referral Network

It is important for a GFI to develop a network of referral sources to meet the varying needs of his or her participants. Instructors should identify allied health professionals who are reputable and aspire to the same professional standards as an ACE Certified Group Fitness Instructor. Potential referral sources include, but are not limited to:

- Instructors of classes outside a GFI's expertise (e.g., tai chi, aquatic fitness, or sports conditioning)
- Personal trainers
- Health coaches
- Certified medical exercise specialists
- Support groups (e.g., bariatric surgery, cancer survivors, and Overeaters Anonymous)
- Massage therapists
- Registered dietitians
- Physical therapists

As the GFI develops a referral network, it is important to research instructors, programs, and/or organizations before recommending any programs or services to a participant. Pertinent questions to ask include: (1) Do they have the proper licensure or certification? (2) Can they provide a list of references? and (3) How many years of experience do they have? The GFI does not want to jeopardize his or her reputation by referring participants to substandard health and fitness "professionals." With proper networking, the GFI may also gain referrals from the other health and fitness professionals within the network.

LEGAL FRAMEWORK

Although most people who teach or administer group fitness programs have received training in exercise instruction, often their knowledge of the law related to their profession is limited. With the continual evolution of the health and fitness industry, GFIs must develop and maintain an understanding of basic legal concepts that apply to the field in which they practice. From employment status and **copyright** law to insurance coverage and **risk management,** learning how these concepts apply to the group fitness setting will help to minimize the risk of injury to participants, decrease the potential for litigation, and mitigate potential damages.

[THINK IT THROUGH]

How much time do you spend thinking about the law and its impact upon your career as a GFI? What specific legal-related questions do you have that pertain to your profession?

LIABILITY AND NEGLIGENCE

The term **liability** refers to responsibility. Legal liability concerns the responsibilities recognized by a court of law. Every GFI who stands in front of a class maintains the responsibilities of recognizing the capacities of, and setting limitations on, participants before they begin and as they continue throughout an exercise program. They also have the added responsibility of ensuring that the facilities and equipment are appropriate and safe before beginning any exercise activity. Although health and fitness professionals simply cannot avoid liability, liabilities may be reduced through adherence to the appropriate **standard of care** and the implementation of certain risk-management principles.

The responsibilities arising from the relationship between the GFI and the participant produce a legal expectation, commonly referred to as the standard of care. This means that the quality of services provided in a fitness setting is commensurate with current professional standards.

Negligence is usually defined as "failure to act as a reasonable and prudent person would act under a similar circumstance." For the GFI, this definition has two important components.

The first deals specifically with actions. "Failure to act" refers to acts of omission as well as acts of commission. In other words, a GFI can be successfully sued for not doing something that should have been done, as well as for doing something that should not have been done. The second part of the definition of negligence pertains to the appropriateness of the action in light of the standard of care, or a "reasonable and prudent" professional standard. In a lawsuit, the court would ask the question, "What would a reasonable, competent, and prudent GFI do in a similar situation?" If other qualified instructors would have acted similarly under the same circumstances, a court would probably not find an instructor's action negligent.

To legally substantiate a charge of negligence, four elements must be shown to exist. As stated by Wong (2010), they are: (1) that the **defendant** (person being sued) had a duty to protect the **plaintiff** (person filing the suit) from injury; (2) that the defendant failed to exercise the standard of care necessary to perform that duty; (3) that such failure was the proximate cause of an injury; and (4) that the injury caused damage to occur to the plaintiff.

 [APPLY WHAT YOU KNOW]

Negligence Example

A GFI is leading a **high-intensity interval training (HIIT)** class in which a participant badly sprains her ankle while following instructions for a series of high-impact exercises. The movement sequence that directly led to the injury consisted of an excessive number of jump squats. If the participant sues the instructor for negligence, the following questions and answers would likely be discussed in court:

▬ *Was it the instructor's duty to provide proper instruction?* Yes, instructors of group fitness classes have a duty to their participants.

▬ *Was that duty satisfactorily performed?* Performing an excessive number of repetitions of a high-intensity, high-impact exercise like jump squats is not usually advocated by group fitness instructors, indicating that the standard of care was likely violated.

▬ *Was the instructor's failure to provide safe instruction the direct cause of the injury?* The plaintiff will likely successfully argue that the injury was directly caused by the excessive repetition of the movement.

▬ *Did actual damages occur?* The plaintiff's doctor will certainly testify that an injury occurred and, at a minimum, damages involving medical care will be sought.

AREAS OF RESPONSIBILITY

The duties assigned to health and fitness professionals vary from one position to another and from organization to organization. Four major areas of responsibility are presented in this section: **health screening,** instruction, supervision, and facilities and equipment. Each area poses unique questions that are important to every certified instructor. ACE's Code of Ethics is helpful in guiding the actions of health and fitness professionals (see Appendix A).

HEALTH SCREENING

A health and fitness professional's responsibility begins when a new participant walks in the door. Most prospective participants will be apparently healthy individuals interested in improving their personal health and fitness. Others, however, may not have exercised in years or may have various health/medical conditions that affect their safety while participating in physical activity. Although most GFIs are not responsible for health screening, it is recommended that facility personnel conduct a pre-participation screening for each participant to document any existing conditions that might affect safe performance in an exercise program (see Chapter 9).

The screening procedure should be valid, simple, cost- and time-efficient, and, most importantly, appropriate for the target population. Screening questionnaires should ideally be interpreted and documented by qualified staff to limit the number of unnecessary medical referrals and avoid barriers to participation. In many cases, the health-history form may indicate that certain individuals should not be participating in certain forms of physical activity or should only participate to a certain level of exertion.

Instructors have been charged with negligence for not accurately assessing available information that could have prevented an injury. Every fitness facility should establish policies and procedures to ensure that each participant's personal history and medical information are taken into account.

> ## ❯❯ HEALTH SCREENING GUIDELINES
>
> Each participant beginning a fitness program should receive a thorough screening. In many facilities and programs, this screening will be performed by someone other than the GFI. Specific risk-management criteria may include the following:
>
> ━━ Evaluation is conducted prior to participating in exercise.
>
> ━━ Screening methods concur with national guidelines (such as those recommended by the American Council on Exercise, American College of Sports Medicine, and American Heart Association).

INSTRUCTION

To conduct a safe and effective exercise class, GFIs are expected to provide instruction that is both adequate and proper. Adequate instruction refers to the amount of direction given to participants before and during activity that is both sufficient and understandable. For example, an instructor who asks a class to perform an exercise without first demonstrating how to do it properly could be found negligent if a participant performs the exercise incorrectly and is injured as a result. Proper instruction, on the other hand, is factually correct and reflects what a reasonable, prudent instructor would provide in the same situation. In other words, an instructor may be liable for a participant's injury resulting from an exercise that was not demonstrated or was demonstrated improperly, or from an unsafe exercise that should not have been included in a group fitness class based on the GFI's standard of care.

In the courtroom, the correctness of instruction is usually assessed by an expert witness who describes the proper procedures for conducting the activity in question. Therefore, the instructional techniques used by a GFI should be consistent with professionally recognized standards. Proper certification from a program accredited by the National Commission for Certifying Agencies (NCCA) or a comparable third-party accreditor of certification programs, as well as appropriate documentation of training (e.g., degrees and continuing education) can enhance a GFI's competence in the eyes of a court, should he or she ever be charged with negligence.

In addition to providing adequate and proper instruction, as discussed in Chapter 8, GFIs should also be careful not to diagnose or suggest treatment for injuries. This includes not only those injuries sustained in class, but also those injuries that occur during other activities. When participants ask for medical advice regarding injuries, GFIs must refer them to the appropriate medical provider. In general, only physicians and certain other healthcare providers are allowed to diagnose and treat injuries.

 [APPLY WHAT YOU KNOW]

Considerations When Offering Advice

Even providing advice that may seem like "common sense" to the GFI can result in potential legal problems, especially when the participant is not familiar with typical injury rehabilitation.

Consider the following situation: When a participant sprained her ankle during a group fitness class, the instructor told her to go home and ice the ankle to reduce the swelling. Because the ice made the injury feel much better, the participant kept her foot in ice water for two hours. As a consequence, several of her toes later had to be amputated because of frostbite.

While this example may be extreme, it serves as a valuable warning, as the instructor could have avoided this unfortunate situation. In an instance like this the best approach would be for the GFI to provide specific instructions (both written and verbal) on the first-aid procedures recommended by the American Heart Association or the American Red Cross and suggest that if the injury did not respond well, then the participant should seek the advice of a physician.

 INSTRUCTION GUIDELINES

A GFI must provide instruction that is both "adequate and proper." To fulfill this standard of care, the following criteria would apply to instruction:

- Instructions or directions provided to participants prior to, and during, activity are sufficient and understandable.

- The GFI conforms to the standard of care (what a reasonable and prudent instructor would provide in the same situation).

SUPERVISION

The GFI is responsible for supervising all aspects of a class. The standards that apply to supervision are the same as those for instruction: adequate and proper. A prerequisite to determining adequate supervision is the ratio of participants to instructors. A prudent instructor should allow a class to be only as large as can be competently monitored. The participant:instructor ratio will, of course, vary with activity, facility, and type of participant. An exercise class of 30 may be appropriate in a large yoga studio, but too big for a Pilates reformer class. Adequate and proper supervision may be different for a class of seasoned participants than for a class of novice exercisers.

>> **SUPERVISION GUIDELINES**

GFIs must perform their supervisory duties in accordance with the following professionally devised and established guidelines:

— Continuous supervision is provided in immediate proximity to the participant to ensure safety.

— Larger groups are supervised from the perimeter of the exercise area to ensure all participants are in full view of the instructor.

— Specific supervision is employed when the activity merits close attention to an individual participant.

FACILITIES AND EQUIPMENT

Safety is the basic issue for a fitness facility. Instructors should continually inspect the environment and ensure that it is free from unreasonable hazards, as discussed in Chapter 7, and that all areas of the facility are appropriate for the specific type of activity to be conducted in that area. For example, dance-based fitness and martial arts classes require a floor surface that will cushion the feet, knees, and legs from inordinate amounts of stress (see Chapter 4).

Some facilities provide locker rooms and showers for participants to use. These areas must be sanitary and the floors must be textured to reduce accidental slipping. Although most GFIs are not responsible for designing and maintaining the fitness facility, any potential problem the GFI detects should be reported and corrected as soon as possible. Until then, appropriate signs should be clearly posted to warn participants of the unsafe conditions, and access to the area should be restricted.

In some cases, a GFI may be assigned to teach in an area of the fitness facility that is unsafe or inappropriate for the activity. Under these circumstances, a prudent instructor would refuse to teach and would document that decision in writing to club or studio management so that constructive action may be taken.

For a program that uses exercise equipment, the legal concerns center primarily on selection, installation, maintenance, and repair. Equipment should meet all appropriate safety and design standards in the industry. If the equipment has been recently purchased from a competent manufacturer and is maintained properly, these standards will probably be met.

Instructors and supervisors should instruct each participant regarding equipment safety. In addition, each instructor and participant should be required to examine the equipment before each use and report any problems immediately (see Chapter 7).

›› FACILITY AND EQUIPMENT GUIDELINES

The central focus is whether the environment is free from unreasonable hazards. Examples of risk-management criteria include the following:

— The floor surface is appropriate for each activity.

— Lighting is adequate for performance of the skill and for supervision.

— Entrances and exits are well marked.

In terms of equipment, the legal concerns center primarily on selection, maintenance, and repair. A risk-management plan should examine the following points:

— Equipment selected meets all safety and design standards within the industry.

— Assembly of equipment follows manufacturers' guidelines.

— A schedule of regular service and repair is established and documented.

— Caution is exercised in relation to recommending equipment.

— Homemade equipment is avoided.

IMPLEMENTATION OF A RISK-MANAGEMENT SYSTEM

There are risks to any activity, but exercise programs carry certain special risks due to the physical movement and exertion often required. GFIs should constantly search for methods to make the environment safer for their participants. Periodically reviewing programs, facilities, and equipment to evaluate potential dangers allows the GFI to decide the best way to minimize potentially costly injuries.

It is critical that facility personnel design, implement, and consistently review a risk-management system. For a complete review of considerations regarding the creation and implementation of policy and staffing concerns, consult the "AHA/ACSM Scientific Statement: Recommendations for Cardiovascular Screening, Staffing, and Emergency Policies at Health/Fitness Facilities" (Balady et al., 1998).

WAIVERS, INFORMED CONSENT, AND AGREEMENT TO PARTICIPATE

The staff members of many facilities attempt to absolve themselves of liability by having all participants sign a liability **waiver** to release the instructor and fitness center from all liability associated with the conduct of an exercise program and any resulting injuries. In some cases, these documents have been of little value because the courts have enforced the specific wording of the waiver and not its intent. In other words, if negligence was found to be the cause of injury, and negligence of the instructor or fitness center was not specifically waived, then the waiver would not be effective. Therefore, waivers must be clearly written and include statements to the effect that the participant waives all claims to damages, even those caused by the negligence of the instructor or fitness center.

Some fitness centers use an **informed consent** form. While this document has many similar components to most waivers, its primary purpose is different. The informed consent form is used to make the dangers of a program or test procedure known to the participant and thereby provide an additional measure of defense against lawsuits.

Obtaining informed consent is very important because GFIs need participants to understand activities and appreciate associated dangers. The following should be an automatic procedure for every person who enters the program, and it should be done before every fitness test:

- Inform the participant of the exercise program or testing procedure, and explain the purpose of each. This written explanation should be thorough and unbiased.

- Inform the participant of the risks involved in the testing procedure or program, along with the possible discomforts.

- Inform the participant of the benefits expected from the testing procedure or program.

- Inform the participant of any alternative programs or tests that may be more advantageous to him or her.

- Solicit questions regarding the testing procedure or exercise program, and give unbiased answers to these inquiries.

- Inform the participant that he or she is free, at any time, to discontinue participation.

- Obtain the written consent of each participant.

Figure 12-1 provides an example of an **agreement to participate** form, which is designed to protect the GFI from a participant claiming to be unaware of the potential risks of physical activity. An agreement to participate is not typically considered a formal **contract**, but rather serves to demonstrate that the participant was made aware of the "normal" outcomes of certain types of physical activity and willingly assumed the risks of participation. Typically, the agreement to participate form is utilized for "class" settings and should detail the nature of the activity, the

Figure 12-1
Sample
agreement to
participate

I, _____, have enrolled in a program of strenuous physical activity including, but not limited to, boot-camp classes and other group fitness activities, which may include the use of various pieces of fitness equipment offered by [name of fitness professional and/or business]. I am aware that participating in these types of activities, even when completed properly, can be dangerous. I agree to follow the verbal instructions issued by the fitness professional. I am aware that potential risks associated with these types of activities include, but are not limited to, death, serious neck and spinal injuries that may result in complete or partial paralysis or brain damage, serious injury to virtually all bones, joints, ligaments, muscles, tendons, and other aspects of the musculoskeletal system, and serious injury or impairment to other aspects of my body, general health, and well-being.

Because of the dangers of participating, I recognize the importance of following the fitness professional's instructions regarding proper techniques and training, as well as other organization rules.

I am in good health and have provided verification from a licensed physician that I am able to undertake a general fitness-training program. I hereby consent to first aid, emergency medical care, and admission to an accredited hospital or an emergency care center when necessary for executing such care and for treatment of injuries that I may sustain while participating in a fitness-training program.

I understand that I am responsible for my own medical insurance and will maintain that insurance throughout my entire period of participation with [name of fitness professional and/or business]. I will assume any additional expenses incurred that go beyond my health coverage. I will notify [name of fitness professional and/or business] of any significant injury that requires medical attention (such as emergency care and hospitalization).

Signed _____

Printed Name_____ Phone Number _____

Address_____

Emergency Contact_____Contact Phone Number _____

Insurance Company_____

Policy #_____ Effective Date _____

Name of Policy Holder_____

potential risks to be encountered, and the expected behaviors of the participant (Cotten & Cotten, 2012). This last consideration is important, as the participant recognizes that he or she may need to follow instructions while participating.

When preparing legal documents, every health and fitness professional should consult with an attorney who has experience and expertise in state and local laws regarding fitness participation. For extensive guidance on many of these issues, consult *IHRSA's Guide to Club Membership and Conduct* (International Health, Racquet and Sportsclub Association, 2005), which provides specific standards, sample forms, and suggested policies and procedures that could be used in risk-management implementation.

The documents referenced and presented in this chapter are designed to serve as a guide to improve understanding. GFIs should not assume that any example included will provide adequate protection in the event of a lawsuit. Please see a local attorney before creating, distributing, and collecting agreements to participate, informed consent forms, and/or waivers.

 [THINK IT THROUGH]

Before beginning the first session of a six-week boot-camp series, you ask new participants to complete a health-history form and sign a liability waiver. One participant says that she does not want to sign any paperwork before "trying out the class" and is very excited to just get started. What potential issues might arise if you do not require the participant to sign the waiver?

LIABILITY INSURANCE

Even after taking precautions, it is important for GFIs to be aware of the importance of insurance. The need for insurance is always present, but as GFIs and their businesses become more financially successful, the importance of insurance increases. Insurance protection provides some peace of mind, as GFIs can feel secure knowing that if someone were to be injured as a result of their actions or if a meritless lawsuit were to occur, insurance coverage would be adequate to compensate that individual for his or her losses.

In general, GFIs should not assume that any of their typically established personal insurance (e.g., auto and home) extends to their professional activities. GFIs need to secure **professional liability insurance** that is specifically designed to cover work within the health and fitness industry. The selected liability insurance policy should cover personal injuries that can occur as a result of an exercise session. Injured participants may sue not only for medical expenses, but also for a variety of other compensation, such as lost wages from being unable to work and pain and suffering. ACE recommends retaining at least $1 million in coverage, as medical expenses can easily cost hundreds of thousands of dollars. In some instances, a higher liability coverage amount may be advisable.

GFIs must understand the specific insurance needs that may

arise given the location of the exercise activities. In each policy, a **rider**—a special addition to typical policy provisions—will explain specific details regarding when and where the insurance policy applies. In cases where GFIs will work outside of a fitness center, it is imperative that the insurance carrier is aware of the professional activities that will occur. In most cases, outdoor classes will require insurance (typically at higher rates) that specifically covers the GFIs for these locations. For GFIs who own their own businesses, insurance should be retained that covers potential problems with the facility as well as the instruction and supervision of the GFI.

[EXPAND YOUR KNOWLEDGE]

Understanding an Umbrella Policy

Most insurance agents now recommend that professionals purchase an **umbrella liability policy,** which provides added coverage for all of the other insurance (e.g., auto, home, and professional liability) that a person may have in place. For example, if a GFI was sued and the judgment exceeded his or her professional liability coverage, the umbrella policy would cover the insurance shortfall. When purchasing an umbrella policy, GFIs should be sure that it covers professional activities associated with group fitness instruction. In addition, every liability policy should be examined to ensure that it covers the GFI while working in various locations (e.g., fitness center and outdoors).

The American Council on Exercise has established relationships with reputable insurance carriers who specialize in insuring professionals within the fitness industry. Visit www.ACEfitness.org/professional-resources/liability-insurance/default.aspx for more information.

OTHER LEGAL CONSIDERATIONS

GFIs are providers of a special service. As a result, they must be familiar with the special aspects of the law that are most frequently encountered in the conduct of their business.

CONTRACTS

Health and fitness professionals must have an adequate knowledge of legal contracts to perform tasks, get paid, and avoid costly legal battles with participants and/or facilities. Some GFIs will want to work as individuals not affiliated with one particular club, while others may want to be employed by a club or fitness center.

Whatever the nature of the work arrangement, a GFI must be aware of the essentials of contract law. Basic contract law indicates that the following elements are necessary to form a binding contract:

- *An offer and acceptance:* Mutual agreement to terms
- *Consideration:* An exchange of items of value
- *Legality:* Acceptable form and subject under the law
- *Capacity:* Such as majority age and mental competency

The general considerations that should be addressed in contracts for use with participants, as well as contracts between health and fitness professionals and clubs for which they intend to work, should include the following:

- *Identification of the parties:* GFI and participant/club
- *Description of the services to be performed:* Group fitness instruction and consultation
- *Compensation:* An agreed upon wage or fee per hour, day, month, or class, and payment method

- *Confidential relationship:* Agreement by each party not to divulge personal or business information gained through the relationship
- *Business status:* Confirmation of employment status
- *Term and termination:* Express definition of the length of the contract and the conditions under which termination is allowed by either party

EMPLOYMENT STATUS

As noted above, another prominent concern for many health and fitness professionals deals with employment status: **independent contractor** versus **employee.** Both of these terms can apply to those who work in a fitness center. However, only the independent contractor status applies to self-employed GFIs working independently from a club. However, most clubs still require independent contractors hired by the club to follow facility rules and to provide proof of liability insurance.

In some instances, owners of fitness centers or clubs have used the term independent contractor for employees. Club owners are often motivated to hire independent contractors in place of regular employees because the facility does not have to provide training, offer medical or other benefits, arrange for social security withholding, or pay into worker's compensation or unemployment funds for independent contractors.

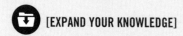 **[EXPAND YOUR KNOWLEDGE]**

Employees versus Independent Contractors

A legal dichotomy exists between regular employees and independent contractors. Most commonly, courts have considered a variety of questions or "tests" to determine if the business relationship in question between a club and a health and fitness professional is that of a regular employee or an independent contractor. These tests can include:

- *The extent of control that, by agreement, the employer can exercise over the details of the work:* The existence of a right to control is indicative of an employer–employee relationship.

- *The method of payment, whether by time or by the job:* Generally, those persons scheduled to be paid on a regular basis at an hourly or weekly rate have been considered employees. Conversely, those paid in a single payment for services rendered have more easily qualified as independent contractors.

- *The length of time for which the person is employed:* Individuals hired for short periods of time (a few days or weeks) have more often been seen as independent contractors, whereas employment periods that extended upward of a full year have been ruled as establishing an employer–employee relationship.

- *The skill required for the provision of services:* When the worker needs limited or no training because of the specialized or technical skills that the employer intends to utilize, the worker will likely be viewed as an independent contractor. Conversely, if an employer provides training to a recently hired individual, that person will more than likely be judged to be an employee.

- *Whether the person employed is in a distinct business or occupation:* If a worker offers services to other employers or clients, a status of independent contractor would probably be found. If, however, the worker only intended to provide services for one employer, and failed to offer the services to others as an independent business, the employee status will likely be found.

- *Whether the employer or the worker provides the equipment:* Independent contractors typically provide and/or utilize their own equipment.

- *Whether the work is a part of the normal business of the employer:* Court rulings have favored classifying individuals as regular employees when services rendered are integral to the business of the employer. Supplemental, special, or one-time services are more likely to be provided by independent contractors.

- *Whether the work is traditionally performed by a specialist in similar businesses:* Employers and employees must examine their field of business to gain an understanding of current practices and align themselves with the prevailing trends.

- *The intent of the parties involved in the arrangement:* The courts will attempt to enforce intent of the parties at the time the agreement was executed. If a professional thought that he or she was hired as an independent contractor, as did the club, it would influence the court's determination, though not guarantee a legal outcome. A clear understanding of the arrangement is critical, but may not completely guarantee how the relationship is perceived by the courts.

The process of determining employment status is marked by careful analysis of the facts and the weighing of interpretations on both sides of the issue. All of the issues addressed in this list have been used in court cases dealing with this matter, each with varying degrees of authority. It is, therefore, imperative that all health and fitness professionals and club owners understand and examine these factors when initiating agreements.

For more specific information on the legal aspects surrounding the independent contractor versus employee issue, consult the guidelines published by the Internal Revenue Service (www.irs.gov).

COPYRIGHT LAW

One of a GFI's major legal responsibilities is compliance with copyright law. All forms of commercially produced creative expression are protected by copyright law, but music is the area most pertinent to instructors. This has become an extremely important issue with the availability of downloadable music. Simply stated, almost all musical compositions that one can hear on the radio or television or buy from music outlets online are owned by artists and studios and are protected by federal copyright law. An instructor who creates a playlist of various downloaded songs he or she has purchased online and then uses that music in a for-profit exercise class—legally speaking, a **public performance**—is in violation of copyright law.

Performance Licenses

To be able to use copyrighted music in an exercise class, one must obtain a performance license from one of the major **performing rights societies**—the **American Society of Composers, Authors and Publishers (ASCAP)**, **Broadcast Music, Inc. (BMI)**, or the **Society of European Stage Authors and Composers (SESAC)**. These organizations vigorously enforce copyright law for their memberships and will not hesitate to sue a health club, studio, or freelance instructor who plays copyrighted music without a license.

Accordingly, most clubs and studios obtain a **blanket license** for their instructors. The license fees for the clubs are determined by the number of participants who attend classes each week, by the number of speakers used in the club, or by whether the club has a single- or multifloor layout.

GFIs who teach as independent contractors at several locations and/or who use their own music may have to obtain their own licenses. They should check with the clubs where they teach to see if each club's blanket license covers their classes. One viable option for instructors is to buy licensed music expressly made for fitness classes, where the copyright holder expressly permits the original music to be used in a class. Another option common for pre-choreographed classes is for clubs to buy "packaged" group fitness programs where all of the advertising, music, and instructor training are provided and the fitness center is allowed to use the name brand of the program in its advertising.

Professional liability insurance will usually not cover an instructor for copyright infringement claims or offer protection in suits involving libel, slander, invasion of privacy, or defamation of character. These sorts of actions may be considered intentional torts and are not typically covered.

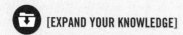**[EXPAND YOUR KNOWLEDGE]**

Obtaining Copyright Protection

Some GFIs may want to obtain copyright protection for certain aspects of their own work, including the following:

■ *Choreographic work:* If an instructor creates more than a simple routine, and publicly distributes (through a dance notation system), performs, or displays the choreography, it can be copyrighted.

■ *Books, videos, and films:* If a choreographed work by an instructor is sold to a publisher, video distributor, or movie studio, that business entity will own the copyright for the material and the instructor will be compensated with either an advance or a certain portion of the proceeds (royalties), or both. Through negotiation with the producing or distributing company, the instructor may be able to retain certain rights to the material.

■ *Compilations of exercise routines:* If an instructor makes an original sequence of routines (i.e., a **compilation**), it may be protected by copyright and licensed to others for a book, video, film, or other presentation form.

■ *Graphic materials:* If an instructor creates pictures, charts, diagrams, informational handouts, or other graphic materials for instructional aides or promotional material, these too may be copyrighted.

For copyright information or applications, write to:
Register of Copyrights
United States Copyright Office
Library of Congress
Washington, D.C. 20559
www.copyright.gov

TRADEMARKS

Though it is important for GFIs to protect their developed intellectual property, it is also imperative that instructors respect the intellectual property of others. Many businesses operate in the fitness industry and their unique names, logos, slogans, and other intellectual property cannot be utilized for commercial purposes without their express written consent. For example, Zumba is a popular company, and as such many participants are familiar with the corporate name and the class format they have created. GFIs, or the health and fitness facilities for which they work, cannot advertise their classes as "Zumba" or "Zumba-like" unless they have successfully completed the Zumba instructor training course and have created the appropriate contractual relationship with Zumba that grants permission to utilize the protected Zumba name.

> It is imperative that instructors respect the intellectual property of others

SHARED-USE SPACE

There is a growing trend in the health and fitness industry to hold workouts in public settings. Often, this means GFIs are holding classes in an outdoor area rather than a controlled, indoor environment. Prior to conducting any form of exercise, the GFI must research the jurisdiction of the potential workout area to determine what is legal to undertake. Often, it is illegal to instruct participants on public beaches, parks, or trails, even if the class offered is donation-based or not-for-profit. It is the GFI's responsibility to know the local laws prior to using these areas.

Once a "legal" outdoor area has been identified and selected for a class offering, the GFI should be sure to understand the potential dangers of the environment before leading a class for participants (see Chapter 4). The GFI should also review the weather forecast for potential likelihood of thunderstorms and other dangerous inclement weather occurrences. If the weather forecast is deemed acceptable for outdoor exercise, the GFI should inspect the workout area before each class to identify any unusual dangers, as discussed in Chapter 7.

Before undertaking any outdoor or public-space classes, the GFI should consult his or her insurance policies to ensure such activities are covered. In addition, a consultation with an attorney may provide insights to better assess the legal ramifications of conducting classes away from a fitness center.

AMERICANS WITH DISABILITIES ACT

Health and fitness professionals can be affected by a variety of legislative mandates. One of the laws that affects the profession is the **Americans with Disabilities Act,** which became law in 1992. Modeled after the Civil Rights Act, it prohibits discrimination on the basis of disability. The law provides for equal treatment and equal access to programs for disabled Americans. The act extends provisions to all areas of public accommodation, including businesses such that all participants, regardless of disability, are guaranteed access to all programs and spaces within the facility. Therefore, it is essential that GFIs make sure that their buildings, equipment, and programs are available to persons with disabilities. Employers must also provide reasonable accommodations for employees with disabilities, including adjusted work stations and equipment as necessary. Therefore, whether a person with a disability is an employee or a participant, steps must be taken to ensure that the professional and business environment is one that respects the dignity, skills, and contributions of that individual.

ENSURING PARTICIPANT CONFIDENTIALITY

When working in the health and fitness industry, GFIs are often exposed to sensitive personal information. Material provided on health screening forms as well as conversations with participants may reveal personal information that should always remain confidential. In order to protect participants' personal data, all individual information should remain secured, away from public access. This may require the GFI to store health screening forms and waivers in a locked file cabinet to prevent unrestricted access. Also, though it may be seen by most as a positive, GFIs must be careful not to share a participant's personal health success story with other participants. Often, "innocent" mistakes are made when a GFI shares a person's weight-loss achievements or other health advancements. Sharing of personal information can not only be against the wishes of a participant but may also potentially against the law. GFIs should acquire express, written consent from a participant before divulging any participant information. With the proliferation of social media, many GFIs should remember that photos of individual or group fitness activities should remain out of the public domain, just like private participant information. Though some state and local laws differ by jurisdiction, photos identifying individual class participants should not be shared or utilized as marketing tools without the consent of the identified participants. In most cases, permission to utilize photos can be obtained when participants first attend the class and provide their health screening information and signed waiver.

ACE PROFESSIONAL PRACTICES AND DISCIPLINARY PROCEDURES

The ACE Professional Practices and Disciplinary Procedures are intended to inform ACE Certified Professionals, candidates for ACE certification, and the public about the ACE application and certification standards relative to professional conduct and disciplinary procedures. ACE may revoke or otherwise take action with regard to the application or certification of an individual in the case of:

- Ineligibility for certification
- Irregularity in connection with any certification examination
- Unauthorized possession, use, access, or distribution of certification examinations, score reports, trademarks, logos, written materials, answer sheets, certificates, **certificant** or applicant files, or other confidential or proprietary ACE documents or materials (registered or otherwise)·
- Material misrepresentation or fraud in any statement to ACE or to the public including, but not limited to, statements made to assist the applicant, certificant, or another to apply for, obtain, or retain certification
- Any physical, mental, or emotional condition of either temporary or permanent nature, including, but not limited to, substance abuse, which impairs or has the potential to impair competent and objective professional performance
- Negligent and/or intentional misconduct in professional work, including, but not limited to, physical or emotional abuse, disregard for safety, or the unauthorized release of confidential information
- The timely conviction, plea of guilty, or plea of *nolo contendere* ("no contest") in connection with a felony or misdemeanor that is directly related to public health and/or fitness instruction or education, and

that impairs competent and objective professional performance. These include, but are not limited to, rape, sexual abuse of a participant, actual or threatened use of a weapon of violence, or the prohibited sale, distribution, or possession with intent to distribute of a controlled substance.

- Failure to meet the requirements for certification or recertification

ACE has developed a three-tiered disciplinary process of review, hearing, and appeals to ensure fair and unbiased examination of alleged violation(s) of the Application and Certification Standards in order to determine the merit of allegations and impose appropriate sanctions as necessary to protect the public and the integrity of the certification process.

 [THINK IT THROUGH]

Given the nature of physical activity and the continual evolution of legal standards, what will you do to continue to remain up-to-date regarding the legal requirements of your profession? What resources can you utilize to not only maintain, but enhance your understanding of the law and its impact on the fitness industry?

SUMMARY

No group fitness class, regardless of how well it is designed and implemented, can completely avoid all potential participant injuries. In an attempt to reduce injuries to participants and minimize the potential legal complications, GFIs and facility management would be wise to adhere to the following guidelines:

— Obtain ongoing professional education and guided practical training under a qualified professional, and maintain current certification from a certification program accredited by the NCCA, or comparable accrediting body.

— Design and instruct classes that reflect current professional standards and guidelines.

— Formulate and enforce policies for the conduct of the class in accordance with professional recommendations, including obtaining documents from prospective participants such as a signed waiver prior to attending class.

— Establish and implement adequate and proper procedures for supervision in all phases of the class.

— Post safety regulations in the facility and ensure that they are rigidly enforced by supervisory personnel.

— Keep the facility free from hazards and maintain adequate free space for class activities.

— Routinely inspect all equipment and facilities and report any potential hazards promptly.

— Formulate policies and guidelines for emergency situations, rehearse the procedures, and require all instructors to have current first-aid, **cardiopulmonary resuscitation (CPR),** and **automated external defibrillator (AED)** training and certification (see Chapter 11).

By applying these recommendations, GFIs can help reduce the probability of injury to participants and limit potential legal liability. Should legal action result from an injury, the facts of the case would be examined to determine whether negligence was the cause. A properly trained, competent, and certified GFI conducting a program that was in accordance with current professional standards would probably prevail.

All GFIs should remember that professional standards in the health and fitness field are continually changing. It is the responsibility of the GFI to remain aware of pertinent legal developments in the industry in addition to keeping abreast of the latest health and fitness research and updated standards and guidelines. By understanding professional and legal responsibilities, GFIs can develop and offer group fitness classes in a way that participants enjoy while limiting instructor liability.

References

Balady, G.J. et al. (1998). AHA/ACSM Scientific Statement: Recommendations for Cardiovascular screening, staffing, and emergency policies at health/fitness facilities: A Joint Position Statement by the American College of Sports Medicine and the American Heart Association. *Circulation,* 97, 2283–2293.

Cotten, D.J. & Cotten, M.B. (2012). *Waivers & Releases of Liability* (8th ed.). Statesboro, Ga.: Sport Risk Consulting.

International Health, Racquet and Sportsclub Association (2005). *IHRSA's Guide to Club Membership and Conduct* (3rd ed.). http://download.ihrsa.org/pubs/club_membership_conduct.pdf

Wong, G. (2010). *Essentials of Sports Law* (4th ed.). Santa Barbara, Calif.: ABC-CLIO.

ACE® CODE OF ETHICS

PROVIDE SAFE AND EFFECTIVE INSTRUCTION

Providing safe and effective instruction involves a variety of responsibilities for ACE Certified Professionals. Safe means that the instruction will not result in physical, mental, or financial harm to the client/participant. Effective means that the instruction has a purposeful, intended, and desired effect toward the client's/participant's goal. Great effort and care must be taken in carrying out the responsibilities that are essential in creating a positive exercise experience for all clients/participants.

Screening

ACE Certified Professionals should have all potential clients/participants complete an industry-recognized health-screening tool to ensure safe exercise participation. If significant risk factors or signs and symptoms suggestive of chronic disease are identified, refer the client/participant to a physician or primary healthcare practitioner for medical clearance and guidance regarding which types of assessments, activities, or exercises are indicated, contraindicated, or deemed high risk. If an individual does not want to obtain medical clearance, have that individual sign a legally prepared document that releases you and the facility in which you work from any liability related to any injury that may result from exercise participation or assessment. Once

the client/participant has been cleared for exercise and you have a full understanding of the client's/participant's health status and medical history, including his or her current use of medications, a formal risk-management plan for potential emergencies must be prepared and reviewed periodically.

Assessment

The main objective of a health assessment is to establish the client's/participant's baseline fitness level in order to design an appropriate exercise program. Explain the risks and benefits of each assessment and provide the client/participant with any pertinent instructions. Prior to conducting any type of assessment, the client/participant must be given an opportunity to ask questions and read and sign an informed consent. The types and order of assessments are dictated by the client's/participant's health status, fitness level, symptoms, and/or use of medications. Remember that each assessment has specific protocols and only those within your scope of practice should be administered. Once the assessments are completed, evaluate and discuss the results objectively as they relate to the client's/participant's health condition and goals. Educate the client/participant and emphasize how an exercise program will benefit the client/participant.

Program Design

You must not prescribe exercise, diet, or treatment, as doing so is outside your scope of practice and implies ordering or advising a medicine or treatment. Instead, it is appropriate for you to design exercise programs that improve components of physical fitness and wellness while adhering to the limitations of a previous injury or condition as determined by a certified, registered, or licensed allied health professional. Because nutritional laws and the practice of dietetics vary in each state, province, and country, understand what type of basic nutritional information is appropriate and legal for you to disseminate to your client/participant. The client's/participant's preferences, and short- and long-term goals, as well as current industry standards and guidelines, must be taken into consideration as you develop a formal yet realistic exercise and weight-management program. Provide as much detail for all exercise parameters such as mode, intensity, type of exercise, duration, progression, and termination points.

Program Implementation

Do not underestimate your ability to influence the client/participant to become active for a lifetime. Be sure that each class or session is well-planned, sequential, and documented. Instruct the client/participant how to safely and properly perform the appropriate exercises and communicate this in a manner that the client/participant will understand and retain. Each client/participant has a different learning curve that will require different levels of attention, learning aids, and repetition. Supervise the client/participant closely, especially when spotting or cueing is needed. If supervising a group of two or more, ensure that you can supervise and provide the appropriate amount of attention to each individual at all times. Ideally, the group will have similar goals and will be performing similar exercises or activities. Position yourself so that you do not have to turn your back to any client/participant performing an exercise.

Facilities

Although the condition of a facility may not always be within your control, you are still obligated to ensure a hazard-free environment to maximize safety. If you notice potential hazards in the health club, communicate these hazards to the client/participant and the facility management. For example, if you notice that the clamps that keep the weights on the barbells are getting rusty and loose, it would be prudent of you to remove them from the training area and alert the facility that immediate repair is required.

Equipment

Obtain equipment that meets or exceeds industry standards and utilize the equipment only for its intended use. Arrange exercise equipment and stations so that adequate space exists between equipment, participants, and foot traffic. Schedule regular maintenance and inspect equipment prior to use to ensure it is in proper working condition. Avoid the use of homemade equipment, as your liability is greater if it causes injury to a person exercising under your supervision.

PROVIDE EQUAL AND FAIR TREATMENT TO ALL CLIENTS/PARTICIPANTS

ACE Certified Professionals are obligated to provide fair and equal treatment for each client/participant without bias, preference, or discrimination against gender, ethnic background, age, national origin, basis of religion, or physical disability.

The Americans with Disabilities Act protects individuals with disabilities against any type of unlawful discrimination. A disability can be either physical or mental, such as epilepsy, paralysis, HIV infection, AIDS, a significant hearing or visual impairment, mental retardation, or a specific learning disability. ACE Certified Professionals should, at a minimum, provide reasonable accommodations to each individual with a disability. Reasonable simply means that you are able to provide accommodations that do not cause you any undue hardship that requires additional or significant expense or difficulty. Making an existing facility accessible by modifying equipment or devices, assessments, or training materials are a few examples of providing reasonable accommodations. However, providing the use of personal items or providing items at your own expense may not be considered reasonable.

This ethical consideration of providing fair and equal treatment is not limited to behavioral interactions with clients/participants, but also extends to exercise programming and other business-related services such as communication, scheduling, billing, cancellation policies, and dispute resolution.

STAY UP-TO-DATE ON THE LATEST HEALTH AND FITNESS RESEARCH AND UNDERSTAND ITS PRACTICAL APPLICATION

Obtaining an ACE certification required you to have broad-based knowledge of many disciplines; however, this credential should not be viewed as the end of your professional development and education. Instead, it should be viewed as the beginning or foundation. The dynamic nature of the health and fitness industry requires you to maintain an understanding of the latest research and professional standards and guidelines and their impact on the design and implementation of exercise programming. To stay informed, make time to review a variety of industry resources such as professional journals, position statements, trade and lay periodicals, and correspondence courses, as well as to attend professional meetings, conferences, and educational workshops.

An additional benefit of staying up-to-date is that it also fulfills your certification renewal requirements for continuing education credit (CEC). To maintain your ACE Certified status, you must obtain an established amount of CECs every two years. CECs are granted for structured learning that takes place within the educational portion of a course related to the profession and presented by a qualified health and fitness professional.

MAINTAIN CURRENT CPR CERTIFICATION AND KNOWLEDGE OF FIRST-AID SERVICES

ACE Certified Professionals must be prepared to recognize and respond to heart attacks and other life-threatening emergencies. Emergency response is enhanced by training and maintaining skills in cardiopulmonary resuscitation (CPR), first aid, and using automated external defibrillators (AEDs), which have become more widely available. An AED is a portable electronic device used to restore normal heart rhythm in a person experiencing a cardiac arrest and can reduce the time to defibrillation before emergency medical services (EMS) personnel arrive. For each minute that defibrillation is delayed, the victim's chance of survival is reduced by 7 to 10%. Thus, survival from cardiac arrest is improved dramatically when CPR and defibrillation are started early.

COMPLY WITH ALL APPLICABLE BUSINESS, EMPLOYMENT, AND INTELLECTUAL PROPERTY LAWS

As an ACE Certified Professional, you are expected to maintain a high level of integrity by complying with all applicable business, employment, and copyright laws. Be truthful and forthcoming with communication to clients/participants, coworkers, and other health and fitness professionals in advertising, marketing, and business practices. Do not create false or misleading impressions of credentials, claims, or sponsorships, or perform services outside of your scope of practice that are illegal, deceptive, or fraudulent.

All information regarding your business must be clear, accurate, and easy to understand for all potential clients/participants. Provide disclosure about the name of your business, physical address, and contact information, and maintain a working phone number and email address. So that clients/participants can make an informed choice about paying for your services, provide detailed information regarding schedules, prices, payment terms, time limits, and conditions. Cancellation, refund, and rescheduling information must also be clearly stated and easy to understand. Allow the client/participant an opportunity to ask questions and review this information before formally agreeing to your services and terms.

Because employment laws vary in each city, state, province, and country, familiarize yourself with the applicable employment regulations and standards to which your business must conform. Examples of this may include conforming to specific building codes and zoning ordinances or making sure that your place of business is accessible to individuals with a disability.

The understanding of intellectual property law and the proper use of copyrighted materials is an important legal issue for all ACE Certified Professionals. Intellectual property laws protect the creations of authors, artists, software programmers, and others with copyrighted materials. The most common infringement of intellectual property law in the fitness industry is the use of music in an exercise class. When commercial music is played in a for-profit exercise class, without a performance or blanket license, it is considered a public performance and a violation of intellectual property law. Therefore, make sure that any music, handouts, or educational materials are either exempt from intellectual property law or permissible under laws by reason of fair use, or obtain express written consent from the copyright holder for distribution, adaptation, or use. When in doubt, obtain permission first or consult with a qualified legal professional who has intellectual property law expertise.

MAINTAIN THE CONFIDENTIALITY OF ALL CLIENT/PARTICIPANT INFORMATION

Every client/participant has the right to expect that all personal data and discussions with an ACE Certified Professional will be safeguarded and not disclosed without the client's/participant's express written consent or acknowledgment. Therefore, protect the confidentiality of all client/participant information such as contact data, medical records, health history, progress notes, and meeting details. Even when confidentiality is not required by law, continue to preserve the confidentiality of such information.

Any breach of confidentiality, intentional or unintentional, potentially harms the productivity and trust of your client/participant and undermines your effectiveness as a fitness professional. This also puts you at risk for potential litigation and puts your client/participant at risk for public embarrassment and fraudulent activity such as identity theft.

Most breaches of confidentiality are unintentional and occur because of carelessness and lack of awareness. The most common breach of confidentiality is exposing or storing a client's personal data in a location that is not secure. This occurs when a client's/participant's file or information is left on a desk, or filed in a cabinet that has no lock or is accessible to others. Breaches of confidentiality may also occur when you have conversations regarding a client's/participant's performance or medical/health history with staff or others and the client's/participant's first name or other identifying details are used.

Post and adhere to a privacy policy that communicates how client/participant information will be used and secured and how a client's/participant's preference regarding unsolicited mail and email will be respected. When a client/participant provides you with any personal data, new or updated, make it a habit to immediately secure this information and ensure that only you and/or the appropriate individuals have access to it. Also, the client's/participant's files must only be accessed and used for purposes related to health and fitness services. If client/

participant information is stored on a personal computer, restrict access by using a protected password. Should you receive any inquiries from family members or other individuals regarding the progress of a client/participant or other personal information, state that you cannot provide any information without the client's/participant's permission. If and when a client/participant permits you to release confidential information to an authorized individual or party, utilize secure methods of communication such as certified mail, sending and receiving information on a dedicated private fax line, or email with encryption.

REFER CLIENTS/PARTICIPANTS TO MORE QUALIFIED HEALTH OR MEDICAL PROFESSIONALS WHEN APPROPRIATE

A fitness certification is not a professional license. Therefore, it is vitally important that ACE Certified Professionals who do not also have a professional license (e.g., physician, physical therapist, registered dietitian, psychologist, or attorney) refer their clients/participants to a more qualified professional when warranted. Doing so not only benefits your clients/participants by making sure that they receive the appropriate attention and care, but also enhances your credibility and reduces liability by defining your scope of practice and clarifying what services you can and cannot reasonably provide.

Knowing when to refer a client/participant is, however, as important as choosing to which professional to refer. For instance, when a client/participant complains of symptoms of muscle soreness or discomfort or exhibits signs of fatigue or lack of energy, it is not an absolute indication to refer your client/participant to a physician. Because continual referrals such as this are not practical, familiarize and educate yourself on expected signs and symptoms, taking into consideration the client's/participant's fitness level, health status, chronic disease, disability, and/or background as he or she is screened and as he or she begins and progresses with an exercise program. This helps you better discern between emergent and non-emergent situations and know when to refuse to offer your services, continue to monitor, and/or make an immediate referral.

It is important that you know the scope of practice for various health professionals and which types of referrals are appropriate. For example, some states require that a referring physician first approve visits to a physical therapist, while other states allow individuals to see a physical therapist directly. Only registered or licensed dietitians or physicians may provide specific dietary recommendations or diet plans; however, a client/participant who is suspected of an eating disorder should be referred to an eating disorders specialist. Refer clients/participants to a clinical psychologist if they wish to discuss family or marital problems or exhibit addictive behaviors such as substance abuse.

Network and develop rapport with potential allied health professionals in your area before you refer clients/participants to them. This demonstrates good will and respect for their expertise and will most likely result in reciprocal referrals for your services and fitness expertise.

UPHOLD AND ENHANCE PUBLIC APPRECIATION AND TRUST FOR THE HEALTH AND FITNESS INDUSTRY

The best way for ACE Certified Professionals to uphold and enhance public appreciation and trust for the health and fitness industry is to represent themselves in a dignified and professional manner. As the public is inundated with misinformation and false claims about fitness products and services, your expertise must be utilized to dispel myths and half-truths about current trends and fads that are potentially harmful to the public.

When appropriate, mentor and dispense knowledge and training to less-experienced fitness professionals. Novice fitness professionals can benefit from your experience and skill as you assist them in establishing a foundation based on exercise science, from both theoretical and practical standpoints. Therefore, it is a disservice if you fail to provide helpful or corrective information—especially when an individual, the public, or other fitness professionals are at risk for injury or increased liability. For example, if you observe an individual using momentum to perform a strength-training exercise, the prudent course of action would be to suggest a modification. Likewise, if you observe a fitness professional in your workplace consistently failing to obtain informed consents before clients/participants undergo fitness testing or begin an exercise program, recommend that he or she

consider implementing these forms to minimize liability.

Finally, do not represent yourself in an overly commercial or misleading manner. Consider the fitness professional who places an advertisement in a local newspaper stating: "Lose 10 pounds in 10 days or your money back!" It is inappropriate to lend credibility to or endorse a product, service, or program founded upon unsubstantiated or misleading claims; thus a solicitation such as this must be avoided, as it undermines the public's trust of health and fitness professionals.

ESTABLISH AND MAINTAIN CLEAR PROFESSIONAL BOUNDARIES

Working in the fitness profession requires you to come in contact with many different people. It is imperative that a professional distance be maintained in relationships with all clients/participants. Fitness professionals are responsible for setting and monitoring the boundaries between a working relationship and friendship with their clients/participants. To that end, ACE Certified Professionals should:

- Never initiate or encourage discussion of a sexual nature

- Avoid touching clients/participants unless it is essential to instruction

- Inform clients/participants about the purpose of touching and find an alternative if the client/participant objects

- Discontinue all touching if it appears to make the client/participant uncomfortable

Take all reasonable steps to ensure that any personal and social contacts between themselves and their clients/participants do not have an adverse impact on the trainer–client, coach–client, or instructor–participant relationship.

If you are unable to maintain appropriate professional boundaries with a client/participant (whether due to your attitudes and actions or those of the client/participant), the prudent course of action is to terminate the relationship and, perhaps, refer the client/participant to another professional. Keep in mind that charges of sexual harassment or assault, even if groundless, can have disastrous effects on your career.

ACE® GROUP FITNESS INSTRUCTOR CERTIFICATION EXAM CONTENT OUTLINE

ATTENTION EXAM CANDIDATES!

When preparing for an ACE certification exam, be aware that the material presented in the *ACE Group Fitness Instructor Handbook*, or any other text or educational materials, may become outdated due to the evolving nature of the fitness and healthcare industries, as well as new developments in current and ongoing research. ACE certifications and the exams one must pass to earn these certifications are based on in-depth job analyses and industry-wide validation surveys.

By design, ACE certification exams assess a candidate's ability to analyze multiple case studies that are representative of the work that a certified professional would encounter on a daily, weekly, or monthly basis, and then to apply knowledge of the most current scientifically based professional standards and guidelines to determine the best solution for the scenario presented. *The dynamic nature of this field requires that ACE certification exams be regularly updated to ensure that they reflect the latest industry findings and research. Therefore, the knowledge, skills, and abilities required to pass these exams are not solely represented in this or any other industry text or educational materials.* In addition to learning the material presented on our website, in this handbook, and in associated educational resources, ACE strongly encourages all exam candidates and health and fitness professionals to keep abreast of new developments, guidelines, and standards from a variety of valid industry sources.

 For the most up-to-date version of the Exam Content Outline, please go to www.ACEfitness.org/GFIexamcontent and download a free PDF.

EXAM CONTENT OUTLINE

The Exam Content Outline is essentially a blueprint for the exam. As you prepare for the ACE Group Fitness Instructor Certification Exam, it is important to remember that each question on the Exam maps directly to one of the Task Statements in this outline.

TARGET AUDIENCE STATEMENT

The ACE Certified Group Fitness Instructor (GFI) plans and leads group fitness classes to promote physical activity as part of a healthy lifestyle. In addition to possessing knowledge of the human body and exercise science, the GFI motivates individuals by incorporating aspects of behavioral psychology into his or her classes, leads groups of exercisers by using teaching techniques suitable for multiple learning styles, and adapts workouts based on the specific needs of the participants.

The following eligibility requirements have been established for individuals to sit for the ACE Group Fitness Instructor Certification Examination:
- Must be at least 18 years of age
- Must hold a current adult cardiopulmonary resuscitation (CPR) certificate, and if living in the U.S.A. or Canada, a current automated external defibrillator (AED) certificate
- Must have completed high school (or the equivalent)

DOMAINS, TASKS, AND KNOWLEDGE AND SKILL STATEMENTS

A Role Delineation Study, or job analysis, was conducted by the American Council on Exercise and Castle Worldwide, Inc., for the ACE Group Fitness Instructor Certification Program. The first step in this process was completed by a panel of subject-matter experts in the various disciplines within the field of group fitness. The primary goal of the panel was to identify the primary tasks performed by professional GFIs in creating, leading, and adapting inclusive group fitness classes of varied formats to help diverse groups of individuals to improve health and fitness, and to make meaningful health behavior changes for sustained results.

The panel first identified the major responsibilities performed by professional GFIs. These responsibilities are defined as "Tasks," and it was determined that the responsibilities of the professional GFI could be described in 13 task statements. These tasks were then grouped into three Performance Domains, or major areas of responsibility.

The Performance Domains are listed here with the percentage indicating the portion of the exam devoted to each Domain:
- Domain I: Class Planning and Design – 32%
- Domain II: Group Leadership and Instruction – 49%
- Domain III: Professional Conduct, Safety, and Risk Management – 19%

Each Performance Domain is composed of Tasks, which detail the job-related functions under that particular Domain. Each Task is further divided into Knowledge and Skill Statements that detail the scope of information and understanding required to perform each Task and explain the skills required to apply that understanding in a practical setting.

The Domains, Task Statements, and Knowledge and Skill Statements identified by the panel of subject-matter experts were presented to a large, nationally representative group of current ACE Certified GFIs through an online survey, and the survey results were used to validate the work of the panel and establish test specifications for the Exam. This completed the Role Delineation Study, with the outcome of this study being the ACE Group Fitness Instructor Certification Exam Content Outline detailed here. Please note that while each question on the Exam maps to one of the Tasks in the Exam Content Outline, not all Knowledge and Skill Statements will be addressed on each exam administration, as there are not enough questions on a certification exam to cover every knowledge and skill statement.

DOMAIN I: CLASS PLANNING AND DESIGN 32%

Task 1

Construct a class outline based on the anticipated target audience and the format and objectives of the class in order to guide the development of the class plan.

Knowledge of:

1. Principles and methods of instructional design
2. Basic group fitness class components (e.g., warm-up, conditioning, cool-down, flexibility)
3. Appropriate exercises for class components (e.g., warm-up, conditioning, cool-down, flexibility)
4. Time management as it relates to the weighting of each component of the class
5. Varied group fitness class formats and objectives (e.g., dance-based, mind-body, indoor cycling, group strength, kickboxing, aqua, boot camp, sports conditioning, senior, pre-/post-natal)
6. Appropriate uses of varied group fitness–related equipment
7. Location and space requirements for varied group fitness class formats and objectives
8. Methods of learning (e.g., visual, verbal, kinesthetic) and their application to group fitness instruction

Skill in:

1. Class planning and instructional design
2. Selecting appropriate exercises for group fitness class components (e.g., warm-up, conditioning, cool-down, flexibility) for varied class formats and objectives (e.g., dance-based, mind-body, indoor cycling, group strength, kickboxing, aqua, boot camp, sports conditioning, senior, pre-/post-natal)
3. Time management as it relates to group fitness class design
4. Establishing appropriate focus (time and effort) for each class component based on group fitness format and objectives
5. Determining appropriate group fitness class formats and design based on expected participant group
6. Selecting appropriate locations for varied group fitness class formats and objectives

Task 2

Select appropriate music, equipment, and apparel taking a variety of factors into consideration (e.g., class format, class objectives, participants) in order to create a safe and effective class.

Knowledge of:

1. Appropriate set-up, preparation and use of various types of group fitness–related equipment (e.g., steps, medicine balls, balance-related tools, cycles, elastic resistance, stability balls, yoga mats)
2. Space requirements for using various types of group fitness–related equipment (e.g., steps, medicine balls, balance-related tools, cycles, elastic resistance, stability balls, yoga mats)
3. Characteristics of music [e.g., beats per minute (bpm), structure, tempos, decibels, lyrics/content] and their relation to group fitness class formats, objectives, and participant groups
4. Appropriate music formats and tempos for varied audiences and group fitness class formats (e.g., step, mind-body, dance-based, indoor cycling)
5. Licensing laws pertaining to music use in fitness settings
6. Audio visual (AV) equipment capabilities and use (e.g., stereo, microphone, lighting)
7. Relationship between exercise intensity and group fitness–related music and equipment

8. Safe selection and use of group fitness–related equipment
9. Characteristics (e.g., breathability, mobility, exercise mode specificity) of fitness-related apparel (e.g., clothing, shoes) and the relation to performance and safety

Skill in:
1. Selecting appropriate group fitness–related equipment as it relates to class format, objectives and physical outcomes
2. Determining space requirement as it relates to equipment use and participation volume in order to provide a safe and enjoyable class experience
3. Selecting appropriate music (e.g., BPM, structure, decibels, lyrics, content) for varied group fitness class participants, formats, and objectives
4. Adhering to laws governing music use in fitness and public settings
5. Musical phrasing and applying movement to music for applicable group fitness class formats
6. Selecting appropriate instructor apparel for performance and professionalism
7. Recommending appropriate apparel for various group fitness class formats to participants

Task 3

Select and sequentially order exercise movements, including appropriate regressions, progressions, and modifications (e.g., postural alignment, form), in order to create safe and effective class experiences for participants.

Knowledge of:
1. Basic components of group fitness classes (e.g., warm-up, conditioning, cool-down, flexibility)
2. Appropriate exercises and movements for the class components of varied group fitness class formats
3. Progressions and regressions for exercises and movements used in various group fitness class formats
4. Exercise modifications that improve effectiveness, safety, and the participant experience
5. Appropriate sequencing of exercises for desired group fitness class formats, objectives, and outcomes
6. Choreography and sequencing principles
7. Health-related components of fitness (e.g., muscular strength, muscular endurance, cardiovascular endurance, flexibility, body composition)
8. Skill-related components of fitness (e.g., balance, agility, speed, power, coordination, reaction time)
9. Principles of training (e.g., overload, specificity, SAID, reversibility, progression, metabolic pathway) and their application to varied group fitness class formats and objectives
10. Applied kinesiology, exercise physiology, biomechanics, and anatomy
11. Current and established guidelines for improving and maintaining cardiorespiratory fitness, muscular strength and endurance, and flexibility
12. Safe and effective exercise movements and functional training principles and their appropriate applications

Skill in:
1. Selecting exercises that target desired skill-related components of fitness (balance, agility, speed, power, coordination, reaction time)
2. Selecting exercises that target desired health-related components of fitness (muscular strength, muscular endurance, cardiovascular endurance, flexibility, body composition)
3. Selecting exercises that incorporate appropriate principles of training (overload, specificity, SAID, reversibility, progression, metabolic pathway) as they relate to the class format and objectives

4. Selecting and sequencing exercises within the basic components of a class (warm-up, conditioning, cool-down, flexibility) as it relates to class format and objectives
5. Determining appropriate exercises and sequencing based on class location, space parameters, and the size, skill, and fitness of the expected participant group
6. Designing exercise sequences, choreography, transitions, and flow to meet desired class objectives
7. Incorporating effective exercise progressions, regressions, and modifications into the class plan
8. Build variety into the class plan to meet the skill- and health-related components needs of the class participants

Task 4
Rehearse and refine the class plan in order to create smooth transitions and a positive class experience that will promote adherence.

Knowledge of:

1. Factors that promote adherence in a group fitness setting
2. Music variables that impact the class plan (e.g., BPM, structure, lyrics/content, applicable music licensing laws)
3. Group fitness class modifications that enhance transitions
4. Choreographic methods (e.g., freestyle vs structural), transitions, and sequential exercise movements
5. Teaching styles (e.g., command, practice, reciprocal, self-check, inclusion) appropriate for a group fitness class
6. Teaching strategies (e.g., slow-to-fast, repetition-reduction, spatial, part-to-whole, simple-to-complex)
7. Various communication and learning styles (visual, auditory, and kinesthetic)
8. Methods for manipulating class intensity (e.g., exercise selection, equipment, music, movement speed)
9. Effective dimensional cueing (verbal, nonverbal, kinesthetic)
10. Methods for demonstrating the use of group fitness–related equipment and appropriate purpose
11. Applied kinesiology, biomechanics, and exercise physiology

Skill in:

1. Determining appropriate music (e.g., BPM, structure, decibels, lyrics, content) for group fitness class components based on class format, intended audience, and expected outcomes
2. Phrasing music and applying movement to music where applicable
3. Incorporating appropriate cueing techniques (verbal, nonverbal, kinesthetic) based on class format to achieve desired class outcomes
4. Determining appropripate transitions and sequences for varied class formats and objectives
5. Identifying elements of group fitness class plans that require modifications based on class format and objectives
6. Recognize need for change and adjustment as it related to environmental factors (e.g., space, heat, cold)
7. Evaluating functionality, efficacy, and quality of the class plan
8. Executing class plan

DOMAIN II: GROUP LEADERSHIP AND INSTRUCTION

49%

Task 1

Conduct pre-class assessments of the space, equipment, environment, and participants in order to identify potential hazards and make appropriate adjustments to the class plan to ensure a safe and effective experience for all participants.

Knowledge of:

1. Environmental factors (e.g., cold, heat, humidity, pollution, altitude, acoustics, exercise floor surface, exercise equipment, class setting) that affect class experience and participant safety
2. Potential hazards in a group fitness class setting (e.g., damaged equipment, wet floor, environmental extremes)
3. Guidelines and recommendations for various group fitness formats and settings
4. Techniques, equipment, space, and environmental requirements for safe and effective exercises
5. Factors that affect equipment safety
6. Class set-up principles
7. Specific exercise guidelines, limitations, and needs for varied special populations groups

Skill in:

1. Identifying hazards in a group fitness class setting
2. Analyzing equipment in relation to class design, placement, and spacing
3. Modifying space, equipment, environmental factors, and class design to provide a safe and effective experience for group fitness participants
4. Recognizing the needs and capabilities of participants from different special population groups
5. Modifying class design to meet the needs of class participants with varying levels of fitness, movement skills, and special needs
6. Adapting class components, exercises, and music to provide an inclusive and fun exercise experience for participants of varying cultural backgrounds and demographics (e.g., age, gender)
7. Adapting class content and/or programming based on specific environmental conditions

Task 2

Implement appropriate introduction and closing activities in order to create a welcoming, positive, and engaging environment and to promote class adherence.

Knowledge of:

1. Factors that create a positive experience for class participants
2. Factors that influence adherence
3. Strategies and methods for providing effective customer service
4. Effective group and interpersonal communication techniques that enhance rapport (e.g., active listening, open-ended questioning, acknowledgement, use of empathy and compassion)
5. Methods for effectively gathering information about participant special needs related to physical activity

Skill in:

1. Delivering opening and closing statements that summarize the class and review objectives
2. Providing quality customer service on an individual and group basis
3. Establishing and developing rapport with and among class participants
4. Establishing an atmosphere of trust and enjoyment
5. Fostering a sense of community among class participants
6. Soliciting feedback from participants
7. Implementing follow-up strategies to help build exercise adherence
8. Gathering information from participant about their special needs related to physical activity

Task 3

Instruct participants on proper movements using demonstration and verbal and nonverbal communication in order to improve participant technique and form, reduce risk of injury, improve performance, and enhance class experience.

Knowledge of:

1. Appropriate body alignment and posture (e.g., neutral spine) during proper execution of exercises
2. Appropriate techniques and situations for cueing movements via touch
3. Correct exercise techniques and movement patterns relevant for a variety of group exercise formats and methods
4. Balance (static and dynamic)
5. Positive and inclusive language
6. Strategies for effective verbal cueing and prevention of vocal stress
7. Teaching techniques (e.g., command, practice, reciprocal, self-check, inclusion) appropriate for a group fitness class
8. Teaching strategies (e.g., slow-to-fast, repetition-reduction, spatial, part-to-whole, simple-to-complex) used to facilitate participant learning
9. Effective communication techniques (e.g., verbal, nonverbal)
10. Cueing techniques (e.g., verbal, visual, kinesthetic)
11. Learning styles (e.g., visual, auditory, kinesthetic)
12. Domains and stages of learning (e.g., cognitive, associative, autonomous)
13. Participant-centered teaching strategies
14. Methods for improving flexibility, exercise, movement, and balance to accommodate various fitness levels

Skill in:

1. Applying effective instructional methods for teaching and correcting exercise techniques, balance, and movements
2. Selecting and implementing appropriate teaching strategies (e.g., slow-to-fast, repetition-reduction, spatial, part-to-whole, simple-to-complex) to accommodate participant fitness, skill levels, cultural background, and class modality
3. Leading exercise through mirroring and matching techniques
4. Selecting appropriate communication styles for various group fitness formats, objectives, and participants
5. Teaching and executing exercises with proper form and technique for each movement
6. Cueing exercise movements, modifications, and transitions

7. Using verbal cuing methods that effectively prevent vocal stress
8. Using various teaching styles (e.g., command, practice, reciprocal, self-check, inclusion) in a group fitness class
9. Implementing appropriate exercise regressions and progressions
10. Manipulating various movements, pieces of equipment, types of music, and teaching styles within any class format
11. Accommodating participants in various stages of learning (i.e., cognitive, associative, autonomous)
12. Teaching multiple options for flexibility, exercise, movement, and balance to accommodate various fitness levels
13. Communicating succinctly and with purpose

Task 4

Coach participants using appropriate methods in order to motivate participants, increase participant confidence, create a positive and inclusive environment, reduce risk of injury, and improve performance.

Knowledge of:
1. Factors that create a positive experience for class participants
2. Factors that influence exercise participation and adherence (e.g., personal, environmental, activity)
3. Effective motivational techniques that engage participants with various skills, limitations, preferences, and expectations
4. Effective group and interpersonal communication techniques that enhance rapport (e.g., active listening, open-ended questioning, acknowledgement, use of empathy and compassion)
5. Transtheoretical stages-of-change model (i.e., precontemplation, contemplation, preparation, action, maintenance)
6. Participant-centered teaching strategies
7. Components of effective feedback
8. Types and appropriate use of feedback (e.g., corrective, value, neutral statements)
9. Varied ability and capabilities within each special-population group

Skill in:
1. Building rapport and trust with class participants (e.g., learning participant names, being accessible and approachable, using culturally appropriate nonverbal communication techniques such as eye contact)
2. Fostering a sense of community and camaraderie among class participants
3. Using effective listening techniques (e.g., minimal encouragement, reflecting, summarizing)
4. Selecting appropriate motivational techniques for desired outcomes
5. Accommodating participants in the various stages of learning and readiness to change
6. Interpreting nonverbal communication
7. Applying appropriate feedback based on participant skill, fitness level, and/or cultural background
8. Providing effective feedback to the class to help participants improve exercise form without negatively impacting self-efficacy and/or adherence
9. Communicating effectively with various personality styles

Task 5

Implement ongoing modifications based on identified needs in order to reduce risk of injury and improve performance.

Knowledge of:

1. Physiological responses and adaptations that result from variations in environmental conditions (e.g., heat, humidity, cold, wind, pollution)
2. Physical signs and symptoms of overexertion, fatigue, and dehydration
3. Exercise guidelines for different special population groups (e.g., youth, older adults, pre-/post-natal, diabetes, obesity, and other diseases, disorders, and disabilities)
4. Training variables that improve performance
5. The relationships of variety, progression, and regression to the prevention of injuries and boredom
6. Factors that increase and reduce injury risk in a group exercise class
7. Strategies for identifying participant needs for specific programming to improve cardiorespiratory fitness, kinesthetic awareness, balance, functional movement, posture, muscular endurance, strength, and flexibility
8. Effective teaching and communication methods for correcting exercise techniques, balance, and movement
9. Methods for manipulating class intensity (e.g., exercise selection, equipment, music, movement speed)
10. Criteria requiring immediate termination of exercise participation

Skill in:

1. Monitoring intensity levels of varied groups of participants in group fitness classes
2. Identifying participants in need of exercise modifications to prevent risk of injury
3. Recognizing the need for progression, regression, and modification of exercise variables to facilitate improved performance and/or reduce the risk of injury
4. Modifying exercise variables (e.g., exercise selection, intensity, duration, recovery) to improve participant performance, adherence, and self-efficacy
5. Regressing and modifying exercises to reduce risk of injury
6. Adapting fitness- and skill-related components of exercise classes to accommodate various fitness levels of participants
7. Adapting class compenents, exercises, and sequencing based on environmental conditions that require exercise program modification
8. Identifying signs and symptoms of overexertion, overexposure, dehydration, and the need to end exercise sessions for individuals and groups
9. Recognizing health issues that require exercise modifications in order for individuals with special needs to safely participant in group exercise classes of varying formats
10. Integrating and modifying programs to meet the needs of participants classified in special-population groups
11. Accommodating participants in the various stages of learning
12. Incorporating various teaching methods (e.g., command, practice, reciprocal, self-check, inclusion) appropriate for a group fitness class
13. Manipulating various exercises, pieces of equipment, types of music, and teaching styles within any class format
14. Observing and interpreting nonverbal communication

Task 6

Educate participants on general health and fitness principles, including the benefits of basic movements, in order to improve performance, reduce risk of injury, and increase participant self-efficacy.

Knowledge of:

1. Methods and reasons for monitoring exercise intensity [e.g., heart rate, talk test, ratings of perceived exertion (RPE), dyspnea scale], and their use, precautions, and limitations
2. Applications and limitations in the calculations of target heart rate: percent of heart-rate reserve, age-predicted maximal heart rate, and measured maximal heart rate
3. Health-related components of fitness (e.g., muscular strength, muscular endurance, cardiovascular endurance, flexibility, body composition)
4. Skill-related components of fitness (e.g., balance, agility, speed, power, coordination, reaction time)
5. Teaching styles (e.g., command, practice, reciprocal, self-check, inclusion) appropriate for a group fitness class
6. Teaching strategies (e.g., slow-to-fast, repetition-reduction, spatial, part-to-whole, simple-to-complex)
7. Various communication and learning styles (visual, auditory, kinesthetic)
8. Effective dimensional cueing (verbal, nonverbal, kinesthetic)
9. Methods for demonstrating the use of group fitness–related equipment and appropriate purpose
10. Effects of acute and regular exercise on health and fitness parameters, and modifiable risk factors
11. General medical conditions and common physical disabilities of special populations
12. Methods used to accommodate various fitness levels
13. Educational techniques for disseminating information
14. Scope of practice

Skill in:

1. Determining pertinent information to disseminate to class participants based on level of interest and information complexity
2. Identifying appropriate healthcare and allied health professionals for referral
3. Teaching groups and individuals about exercise science–related topics
4. Teaching class participants techniques for self-monitoring exercise intensity (e.g., talk test, heart rate, RPE, dyspnea scale)
5. Providing effective feedback to the class to help participants improve exercise form without negatively impacting self-efficacy and/or adherence
6. Modifying teaching styles and methods to meet the needs of class participants
7. Demonstrating proper exercise techiques
8. Cueing (verbal, nonverbal, kinesthetic) proper exercise techniques, intensities, sequences, and transitions

DOMAIN III: PROFESSIONAL CONDUCT, SAFETY, AND RISK MANAGEMENT 19%

Task 1

Review class objectives and evaluate feedback from a variety of sources (e.g., participant feedback, observation, self-assessment) in order to make improvements to future class experiences.

Knowledge of:

1. Effective strategies for evaluating and revising goals and objectives
2. Effective communication, coaching, and teaching strategies
3. Feedback types and methods (e.g., positive, negative, performance, immediate, specific)
4. Strategies for evaluating effectiveness in meeting class objectives in order to identify successes and areas for improvement
5. Strategies and methods for building adherence (e.g., building rapport, being approachable, creating a community)
6. Concepts of variety and progression as they relate to the prevention of injury and boredom
7. Factors that create a positive and compelling experience for participants
8. Components of a class plan (e.g., warm-up, conditioning, cool-down, flexibility)
9. Group fitness class formats and related exercise selection
10. Fair and equal treatment for all participants
11. Methods used to accommodate various fitness levels
12. Characteristics of the well-qualified fitness instructor
13. Strategies to facilitate conflict resolution

Skill in:

1. Interpreting and evaluating achievement of objectives within a class plan
2. Interpreting and evaluating participant progress
3. Collaborating with participants to modify a class plan
4. Gathering feedback from a variety of sources (e.g., participants, observation, supervisors, self)
5. Using appropriate feedback to improve a class plan
6. Determining class variables that require modification
7. Manipulating various exercises (e.g., movement, intensity, sequence), equipment, music, and teaching styles for future class plans
8. Providing an inclusive class environment
9. Addressing and alleviating conflict resolution

Task 2

Maintain and enhance competency by staying current on scientifically based research and best practices using credible resources (e.g., continuing education, professional organizations, industry journals) in order to provide safe and effective classes.

Knowledge of:

1. Appropriate agencies and organizations that establish and publish scientifically based health and fitness standards and guidelines for the general public and special populations (e.g., USDA, ACOG, ACE, NIH)
2. Available and credible resources for academically sound information
3. Scope of practice for ACE Certified Group Fitness Instructors
4. Available and credible continuing education providers and programs (e.g., conferences, workshops, college/university courses, online courses, home study courses)
5. Appropriate uses of technology and equipment in a group fitness setting
6. Reputable sources for product and service information

Skill in:

1. Identifying credible resources for fitness-related standards, guidelines, research, and continuing education
2. Determining information that is pertinent to the class plan and participants
3. Identifying and applying appropriate uses of technology and equipment in a group fitness setting
4. Determining appropriate action within the GFI's scope of practice

Task 3

Adhere to recognized standards, guidelines, policies, laws, and regulations, including making appropriate referrals when necessary, in order to protect participants, instructors, and other relevant parties and to manage risk and liability.

Knowledge of:

1. Industry guidelines, appropriate laws, and facility procedures relating to safety, risk management, emergencies, and injuries in fitness facilities and/or group exercise classes (indoor and outdoor)
2. Standards, laws, and regulations governing confidentiality
3. Medical conditions that affect a participant's ability to exercise safely in class (e.g., diabetes, hypertension, heart disease, arthritis, osteoporosis)
4. Physiological responses to and recommendations for exercising in various environmental conditions (e.g., heat, cold, humidity, altitude, pollution)
5. Basic procedures for injury management and emergency response within the GFI's scope of practice (e.g., CPR, AED, basic first aid, RICE)
6. Procedures for documenting accidents, injuries, and incident reports, while safeguarding participant confidentiality
7. Appropriate insurance protections (e.g., professional liability insurance, general liability insurance, workers' compensation insurance, health and disability insurance) for group fitness professionals, participants, and other relevant parties in a variety of settings (e.g., indoors, pool, outdoors)
8. Scope of practice for ACE Certified Group Fitness Instructors
9. American Council on Exercise Professional Practices and Disciplinary Procedures
10. Professional boundaries for maintaining participant confidentiality and instructor privacy
11. Appropriate use of social media (e.g., professional boundaries)
12. Music licensing copyright laws

Skill in:

1. Utilizing various methods for monitoring intensity (e.g., RPE, heart rate, dyspnea) to prevent overexertion in regular class and adverse environmental conditions
2. Identifying signs and symptoms of overexertion and making appropriate modifications
3. Administering basic injury-management procedures, and completing appropriate reports (e.g., incident reports)
4. Safeguarding confidential information
5. Carrying out facility/location emergency management procedures
6. Following industry guidelines to minimize risk for the GFI and class participants (e.g., adequate warm-up and cool-down, recognizing potential hazards, providing proper instruction)
7. Determining appropriate insurance and levels of coverage necessary for the GFI based upon the teaching facility and class logistics
8. Referring participants to more qualified fitness, medical, or health professionals when appropriate
9. Determining appropriate action within the GFI's scope of practice
10. Applying appropriate and professional use of social media, music and trademarks

PRINCIPLES OF NUTRITION FOR THE GROUP FITNESS INSTRUCTOR

NATALIE DIGATE MUTH

Many participants aspire to improve their fitness and optimize their health, but on a day-to-day basis struggle to maintain a healthful diet and commit to an exercise program. An ACE Certified Group Fitness Instructor (GFI) has the difficult but rewarding task of helping to translate the federal government's nutrition advice into easily understood action items for individual participants and groups of participants.

DIETARY REFERENCE INTAKES

Much of the advice contained within the *2015–2020 Dietary Guidelines for Americans* (8th ed.) [U.S. Department of Agriculture (USDA), 2015] and MyPlate is based upon **Dietary Reference Intakes (DRIs)**. It used to be that dietary recommendations were based simply off of the **Recommended Dietary Allowance (RDA),** or the amount of a particular nutrient that would be sufficient to prevent deficiency in 97 to 98% of the population. However, in 2000, the Food and Nutrition Board of the Institute of Medicine (IOM) released the complete set of DRIs to help nutrition professionals better assess and plan diets. DRI is a generic term used to refer to four types of reference values:

- Recommended Dietary Allowance (RDA): The level of intake of a nutrient that is adequate to meet the known needs of practically all healthy persons

- **Estimated Average Requirement (EAR):** An adequate intake in 50% of an age- and gender-specific group

- **Tolerable Upper Intake Level (UL):** The maximal intake that is unlikely to pose a risk of adverse health effects to almost all individuals in an age- and gender-specific group

- **Adequate Intake (AI):** A recommended nutrient intake level that, based on research, appears to be sufficient for good health; used when the RDA cannot be based on an EAR

All of the abbreviations and accompanying definitions that make up the DRIs can be confusing, even for the most seasoned nutrition experts. To help clear up the confusion, note that the RDA and the EAR should be considered together. If a person's intake falls well below the EAR, it is likely that person does not consume enough of the nutrient. If the level is between the EAR and the RDA, then it is likely the participant consumes enough of the nutrients (50%+ likelihood). If the level is at or above the RDA, then the participant almost certainly consumes a sufficient amount (since the RDA covers 97 to 98% of the population).

If the nutrient has not been adequately studied and too little information is available to determine an EAR (a level good enough for 50% of the population), then it is also not possible to determine an RDA (a level good enough for 97 to 98% of the population). In these cases, the AI is published. If a participant's intake is at or exceeds the AI, then it is very likely that he or she consumes enough of the nutrient to prevent deficiency. If intake is below the AI, then it is possible (but not certain) that the participant is deficient in that nutrient.

Comparing a person's usual intake of a nutrient to the UL helps to determine whether he or she is at risk of nutrient toxicity. The UL is set so that even the most sensitive people should not have an adverse response to a nutrient at intake levels near the UL. Thus, many people who have intakes above the UL may never experience a nutrient toxicity, though it is difficult to assess which participants may be most and least at risk for a nutrient overdose.

Ultimately, "how much you should eat" is an approximation based on a series of probabilities that are known collectively as the DRIs. DRIs for specific nutrients are available at www.iom.edu/dris and are described in this appendix.

DIETARY GUIDELINES

The *Dietary Guidelines* are written by a panel of nutrition experts from a variety of fields, such as dietetics, medicine, and public health, who review the nutrition-related scientific literature to develop the latest evidence-based nutrition recommendations for good health. This committee of experts develops a report that is made available to the public and federal agencies for comment. The feedback is reviewed and, when deemed appropriate by congress, incorporated into the document. Once published, the document is intended to be used by health professionals and government officials to develop educational materials and design and implement nutrition-related programs.

While the following section outlines the key content provided in the *Dietary Guidelines,* all GFIs should take the time to read the *Guidelines* in full and familiarize themselves with the many tools offered at www.health.gov/dietaryguidelines. Note that the *Guidelines* are updated every five years, so it is essential that all health and fitness professionals visit the website periodically to ensure their knowledge is up-to-date.

Though the development of the *Guidelines* is influenced by political pressures, efforts are made to ultimately publish scientifically supported evidence for optimal nutrition for the generally healthy population. As such, the *Dietary Guidelines* generally reflect the best evidence on how to eat for optimal health for Americans aged two and older, including those at increased risk of chronic disease. The statements for which there is strongest scientific support are noted within the *Dietary Guidelines* and are emphasized in this chapter.

Most GFIs realize that sharing information contained within the *Dietary Guidelines* is within their **scope of practice**; however, few appreciate the quantity and depth of the nutrition information available. Though the *Guidelines* do not typically reflect the latest nutrition trends and controversies, they do provide quality nutrition information supported by solid scientific evidence.

The major nutrition information, how it pertains to the GFIs, and how they can translate this information into programs, tip sheets, and value-added services for participants are described here. Readers are referred to www.health.gov/dietaryguidelines for a full review of the report.

BALANCING CALORIES TO MANAGE WEIGHT

Every GFI understands that the balance of calories in and calories out determines weight status—if more energy is consumed than expended, a person gains weight; if intake equals output, a person maintains weight; and if energy out exceeds calories in, then a person loses weight. The *Guidelines* offer GFIs an opportunity to take this concept to the next level and share specific nutrition strategies to help a participant manage weight.

WEIGHT-MANAGEMENT RECOMMENDATIONS FOR SPECIAL POPULATIONS

One of the most common reasons participants seek out the services of GFIs is for help with managing weight. The following list briefly explains how GFIs should address those issues for special populations:

- *Adults with obesity [**body mass index (BMI)** ≥30 kg/m²]:* Change eating and activity to lose weight and prevent additional weight gain.

- *Adults who are overweight (BMI ≥25 kg/m²):* Avoid additional weight gain and lose weight, especially for those individuals at increased risk for cardiovascular disease. Major risk factors for cardiovascular disease, in addition to **overweight** and **obesity,** include elevated **cholesterol, type 2 diabetes, hypertension, metabolic syndrome,** physical inactivity, and tobacco use.

- *Children with overweight or obesity (BMI percentile for age and gender >85% or >95%, respectively):* Change nutrition and physical-activity patterns so that the BMI-for-age percentile does not increase over time. In essence, this recommendation advises *against* weight loss for most children, but rather promotion of weight maintenance as a child grows taller, effectively reducing BMI. A GFI who works with children should gain competence in understanding and plotting BMI-for-age so as to understand the criteria for determining overweight and obesity in children and to monitor a child's status over time. A GFI who works with a child who is affected with overweight or obesity will also benefit from close communication with the child's parents and pediatrician, with the permission of the child and his or her family.

■ *Pregnant women:* Follow the weight-gain recommendations provided by the 2009 IOM report, which states that underweight women should gain 28 to 40 pounds (13 to 18 kg), normal-weight women should gain 25 to 35 pounds (11 to 16 kg), overweight women should gain 15 to 25 pounds (7 to 11 kg), and women with obesity should gain 11 to 20 pounds (5 to 9 kg) (IOM, 2009).

■ *Overweight older adults (65 years and older):* Avoid additional weight gain. Older adults with obesity and cardiovascular disease risk factors should aim to lose weight to benefit health and reduce the risk of chronic disease and disability.

DETERMINING CALORIE AND NUTRIENT NEEDS

The *Dietary Guidelines* offer a fairly detailed table to help determine typical calorie needs. Note that the low end of the range provided is for a sedentary person, while the high end of the range is for a very active person. For example, a 25-year-old sedentary male needs approximately 2,400 calories each day, while an active male of the same age needs around 3,000 calories. Online tools for helping the participant estimate caloric needs are also available through the MyPlate portal (see page 259).

> This and other tables featured in the *2015– 2020 Dietary Guidelines* are available as free PDFs at www.ACEfitness. org/GFIresources.

The IOM has established a range, known as the **Acceptable Macronutrient Distribution Range (AMDR),** for the percentage of calories that should come from **carbohydrates, protein,** and **fat** for both optimal health and reduction of chronic disease risk (Table 1). While many weight-loss diets purport success based on variations from these recommendations, strong evidence

Table 1

RECOMMENDED MACRONUTRIENT PROPORTIONS BY AGE

	CARBOHYDRATE	PROTEIN	FAT
Young children (1–3 years)	45–65%	5–20%	30–40%
Older children and adolescents (4–18 years)	45–65%	10–30%	25–35%
Adults (19 and older)	45–65%	10–35%	20–35%

Source: Institute of Medicine (2002). *Dietary Reference Intakes for Energy, Carbohydrate, Fiber, Fat, Fatty Acids, Cholesterol, Protein, and Amino Acids.* Washington, D.C.: The National Academies Press.

supports that it is not the relative proportion of macronutrients that determines long-term weight-loss success, but rather calorie content and whether a person can maintain the intake over time.

Americans should take into consideration the types of carbohydrates, proteins, and fats consumed to meet needs. While the **glycemic index (GI)** and **glycemic load (GL)** of carbohydrates are frequently discussed, strong evidence shows that these factors are not associated with body weight. The *Dietary Guidelines* advise that Americans get the majority of carbohydrates from natural, unprocessed foods such as whole grains, beans and peas, vegetables, and fruits rather than refined grains and added sugars. The best protein sources are lean meats and plant proteins rather than red meats and other animal protein sources that are high in **saturated fat.** The healthiest fats are **monounsaturated fat** and **polyunsaturated fat,** which are found in seafood, nuts, seeds, and oils.

Taken together, a person's approximate caloric needs multiplied by the percentage of calories from each of the macronutrients can help to estimate the number of grams of carbohydrate, protein, and fat that should be consumed in a day, based on the *Dietary Guidelines*.

UNDERSTANDING CURRENT INTAKE

The *Dietary Guidelines* strongly encourage individuals to monitor dietary intake. Several tools are available to do this. While most GFIs are not qualified to analyze dietary logs, there are tools available to help track a participant's intake and provide an analysis of dietary quality, while staying within the scope of practice. For instance, the free USDA SuperTracker tool is an excellent method to monitor intake (see page 259).

[DO THE MATH]

Macronutrient Needs Sample Problem

One of your participants, a 30-year-old moderately active man named Carlos, is trying to determine how much of the three macronutrients he should be eating on a daily basis in order to adhere to the *Dietary Guidelines* you discussed with him after one of your classes. Use the following information to determine how many grams of carbohydrate, protein, and fat Carlos should be eating each day:

According to the *Dietary Guidelines,* Carlos should be consuming approximately 2,600 calories per day, and his diet should consist of 45–65% carbohydrate, 10–35% protein, and 20–35% fat. For example:

Carbohydrate: 2,600 calories x 0.55 = 1,430 calories

Protein: 2,600 calories x 0.25 = 650 calories

Fat: 2,600 calories x 0.20 = 520 calories

Answers:

Convert calories to grams (1 gram of carbohydrate = 4 calories; 1 gram of protein = 4 calories; and 1 gram of fat = 9 calories).

This participant should consume the following:

Carbohydrate: 1,430 calories / 4 = 358 grams

Protein: 650 calories / 4 = 163 grams

Fat: 520 calories / 9 = 58 grams

NUTRITION STRATEGIES TO MANAGE WEIGHT

The following evidence-based tips are important to share with participants and incorporate into nutrition education offerings to help a participant manage weight:

■ **Portion** size is directly related to weight status. Smaller portion size contributes to weight loss, so participants should pay careful attention to this variable.

■ Decrease visits to fast-food and quick-service restaurants. People who eat at these establishments one or more times per week are at high risk of weight gain, overweight, and obesity.

■ Aim for a calorie deficit of 500 calories per day, either through increased physical activity or decreased caloric intake or a combination of the two. Smaller deficits will also contribute to weight loss over time.

■ Increase intake of whole grains, vegetables, and fruit. Moderate evidence suggests that adults who eat more high-**fiber** whole grains, fruits, and vegetables have lower body weight than their peers who eat fewer **servings** of these types of foods.

■ Decrease intake of sugar-sweetened beverages. Strong evidence supports that children and adolescents who consume more sugary drinks have higher body weight

(USDA, 2010). Sugar-sweetened beverages are nutrient-poor and calorie-rich, and the *Dietary Guidelines* advise that they should be consumed only when other nutrient needs have been met, without exceeding daily calorie needs. Decreasing intake of sodas, juice, high-calorie mixtures used to make alcohol drinks, and other sugar-sweetened beverages can help to create a caloric deficit. Excessive alcohol intake is also associated with weight gain. At 7 calories per gram, alcohol is very high in calories with little or no nutrient value.

■ Eat breakfast. Eating breakfast is associated with weight loss and improved nutrient intake, while skipping breakfast is associated with excess body weight, especially in children and adolescents.

In addition to strategies highlighting specific types of foods or food groups or behavioral strategies to manage caloric intake, participants benefit from adopting an overall healthy eating plan to optimize health and manage weight.

PHYSICAL-ACTIVITY CONSIDERATIONS

GFIs understand the importance of physical activity in weight management. The *Dietary Guidelines* include a discussion of physical activity and its important role in contributing to calorie

balance. They also make a key recommendation that individuals adhere to the *2008 Physical Activity Guidelines for Americans,* a document that all GFIs should study (visit www.health.gov/paguidelines/ for a review) (U.S. Department of Health & Human Services, 2008). Additionally, GFIs can read more about how physical activity pertains to weight loss in the American College of Sports Medicine's Position Stand: "Appropriate Physical Activity Intervention Strategies for Weight Loss and Prevention of Weight Regain for Adults" (Donnelly et al., 2009). Importantly, limiting screen time to fewer than two hours per day and avoiding eating while watching TV can help to avoid excess weight gain.

BEHAVIORAL STRATEGIES TO MANAGE WEIGHT

The *Dietary Guidelines* also emphasize the importance of behavioral strategies in helping to manage weight, especially monitoring what, when, why, and how much people eat.

FOOD COMPONENTS AND FOODS TO REDUCE

- *Sodium:* <2,300 mg per day. Those who have prehypertension or hypertension should aim for sodium intake <1,500 mg per day.

- *Saturated fatty acids:* <10% of calories per day. Replace saturated fats with monounsaturated and polyunsaturated fat, such as those found in certain oils extracted from plants (e.g., olive, peanut, and soybean oils).

- *Trans fat:* Aim for zero intake by limiting foods with trans fats, partially hydrogenated oil, and other saturated fats.

- *Added sugars:* Limit to <10% of total caloric intake.

- *Refined grains:* Limit consumption, especially from foods that contain solid fats, added sugars, and sodium.

- *Alcohol:* If consumed, limit to one drink per day for women and two drinks per day for men.

FOOD COMPONENTS AND NUTRIENTS TO INCREASE

- *Vegetables and fruits:* Vegetables and fruits are high in **vitamins, minerals,** and fiber while being low in calories. People should eat a variety of whole fruits, as well as a variety of vegetables from all subgroups: dark green, red, and orange, legumes (beans and peas), starchy, and other.

- *Whole grains:* Whole grains are naturally rich in nutrients, including **iron,** magnesium, selenium, B vitamins, and dietary fiber. At least half of grains consumed should be whole grains.

- *Milk and milk products:* While not necessary to meet nutrient needs, milk and milk products contain many nutrients, including calcium, vitamin D, and potassium. People should choose fat-free or low-fat dairy products.

- *Seafood, nuts, and seeds:* These foods are high in protein, B vitamins, vitamin E, iron, zinc, magnesium, and healthy oils. Seafood is particularly high in **omega-3 fatty acids.** People should eat a variety of protein foods, including seafood, lean meats and poultry, eggs, legumes, nuts, seeds, and soy products.

- *Dietary fiber:* Dietary fiber increases feelings of fullness, promotes normal bowel function, and may help decrease the risk of cardiovascular disease, obesity, and type 2 diabetes.

- *Vitamins and minerals:*
  - ✔ Potassium
  - ✔ Calcium
  - ✔ Vitamin D
  - ✔ Iron
  - ✔ Folate
  - ✔ Vitamin B12

COMMON FEATURES OF HEALTHY EATING PATTERNS

While health eating patterns can exist in many different forms, they tend to share some common features. These features include:

- High in vegetables and fruits

- High in whole grains

- Moderate amounts of foods high in protein, including seafood, beans and peas, nuts, seeds, soy products, meat, poultry, and eggs

- Small amounts of added sugars

- More oils than solid fats

- Low in full-fat (whole) milk and milk products (though some healthy eating patterns include high amounts of low-fat and fat-free milk and milk products)

The reality is that very few Americans eat in line with these healthy eating patterns. Figure 1 shows the typical American intake compared with the recommendations. The GFI could target any or all of these areas as opportunities for positive nutrition changes when working with participants.

Figure 1
How do typical American diets compare to recommended intake levels of limits?

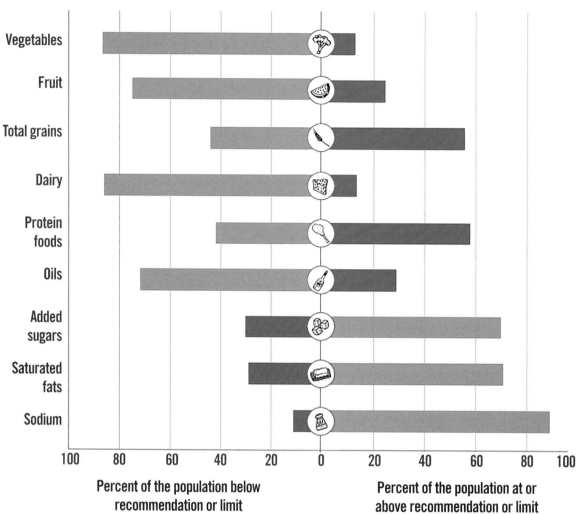

| | Intake below recommendation or above limit | | Intake at/below recommendation or below limit |

Percent of the population below recommendation or limit

Percent of the population at or above recommendation or limit

Note: The center (0) line is the goal or limit. For most, those represented by the orange sections of the bars, shifting toward the center line will improve their eating pattern.

Data sources: What We Eat in America, NHANES 2007-2010 for average intakes by age-sex group. Healthy U.S.-Style Food Patterns, which vary based on age, sex, and activity level, for recommended intakes and limits.

Moreover, the GFI may share information about any of the three healthful eating plans contained within the *Dietary Guidelines:* the USDA food patterns and **vegan/vegetarian** variations (intended to represent the *Dietary Guidelines*), the **Mediterranean eating plan** (associated with decreased cardiovascular risk and increased longevity), or the **DASH eating plan** (developed to prevent hypertension and other cardiovascular risk factors).

The tools and templates contained within the *Dietary Guidelines* allow the GFI to help participants identify their caloric needs, choose a healthful eating plan at the necessary caloric level, and then develop specific menus and meal plans to follow a chosen eating plan. The *Dietary Guidelines* form the basis for the online SuperTracker, which goes through this process electronically (www.supertracker.usda.gov).

MYPLATE

One tool that the federal government employs in an effort to translate recommendations into action is an icon representing a healthy eating plan (Figure 2). Up until 2011, the icon was a pyramid—first the Food Guide Pyramid and then MyPyramid. MyPyramid was a short-lived dietary tool, retired after just five years in favor of the current simpler icon.

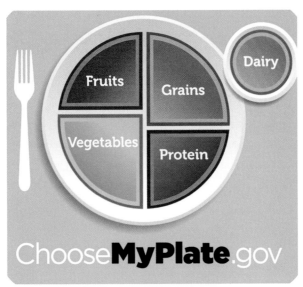

Figure 2
MyPlate

Based on the *Dietary Guidelines,* MyPlate is an interactive online tool (www.ChooseMyPlate.gov). MyPlate simplifies the government's nutrition messages into an easily understood and implemented graphic—a dinner plate divided into four sections: fruits, vegetables, protein, and grains accompanied by a glass of 1% (low-fat) or non-fat milk. The goal is to influence Americans to eat a more balanced diet by encouraging people to make their plate 50% fruits and vegetables. Furthermore, a GFI can search the MyPlate website to find free downloadable materials to help facilitate the nutrition education process with their participants.

On the website www.supertracker.usda.gov, consumers can input their age, gender, height, weight, and physical-activity level to get an individualized eating plan to meet caloric needs. The program calculates estimated energy expenditure based on this demographic information. Within seconds, users are categorized into one of 12 different energy levels (anywhere from 1,000 to 3,200 calories) and are given the recommended number of servings—measured in cups and ounces—to eat from each of the five food groups (vegetables, fruit, protein, grains, and dairy). A number of empty calories [those attained from **solid fats and added sugars (SoFAS)**] is also allocated for

that individual. By following these recommendations, users have a sound diet for disease prevention and weight maintenance based on their personalized needs. This free tool is a beneficial starting point for recreational athletes, as well as the general population. Overall, MyPlate encourages people to:

- Balance calories from an energy intake vs. energy output perspective.
- Enjoy food, but eat fewer calories.
- Eat more vegetables, fruits, whole grains, and fat-free or 1% milk dairy products for adequate potassium, calcium, vitamin D, and fiber.
- Make half their plate fruits and vegetables.
- Switch to fat-free or low-fat (1%) milk.
- Make half their grains whole grains.
- Eat fewer foods high in solid (typically saturated and trans) fat, added sugars, and salt.
- Compare sodium in foods and then choose the lower-sodium versions.
- Drink water instead of sugary drinks to help cut sugar and unnecessary calories.

FOOD LABELS

For people to make health nutrition decisions, they first have to be able to understand which nutrients contribute to a healthy diet, and second, know which foods contain those nutrients. While the bulk of a healthy diet is made up of whole, unprocessed foods that do not carry food labels, there are processed or prepared foods (e.g., low-fat milk and milk products) that can be part of a healthy diet that do have food labels. The food label, a required component of nearly all packaged foods, can help people turn knowledge into action. It can also be a source of confusion and misunderstanding.

READING THE NUTRITION LABEL

While the nutrition label provides a large amount of useful nutrition information, it can also be a source of confusion for many consumers. A GFI can play an important role in helping consumers effectively use the nutrition label to guide them in making healthy choices.

A STEPWISE APPROACH

A GFI can advise individuals to dissect the food label (Figure 3) by taking a stepwise approach. Start from the top with the serving size and the number of servings per container. In general, serving sizes are standardized so that consumers can compare similar products, such as Triscuits and Wheat Thins or natural applesauce and sweetened applesauce (although this is not always the case). All of the nutrient amounts listed on the food label are for one serving, so it is important to determine how many servings are actually being consumed to accurately assess nutrient intake.

Next, consumers should look at the total calories and calories from fat. The total calories indicate how much energy a person gets from a particular food. Americans tend to consume too many calories, and too many calories from fat, without meeting daily nutrient requirements. This part of the nutrition label is the most important factor for weight control. In general, 40 calories per serving is considered low, 100 calories is moderate, and 400 or more calories is considered high.

The next two sections of the label note the nutrient content of the food product. Consumers should try to minimize intake of the first three nutrients listed—fat (especially saturated and **trans fat**), cholesterol, and sodium—and aim to consume adequate amounts of fiber, as well as vitamins and minerals, especially vitamin A, vitamin C, calcium, and iron. The food label includes the total amount of sugars (natural and added). Though the label does not separately identify added sugars, natural sugars are found primarily in milk and fruit. Therefore, if the food item does not belong to either of those two food groups, the amount of sugar contained in the product approximates added sugar. For foods that contain milk or fruit, added sugars can be identified in the ingredients list.

The **percent daily values (PDV)** are listed for key nutrients to make it easier to compare products (just make sure that the serving sizes are similar), evaluate **nutrient content claims** (does 1/3 reduced-sugar cereal really contain less carbohydrate than a similar cereal of a different brand?), and make informed dietary tradeoffs (e.g., balance consumption of a high-fat product for lunch with lower-fat products throughout the rest of the day). In general, 5% daily value or less is considered low, while 20% daily value or more is considered high.

The footnote at the bottom of the label reminds consumers that all PDV are based on a 2,000-calorie diet. Individuals who need more or fewer calories should adjust recommendations accordingly. For example, 3 grams of fat provides 5% of the recommended amount for someone on a 2,000-calorie diet, but 7% for someone on a 1,500-calorie diet. The footnote also includes daily values for nutrients to limit (total fat, saturated fat, trans fat, cholesterol, and sodium), recommended carbohydrate intake for a 2,000-calorie diet (60% of calories), and minimal fiber recommendations for 2,000- and 2,500-calorie diets.

Legislation also requires food manufacturers to list all potential food **allergens** on food packaging. The most common food

Figure 3
Nutrition facts label

Serving Size
Is your serving the same size as the one on the label? If you eat double the serving size listed, you need to double the nutrient and calorie values. If you eat one-half the serving size shown here, cut the nutrient and calorie values in half.

Calories
Are you overweight? Cut back a little on calories. Look here to see how a serving of the food adds to your daily total. A 5'4", 138-lb active woman needs about 2,200 calories each day. A 5'10", 174-lb active man needs about 2,900.

Total Carbohydrate
Carbohydrates are in foods like bread, potatoes, fruits, and vegetables. Choose these often! They provide more nutrients than sugars like soda pop and candy.

Dietary Fiber
Grandmother called it "roughage," but her advice to eat more is still up-to-date! That goes for both soluble and insoluble kinds of dietary fiber. Fruits, vegetables, whole-grain foods, beans, and peas are all good sources and can help reduce the risk of heart disease and cancer.

Protein
Most Americans get more than they need. Where there is animal protein, there is also fat and cholesterol. Eat small servings of lean meat, fish, and poultry. Use skim or low-fat milk, yogurt, and cheese. Try vegetable proteins like beans, grains, and cereals.

Vitamins and Minerals
Your goal here is 100% of each for the day. Don't count on one food to do it all. Let a combination of foods add up to a winning score.

Total Fat
Fat is calorie-dense and, if consumed in large portions, can increase the risk of weight problems. While once vilified, most fat, in and of itself, is not bad.

Saturated Fat
Saturated fat is part of the total fat in food. It is listed separately because it is an important player in raising blood cholesterol and your risk of heart disease. Eat less!

Trans Fat
Trans fat works a lot like saturated fat, except it is worse. This fat starts out as a liquid unsaturated fat, but then food manufacturers add some hydrogen to it, turning it into a solid saturated fat (that is what "partially hydrogenated" means when you see it in the food ingredients). They do this to increase the shelf-life of the product, but in the body the trans fat damages the blood vessels and contributes to increasing blood cholesterol and the risk of heart disease.

Cholesterol
Too much cholesterol—a second cousin to fat—can lead to heart disease in some people. Aim to eat less than 300 mg each day.

Sodium
You call it "salt," the label calls it "sodium." Either way, it may add up to high blood pressure in some people. So, keep your sodium intake low—less than 2,300 mg each day. (The American Heart Association recommends no more than 3,000 mg of sodium per day for healthy adults.)

Daily Value
Feel like you are drowning in numbers? Let the Daily Value be your guide. Daily Values are listed for people who eat 2,000 calories each day. If you eat more, your personal daily value may be higher than what's listed on the label. If you eat less, your personal daily value may be lower. For fat, saturated fat, cholesterol, and sodium, choose foods with a low % Daily Value. For total carbohydrates, dietary fiber, vitamins, and minerals, your daily value goal is to reach 100% of each.

Nutrition Facts
Serving Size ½ cup (114g)
Servings Per Container 4

Amount Per Serving

Calories 90 — Calories from Fat 30

% Daily Value*

Total Fat 3g	**5%**
Saturated Fat 0g	0%
Trans Fat 0g	0%
Cholesterol 0mg	0%
Sodium 300mg	13%
Total Carbohydrate 13g	4%
Dietary Fiber 3g	12%
Sugars 3g	
Protein 3g	

Vitamin A	80%	•	Vitamin C	60%
Calcium	4%	•	Iron	4%

*Percent Daily Values are based on a 2,000 calorie diet. Your daily values may be higher or lower depending on your calorie needs:

	Calories	2,000	2,500
Total Fat	Less than	65g	80g
Sat Fat	Less than	20g	25g
Cholesterol	Less than	300mg	300mg
Sodium	Less than	2,400mg	2,400mg
Total Carbohydrate		300g	375g
Fiber		25g	30g

Calories per gram:
Fat 9 • Carbohydrate 4 • Protein 4

Ingredients: This portion of the label lists all of the foods and additives contained in a product, in order from the most prevalent ingredient to the least.

Allergens: This portion of the ingredient label identifies which of the most common allergens may be present in the product.

(More nutrients may be listed on some labels)

mg = milligrams (1,000 mg = 1 g)
g = grams (about 28 g = 1 ounce)

allergens are fish, shellfish, soybean, wheat, egg, milk, peanuts, and tree nuts. This information usually is included near the list of ingredients on the package. Clearly, this information is especially important to participants with food allergies. For participants who follow a gluten-free diet, this is also an easy way to identify if wheat is a product ingredient.

Carefully review the ingredients list. Note that the ingredient list is in decreasing order of substance weight in the product. That is, the ingredients that are listed first are the most abundant ingredients in the product. The ingredient list is useful to help identify whether or not the product contains trans fat, solid fats, added sugars, whole grains, and refined grains.

- *Trans fat:* Although trans fat is included in the "fat" section of the nutrition label, if the product contains <0.5 grams per serving, the manufacturer does not need to claim it. However, if a product contains "partially hydrogenated oils," then the product contains trans fat.

- *Solid fats:* If the ingredient list contains beef fat, butter, chicken fat, coconut oil, cream, hydrogenated oils, palm kernel oils, pork fat (lard), shortening, or stick margarine, then the product contains solid fats.

- *Added sugars:* Ingredients signifying added sugars include anhydrous dextrose, brown sugar, confectioner's powdered sugar, corn syrup, corn syrup solids, dextrin, fructose, high-fructose corn syrup, honey, invert sugar, lactose, malt syrup, maltose, maple syrup, molasses, nectar, pancake syrup, raw sugar, sucrose, sugar, white granulated sugar, cane

juice, evaporated corn sweetener, fruit juice concentrate, crystal dextrose, **glucose,** liquid fructose, sugar cane juice, and fruit nectar. In many cases, products contain multiple forms of sugar.

- *Whole grains:* To be considered 100% whole grain, the product must contain all of the essential parts of the original kernel—the bran, germ, and endosperm. When choosing products, the whole grain should be the first or second ingredient. Examples of whole grains include brown rice, buckwheat, bulgur (cracked wheat), millet, oatmeal, popcorn, quinoa, rolled oats, whole-grain sorghum, whole-grain triticale, whole-grain barley, whole-grain corn, whole oats/oatmeal, whole rye, whole wheat, and wild rice.

- *Refined grains:* Refined grains are listed as "enriched." If the first ingredient is an enriched grain, then the product is not a whole grain. This is one way to understand whether or not a "wheat bread" is actually whole wheat or a refined product.

While the food label is found on the side or the back of products, other health and nutrition claims are often visibly displayed on the front of the package, as described previously. Though the FDA regulates these claims, they frequently are a source of confusion. Consumers should be skeptical of front-of-package claims and evaluate them on a case-by-case basis. A loophole allowing "qualified health claims" has paved the way for manufacturers to claim unproven benefits to products, as long as the label states the claim is supported by very little scientific evidence.

 [DO THE MATH]

Nutrition Label Sample Problem

Using the nutrition label from Figure 3, determine (1) the number of calories per container; (2) the calories from carbohydrate, protein, and fat per serving; and (3) the percentage of calories from carbohydrate, protein, and fat.

90 calories per serving x 4 servings per container = 360 calories per container

Carbohydrate: 13 grams carbohydrate per serving x 4 calories per gram = 52 calories per serving from carbohydrate

Protein: 3 grams protein per serving x 4 calories per gram = 12 calories per serving from protein

Fat: 3 grams fat per serving x 9 calories per gram = 27 calories per serving from fat

[*Note:* The nutrition label does these calculations for you and lists the calories from fat on the label. On this label, it states that the product contains the rounded number 30 calories from fat vs. the calculated 27 calories from fat. Also note that the total calories is 91 per the calculations but the label rounds to 90.]

Carbohydrate: 52 calories from carbohydrate/91 calories = 57% carbohydrate

Protein: 12 calories from protein/91 calories = 13% protein

Fat: 27 calories from fat/91 calories = 30% fat

NUTRITION AND HYDRATION FOR SPORTS AND FITNESS

Optimal nutrition and hydration and a successful and progressive physical fitness program go hand-in-hand. Participants will not only enhance their health, but also improve their athletic performance with conscientious fueling and refueling to maintain optimal performance and overall health.

CARBOHYDRATES AND SPORTS NUTRITION

The EAR for carbohydrates is 100 grams (about seven servings) for children and nonpregnant, nonlactating adults; 135 grams (about nine servings) for pregnant women; and 160 grams (about 11 servings) for lactating women. The Academy of Nutrition and Dietetics (A.N.D.) [formerly the American Dietetic Association (ADA)] recommends that athletes consume 3 to 5 g/lb (6 to 10 g/kg) of body weight per day depending on their total daily energy expenditure, type of exercise performed, gender, and environmental conditions, to maintain blood glucose levels during exercise and to replace muscle **glycogen** (Rodriguez, Di Marco, & Langley, 2009).

[EXPAND YOUR KNOWLEDGE]

Food Models and Portion Estimates

Recommendations are often provided in terms of the number of servings needed to meet a participant's needs, so it is important that the GFI is able to effectively estimate intake and teach participants how to do it.

A portion is the amount of food a person chooses to eat, while a serving is a standardized amount of a food used to estimate and/or evaluate one's intake. Increases in portion sizes have been frequently cited as an important contributing factor to the growing rates in obesity seen over the past several decades (Figure 4). Portions are very difficult for some to estimate, and correct estimates could mean the difference between a 1,400-calorie diet and a 2,200-calorie diet.

A GFI can assist participants in a number of ways when estimating their portions. The guidelines presented in Table 2 can be used to help participants more accurately determine the amount of food that they are consuming. Comparing food portions to common items is also a helpful way for participants to visualize the foods they eat, adopt better habits, and eat more appropriate food amounts. For example, in Table 2, servings are compared to common household items for reference.

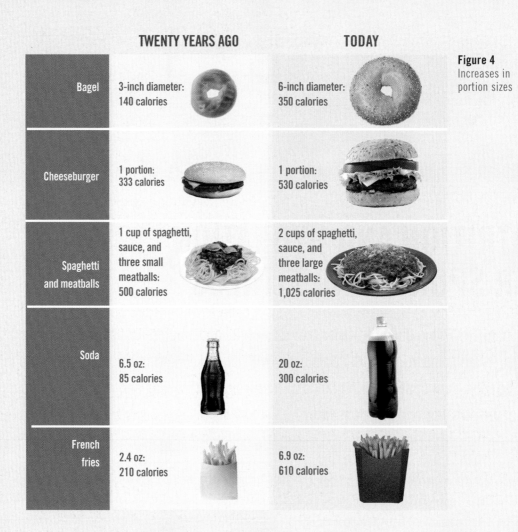

TWENTY YEARS AGO

TODAY

Figure 4
Increases in portion sizes

Bagel	3-inch diameter: 140 calories	6-inch diameter: 350 calories
Cheeseburger	1 portion: 333 calories	1 portion: 530 calories
Spaghetti and meatballs	1 cup of spaghetti, sauce, and three small meatballs: 500 calories	2 cups of spaghetti, sauce, and three large meatballs: 1,025 calories
Soda	6.5 oz: 85 calories	20 oz: 300 calories
French fries	2.4 oz: 210 calories	6.9 oz: 610 calories

Table 2

ESTIMATING PORTION SIZE

FOOD GROUP	KEY MESSAGE	WHAT COUNTS?	LOOKS LIKE …
Grains	Make half your grains whole.	1 oz equivalent = 1 slice of bread 1 cup of ready-to-eat cereal ½ cup cooked rice, pasta, or cooked cereal 5 whole-wheat crackers	CD cover A baseball ½ a baseball
Vegetables	Vary your veggies. Make half your plate fruits and vegetables.	1 cup = 1 cup of raw or cooked vegetable 2 cups of raw leafy salad greens 1 cup of vegetable juice	Baseball Softball
Fruits	Make half your plate fruits and vegetables.	1 cup = 1 cup raw fruit ½ cup dried fruit 1 cup 100% fruit juice	Tennis ball 2 golf balls
Milk	Switch to fat-free or low-fat (1%) milk.	1 cup = 1 cup of milk, yogurt, or soy milk 1.5 ounces of natural cheese or 2 ounces of processed cheese	Baseball 1½ 9-volt batteries
Protein Foods	Choose lean proteins.	1 ounce = 1 oz of meat, poultry, or fish ¼ cup cooked dry beans 1 egg 1 Tbsp peanut butter ½ oz nuts or seeds 2 Tbsp hummus	Deck of cards for lean meats (3 oz); checkbook = 3 oz fish ½ golf ball ½ of a Post-it note Golf ball
Oils	Choose liquid oils and avoid solid fats.	3 tsp = 1 Tbsp vegetable oils ½ medium avocado 1 oz peanuts, mixed nuts, cashews, almonds, or sunflower seeds	Tip of thumb

For more specific amounts, please visit www.ChooseMyPlate.gov.

PROTEIN AND SPORTS NUTRITION

While low-carbohydrate/high-protein diets, such as the Atkins and South Beach plans, are no longer the hottest trend, "high-protein" diets (eating plans on the higher end of the AMDR for protein of 10 to 35%) of calories seem to be just as good as, if not better than, high-carbohydrate diets for weight loss and health benefits (Champagne et al., 2011). A high-protein diet can even help to optimize athletic performance (and muscle strengthening) due to the important role of protein in both muscle building and tissue repair. It should be noted that the effects of protein are enhanced if it is consumed around the time of the physical activity. Protein intake during exercise probably does not offer any additional performance benefit if sufficient

amounts of carbohydrate—the body's preferred energy source—are consumed. However, for endurance athletes who need to consume adequate calories to fuel extended training sessions, or for any exerciser striving to lose weight, protein can help preserve lean muscle mass when combined with resistance-type exercise and ensure that most weight loss comes primarily from fat rather than lean tissue.

The average person requires 0.8 to 1.0 g/kg of body weight of protein per day (0.4 to 0.5 g/lb). Athletes need anywhere from 1.2 to 1.7 g/kg (0.5 to 0.8 g/lb), depending on gender, age, and type and intensity of the exercise (less for endurance athletes and more for strength or power athletes) (Rodriguez, Di Marco, & Langley, 2009). Participants can ensure adequate protein consumption if recommendations are based on the AMDR of 10 to 35% of daily energy intake (IOM, 2005). Table 3 shows the total protein intake at various levels of energy intake within the AMDR for protein. Recommended protein intakes are best met through diet, though many athletes (particularly those who focus on strength and power activities) do turn to **whey**- or **casein**-based protein powders and other supplements to boost protein intake.

Several factors come into play when choosing the "best" type of protein from food, including protein quality, health benefits, dietary restrictions, cost, convenience, and taste. While no one type of protein is best for everyone, keep these considerations in mind:

▬ *Protein quality varies.* Similar to lean meats, poultry, and fish, such proteins as whey, casein, egg, soy, and chia contain all of the **essential amino acids** in relatively adequate amounts and are easily digested and absorbed. Fruits, vegetables, grains, and nuts are incomplete proteins and must be combined over the day to ensure adequate intake of each of the essential amino acids (Figure 5).

▬ *Different types of proteins are better at different times.* Many athletes consume the milk proteins whey and casein in an effort to maximize muscle building. Whey protein— the liquid remaining after milk has been curdled and strained—is rapidly digested, resulting in a short burst of amino acids into the bloodstream. Whey is known for its ability to stimulate muscle protein synthesis, even more so than casein and soy. Casein—the protein that gives milk its white color and accounts for the majority of milk

Table 3

PROTEIN INTAKE (GRAMS) AT VARIOUS LEVELS OF ENERGY INTAKE

ENERGY INTAKE (KCAL/D)	LOW-PROTEIN DIET (<10% KCAL)	AVERAGE DIET (~15% KCAL)	HIGH-PROTEIN DIET (≥20% KCAL)	VERY-HIGH PROTEIN DIET (≥30% KCAL)
1,200	30	45	60	90
2,000	50	75	100	150
3,000	75	112	150	225

Note: Each gram of protein contains 4 calories.

Reprinted with permission from the American Heart Association, Inc.; St. Jeor, S.T. et al. (2001). Dietary protein and weight reduction: A statement for healthcare professionals from the nutrition committee of the Council on Nutrition, Physical Activity, and Metabolism of the American Heart Association. *Circulation,* 104, 1869–1874.

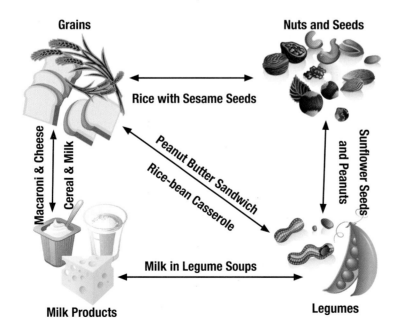

Grains

Nuts and Seeds

Rice with Sesame Seeds

Macaroni & Cheese

Cereal & Milk

Peanut Butter Sandwich

Rice-bean Casserole

Sunflower Seeds and Peanuts

Milk in Legume Soups

Milk Products

Legumes

Figure 5
Protein complementarity chart

Source: Lappé, F.M. (1992). *Diet for a Small Planet.* New York: Ballantine Books.

protein—is slowly digested, resulting in a more prolonged release of amino acids lasting up to hours. If the goal is for amino acids to be readily available for muscle regeneration immediately following a workout, an athlete may consider timing protein intake accordingly to best maximize muscle building and repair. In any case, the GFI should feel comfortable sharing credible information with participants, but should not recommend or advise participants to follow a specific diet regimen or take supplements.

▬ *More is not always better.* Total daily protein intake should not be excessive. Protein consumption beyond recommended amounts is unlikely to result in further muscle gains because the body has a limited capacity to use amino acids to build muscle. Most studies suggest that there is a threshold effect of 1.6 to 1.7 g/kg protein (Rosenbloom & Coleman, 2012). Beyond that amount, there is no further increase in skeletal muscle protein synthesis. In fact, consumption of protein beyond 1.6 to 1.7 g/kg promotes increased amino acid **catabolism** and protein oxidation, and may provide excess caloric intake that is stored as fat (Moore et al., 2009).

Ultimately, the science is still evolving regarding the best amounts, mechanisms, and methods of protein intake. However, it seems that when combined with regular exercise and an overall healthy lifestyle, an appropriate amount of protein can help participants maintain or gain muscle mass.

FATS AND SPORTS NUTRITION

Fat is an important source of energy, fat-soluble vitamins, and **essential fatty acids.** Athletes should consume a comparable proportion of food from fat as the general population—that is, 20 to 35% of total calories. There is no evidence for performance benefit from a very low-fat diet (<15% of total calories) or from a high-fat diet (Rodriguez, Di Marco, & Langley, 2009).

FUELING BEFORE AND AFTER EXERCISE

Physically active individuals need the right types and amounts of food before and after group fitness classes to maximize the amount of energy available to fuel optimal performance and minimize the amount of gastrointestinal distress.

PRE-EXERCISE FUELING

The two main goals of a pre-exercise snack are to (1) optimize

glucose availability and glycogen stores and (2) provide the fuel needed to support exercise performance. Keeping this in mind, in the days up to a week before a strenuous endurance effort, an athlete should consider what nutritional strategies might set the stage for optimal performance. For example, an individual preparing for a long endurance event might consider the pros and cons of carbohydrate loading. On the day of the event or an important training session, the athlete should aim to eat a meal about four to six hours prior to the workout to minimize gastrointestinal distress and optimize performance. Four hours after eating, the food will already have been digested and absorbed; now liver and muscle glycogen levels are increased. To translate this into an everyday, practical recommendation, athletes who plan to work out for an extended duration in the early afternoon should be certain to eat a wholesome, carbohydrate-rich breakfast. Those who exercise in the early morning may benefit from a carbohydrate-rich snack before going to bed.

Some research also suggests that eating a relatively small carbohydrate- and protein-containing snack (e.g., 50 grams of carbohydrate and 5 to 10 grams of protein) 30 to 60 minutes before exercise helps increase glucose availability near the end of long-duration workout and helps to decrease exercise-induced protein catabolism (Kreider et al., 2010). The exact timing and size of the snack for peak performance will vary by individual and type of exercise. As a general rule, individuals should try out any snacks or drinks with practice sessions and workouts prior to relying on them to help athletic performance during competition. In general, a pre-exercise or pre-workout meal or snack should be:

▬ Relatively high in carbohydrate to maximize blood glucose availability (*Note:* Although no DRIs exist for pre-exercise carbohydrate intake, most credible sources recommended 1.0 to 4.5 g of carbohydrate per kg of body weight depending on the type of food and the time of the exercise or event.)

▬ Relatively low in fat and fiber to minimize gastrointestinal distress and facilitate gastric emptying

▬ Moderate in protein

▬ Approximately 400 to 800 calories—an amount that should fuel the exercise without causing noticeable sluggishness or fullness

▬ Well-tolerated by the individual

POST-EXERCISE REPLENISHMENT

The main goal of post-exercise fueling is to replenish glycogen stores and facilitate muscle repair. The average participant training at moderate intensities every few days does not need any aggressive post-exercise replenishment. Normal dietary practices following exercise will facilitate recovery within 24 to 48 hours. But athletes following vigorous training regimens, especially those who will participate in multiple training sessions in a single day (e.g., triathletes or athletes participating in training camp for a team sport), benefit from strategic refueling. Studies show that the best post-workout meals include mostly carbohydrates accompanied by some protein (Kreider et al., 2010). Refueling should begin within 30 minutes after exercise and be followed by a high-carbohydrate meal within two hours (Kreider et al., 2010). The carbohydrates replenish the used-up energy that is normally stored as glycogen in muscle and liver. The protein helps to rebuild the muscles that were fatigued with exercise. A carbohydrate intake of 1.5 g/kg of body weight in the first 30 minutes after exercise and then every two hours for four to six hours is recommended (Rodriguez, Di Marco, & Langley, 2009). After that, the athlete can resume his or her typical, balanced diet. Of course, the amount of refueling necessary depends on the intensity and duration of the training session. A long-duration, low-intensity workout may not require such vigorous replenishment.

 [APPLY WHAT YOU KNOW]

Post-workout Snack and Meal Ideas

In the several hours following a prolonged and strenuous workout, consuming snacks and meals high in carbohydrate with some protein can set the stage for optimal glycogen replenishment and subsequent performance. Here are a few snack and meal ideas that fit the bill:

Snack 1: In the first several minutes after exercise, consume 16 oz of Gatorade or other sports drink, a power gel such as a Clif Shot or GU, and a medium banana. This quickly begins to replenish muscle carbohydrate stores.

Carbohydrates: 73 g; Protein: 1 g; Calories: 290

Snack 2: After cooling down and showering, grab another quick snack such as 12 oz of orange juice and ¼ cup of raisins.

Carbohydrates: 70 g; Protein 3 g; Calories: 295

Small meal appetizer: Enjoy a spinach salad with tomatoes, chickpeas, green beans, and tuna and a whole-grain baguette.

Carbohydrates: 70 g; Protein: 37 g; Calories: 489

Small meal main course: Replenish with whole-grain pasta with diced tomatoes.
Carbohydrates: 67 g; Protein: 2 g; Calories: 292

Dessert: After allowing ample time for the day's snacks and meals to digest, finish your refueling program with one cup of frozen yogurt and berries.

Carbohydrates: 61 g; Protein: 8 g; Calories: 280

FLUID AND HYDRATION BEFORE, DURING, AND AFTER EXERCISE

When it comes to fluid balance during exercise, it seems like the proverbial double-edged sword: Drinking too little can lead to **dehydration**—a scary condition exercisers have been cautioned against in every text, handout, and presentation on fluid replacement. But drinking too much plain water—out of fear of not drinking enough—could lead to **hyponatremia** (i.e., low sodium in the blood), a condition less well known and understood, but equally frightening. Here is the good news: the body is very good at handling and normalizing large variations in fluid intake. For this reason, severe hyponatremia and dehydration are rare and generally affect very specific high-risk populations during specific types of activities. Both conditions are highly preventable. To prevent dehydration and hyponatremia, the goal is to drink just the right amount of fluid and/or electrolytes before, during, and after exercise to maintain a state of euhydration, which is a state of "normal" body water content—the perfect balance between "too much" and "not enough" fluid intake (Table 4).

Table 4

FLUID-INTAKE RECOMMENDATIONS DURING EXERCISE

2 hours prior to exercise, drink 500–600 mL (17–20 oz)
Every 10–20 minutes during exercise, drink 200–300 mL (7–10 oz) or, preferably, drink based on sweat losses
Following exercise, drink 450–675 mL for every 0.5 kg body weight lost (or 16–24 oz for every pound)

Source: Casa, D.J. et al. (2000). National Athletic Trainers' Association: Position statement: Fluid replacement for athletes. *Journal of Athletic Training,* 35, 212–224.

HYDRATION PRIOR TO EXERCISE

Most people begin exercise euhydrated with little need for a rigorous prehydration regimen. However, if fewer than eight to 12 hours have elapsed since the last intense training session or fluid intake has been inadequate, the athlete may benefit from a prehydration program.

An athlete should begin prehydrating about four hours prior to the exercise session. The athlete should aim to slowly consume about 5 to 7 mL (0.17 to 0.23 oz) of fluid per 1 kg (2.2 lb) of body weight. If after two hours of prehydration no urine is produced or if the urine is dark or highly concentrated, the individual should aim to drink an additional 3 to 5 mL (0.1 to 0.17 oz) of fluid per 1 kg (2.2 lb) of body weight two hours before the event. Drinking fluid that contains 20 to 50 milliequivalents/liter (mEq/L) (460 to 1150 mg/L) of sodium or consuming salt-containing snacks at this time helps stimulate thirst and retain the consumed fluids (Sawka et al., 2007). Some athletes may try to hyperhydrate with glycerol-containing solutions that act to expand the extra- and intra-cellular spaces. While glycerol may be advantageous for certain athletes who meet specific criteria, glycerol is unlikely to be advantageous for athletes who will experience no to mild dehydration during exercise (loss of <2% body weight) and glycerol use may in fact contribute to increased risk of hyponatremia (van Rosendal et al., 2010).

HYDRATION DURING EXERCISE

The goal of fluid intake during exercise is to prevent performance-diminishing or health-altering effects from dehydration or hyponatremia. A GFI can share the following guidelines with participants:

- *Aim for a 1:1 fluid replacement to fluid loss ratio.* Ideally, exercisers should consume the same amount of fluid as they lose in sweat. An easy way to assess post-exercise hydration is to compare pre- and post-exercise body weight. The goal is to avoid weight loss greater than 2%. There is no one-size-fits-all recommendation, though if determining individual needs is not feasible, athletes should aim to drink 0.4 to 0.8 L/h (8 to 16 oz/h), with the higher rate for faster, heavier athletes in a hot and humid environment and the lower rate for slower, lighter athletes in a cool environment (Sawka et al., 2007). Because people sweat at varying rates and exercise at different intensities, this range may not be appropriate for everyone. However, when individual assessment is not possible, this recommendation works for most people.

For information on sports drinks and hydration guidelines for longer-endurance training, refer to the *ACE Fitness Nutrition Manual* (Muth, 2013).

POST-EXERCISE HYDRATION

Following exercise, the athlete should aim to correct any fluid imbalances that occurred during the exercise session. This includes consuming water to restore hydration, carbohydrates to replenish glycogen stores, and electrolytes to speed rehydration. If the athlete will have at least 12 hours to recover before the next strenuous workout, rehydration with the usual meals and snacks and water should be adequate. The sodium in the foods will help retain the fluid and stimulate thirst. If rehydration needs to occur quickly, the athletes should drink about 1.5 L of fluid for each kilogram (or 0.70 L of fluid for each pound) of body weight lost (Sawka et al., 2007). This will be enough to restore lost fluid and also compensate for increased urine output that occurs with rapid consumption of large amounts of fluid. A severely dehydrated athlete (>7% body weight loss) with symptoms (nausea, vomiting, or diarrhea) may need intravenous fluid replacement. Those at greatest risk of hyponatremia should be careful not to consume too much water following exercise and instead should focus on replenishing sodium.

SUMMARY

Federal, state, and local governments play a large role in researching and understanding the major components of an optimal diet, promoting an optimal eating plan, developing food policy agendas, regulating the safety and quality of food available, and funding nutritional programs. A thorough understanding of state and federal dietary recommendations and policies offers the GFI a basis from which to make general nutrition recommendations while staying within his or her scope of practice.

The macronutrients play a major role in supporting performance for an active individual. Understanding carbohydrate, protein, and fat recommendations for active individuals and athletes will help GFIs educate their participants on the most beneficial fueling options to enhance their workouts and support recovery. Furthermore, educating participants on appropriate hydration practices can be helpful for improving performance and, more importantly, preventing fluid-related illness.

References

Casa, D.J. et al. (2000). National Athletic Trainers' Association position statement: Fluid replacement for athletes. *Journal of Athletic Training,* 35, 212–224.

Champagne, C.M. et al. (2011). Dietary intakes associated with successful weight loss and maintenance during the Weight Loss Maintenance Trial. *Journal of the American Dietetic Association,* 111, 12, 1826–1835.

Donnelly, J.E. et al. (2009). American College of Sports Medicine position stand: Appropriate physical activity intervention strategies for weight loss and prevention of weight regain for adults. *Medicine & Science in Sports & Exercise,* 41, 2, 459–471.

Institute of Medicine (2009). *Report Brief: Weight Gain During Pregnancy: Reexamining the Guidelines.* www.iom.edu/pregnancyweightgain

Institute of Medicine (2005). *Dietary Reference Intakes for Energy, Carbohydrate, Fiber, Fat, Fatty Acids, Cholesterol, Protein, and Amino Acids.* Washington, D.C.: National Academy Press.

Institute of Medicine (2002). *Dietary Reference Intakes for Energy, Carbohydrate, Fiber, Fat, Fatty Acids, Cholesterol, Protein, and Amino Acids.* Washington, D.C.: National Academies Press.

Kreider, R.B. et al. (2010). ISSN exercise & sport nutrition review: Research & recommendations. *Journal of the International Society of Sports Nutrition, 7,* 7.

Lappé, F.M. (1992). *Diet for a Small Planet.* New York: Ballantine Books.

Moore, D.R. et al. (2009). Ingested protein dose response of muscle and albumin protein synthesis after resistance exercise in young men. *American Journal of Clinical Nutrition, 89,* 1, 161–168.

Muth, N.D. (2013). *ACE Fitness Nutrition Manual.* San Diego: American Council on Exercise.

Rodriguez, N.R., Di Marco, N.M., & Langley, S. (2009). American College of Sports Medicine position stand: Nutrition and athletic performance. *Medicine & Science in Sports & Exercise,* 41, 709–731.

Rosenbloom, C. & Coleman, E. (Eds.) (2012). *Sports Nutrition: A Practice Manual for Professionals* (5th ed.). Washington, D.C.: Academy of Nutrition and Dietetics.

Sawka, M.N. et al. (2007). American College of Sports Medicine position stand: Exercise and fluid replacement. *Medicine & Science in Sports & Exercise,* 39, 2, 377–390.

St. Jeor, S.T. et al. (2001). Dietary protein and weight reduction: A statement for healthcare professionals from the nutrition committee of the Council on Nutrition, Physical Activity, and Metabolism of the American Heart Association. *Circulation,* 104, 1869–1874.

U.S. Department of Agriculture (2015). *2015–2020 Dietary Guidelines for Americans* (8th ed.). www.health.gov/dietaryguidelines

U.S. Department of Agriculture, Agriculture Research Service and U.S. Department of Health & Human Services, Centers for Disease Control and Prevention (2010). *What We Eat in America.* www.ars.usda.gov/Services/docs.htm?docid=13793

U.S. Department of Health & Human Services (2008). *2008 Physical Activity Guidelines for Americans: Be Active, Healthy and Happy.* www.health.gov/paguidelines/

van Rosendal, S.P. et al. (2010). Guidelines for glycerol use in hyperhydration and rehydration associated with exercise. *Sports Medicine,* 40, 2, 113–129.

Suggested Reading

Institute of Medicine (2005). *Dietary Reference Intakes for Energy, Carbohydrate, Fiber, Fat, Fatty Acids, Cholesterol, Protein, and Amino Acids.* Washington, D.C.: National Academy Press.

Kreider R.B. et al. (2010). ISSN exercise & sport nutrition review: Research & recommendations. *Journal of the International Society of Sports Nutrition, 7,* 7.

Rodriguez, N.R., Di Marco, N.M., & Langley, S. (2009). American College of Sports Medicine position stand: Nutrition and athletic performance. *Medicine & Science in Sports & Exercise,* 41, 709–731.

Sawka, M.N. et al. (2007). American College of Sports Medicine position stand: Exercise and fluid replacement. *Medicine & Science in Sports & Exercise,* 39, 2, 377–390.

U.S. Department of Agriculture (2015). *2015–2020 Dietary Guidelines for Americans* (8th ed.). www.health.gov/dietaryguidelines

ACE® POSITION STATEMENT ON NUTRITION SCOPE OF PRACTICE FOR FITNESS PROFESSIONALS

It is the position of the American Council on Exercise (ACE) that fitness professionals not only can but should share general nonmedical nutrition information with their clients/participants. In the current climate of an epidemic of obesity, poor nutrition, and physical inactivity paired with a multibillion dollar diet industry and a strong interest among the general public in improving eating habits and increasing physical activity, fitness professionals are on the front lines in helping the public to achieve healthier lifestyles. Fitness professionals provide an essential service to their clients/participants, the industry, and the community at large when they are able to offer credible, practical, and relevant nutrition information to clients/participants while staying within their professional scope of practice.

Ultimately, an individual fitness professional's scope of practice as it relates to nutrition is determined by state policies and regulations, education and experience, and competencies and skills. While this implies that the nutrition-related scope of practice may vary among fitness professionals, there are certain actions that are within the scope of practice of all fitness professionals.

For example, it is within the scope of practice of all fitness professionals to share dietary advice endorsed or developed by the federal government, especially the *Dietary Guidelines for Americans* (www.health.gov/dietaryguidelines) and the MyPlate recommendations (www.ChooseMyPlate.gov).

Fitness professionals who have passed National Commission for Certifying Agencies (NCCA)– or American National Standards Institute (ANSI)–accredited certification programs that provide basic nutrition information, such as those provided by ACE, and those who have undertaken nutrition continuing education, should also be prepared to discuss:

— Principles of healthy nutrition and food preparation

— Food to be included in the balanced daily diet

— Essential nutrients needed by the body

— Actions of nutrients on the body

— Effects of deficiencies or excesses of nutrients

— How nutrient requirements vary through the lifecycle

— Information about nutrients contained in foods or supplements

Fitness professionals may share this information through a variety of venues, including cooking demonstrations, recipe exchanges, development of handouts and informational packets, individual or group classes and seminars, or one-on-one encounters.

Fitness professionals who do not feel comfortable sharing

this information are strongly encouraged to undergo continuing education to further develop nutrition competency and skills and to develop relationships with registered dietitians or other qualified health professionals who can provide this information. It is within the fitness professional's scope of practice to distribute and disseminate information or programs that have been developed by a registered dietitian or medical doctor.

The actions that are outside the scope of practice of fitness professionals include, but may not be limited to, the following:

- Individualized nutrition recommendations or meal planning other than that which is available through government guidelines and recommendations, or has been developed and endorsed by a registered dietitian or physician

- Nutritional assessment to determine nutritional needs and nutritional status, and to recommend nutritional intake

- Specific recommendations or programming for nutrient or nutritional intake, caloric intake, or specialty diets

- Nutritional counseling, education, or advice aimed to prevent, treat, or cure a disease or condition, or other acts that may be perceived as medical nutrition therapy

- Development, administration, evaluation, and consultation regarding nutritional care standards or the nutrition care process

- Recommending, prescribing, selling, or supplying nutritional supplements to clients/participants

- Promotion or identification of oneself as a "nutritionist" or "dietitian"

Engaging in these activities can place a client's/participant's health and safety at risk and possibly expose the fitness professional to disciplinary action and litigation. To ensure maximal client/participant safety and compliance with state policies and laws, it is essential that the fitness professional recognize when it is appropriate to refer to a registered dietitian or physician. ACE recognizes that some fitness and health clubs encourage or require their employees to sell nutritional supplements. If this is a condition of employment, ACE suggests that fitness professionals:

- Obtain complete scientific understanding regarding the safety and efficacy of the supplement from qualified healthcare professionals and/or credible resources. Note: Generally, the Office of Dietary Supplements (ods. od.nih.gov), the National Center for Complementary and Alternative Medicine (nccam.nih.gov), and the Food and Drug Administration (FDA.gov) are reliable places to go to examine the validity of the claims as well as risks and benefits associated with taking a particular supplement. Since the sites are from trusted resources and in the public domain, fitness professionals can freely distribute and share the information contained on these sites.

- Stay up-to-date on the legal and/or regulatory issues related to the use of the supplement and its individual ingredients.

- Obtain adequate insurance coverage should a problem arise.

GLOSSARY

Abduction Movement away from the midline of the body.

Abrasion A scraping away of a portion of the skin or mucous membrane.

Accent Emphasis on a given beat.

Acceptable Macronutrient Distribution Range (AMDR) The range of intake for a particular energy source that is associated with reduced risk of chronic disease while providing intakes of essential nutrients.

Action The stage of the transtheoretical model of behavioral change during which the individual is actively engaging in a behavior that was started less than six months ago.

Active listening Mode of listening in which the listener is concerned about the content, intent, and feelings of the message.

Activities of daily living (ADL) Activities normally performed for hygiene, bathing, household chores, walking, shopping, and similar activities.

Add-in strategy *See* Part-to-whole teaching strategy.

Adduction Movement toward the midline of the body.

Adenosine trisphosphate (ATP) A high-energy phosphate molecule required to provide energy for cellular function. Produced both aerobically and anaerobically and stored in the body.

Adequate Intake (AI) A recommended nutrient intake level that, based on research, appears to be sufficient for good health.

Adherence The extent to which people follow their plans or treatment recommendations. Exercise adherence is the extent to which people follow an exercise program.

Aerobic system The energy pathway that uses oxygen, fats, carbohydrate, and sometimes proteins for re-synthesizing adenosine triphosphate (ATP) for prolonged energy use.

Affective domain One of the three domains of learning; involves the learning of emotional behaviors.

Agonist The muscle directly responsible for observed movement; also called the prime mover.

Agreement to participate Signed document that indicates that the participant is aware of inherent risks and potential injuries that can occur from participation.

Allergen A substance that can cause an allergic reaction by stimulating type-1 hypersensitivity in genetically susceptible individuals.

Ambient temperature The temperature of the surrounding air; room temperature.

American Society of Composers, Authors and Publishers (ASCAP) One of two performing rights societies in the United States that represent music publishers in negotiating and collecting fees for the nondramatic performance of music.

Americans with Disabilities Act Civil rights legislation designed to improve access to jobs, work places, and commercial spaces for people with disabilities.

Anaerobic Without the presence of oxygen.

Anatomy The brand of science concerned with the bodily structure of humans, animals, and other living organisms.

Antagonist The muscle that acts in opposition to the contraction produced by an agonist (prime mover) muscle.

Anterior Anatomical term meaning toward the front. Same as ventral; opposite of posterior.

Anxiety A state of uneasiness and apprehension; occurs in some mental disorders.

Arthritis Inflammation of a joint; a state characterized by the inflammation of joints.

Articular cartilage Cartilage covering the ends of the bones inside diarthroidial joints; allows the ends of the bones to glide without friction.

Associative stage of learning The second stage of learning a motor skill, when performers have mastered the fundamentals and can concentrate on skill refinement.

Asthma A chronic inflammatory disorder of the airways that affects genetically susceptible individuals in response to various environmental triggers such as allergens, viral infection, exercise, cold, and stress.

Atherosclerosis A specific form of arteriosclerosis characterized by the accumulation of fatty material on the inner walls of the arteries, causing them to harden, thicken, and lose elasticity.

Athletic trainer A healthcare professional who collaborates with physicians and specializes in providing immediate intervention when injuries occur and helping athletes and clients in the prevention, assessment, treatment, and rehabilitation of emergency, acute, and chronic medical conditions involving injury, impairment, functional limitations, and disabilities.

Atrophy A reduction in muscle size (muscle wasting) due to inactivity or immobilization.

Automated external defibrillator (AED) A portable electronic device used to restore normal heart rhythms in victims of sudden cardiac arrest.

Autonomous stage of learning The third stage of learning a motor skill, when the skill has become habitual or automatic for the performer.

Avulsion A wound involving forcible separation or tearing of tissue from the body.

Baroreceptor A sensory nerve ending that is stimulated by changes in pressure, as those in the walls of blood vessels.

Base of support (BOS) The areas of contact between the feet and their supporting surface and the area between the feet.

Beats Regular pulsations that have an even rhythm and occur in a continuous pattern of strong and weak pulsations.

Biomechanics The mechanics of biological and muscular activity.

Blanket license A certificate or document granting permission that varies and applies to a number of situations.

Blood pressure (BP) The pressure exerted by the blood on the walls of the arteries; measured in millimeters of mercury (mmHg) with a sphygmomanometer.

Body composition The makeup of the body in terms of the relative percentage of fat-free mass and body fat.

Body fat A component of the body, the primary role of which is to store energy for later use.

Body mass index (BMI) A relative measure of body height to body weight used to determine levels of weight, from underweight to extreme obesity.

Broadcast Music Inc. (BMI) One of two performing rights societies in the U.S. that represent music publishers in negotiating and collecting fees for the nondramatic performance of music.

Bursitis Swelling and inflammation in the bursa that results from overuse.

Carbohydrate The body's preferred energy source. Dietary sources include sugars (simple) and grains, rice, potatoes, and beans (complex). Carbohydrate is stored as glycogen in the muscles and liver and is transported in the blood as glucose.

Cardiac output The amount of blood pumped by the heart per minute; usually expressed in liters of blood per minute.

Cardiopulmonary resuscitation (CPR) A procedure to support and maintain breathing and circulation for a person who has stopped breathing (respiratory arrest) and/or whose heart has stopped (cardiac arrest).

Cardiorespiratory endurance The capacity of the heart, blood vessels, and lungs to deliver oxygen and nutrients to the working muscles and tissues during sustained exercise and to remove metabolic waste products that would result in fatigue.

Cardiorespiratory fitness The ability to perform large muscle movement over a sustained period; related to the capacity of the heart-lung system to deliver oxygen for sustained energy production. Also called cardiorespiratory endurance or aerobic fitness.

Cardiovascular disease (CVD) A general term for any disease of the heart, blood vessels, or circulation.

Carpal tunnel syndrome A pathology of the wrist and hand that occurs when the median nerve, which extends from the forearm into the hand, becomes compressed at the wrist.

Casein The main protein found in milk and other dairy products.

Catabolism Metabolic pathways that break down molecules into smaller units and release energy.

Center of gravity (COG) *See* Center of mass (COM).

Center of mass (COM) The point around which all weight is evenly distributed; also called center of gravity.

Certificant An individual who has earned a credential awarded through a certification program.

Cholesterol A fatlike substance found in the blood and body tissues and in certain foods. Can accumulate in the arteries and lead to a narrowing of the vessels (atherosclerosis).

Choreography The art of designing sequences of movements.

Chronic disease Any disease state that persists over an extended period of time.

Chronic obstructive pulmonary disease (COPD) A condition, such as asthma, bronchitis, or emphysema, in which there is chronic obstruction of air flow.

Closed-kinetic-chain exercises Movements where the distal segment is more fixed; generally considered more functional, as they mimic daily activities closely.

Cognitive domain One of the three domains of learning; describes intellectual activities and involves the learning of knowledge.

Cognitive stage of learning The first stage of learning a motor skill when performers make many gross errors and have extremely variable performances.

Command style of teaching A teaching style in which the instructor makes all decisions about rhythm, posture, and duration while participants follow the instructor's directions and movements.

Compilations Original, copyrightable sequences or a program of dance steps or exercise routines that may or may not be copyrightable individually.

Compound fracture A fracture in which the broken bone is exposed through a wound in the skin.

Concentric A type of isotonic muscle contraction in which the muscle develops tension and shortens when stimulated.

Contemplation The stage of the transtheoretical model of behavioral change during which the individual is weighing the pros and cons of behavioral change.

Contract A binding agreement between two or more persons that is enforceable by law composed of an offer, acceptance, and consideration (or what each party puts forth to make the agreement worthwhile).

Contusion A wound, such as a bruise, in which the skin is not broken; often resulting in broken blood vessels and discoloration.

Convection The transfer of heat through surrounding air or water molecules.

Copyright The exclusive right, for a certain number of years, to perform, make, and distribute copies and otherwise use an artistic, musical, or literary work.

Coronary artery disease (CAD) *See* Coronary heart disease (CHD).

Coronary heart disease (CHD) The major form of cardiovascular disease; results when the coronary arteries are narrowed or occluded, most commonly by atherosclerotic deposits of fibrous and fatty tissue; also called coronary artery disease (CAD).

Creatine phosphate (CP) A storage form of high-energy phosphate in muscle cells that can be used to immediately resynthesize adenosine triphosphate (ATP).

Creatine phosphate system The energy pathway that consists of adenosine triphosphate (ATP) and phosphocreatine (PCr); provides immediate energy (between 10 and 15 seconds) through the breakdown of these stored high-energy phosphates.

Cryotherapy Treatment of a disorder with ice or by freezing.

Cueing Visual or verbal techniques, using hand signals or concise words, to inform participants of upcoming movements.

Cultural competence The ability to communicate and work effectively with people from different cultures.

DASH eating plan *See* Dietary Approaches to Stop Hypertension eating plan.

Deep vein thrombosis A blood clot in a major vein, usually in the legs and/or pelvis.

Defendant The party in a lawsuit who is being sued or accused.

Dehydration The process of losing body water; when severe can cause serious, life-threatening consequences.

Depression 1. The action of lowering a muscle or bone or movement in an inferior or downward direction. 2. A condition of general emotional dejection and withdrawal; sadness greater and more prolonged than that warranted by any objective reason.

Diabetes *See* Diabetes mellitus.

Diabetes mellitus A disease of carbohydrate metabolism in which an absolute or relative deficiency of insulin results in an inability to metabolize carbohydrates normally.

Diabetic shock Severe low blood sugar associated with diabetes, with symptoms that include fatigue, lightheadedness, or fainting.

Diastasis recti A separation of the recti abdominal muscles along the midline of the body.

Diastolic blood pressure (DBP) The pressure in the arteries during the relaxation phase (diastole) of the cardiac cycle; indicative of total peripheral resistance.

Dietary Approaches to Stop Hypertension (DASH) eating plan An eating plan designed to reduce blood pressure; also serves as an overall healthy way of eating that can be adopted by nearly anyone; may also lower risk of coronary heart disease.

Dietary Reference Intake (DRI) A generic term used to refer to three types of nutrient reference values: Recommended Dietary Allowance (RDA), Estimated Average Requirement (EAR), and Tolerable Upper Intake Level (UL).

Distal Farthest from the midline of the body, or from the point of origin of a muscle.

Dorsiflexion Movement of the foot up toward the shin.

Double-time A means of adding challenge to a choreographed workout routine that involves the performance of movement twice as fast as in an earlier section.

Downbeat The regular strong pulsation in music occurring in a continuous pattern at an even rhythm.

Dynamic flexibility The ability to move the joints through their full, intended ranges of motion fluidly or quickly without undue stress or strain.

Dyspnea Shortness of breath; a subjective difficulty or distress in breathing.

Dyspnea scale A subjective four-point scale that reflects an individual's perception of the difficulty of breathing during physical activity, with 1 reflecting mild difficulty that is noticeable to the exerciser but not an observer, and 4 reflecting severe difficulty that forces the individual to stop exercising.

Eccentric A type of isotonic muscle contraction in which the muscle lengthens against a resistance when it is stimulated; sometimes called "negative work" or "negative reps."

Electrocardiogram (ECG or EKG) A recording of the electrical activity of the heart.

Empathy Understanding what another person is experiencing from his or her perspective.

Emphysema An obstructive pulmonary disease characterized by the gradual destruction of lung alveoli and the surrounding connective tissue, in addition to airway inflammation, leading to reduced ability to effectively inhale and exhale.

Employee A person who works for another person in exchange for financial compensation. An employee complies with the instructions and directions of his or her employer and reports to them on a regular basis.

Essential amino acids Eight to 10 of the 23 different amino acids needed to make proteins. Called essential because the body cannot manufacture them; they must be obtained from the diet.

Essential fatty acids Fatty acids that the body needs but cannot synthesize; includes linolenic (omega-3) and linoleic (omega-6) fatty acids.

Estimated Average Requirement (EAR) An adequate intake in 50% of an age- and gender-specific group.

Evaporation The process by which molecules in a liquid state (e.g., water) spontaneously become gaseous (e.g., water vapor).

Eversion Rotation of the foot to direct the plantar surface outward; occurs in the frontal plane.

Exercise dependence A state in which physical activity is extreme in frequency and duration, relatively resistant to change, and is associated with an irresistible impulse to continue exercise despite injury, illness, or fatigue.

Exercise evaluation A process of evaluating an exercise or movement based on its effectiveness and safety.

Exercise-induced asthma (EIA) *See* Exercise-induced bronchospasm (EIB).

Exercise-induced bronchospasm (EIB) Transient and reversible airway narrowing triggered by vigorous exercise; also called exercise-induced asthma (EIA).

Extension The act of straightening or extending a joint, usually applied to the muscular movement of a limb.

Extrinsic feedback Information received from an external source (such as another person) about a completed task (such as an exercise).

Extrinsic motivation Motivation that comes from external (outside of the self) rewards, such as material or social rewards.

Fascia Strong connective tissue that performs a number of functions, including developing and isolating the muscles of the body and providing structural support and protection. Plural = Fasciae.

Fat An essential nutrient that provides energy, energy storage, insulation, and contour to the body. 1 gram of fat equals 9 kcal.

Fatigue The decline in ability of a muscle to generate force.

Fatty acid A long hydrocarbon chain with an even number of carbons and varying degrees of saturation with hydrogen.

Feedback An internal response within a learner; during information processing, it is the correctness or incorrectness of a response that is stored in memory to be used for future reference. Also, verbal or nonverbal information about current behavior that can be used to improve future performance.

Fiber Carbohydrate chains the body cannot break down for use and which pass through the body undigested.

First ventilatory threshold (VT1) Intensity of aerobic exercise at which ventilation starts to increase in a nonlinear fashion in response to an accumulation of metabolic by-products in the blood.

Flexibility The ability to move joints through their normal full ranges of motion.

Flexion The act of moving a joint so that the two bones forming it are brought closer together.

Frontal plane A longitudinal section that runs at a right angle to the sagittal plane, dividing the body into anterior and posterior portions.

Glucose A simple sugar; the form in which all carbohydrates are used as the body's principal energy source.

Glycemic index (GI) A ranking of carbohydrates on a scale from 0 to 100 according to the extent to which they raise blood sugar levels.

Glycemic load (GL) A measure of glycemic response to a food that takes serving size into consideration; GL = Glycemic index x Grams of carbohydrate/100.

Glycogen The chief carbohydrate storage material; formed by the liver and stored in the liver and muscle.

Glycolytic anaerobic system The energy pathway that uses glycogen to produce power, but not quite as much or as quickly as the creatine phosphate system.

Golgi tendon organ (GTO) A sensory organ within a tendon that, when stimulated, causes an inhibition of the entire muscle group to protect against too much force.

Ground reaction forces The force exerted by the ground on a body in contact with it.

Half-time A means of reducing the challenge of a portion of choreography that involves performing a movement at half of the usual speed; often used when teaching new movements.

Health Insurance Portability and Accountability Act (HIPAA) Enacted by the U.S. Congress in 1996, HIPAA requires the U.S. Department of Health & Human Services (HHS) to establish national standards for electronic health care information to facilitate efficient and secure exchange of private health data. The Standards for Privacy of Individually Identifiable Health Information ("Privacy Rule"), issued by the HHS, addresses the use and disclosure of individuals' health information—called "protected health information"—by providing federal protections and giving patients an array of rights with respect to personal health information while permitting the disclosure of information needed for patient care and other important purposes.

Health perception An individual's perception of his or her relative level of wellness and illness.

Health screening A vital process that identifies individuals at high risk for exercise-induced heart problems that need to be referred to appropriate medical care as needed.

Heart rate (HR) The number of heart beats per minute.

Heart-rate reserve (HRR) The reserve capacity of the heart; the difference between maximal heart rate and resting heart rate. It reflects the heart's ability to increase the rate of beating and cardiac output above resting level to maximal intensity.

Heat cramps A mild form of heat-related illness that generally occurs during or after strenuous physical activity and is characterized by painful muscle spasms.

Heat exhaustion The most common heat-related illness; usually the result of intense exercise in a hot, humid environment and characterized by profuse sweating, which results in fluid and electrolyte loss, a drop in blood pressure, lightheadedness, nausea, vomiting, decreased coordination, and often syncope (fainting).

Heat stroke A medical emergency that is the most serious form of heat illness due to heat overload and/or impairment of the body's ability to dissipate heat; characterized by high body temperature (>104° F or 40° C), dry, red skin, altered level of consciousness, seizures, coma, and possibly death.

High-intensity interval training (HIIT) An exercise strategy alternating periods of short, intense anaerobic exercise with less-intense recovery periods.

Hyperextension Extension of an articulation beyond anatomical position.

Hyperflexion Flexion of an articulation beyond anatomical position.

Hyperglycemia An abnormally high content of glucose (sugar) in the blood (above 100 mg/dL).

Hypertension High blood pressure, or the elevation of resting blood pressure above 140/90 mmHg.

Hypertensive *See* Hypertension.

Hyperthermia Abnormally high body temperature.

Hypoglycemia A deficiency of glucose in the blood commonly caused by too much insulin, too little glucose, or too much exercise. Most commonly found in the insulin-dependent diabetic and characterized by symptoms such as fatigue, dizziness, confusion, headache, nausea, or anxiety.

Hyponatremia Abnormally low levels of sodium ions circulating in the blood; severe hyponatremia can lead to brain swelling and death.

Hypothermia Abnormally low body temperature.

Iliotibial band friction syndrome (ITBFS) A repetitive overuse condition that occurs when the distal portion of the iliotibial band rubs against the lateral femoral epicondyle.

Impingement A trapping or crushing of soft tissues in a joint, such as tendons and bursa in the shoulder.

Independent contractor A person who conducts business on his or her own on a contract basis and is not an employee of an organization.

Inferior Located below.

Informed consent A written statement signed by a participant prior to testing that informs him or her of testing purposes, processes, and all potential risks and discomforts.

Insulin A hormone released from the pancreas that allows cells to take up glucose.

Insulin resistance An inability of muscle tissue to effectively use insulin, where the action of insulin is "resisted" by insulin-sensitive tissues.

Intrinsic feedback Feedback provided by the participants themselves; the most important type of feedback for long-term program adherence.

Intrinsic motivation Motivation that comes from internal states, such as enjoyment or personal satisfaction.

Inversion Rotation of the foot to direct the plantar surface inward; occurs in the frontal plane.

Iron An essential dietary mineral necessary for the transport of oxygen (via hemoglobin in red blood cells) and for oxidation by cells; deficiency causes anemia; found in meat, poultry, eggs, vegetables, and cereals (especially those fortified with iron).

Ischemia A decrease in the blood supply to a bodily organ, tissue, or part caused by constriction or obstruction of the blood vessels.

Isometric A type of muscular contraction in which the muscle is stimulated to generate tension but little or no joint movement occurs.

Joint capsule A ligamentous sac that surrounds the articular cavity of a freely movable joint.

Joint stability The ability to maintain or control joint movement or position.

Kinesthetic awareness The perception of body position and movement in space.

Kinetic chain The concept that joints and segments have an effect on one another during movement.

Knowledge of results The motivational impact of feedback provided to a person learning a new task or behavior indicating the outcomes of performance.

Kyphosis Excessive posterior curvature of the spine, typically seen in the thoracic region.

Laceration A jagged, irregular cut or tear in the soft tissues, usually caused by a blow. Because of extensive tissue destruction, there is a great potential for contamination and infection.

Lactic acid A metabolic by-product of anaerobic glycolysis; when it accumulates it decreases blood pH, which slows down enzyme activity and ultimately causes fatigue.

Lapses The expected slips or mistakes that are usually discreet events and are a normal part of the behavior-change process.

Lateral Away from the midline of the body, or the outside.

Laxity Lacking in strength, firmness, or resilience; joints that have been injured or overstretched may exhibit laxity.

Layering A method of choreography wherein the instructor starts with a base move and then layers on one new element at a time.

Lever A rigid bar that rotates around a fixed support (fulcrum) in response to an applied force.

Liability Legal responsibility.

Ligament A strong, fibrous tissue that connects one bone to another.

Lipid The name for fats used in the body and bloodstream.

Lordosis Excessive anterior curvature of the spine that typically occurs at the low back (may also occur at the neck).

Maintenance The stage of the transtheoretical model of behavioral change during which the individual is incorporating the new behavior into his or her lifestyle and has been doing so for more than six months.

Matching In choreography, where one exercise ends, another starts.

Maximal heart rate (MHR) The highest heart rate a person can attain. Sometimes abbreviated as HRmax.

Measure One group of beats in a musical composition marked by the regular occurrence of the heavy accent.

Medial Toward the midline of the body, or the inside.

Mediterranean eating plan An eating plan generally characterized by increased consumption of olive oil, complex carbohydrates, vegetables, and fish, and decreased red meat and pork consumption.

Mending In choreography, stringing two exercises or movements together.

Metabolic syndrome (MetS) A cluster of factors associated with increased risk for coronary heart disease and diabetes—abdominal obesity indicated by a waist circumference ≥40 inches (102 cm) in men and ≥35 inches (88 cm) in women; levels of triglyceride ≥150 mg/dL (1.7 mmol/L); high-density lipoprotein levels <40 and 50 mg/dL (1.0 and 1.3 mmol/L) in men and women, respectively; blood-pressure levels ≥130/85 mmHg; and fasting blood glucose levels ≥100 mg/dL (5.6 mmol/L).

Meter The organization of beats into musical patterns or measures.

Mineral An inorganic substance needed in the diet in small amounts to help regulate bodily functions.

Mirroring In group fitness classes, the practice of an instructor facing the class while teaching movements so that the participants can make direct eye contact with the instructor and see a "mirror image," rather than looking at the instructor's back.

Mobility The degree to which an articulation is allowed to move before being restricted by surrounding tissues.

Monounsaturated fat *See* Monounsaturated fatty acid.

Monounsaturated fatty acid A type of unsaturated fat (liquid at room temperature) that has one open spot on the fatty acid for the addition of a hydrogen atom (e.g., oleic acid in olive oil).

Motivation The psychological drive that gives purpose and direction to behavior.

Motor skill The degree to which movements using agility, balance, and coordination are executed.

Motor unit A motor nerve and all of the muscle fibers it stimulates.

Muscle spindle The sensory organ within a muscle that is sensitive to stretch and thus protects the muscle against too much stretch.

Muscular endurance The ability of a muscle or muscle group to exert force against a resistance over a sustained period of time.

Muscular strength The maximal force a muscle or muscle group can exert during contraction.

Musical phrase A short musical passage; used as a means of choreographing movement to a piece of music.

Myocardial infarction (MI) An episode in which some of the heart's blood supply is severely cut off or restricted, causing the heart muscle to suffer and die from lack of oxygen. Commonly known as a heart attack.

Myocardium Muscle of the heart.

National Commission of Certifying Agencies (NCCA) An organization created to help ensure the health, welfare, and safety of the public through the accreditation of a variety of certification programs/organizations that assess professional competence; part of the Institute for Credentialing Excellence (ICE).

Negligence Failure of a person to perform as a reasonable and prudent professional would perform under similar circumstances.

Neuromuscular efficiency The ability of the neuromuscular system to allow muscles that produce movement and muscles that provide stability to work together synergistically as an integrated functional unit.

Neuropathy Any disease affecting a peripheral nerve. It may manifest as loss of nerve function, burning pain, or numbness and tingling.

Nutrient A component of food needed by the body. There are six classes of nutrients: water, minerals, vitamins, fats, carbohydrates, and protein.

Nutrient content claim Statement of the implied health benefits of a product that describes the level of a nutrient in a product using terms like "free," "high," or "low," or compared to another product using terms like "more," "reduced," and "lite."

Obesity An excessive accumulation of body fat. Usually defined as more than 20% above ideal weight, or over 25% body fat for men and over 32% body fat for women; also can be defined as a body mass index of ≥30 kg/m^2 or a waist girth of ≥40 inches (102 cm) in men and ≥35 inches (89 cm) in women.

Occupational therapist A healthcare provider specializing in treatments that help people who suffer from mentally, physically, developmentally, or emotionally disabling conditions to develop, recover, or maintain daily living and work skills that include improving basic motor functions and reasoning abilities.

Omega-3 fatty acid An essential fatty acid that promotes a healthy immune system and helps protect against heart disease and other diseases; found in egg yolk and cold water fish and shellfish like tuna, salmon, mackerel, cod, crab, shrimp, and oyster. Also known as linolenic acid.

Open-ended question A question that does not allow for a simple one-word answer (yes/no); designed to encourage a full, meaningful answer using the subject's own knowledge and/or feelings.

Orthostatic hypotension A drop in blood pressure associated with rising to an upright position.

Osteoarthritis (OA) A degenerative disease involving a wearing away of joint cartilage. This degenerative joint disease occurs chiefly in older persons.

Osteoporosis A disorder, primarily affecting postmenopausal women, in which bone density decreases and susceptibility to fractures increases.

Osteoporotic fracture Bone fracture that occurs in individuals with compromised bone mass density; most common at the spine, hip, and wrist.

Overexertion Pushing oneself past the point of volitional control or exceeding the limits of one's abilities.

Overload The principle that a physiological system subjected to above-normal stress will respond by increasing in strength or function accordingly.

Overtraining Constant intense training that does not provide adequate time for recovery; symptoms include increased resting heart rate, impaired physical performance, reduced enthusiasm and desire for training, increased incidence of injuries and illness, altered appetite, disturbed sleep patterns, and irritability.

Overuse injury An injury caused by activity that places too much stress on one area of the body over an extended period.

Overweight A term to describe an excessive amount of weight for a given height, using height-to-weight ratios.

Part-to-whole teaching strategy A teaching strategy involving breaking a skill down into its component parts and practicing each skill in its simplest form before placing several skills in a sequence.

Patching In choreography, adding an additional movement between two exercises or movements for a seamless transition.

Patellofemoral pain syndrome (PFPS) A degenerative condition of the posterior surface of the patella, which may result from acute injury to the patella or from chronic friction between the patella and the groove in the femur through which it passes during motion of the knee.

Pedagogy Method and style of education, including the study and practice of how best to teach.

Percent daily value (PDV) A replacement for the percent Recommended Dietary Allowance (RDA) on the newer food labels. Gives information on whether a food item has a significant amount of a particular nutrient based on a 2,000-calorie diet.

Performance standard A level of expectation concerning the performance of a task achieved by an individual, group, or organization according to pre-established requirements and/or specifications.

Performing rights society An organization to which the copyright or publisher assigns the nondramatic performing rights in a musical composition.

Peripheral arterial disease All diseases caused by the obstruction of large peripheral arteries, which can result from atherosclerosis, inflammatory processes leading to stenosis, an embolism, or thrombus formation.

Peripheral heart disease Circulation disorders that affect blood vessels outside of the heart and brain, most commonly of the lower extremity.

Phosphagen system A system of transfer of chemical energy from the breakdown of creatine phosphate to regenerate adenosine triphosphate (ATP).

Physical Activity Readiness Questionnaire (PAR-Q) A brief, self-administered medical questionnaire recognized as a safe pre-exercise screening measure for low-to-moderate (but not vigorous) exercise training.

Physical therapist A healthcare provider specializing in treatments that help restore function, improve mobility, relieve pain, and prevent or limit permanent physical disabilities in patients of all ages suffering from medical problems, injuries, diseases, disabilities, or other health-related conditions.

Plaintiff A party who brings a suit against another party in a court of law.

Planes of motion The conceptual planes in which the body moves; called the sagittal, frontal, and transverse planes; often used as a way to describe anatomical movement.

Plantar fasciitis Inflammation of the plantar fascia, a broad band of connective tissue running along the sole of the foot; caused by stretching or tearing the tissue, usually near the attachment at the heel.

Plantar flexion Distal movement of the plantar surface of the foot; opposite of dorsiflexion.

Plyometrics High-intensity movements, such as jumping, involving high-force loading of body weight during the landing phase of the movement that take advantage of the stretch-shortening cycle.

Polyunsaturated fat *See* Polyunsaturated fatty acid.

Polyunsaturated fatty acid A type of unsaturated fat (liquid at room temperature) that has two or more spots on the fatty acid available for hydrogen (e.g., corn, safflower, and soybean oils).

Portion The amount of a food or beverage consumed by an individual in one sitting.

Posterior Toward the back or dorsal side.

Postural hypotension *See* Orthostatic hypotension.

Posture The arrangement of the body and its limbs.

Practice style of teaching A teaching style that provides opportunities for individualization and includes practice time and individualized instructor feedback.

Pre-choreographed classes Group fitness classes offered by companies that create choreography that is packaged and utilized by instructors who have completed the training necessary to provide the specialized classes.

Precontemplation The stage of the transtheoretical model of behavioral change during which the individual is not yet thinking about changing.

Prediabetes The state in which some but not all of the diagnostic criteria for diabetes are met (e.g., blood glucose levels are higher than normal but are not high enough for a diagnosis of diabetes).

Preparation The stage of the transtheoretical model of behavioral change during which the individual is getting ready to make a change.

Prime mover A muscle responsible for a specific movement. Also called an agonist.

Professional liability insurance Insurance to protect a trainer/instructor against professional negligence or failure to perform as a competent and prudent professional would under similar circumstances.

Progression The systematic process of applying overload. For example, in resistance training, more resistance is added to progress the training stimulus.

Progressive overload The gradual increase of physiological stress placed on the body during a program of exercise training.

Pronation Internal rotation of the forearm causing the radius to cross diagonally over the ulna and the palm to face posteriorly.

Prone Lying flat, with the anterior aspect of the body facing downward.

Proprioception Sensation and awareness of body position and movements.

Protein A compound composed of a combination 20 amino acids that is the major structural component of all body tissue.

Proximal Nearest to the midline of the body or point of origin of a muscle.

Psychomotor domain One of three domains in Bloom's taxonomy of learning comprised of physical movement, coordination, and use of the motor-skill.

Public performance Playing a recording of a copyrighted musical composition at a place where a substantial number of persons outside of a normal circle of a family and its social acquaintances are gathered.

Pulse rate The wave of pressure in the arteries that occurs each time the heart beats.

Puncture A piercing wound from a sharp object that makes a small hole in the skin.

Range of motion (ROM) The number of degrees that an articulation will allow one of its segments to move.

Rapport A relationship marked by mutual understanding and trust.

Ratings of perceived exertion (RPE) A scale, originally developed by noted Swedish psychologist Gunnar Borg, that provides a standard means for evaluating a participant's perception of exercise effort. The original scale ranged from 6 to 20; a revised category ratio scale ranges from 0 to 10.

Recommended Dietary Allowance (RDA) The levels of intake of essential nutrients that, on the basis of scientific knowledge, are judged by the Food and Nutrition Board to be adequate to meet the known needs of practically all healthy persons.

Recovery heart rate The number of heart beats per minute following the cessation of vigorous physical activity. As cardiorespiratory fitness improves, the heart rate returns to resting levels more quickly.

Registered dietitian (RD) A food and nutrition expert that has met the following criteria: completed a minimum of a bachelor's degree at a U.S. accredited university, or other college coursework approved by the Commission on Accreditation for Dietetics Education (CADE); completed a CADE-accredited supervised practice program; passed a national examination; and completed continuing education requirements to maintain registration.

Regression Offering participants ways or modifications to decrease the intensity or complexity of an exercise or movement.

Rehearsal move A movement typically performed during the warm-up in a group fitness class that mimics an upcoming conditioning exercise and helps prepare the neuromuscular system for increased intensity.

Relapse In behavioral change, the return of an original problem after many lapses (i.e., slips or mistakes) have occurred.

Relaxin A hormone of pregnancy that relaxes the pelvic ligaments and other connective tissue in the body.

Repetition-reduction teaching strategy Teaching strategy involving reducing the number of repetitions that make up a movement sequence.

Resting heart rate (RHR) The number of heart beats per minute when the body is at complete rest; usually counted first thing in the morning before any physical activity.

Reversibility The principle of exercise training that suggests that any improvement in physical fitness due to physical activity is entirely reversible with the discontinuation of the training program.

Rhabdomyolysis The breakdown of muscle fibers resulting in the release of muscle fiber contents into the circulation. Some of these are toxic to the kidney and frequently result in kidney damage.

Rheumatoid arthritis (RA) An autoimmune disease that causes inflammation of connective tissues and joints.

Rhythm A strong, regular, repeated pattern of movement or sound.

Rider Specific additions to a standard insurance policy.

Risk management Minimizing the risks of potential legal liability.

Sagittal plane The longitudinal plane that divides the body into right and left portions.

Sarcopenia Decreased muscle mass; often used to refer specifically to an age-related decline in muscle mass or lean-body tissue.

Saturated fat *See* Saturated fatty acid.

Saturated fatty acid A fatty acid that contains no double bonds between carbon atoms; typically solid at room temperature and very stable.

Scapular plane A shoulder angle about halfway between the sagittal plane and the frontal plane, which represents approximately 30–45 degrees of shoulder flexion. This angle is in line with the orientation of the scapula as it rests naturally against the rib cage and helps protect the shoulder joint during overhead movements.

Scoliosis Excessive lateral curvature of the spine.

Scope of practice The range and limit of responsibilities normally associated with a specific job or profession.

Second ventilatory threshold (VT2) A metabolic marker that represents the point at which high-intensity exercise can no longer be sustained due to an accumulation of lactate.

Sedentary Doing or requiring much sitting; minimal activity.

Seizure A sudden attack of illness, especially a stroke or an epileptic fit, that typically involves spasms or convulsions.

Self-check style of teaching A teaching style that relies on individual performers to provide their own feedback.

Self-efficacy One's perception of his or her ability to change or to perform specific behaviors (e.g., exercise).

Self–myofascial release (SMR) The act of rolling one's own body on a round foam roll or other training tool, massaging away restrictions to normal soft-tissue extensibility.

Serving The amount of food used as a reference on the nutrition label of that food; the recommended portion of food to be eaten.

Shear force Any force that causes slippage between a pair of contiguous joints or tissues in a direction that parallels the plane in which they contact.

Shin splints A general term for any pain or discomfort on the front or side of the lower leg in the region of the shin bone (tibia).

Shock A life-threatening condition that occurs when the body is not getting enough blood flow.

Simple-to-complex teaching strategy Advanced teaching strategy that treats a sequence of movement patterns as a whole, teaching small changes (adding small amounts of complexity) to progressively challenge the exercise participant.

Slow-to-fast teaching strategy Teaching strategy used to allow participants to learn complex movement at a slower pace, emphasizing proper placement or configuration of a movement pattern (e.g., teaching a movement at half-tempo).

SMART goal A properly designed goal; SMART stands for specific, measurable, attainable, relevant, and time-bound.

Social support The perceived comfort, caring, esteem, or help an individual receives from other people.

Society of European Stage Authors and Composers (SESAC) A performing rights organization designed to represent songwriters

and publishers and their right to be compensated for having their music performed in public.

Solid fats and added sugars (SoFAS) SoFAS are added to foods or beverages to make them more appealing, but they also can add a lot of calories. The foods and beverages with SoFAS provide the most empty calories for Americans.

Spatial awareness Being aware of oneself in space along with other objects in the immediate surroundings.

Specificity Exercise training principle explaining that specific exercise demands made on the body produce specific responses by the body; also called exercise specificity.

Sprain A traumatic joint twist that results in stretching or tearing of the stabilizing connective tissues; mainly involves ligaments or joint capsules, and causes discoloration, swelling, and pain.

Stability Characteristic of the body's joints or posture that represents resistance to change of position.

Stages-of-change model A lifestyle-modification model that suggests that people go through distinct, predictable stages when making lifestyle changes: precontemplation, contemplation, preparation, action, and maintenance. The process is not always linear.

Standard of care Appropriateness of an exercise professional's actions in light of current professional standards and based on the age, condition, and knowledge of the participant.

Steady-state exercise A state of aerobic exercise in which the intensity remains consistent, as opposed to alternating between higher and lower intensities.

Strain A stretch, tear, or rip in the muscle or adjacent tissue such as the fascia or tendon.

Stretch reflex An involuntary motor response that, when stimulated, causes a suddenly stretched muscle to respond with a corresponding contraction.

Stroke A sudden and often severe attack due to blockage of an artery into the brain.

Subchondral bone Bone structure that lies under articular cartilage and contains marrow.

Superior Located above.

Supination External rotation of the forearm (radioulnar joint) that causes the palm to face anteriorly.

Supine Lying face up (on the back).

Syncopation Temporary shifts in the normal pattern of stressed to unstressed beats or parts of beats.

Synovial fluid Transparent, viscous lubricating fluid found in joint cavities, bursae, and tendon sheaths.

Systolic blood pressure (SBP) The pressure exerted by the blood on the vessel walls during ventricular contraction.

Talk test A method for measuring exercise intensity using observation of respiration effort and the ability to talk while exercising.

Target heart rate (THR) Number of heart beats per minute that indicate appropriate exercise intensity levels for each individual; also called training heart rate.

Telemetry The process by which measured quantities from a remote site are transmitted to a data-collection point for recording and processing, such as what occurs during an electrocardiogram.

Tempo The rate of speed of music, usually expressed in beats per minute.

Tendinitis Inflammation of a tendon. Also called tendonitis.

Tendon A band of fibrous tissue forming the termination of a muscle and attaching the muscle to a bone.

Tennis elbow Pain on the outside of the elbow at the attachment of the forearm muscles; lateral epicondylitis.

Testosterone In males, the steroid hormone produced in the testes; involved in growth and development of reproductive tissues, sperm, and secondary male sex characteristics.

Three-dimensional cueing The process of delivering multiple pieces of information simultaneously, all while addressing the three learning styles (i.e., verbal, visual, and kinesthetic).

Tolerable Upper Intake Level (UL) The maximum intake of a nutrient that is unlikely to pose risk of adverse health effects to almost all individuals in an age- and gender-specific group.

Trans fat *See* Trans fatty acid.

Trans fatty acid An unsaturated fatty acid that is converted into a saturated fat to increase the shelf life of some products.

Transition The process of smoothly sequencing together two or more exercises or movements to minimize disruption in intensity or position and maximize the student experience.

Transtheoretical model of behavioral change (TTM) A theory of behavior that examines one's readiness to change and identifies five stages: precontemplation, contemplation, preparation, action, and maintenance. Also called the stages-of-change model.

Transverse plane Anatomical term for the imaginary line that divides the body, or any of its parts, into upper (superior) and lower (inferior) parts. Also called the horizontal plane.

Triglyceride Three fatty acids joined to a glycerol (carbon and hydrogen structure) backbone; how fat is stored in the body.

Type 1 diabetes *See* Type 1 diabetes mellitus (T1DM).

Type 1 diabetes mellitus (T1DM) Form of diabetes caused by the destruction of the insulin-producing beta cells in the pancreas, which leads to little or no insulin secretion; generally develops in childhood and requires regular insulin injections; formerly known as insulin-dependent diabetes mellitus (IDDM) and childhood-onset diabetes.

Type 2 diabetes *See* Type 2 diabetes mellitus (T2DM).

Type 2 diabetes mellitus (T2DM) Most common form of diabetes; typically develops in adulthood and is characterized by a reduced sensitivity of the insulin target cells to available insulin; usually associated with obesity; formerly known as non-insulin-dependent diabetes mellitus (NIDDM) and adult-onset diabetes.

Umbrella liability policy Insurance that provides additional coverage beyond other insurance such as professional liability, home, automobile, etc.

Upbeat The deemphasized beat in a piece of music.

Valsalva maneuver A strong exhaling effort against a closed glottis, which builds pressure in the chest cavity that interferes with the return of the blood to the heart; may deprive the brain of blood and cause lightheadedness or fainting.

Vegan A vegetarian who does not consume any animal products, including dairy products such as milk and cheese.

Vegetarian A person who does not eat meat, fish, poultry, or products containing these foods.

Vitamin An organic micronutrient that is essential for normal physiologic function.

$\dot{V}O_2$max Considered the best indicator of cardiovascular endurance, it is the maximum amount of oxygen (mL) that a person can use in one minute per kilogram of body weight. Also called maximal oxygen uptake and maximal aerobic capacity.

$\dot{V}O_2$reserve ($\dot{V}O_2$R) The difference between $\dot{V}O_2$max and $\dot{V}O_2$ at rest; used for programming aerobic exercise intensity.

Waiver Voluntary abandonment of a right to file suit; not always legally binding.

Whey The liquid remaining after milk has been curdled and strained; high in protein and carbohydrates.

INDEX

Diabetic shock, 194

Diaphragmatic breathing, 148

Diastolic blood pressure (DBP), 145

Dietary Guidelines, 254–258
    MyPlate, 259, 259f
    weight management, 254–257

Dietary Reference Intakes, 253

Disciplinary procedures, ACE, 227

Domains of learning, 134–135
    affective, 135
    cognitive, 134
    psychomotor, 135

Dorsal, 35f

Dorsiflexion, 36

Double-time, 139

Downbeat, 66

DRILLS, 140

Duffel bag checklist, 120

Dynamic flexibility, arthritis, 150

Dynamic movement, appropriate, 23

Dyspnea, asthma, 147

Dyspnea scale, 68, 72
    asthma monitoring, 148

E

Eating
    after class, 122
    food models, 264
    foods to reduce, 257
    healthy patterns, 257, 258f
    macronutrient needs, 255, 255t,
        256
    MyPlate, 259, 259f
    nutrients to increase, 257
    post-exercise fueling, 268
    pre-exercise fueling, 267

Eccentric movement, rhythm and, 171

Education, continuing, 14–15, 211

Elderly participants, 155–156

Emergencies, medical, 190–194. *See
    also* Medical emergencies

Emergency medical services (EMS),
    activating, 190, 198

Emergency response, 196–197

Emergency situations, potential, 102

Employees, 221–222

Employment status, 221–222

Endurance
    cardiorespiratory, 27, 27t
    muscular, 27, 27t

Energy pathways, 39, 39f

Environment, 97

Environmental emergencies, 194, 194t

Environmental temperature, 59–61
    cold, 61
    heat, 59–60, 59t, 60t
    prenatal participants, 158

Equipment, 64
    common issues, 114
    fit check, 202
    lack of, adapting to, 119
    lack of, conflict resolution, 180
    responsibilities, 217
    setting up, 114
    set-up of, 116
    youth, 157

Erector spinae, 46f

Essential fatty acids, 267

Estimated Average Requirement (EAR),
    253

Ethics, ACE Code of, 13, 232–236

Evaluation
    exercise, class blueprint, 86
    pre-class, 118

Evaporation
    cold-temperature exercise, 61
    youth, 157

Eversion, ankle, 36

Evidence-based recommendations
    aerobic exercise, 28t
    resistance exercise, 29t

Execution, 169

Exercise addiction, 195

Exercise area assessment, 113

Exercise dependence, 195

Exercise evaluation, 86

Exercise-induced asthma (EIA), 147

Exercise order, 89–90

Exercise-related injuries, 190

Exercise room, 58

Exercise surface, 58

Expectations, managing participant,
    106

Extension, 36

Extensors, hip, 45f

External oblique, 46f

External rotators, myofascial release,
    87, 87f

Extrinsic feedback, 176

Extrinsic motivation, 102

F

Facilities
    access, participation and
        adherence, 97
    exercise area assessment, 113
    exercise room, 58
    exercise surface, 58
    policies and procedures, 204
    responsibilities, 217
    shared-use space, 225

Fat-free mass, 27t

Fat mass, 27t

Fats
    to avoid, 257, 258f
    energy from, 39
    sports nutrition, 267
    types and healthiest, 255, 257,
        258f

Feedback, 176–180
    from colleagues, 180
    extrinsic, 176
    importance, 137
    intrinsic, 176
    observational assessments, 176
    from participants, 179–180
    posture and movement
        assessment,
        176–177, 177f
    providing, 176–178
    from supervisors, 180

First ventilatory threshold (VT1), 39, 39f
    talk test, 70

Fitness, physical
    definition, 27
    health-related, 27, 27t
    skill-related, 28, 28t

Five primary movement patterns, 36,
    37f

Five senses, compelling experiences,
    105

Flexibility, 27, 27t
    dynamic, arthritis, 150

Flexion, 36
    dorsiflexion, 36
    plantar, 36

I

Icing, 197

I formation, 82, 82f

Iliacus, 45f

Iliocostalis, 46f

Iliotibial band, 45f

Iliotibial (IT) band friction syndrome, 192t

Impingements, 192t

Incident management, 196–198
    EMS, activating, 198
    general procedures, 197
    icing injuries, 197
    RICE, 197

Inclusive experiences, fostering, 142–162
    arthritis, 149–150, 149f
    cardiac conditions, 145–146, 146t
    diabetes mellitus, 150–152
        (*See also* Diabetes mellitus)
    heart-rate response, medications on, 160, 161t
    low-back pain, 153–154, 154f
    older adults, 155–156
    prenatal and postpartum participants, 158–159
    privacy, participant, 144
    pulmonary conditions, 147–148, 148t
    screening, pre-participation, 144
    youth, 157

Independent contractors, 221–222

Inferior, 35f, 36

Informed consent, 199, 218

Initial onsite procedures and responsibilities, 113–118
    arrangement and positioning, 115, 115f
    audience, 118
    bike fit, 117, 117f
    equipment set-up, 116
    room/exercise area, 113
    set up music and equipment, 114

Injuries, 190–194. *See also* specific types
    acute vs. chronic, 190
    exercise-related, 190
    icing, 197
    monitoring, 97
    musculoskeletal, acute, 191, 191t

potential, noticing, 102
signs and symptoms, 190
soft-tissue, 194

Injury prevention, 199–204
    informed consent, 199
    new class formats, 199
    Physical Activity Readiness Questionnaire, 203, 204f
    policies and procedures, facility, 204
    pre-screening questionnaires, 199
    responsibilities, 199
    risk factors, 200–203, 200t, 201t

Innovation, 4

Institute for Credentialing Excellence (ICE), 7

Instruction, enhancing strategies, 166–182
    analyzing intensity and monitoring progress, 175
    burnout, avoiding, 182
    class education, 172–173
    conflict resolution, 180–181
    corrections, making, 174–175
    feedback, 176–180 (*See also* Feedback)
    movement education, 168
    teaching methodology, 168–171 (*See also* Teaching methodology)
    teaching styles, 168

Instructional focus (teaching style)
    command, 133
    practice, 133
    self-check, 133

Instruction responsibilities, 215

Instructor's eye, 189

Insulin reaction, 151t

Insurance
    Health Insurance Portability and Accountability Act, 144, 198
    liability, 220
    rider, 220
    umbrella policy, 220

Intake
    Acceptable Macronutrient Distribution Range, 255
    Adequate Intake, 253
    current, 255
    Dietary Reference Intakes, 253
    fluid, 60, 60t, 268–269
    Tolerable Upper Intake Level, 253

Intensity, exercise
    analyzing, 175
    monitoring, 68–73 (*See also* Monitoring intensity)
    participation and adherence, 97
    scaling, 87

Internal oblique, 46f

International Health, Racquet and Sportsclub Association (IHRSA), 7

Interpersonal issues, participant, 181

Interval-based treadmill class, 91

Intrinsic feedback, 176

Intrinsic motivation, 102

Inversion, ankle, 36

Isometric exercise, with hypertension, 146

J

Joint mobility, 34, 35f

Joint stability, 34, 35f

K

Karvonen formula, 70

Key considerations, group fitness classes, 56–73. *See also* Class considerations, group fitness

Kinesthetic awareness, 104
    heightening participants', 135
    teaching, 174

Kinesthetic learners, 131

Kinetic chain, 34, 35f, 81
    stability and mobility, 34, 35f

Knee extension, agonist-antagonist pair, 91

Knee flexion, agonist-antagonist pair, 91

Knee issues, 121

Kneeling, 50f

Kneeling prisoner rotations, warm-up, 82, 83f

Knowledge
    ACE GFI, 12
    on participation and adherence, 96

Knowledge-based certificates, 8

Kyphosis, 49, 49f

50f–51f
energy pathways, 39, 39f
five primary movement patterns, 36, 37f
movement in three planes, 34–36, 35f–37f
reorganizing, 175
stability and mobility, kinetic chain, 34, 35f
three-zone intensity model, 39, 39f

Movement education, 168

Movement patterns, five primary, 36, 37f

Multilevel classes, teaching, 140

Multiplanar training, 85

Muscles, 43, 43f–48f
anterior tibialis, 44f
atrophy, arthritis, 149, 149f
gastrocnemius, 44f
hamstrings, 44f
hyperextension, 43
hyperflexion, 43
pelvic floor, 43f
quadriceps, 44f
soleus, 44f
transverse abdominis, 43f

Muscle spindles, 25, 25f

Muscular endurance, 27, 27t

Muscular strength
adults, 27, 27t
youth, 157

Musculoskeletal conditions, chronic, 190, 192, 192t

Musculoskeletal injuries, acute, 191, 191t

Music, 65–67
accent, 66
compelling experiences, 105
components and tempo, 66–67, 67t
conflict resolution, 180–181
copyright law, 223–224
movement integration, 66
purposes, 65
rhythm, 171
set up, 114
tempo, 171
volume, 65

Musical phrases, 67

Myocardial infarction (MI), 145

Myocardium, 145

Myofascial release, 87, 87f

Myostatic stretch reflex, 25, 25f

MyPlate, 259, 259f

N

Names, learning, 98–99

National Commission for Certifying Agencies (NCCA), 5

National Organization for Competency Assurance (NOCA), 7

Negligence, 213

Neuromuscular balance, 38

Neuromuscular efficiency, 23

Neutral posture, 48

New class formats, injury prevention, 199

New participation, pre-class evaluation, 118

Nonverbal communication skills, 99

Nutrient needs, 255, 255t
determining, 255, 255t
nutrients to increase, 257
sample problem, 256

Nutrition, 252–269
ACE Position Statement on Nutrition Scope of Practice for Fitness Professionals, 272–273
carbohydrates, 263
dietary guidelines, 254–258 (See also Dietary Guidelines)
dietary reference intakes, 253
fats, 267
fluid and hydration, 60, 60t, 268–269, 269t
food labels, 260–262, 261f
food models, 264
fueling, post-exercise, 268
fueling, pre-exercise, 267
MyPlate, 259
portion estimates, 264, 264f, 265t
protein, 265–267, 266f, 266t
weight management, 254–258 (See also Weight management)

Nutrition labels, 260–262, 261f

O

Obesity
adults, 254
children, 254–255

Objectives, class, 79

Obliques, 46f

Odors, 181

O formation, 82, 82f

Older adults, 155–156

Opening statement, 106

Orthostatic hypotension, 90, 146

Osteoarthritis, 149–150, 149f

Osteoporosis, 156

Overhead-activity, modifications, 202

Overload
progressive, 30
rhythm on, 171

Overstretching, passive, 25, 25f

Overweight
adults, 254
children, 254–255
older adults, 254, 255

P

Parallel lines arrangement, 115, 115f

PAR-Q, 203, 204f

Participants, recruiting and retaining, 107

Participation and adherence
environmental, 97
personal attributes, 96–97
physical-activity, 97

Partner exercises, conflict, 181

Part-to-whole teaching strategy, 138

Passive overstretching, 25, 25f

Patching, 170

Patellofemoral pain syndrome, 192t

Pectineus, 46f

Pectoralis major, 47f

Pelvic floor, 48
maneuvers, 48
muscles, 43f

Performance, 173

Performance licenses, 223

Performance standard, 137

Performing rights societies, 223

Peripheral heart disease, 145

Personal attributes, 96–97

Phases
cardiorespiratory training, 40, 41f
functional movement and resistance training, 40, 41f

Phosphagen system, 39

Phrase, musical, 67

Physical-activity factors, 97

Physical Activity Readiness
Questionnaire (PAR-Q),
203, 204f

Physical fitness. *See also* specific
topics
definition, 27
health-related, 27, 27t
skill-related, 28, 28t

Plaintiff, 213

Plan, class, 80–88, 80f. *See also* Class
plan, designing

Planes
of motion, 34–36, 35f–37f
three, movement in, 34–36,
35f–37f

Plank, 51f

Plank, reverse, 51f

Plantar fasciitis, 192t

Plantar flexion, 36

Plyometrics, exercise order, 89

Plyometric training, 20

Policies and procedures, facility, 204

Polyunsaturated fat, 255

Portion estimates, 264, 264f, 265t

Positioning, participant, 115, 115f

Positions, body. *See also* specific types
10 basic, 50, 50f–51f

Post-conditioning cool-down, 24–26,
25f

Postpartum depression, 195

Postpartum participants, 158–159

Postural hypotension, 90, 146

Posture
assessing, 176–177, 177f
importance, 48
neutral, 48
pre-class evaluation, 118

Power, 28, 28t

Practice style of teaching, 133

Pre-class evaluation, 118

Precontemplation stage, 100, 101t

Prediabetes, 150

Pregnancy
emergencies, 195
prenatal participants, 158–159
weight management, 254, 255

Preparation, class, day-of, 110–122.
See also Day-of class

preparation

Preparation stage, 100, 101t

Pre-participation screening, 144

Pre-screening questionnaires, 199

Prevention, injury, 199–204. *See also*
Injury prevention

Prime mover, 91

Professional certification, 8

Professional conduct, 210–212
best practices, 211
continuing education, 211
referrals and referral network,
211–212

Professionalism, 112

Professional practices, ACE, 227

Professional responsibilities, 13,
214–217. *See also* Legal
guidelines
advice, offering, 215
facilities and equipment, 217
health screening, 214
instruction, 215
insurance, liability, 220
insurance, rider, 220
insurance, umbrella, 220
risk-management system,
218–219
supervision, 216
umbrella policy, 220

Professional responsibility areas,
214–217
advice, offering, 215
facilities and equipment, 217
health screening, 214
instruction, 215
supervision, 216

Programming balance, 38

Progress, monitoring, 175

Progressions, 20, 41
appropriate, 87
teaching, 168
use, 175

Progressive overload, 30

Prone, 51f

Proprioception, elderly, 156
Protein
energy from, 39
sports nutrition, 265–267, 266f,
266t

Psoas major, 45f

Psoas minor, 45f

Psychological traits, 96

Psychomotor domain, 135

Puberty, 157

Public performance, 223

Pulling movement, upper-body, 36, 37f

Pulmonary conditions, 147–148
asthma, 147–148, 148t
chronic obstructive pulmonary
disease, 147
exercise, 148

Pulse rate monitoring, 69, 69f

Punctuality, 112

Punctures, 194

Purpose, class, 78

Pursed-lip breathing, 148

Pushing movement, upper-body, 36,
37f

Q

Q-signs, aerobic, 129, 129f

Quadratus lumborum, 47f

Quadriceps muscle, 44f
myofascial release, 87, 87f

Quadriceps stretch, 24, 25f

Quadruped, 50f

Questionnaires
Physical Activity Readiness
Questionnaire, 203,
204f
pre-screening, 199

Questions, frequently asked, 121–122

R

Radial heart-rate monitoring, 69, 69f

Range of motion (ROM)
arthritis, 149
avoiding extreme, 202
balance, 38
in executing, 169

Rapport, 40, 41f
audience, 118
behavior change, 98–99
building, 168
mirroring, 131

Ratings of perceived exertion (RPE
scale), 68, 69, 69t,
71–72, 71t
asthma, 147

Vests, weighted, 87

Visual cues
    aerobic Q-signs, 129, 129f
    delivering, 131
    exercise classes, 130, 130f
    mirroring, 131

Visual learners, 129–130, 129f, 130f

Voice care tips, 128

Volume, music, 65

W

Waivers, 218

Warm-up, 23, 81–84
    arm circles and standing diagonals,
        82, 84f
    birddog, 82, 82f
    cat-camel, 82, 82f
    glute bridge, 82, 83f
    I, Y, W, O formations, 82, 82f
    kneeling prisoner rotations, 82, 83f
    rehearsal moves, 84
    standing ankle mobilization, 82, 83f

Warning signs
    awareness, 73
    recognizing, 188–189

Weighted vests, 87

Weight management, 254–257
    balancing calories, 255
    calorie and nutrient needs, 255–256,
        255t
    current intake, 255
    glycemic index and glycemic load, 255
    nutrition strategies, 256
    in obese adults, 254
    in obese children, 254–255
    in overweight adults, 254
    in overweight children, 254–255
    in overweight older adults, 254
    in pregnancy, 254
    weight loss recommendations, 122

W formation, 82, 82f

Work-to-recovery ratios, 90

Y

Y formation, 82, 82f

Yoga
    bone anatomical cues, 43t
    class themes, 104–105
    hot, 60
    stretching, 26

Z

Zumba, 224

ABOUT THE AUTHORS

JESSICA MATTHEWS, M.S., E-RYT 500, is assistant professor of health and exercise science at Miramar College and associate kinesiology faculty at MiraCosta College in San Diego, Calif. She has developed and implemented comprehensive 200- and 500-hour yoga teacher training programs at the college level, in addition to teaching courses ranging from applied kinesiology to exercise leadership. Matthews serves as Senior Advisor for Health and Fitness Education for the American Council on Exercise® (ACE®), developing and delivering educational content in the form of textbooks, articles, videos, and online courses. She also presents lectures and workshops at conferences and events worldwide, including courses in the areas of health coaching and behavioral change. Additionally, Matthews is a freelance wellness writer and contributing fitness editor for *SHAPE* magazine, as well as a featured health and fitness expert and guest host on OWNTV's web-based series #OWNSHOW. She regularly contributes to numerous publications and media outlets, including CNN, *Yoga Journal, Health* magazine, NPR, and *The Washington Post.* An ACE Certified Health Coach, Personal Trainer, and Group Fitness Instructor, Matthews has a bachelor's degree in physical education from Coastal Carolina University and a master's degree in physical education from Canisius College. She is currently completing a doctorate in behavioral health through Arizona State University.

SABRENA JO, M.S., has been actively involved in the fitness industry since 1987. An ACE Certified Group Fitness Instructor, Personal Trainer, and Health Coach, Jo teaches group exercise, owns and operates her own personal-training business, has managed fitness departments in commercial facilities, and lectured to university students and established fitness professionals. Jo serves as Senior Advisor for Health and Fitness Education for the American Council on Exercise® (ACE®), developing and delivering educational content in the form of textbooks, articles, videos, and online courses. She has a bachelor's degree in exercise science as well as a master's degree in physical education from the University of Kansas, and has numerous certifications in exercise instruction. Jo acts as a spokesperson for the American Council on Exercise (ACE) and is involved in curriculum development for ACE continuing education programs. Additionally, Jo presents lectures and workshops to fitness professionals nationwide and has authored chapters in numerous ACE texts.

SHANNAN LYNCH, PH.D., CSCS, HFS, FISSN, is a veteran of the health, exercise science, sports medicine, and nutrition industries, with experience in both the applied and program development spaces. Dr. Lynch's career path has exposed her to multiple categories within the field, including sports performance, fitness, corporate wellness, program design and continuing education for fitness professionals, online curriculum design, sports nutrition, management, operations, and customer service. Dr. Lynch earned her Ph.D. in health sciences with a focus in sports nutrition and human performance, as well as ancillary studies in health education and research; a M.S. degree in human movement with a specialty in sports conditioning; and a B.S. degree in nutritional sciences. In addition to her academic background, she has earned several recognizable industry certifications: Health and Fitness Specialist (HFS) – American College of Sports Medicine; Certified Strength and Conditioning Specialist (CSCS) – National Strength and Conditioning Association; and Fellow of the International Society of Sports Nutrition (FISSN). Dr. Lynch is a master instructor for Kettlebell Concepts, serves on two scientific advisory boards, sits on the editorial board of the *Journal of the International Society of Sports Nutrition,* and lectures regularly at global exercise science and nutrition conventions and conferences